ONE
PRESENTS

モ ブ サ イ コ 1 0 0

MOB PSYCHO 100

VOLUME 3

DARK HORSE MANGA

W9-DHS-244

MOB PSYCHO 100
VOLUME 3
Translated by
KUMAR SIVASUBRAMANIAN
Lettering and Retouch by
JOHN CLARK
Edited by
CARL GUSTAV HORN

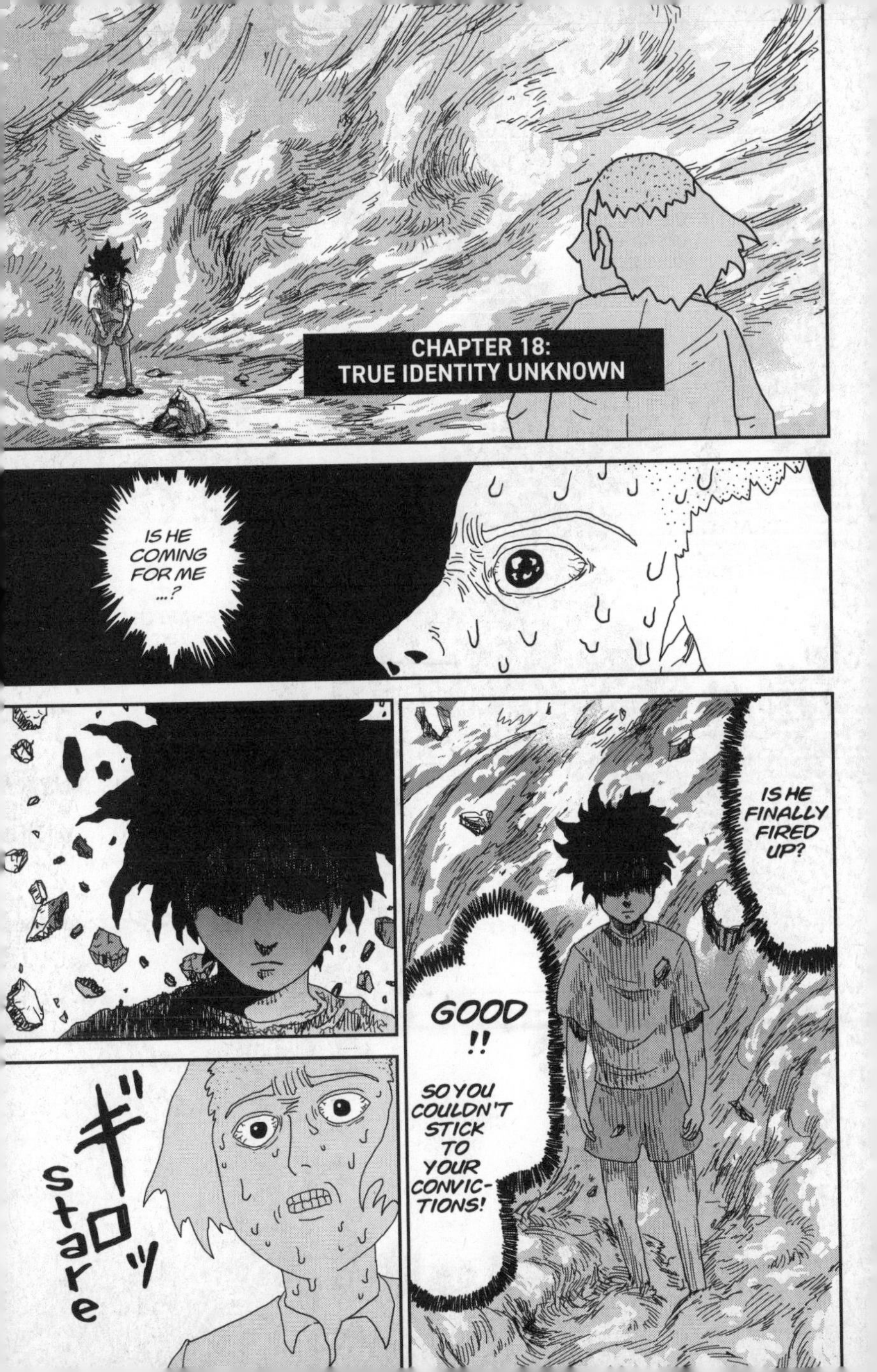
CHAPTER 18:
TRUE IDENTITY UNKNOWN
IS HE COMING FOR ME ...?
IS HE FINALLY FIRED UP?
GOOD !!
SO YOU COULDN'T STICK TO YOUR CONVIC-TIONS!
ギロッ
stare

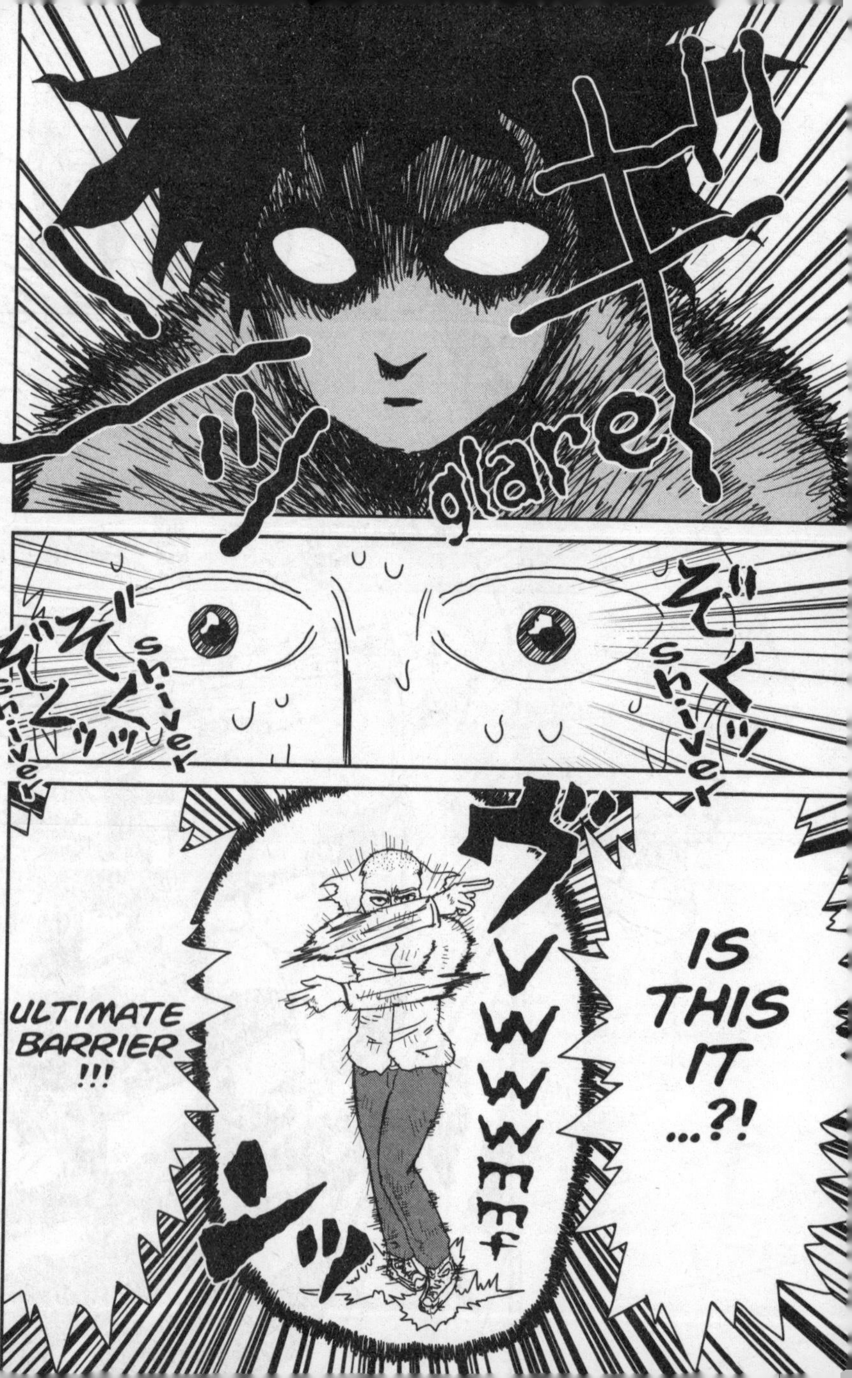
glare
shiver
shiver
shiver
IS THIS IT ...?!
VWWWmmf
ULTIMATE BARRIER !!!

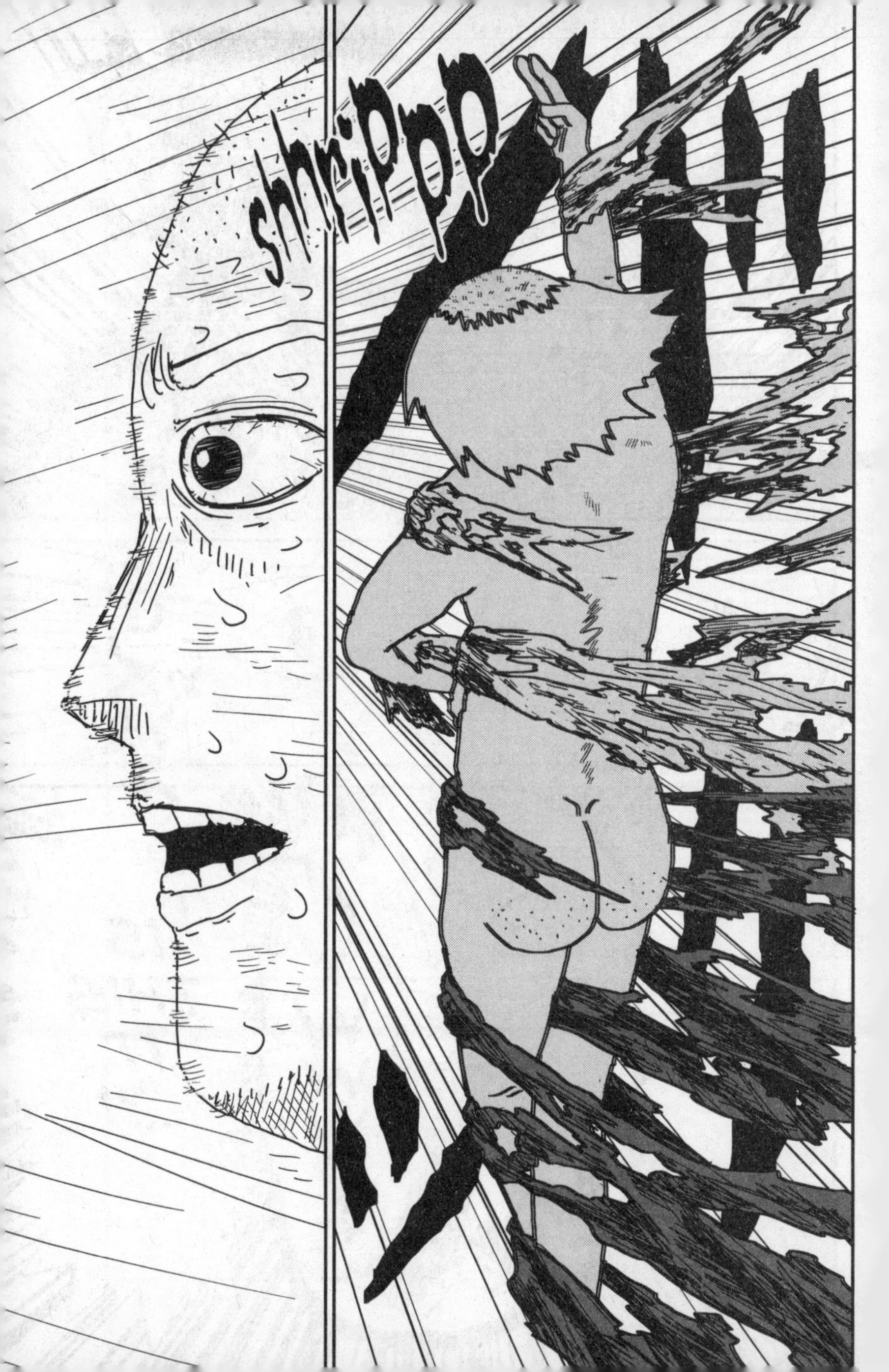
shhriPPP

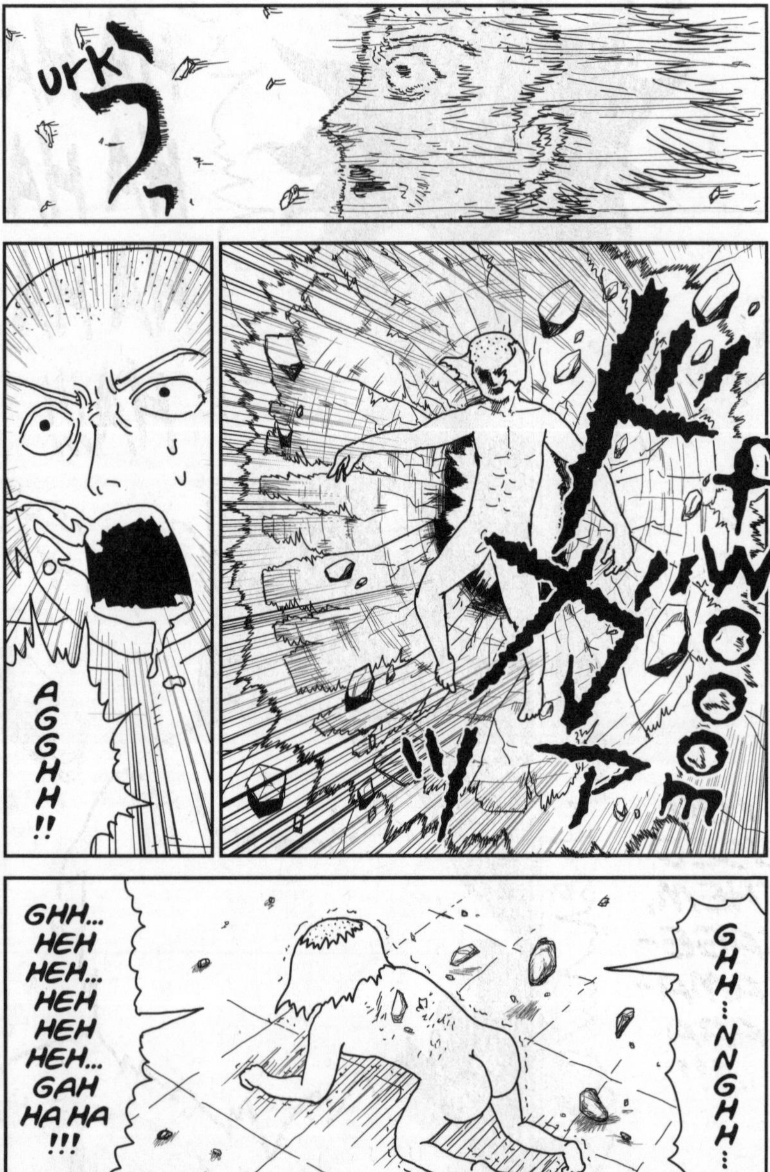
urk
fwooom
AGGHH!!
GHH... NNGHH...
GHH... HEH HEH... HEH HEH HEH... GAH HA HA!!!

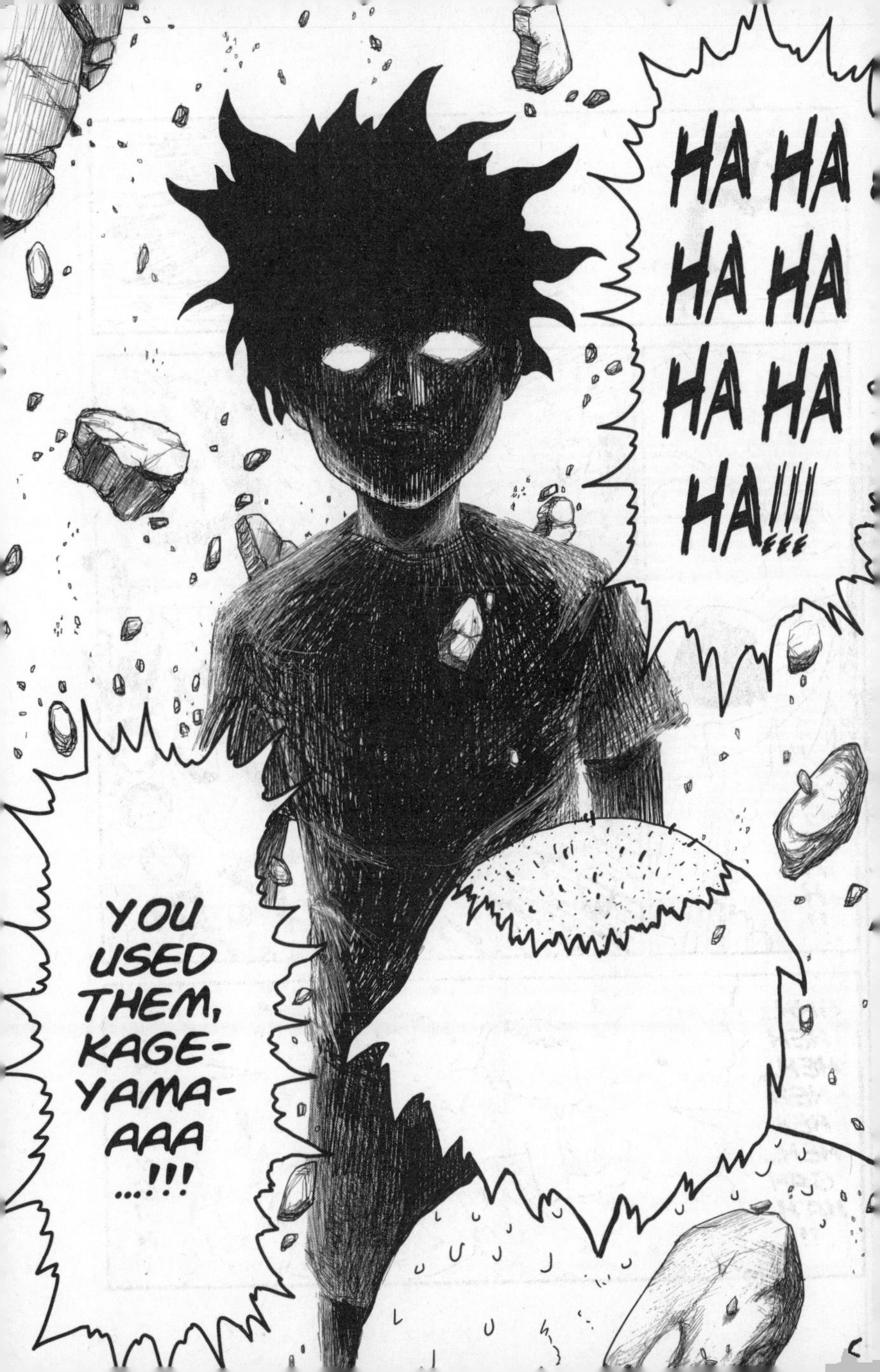
HA HA HA HA HA HA HA!!!
YOU USED THEM, KAGE-YAMA-AAA ...!!!

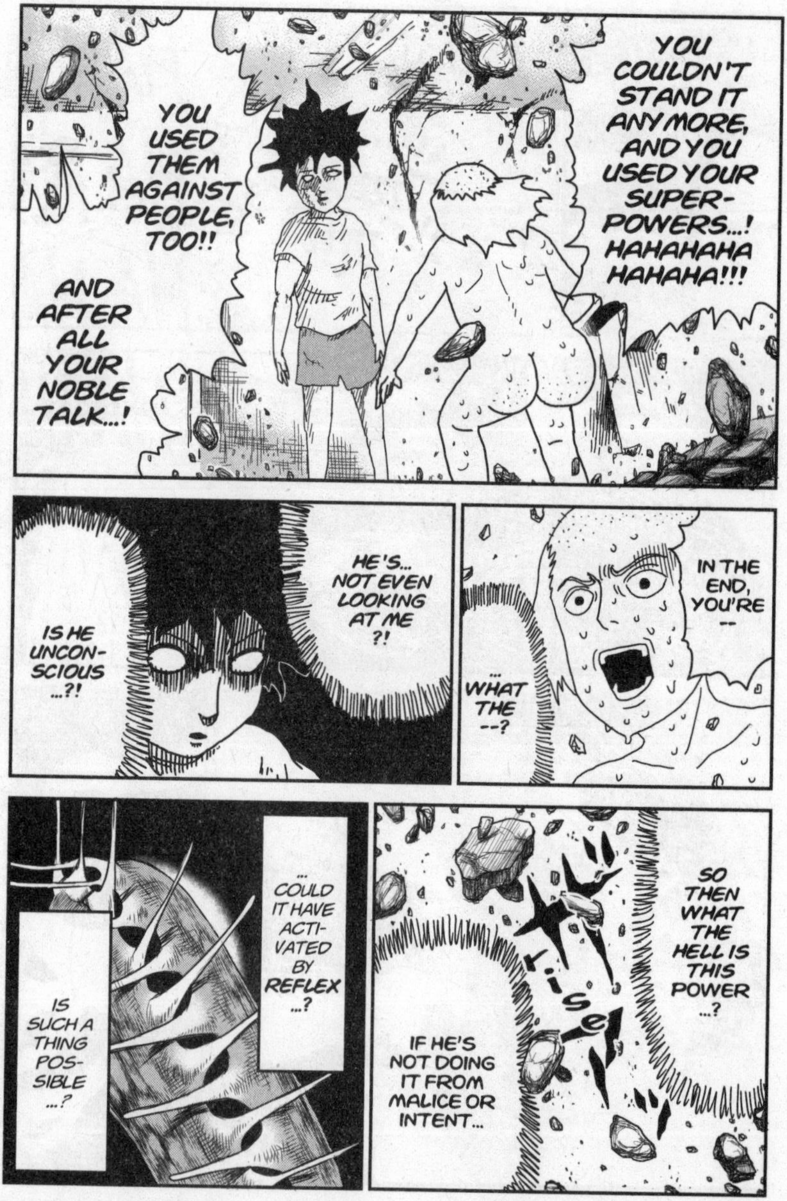
YOU COULDN'T STAND IT ANY MORE, AND YOU USED YOUR SUPER-POWERS...! HAHAHAHA HAHAHA!!!
YOU USED THEM AGAINST PEOPLE, TOO!!
AND AFTER ALL YOUR NOBLE TALK...!
IN THE END, YOU'RE --
... WHAT THE --?
HE'S... NOT EVEN LOOKING AT ME ?!
IS HE UNCON-SCIOUS ...?!
SO THEN WHAT THE HELL IS THIS POWER ...?
rise
IF HE'S NOT DOING IT FROM MALICE OR INTENT...
... COULD IT HAVE ACTI-VATED BY REFLEX ...?
IS SUCH A THING POS-SIBLE ...?

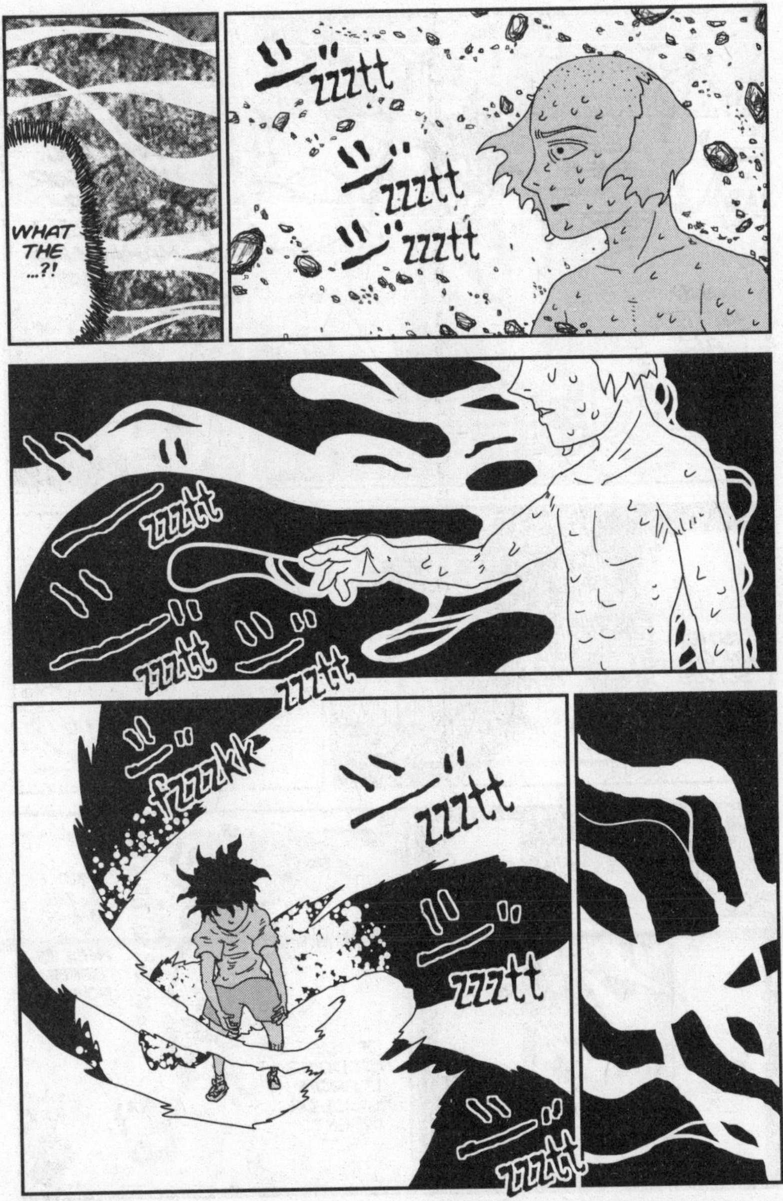
zzztt
zzztt
zzztt
WHAT THE ...?!
zzzztt
zzztt
zzztt
zzztt
fzzzkk
zzztt
zzztt
zzztt

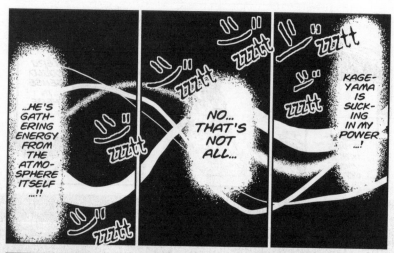

KAGE-YAMA IS SUCK-ING IN MY POWER ...!
NO... THAT'S NOT ALL...
...HE'S GATH-ERING ENERGY FROM THE ATMO-SPHERE ITSELF ...!!
SO HE HAS THE CAPACITY TO ABSORB SUCH MAMMOTH ENERGY...
...BUT HIS SELF-IDENTITY NOW IS ABSENT... GONE.
WHICH MEANS, IN THIS STATE...
THAT CAPACITY IS ACTING OF ITS OWN ACCORD ...?
THEN HE CAN'T BE THAT BIG A THREAT...
BUT...

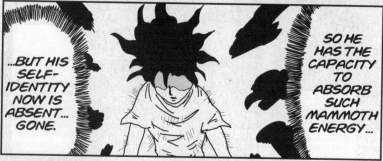

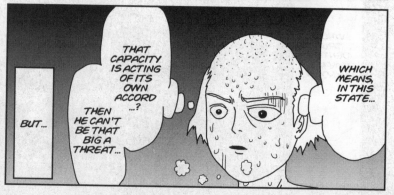

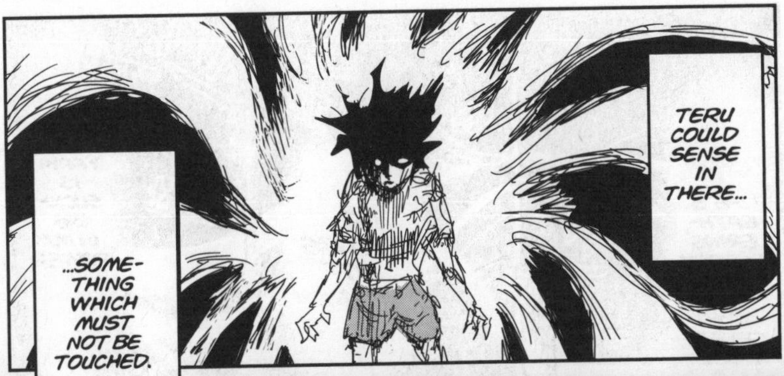
TERU COULD SENSE IN THERE...
...SOME-THING WHICH MUST NOT BE TOUCHED.
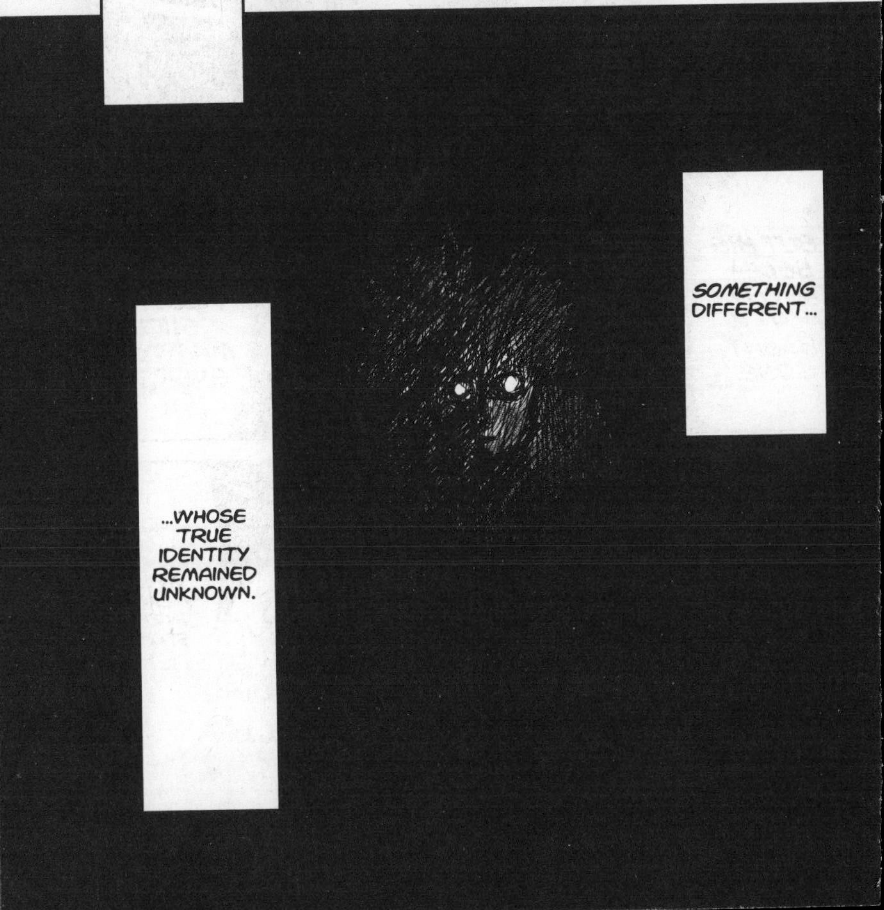
SOMETHING DIFFERENT...
...WHOSE TRUE IDENTITY REMAINED UNKNOWN.

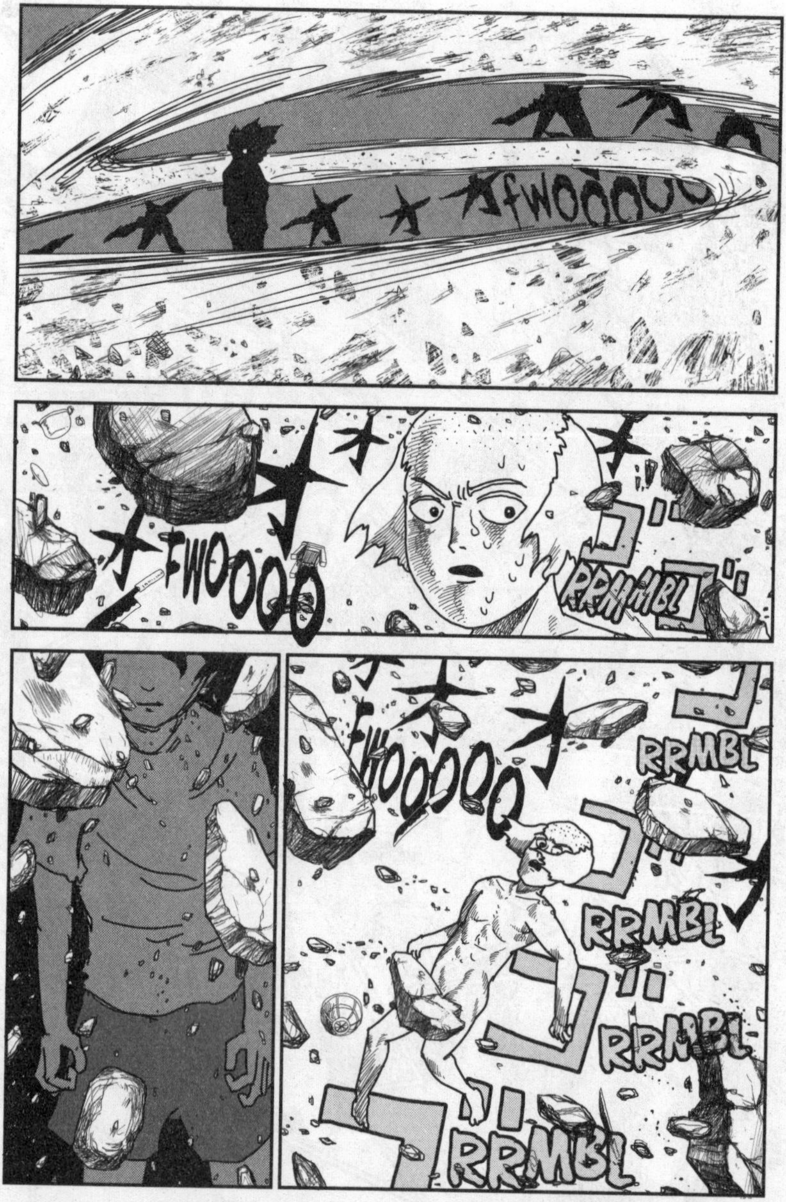
fWOOOOO
RRMMBL
FWOOOO
FWOOOOO
RRMBL
RRMBL
RRMBL
RRMBL

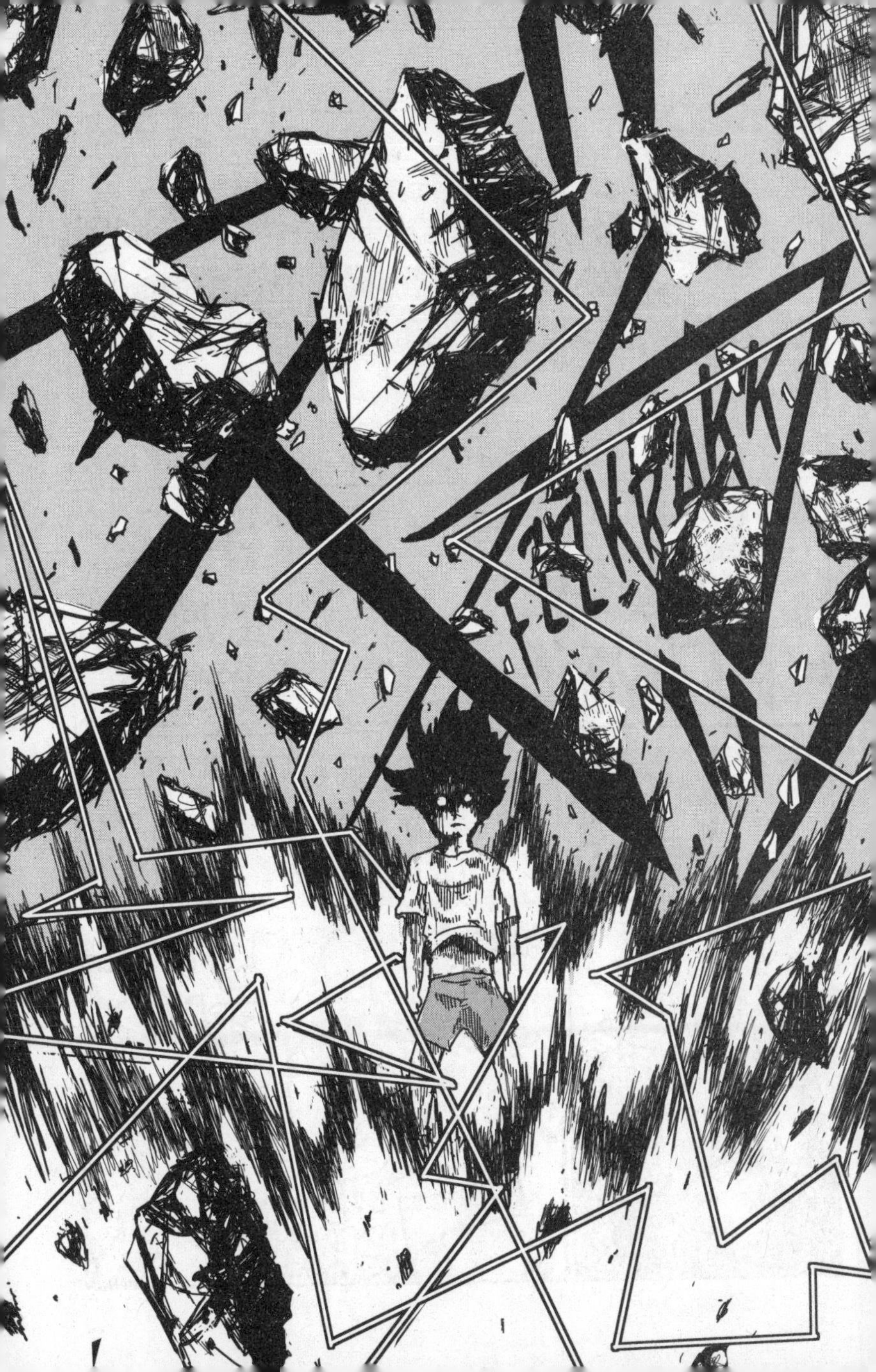
ZZKRAKK

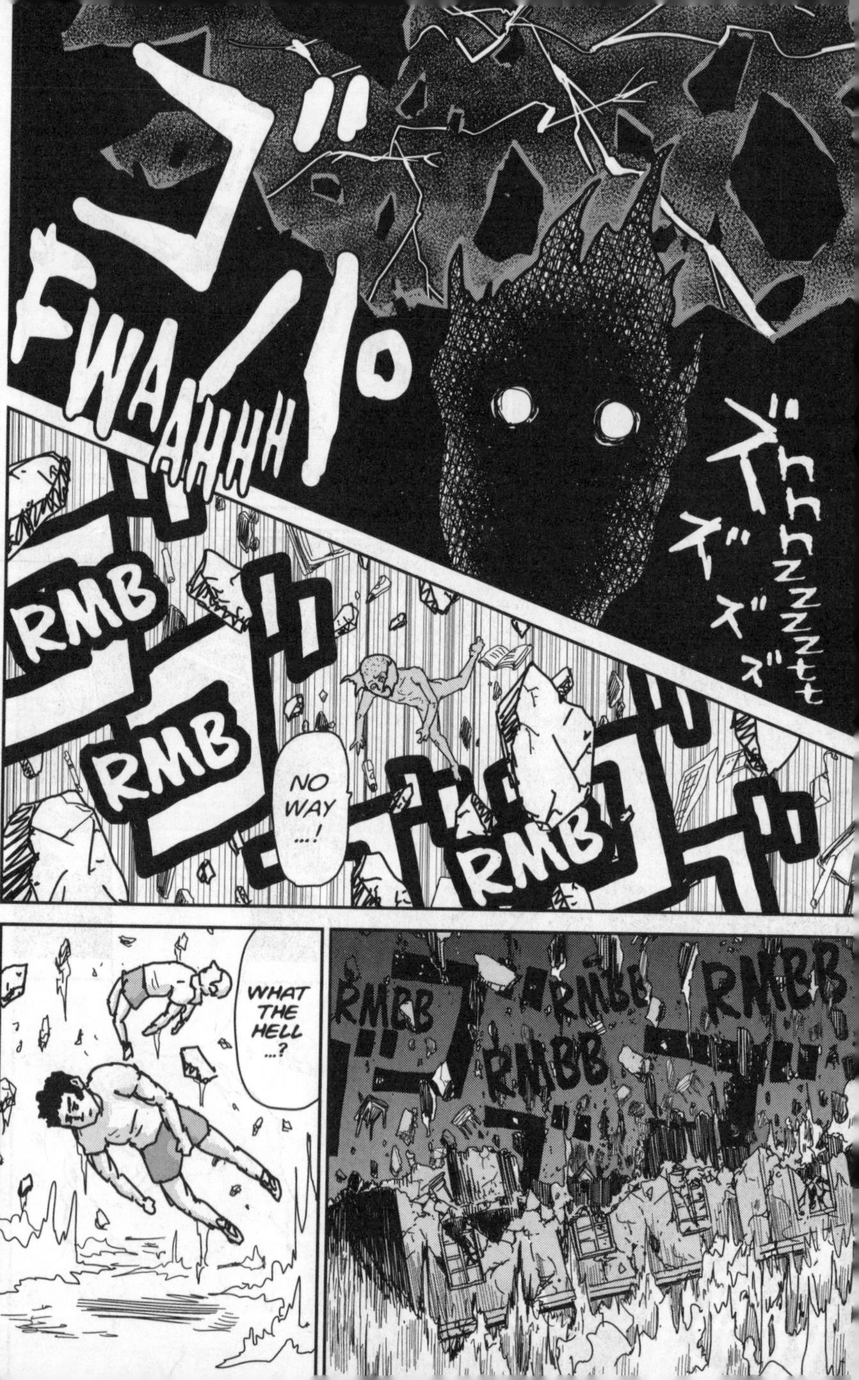
FWAAHHH!
RMB
RMB
NO WAY...!
RMB
RMBB
RMBB
RNBB
RMBB
WHAT THE HELL...?

ROAARR

ROAARR

RMBBL

RMBBL

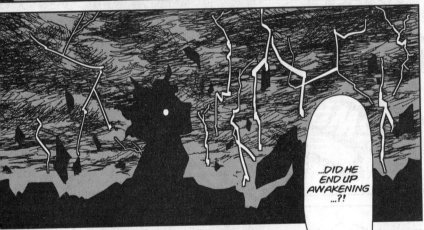

...DID HE END UP AWAKENING...?!

...AHHH!

RMBB

RMBB

AGGH...

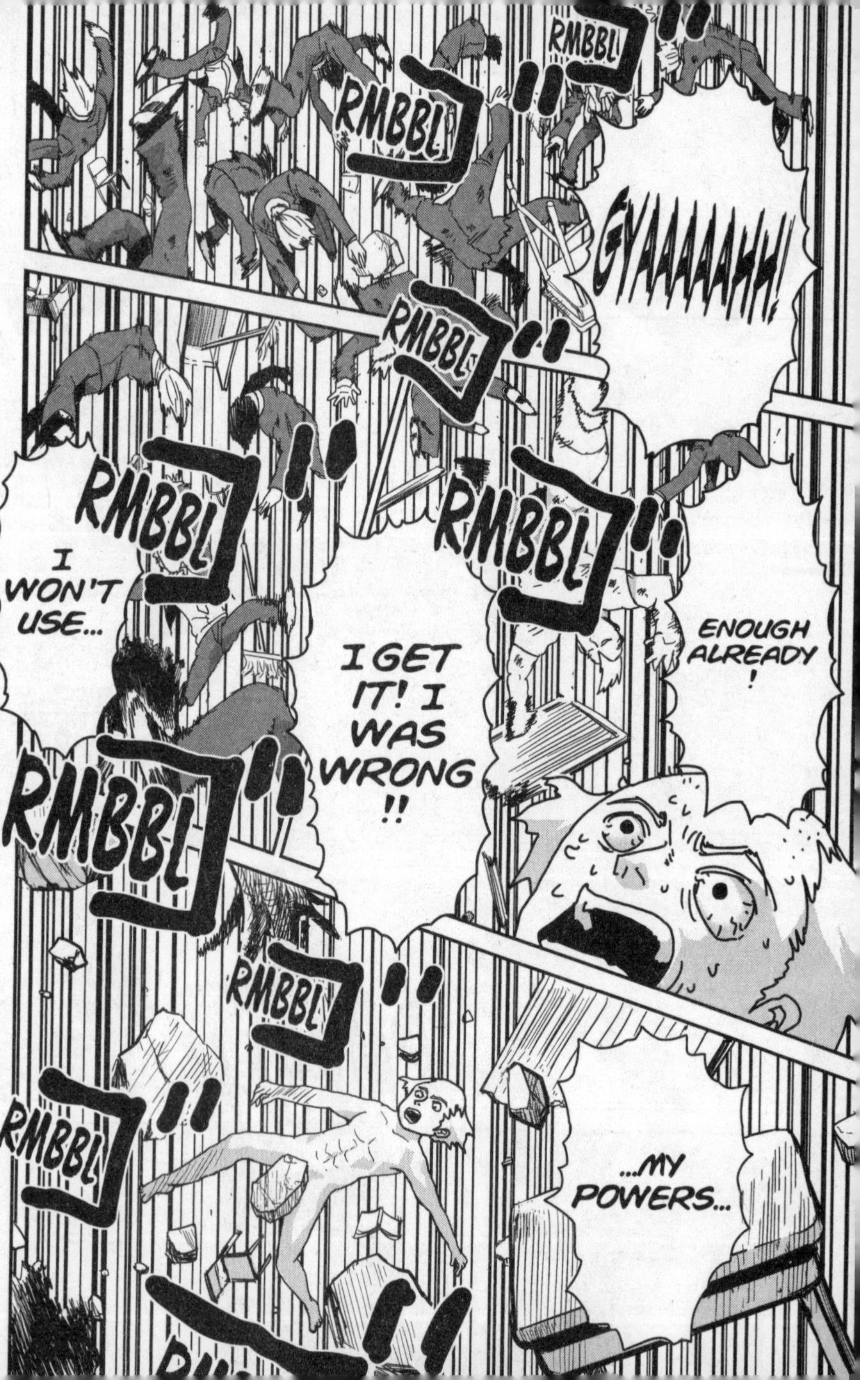
RMBBL
RMBBL
GYAAAAAHH!
RMBBL
RMBBL
RMBBL
ENOUGH ALREADY!
I GET IT! I WAS WRONG!!
I WON'T USE...
RMBBL
RMBBL
...MY POWERS...
RMBBL

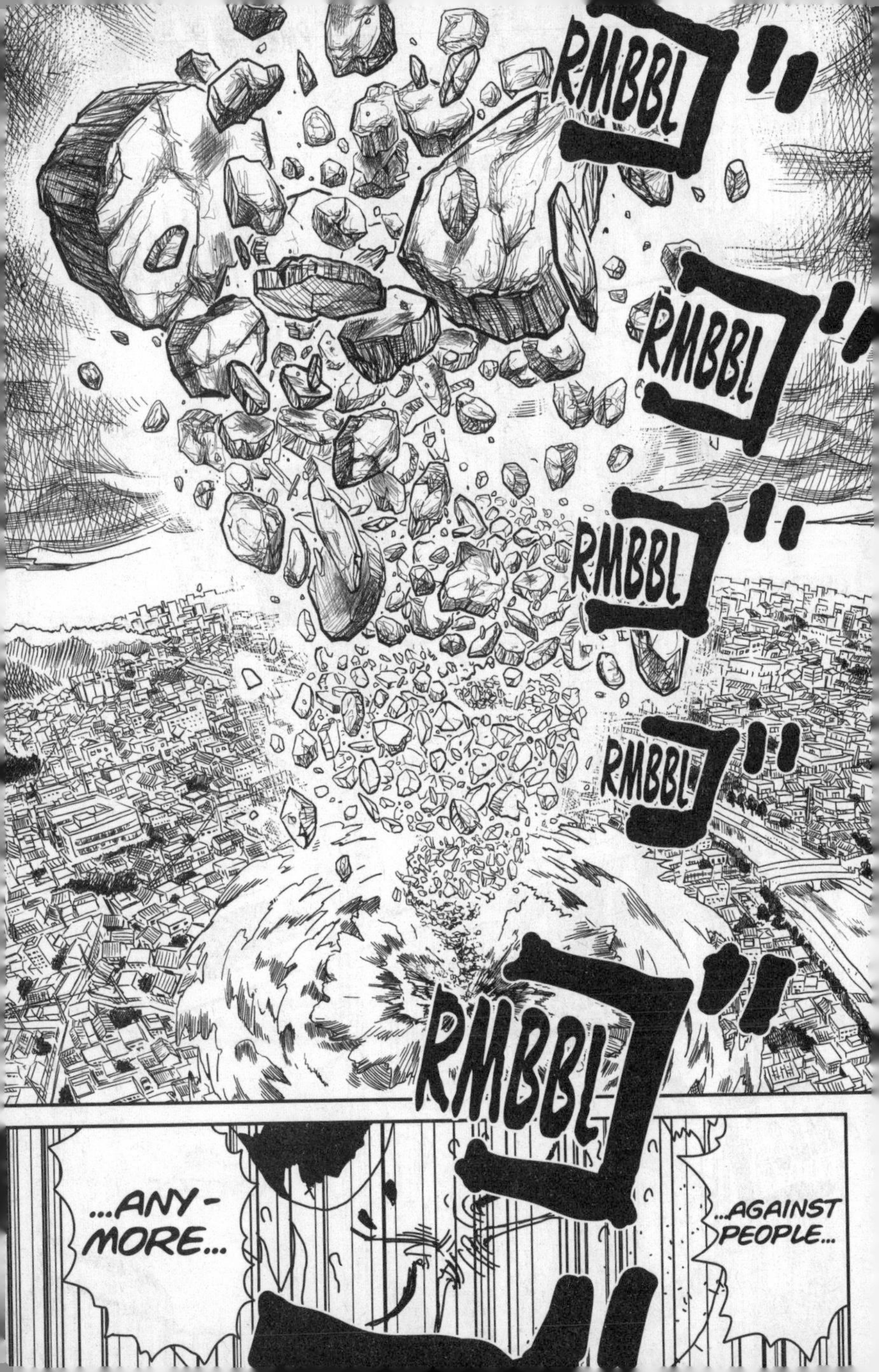
RMBBL
RMBBL
RMBBL
RMBBL
RMBBL
...AGAINST PEOPLE...
...ANY-MORE...

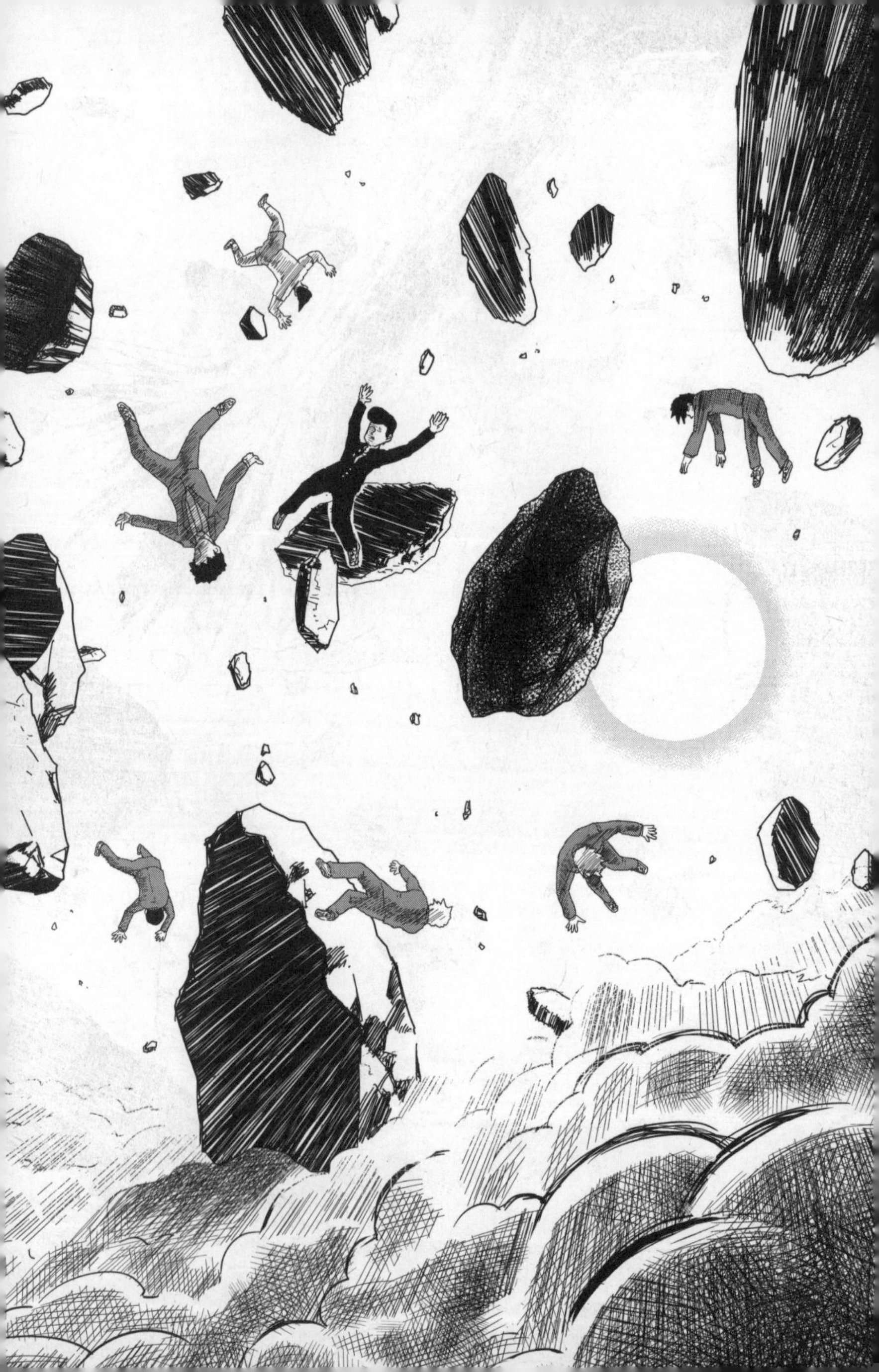

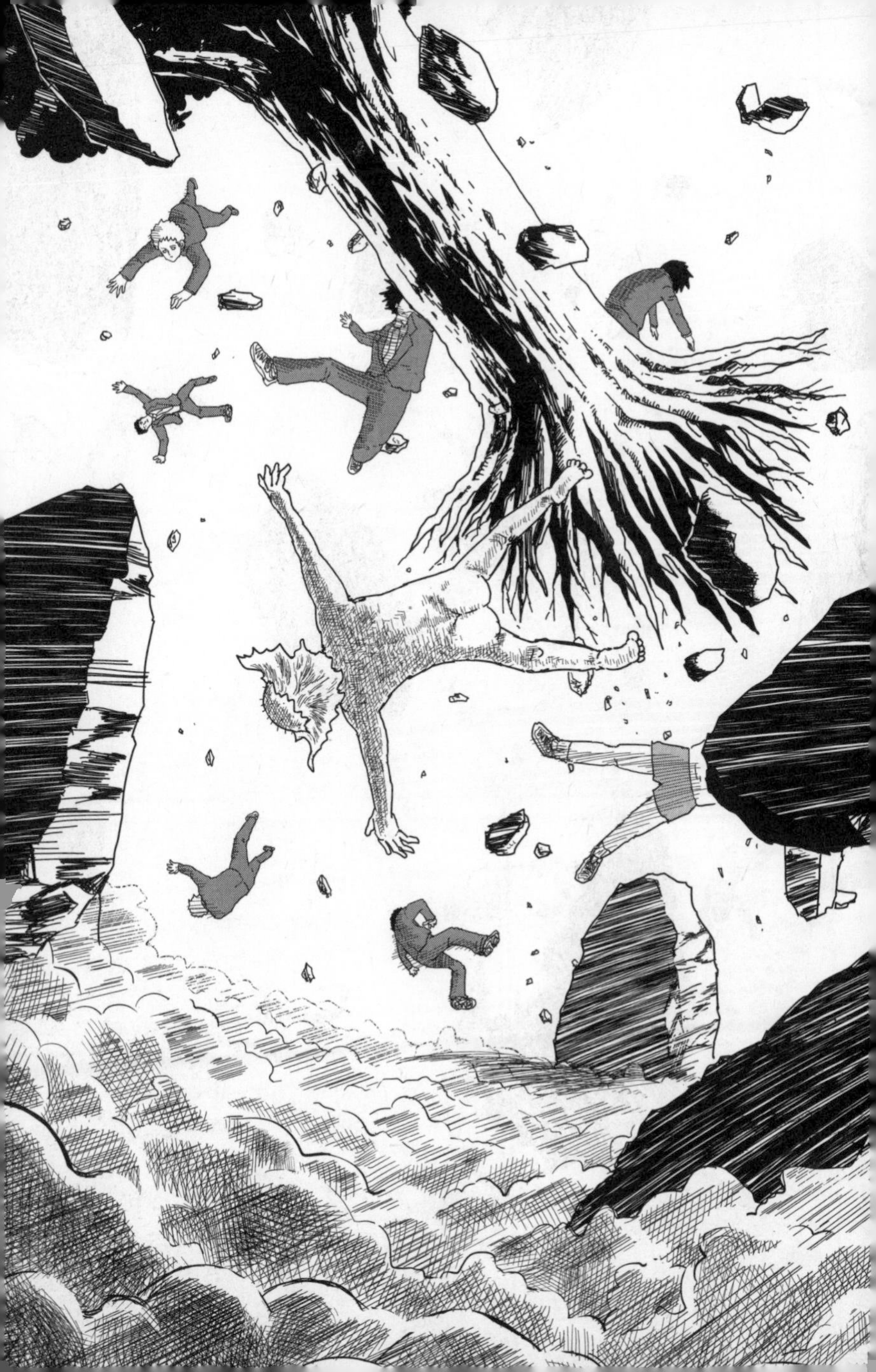

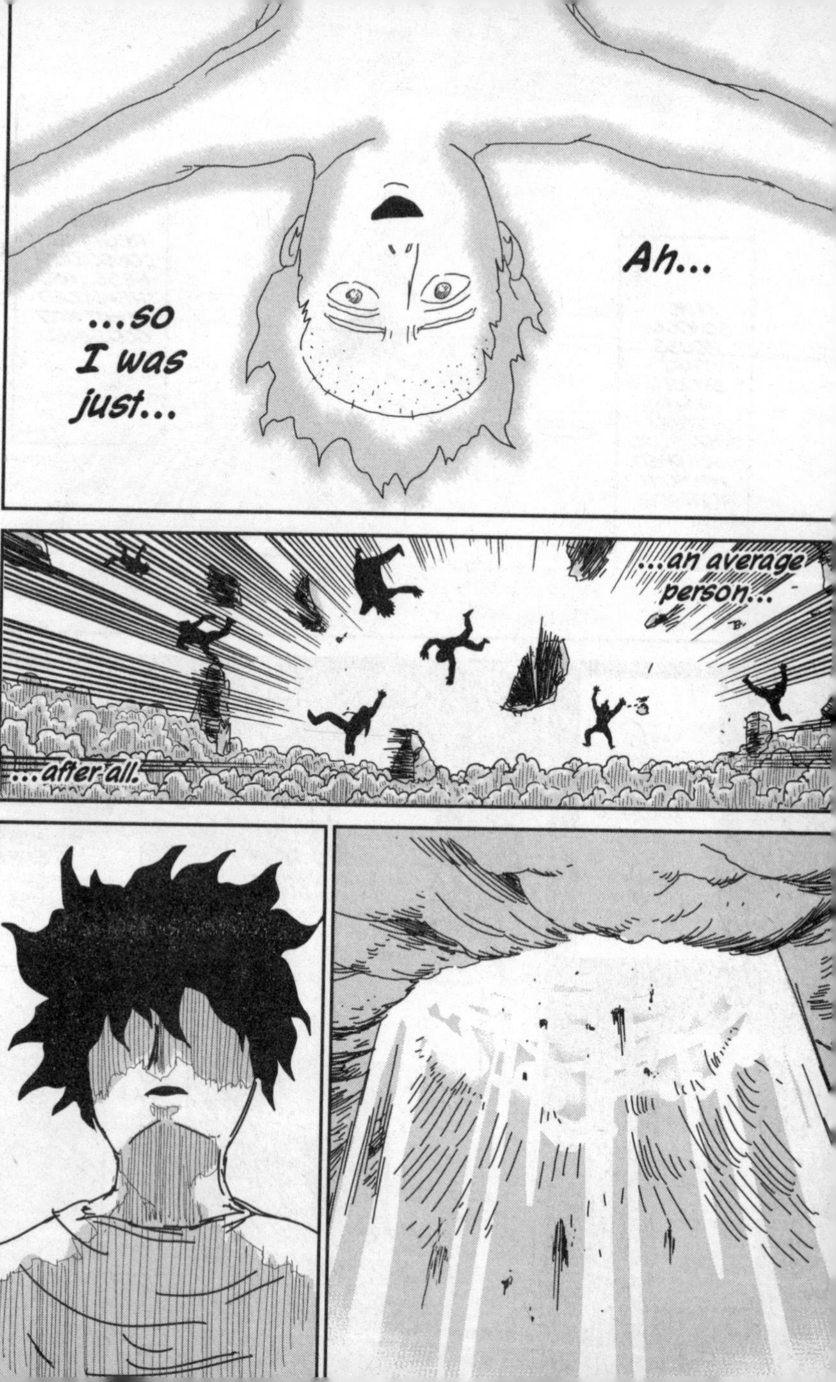
Ah...
...so I was just...
...an average person...
...after all.

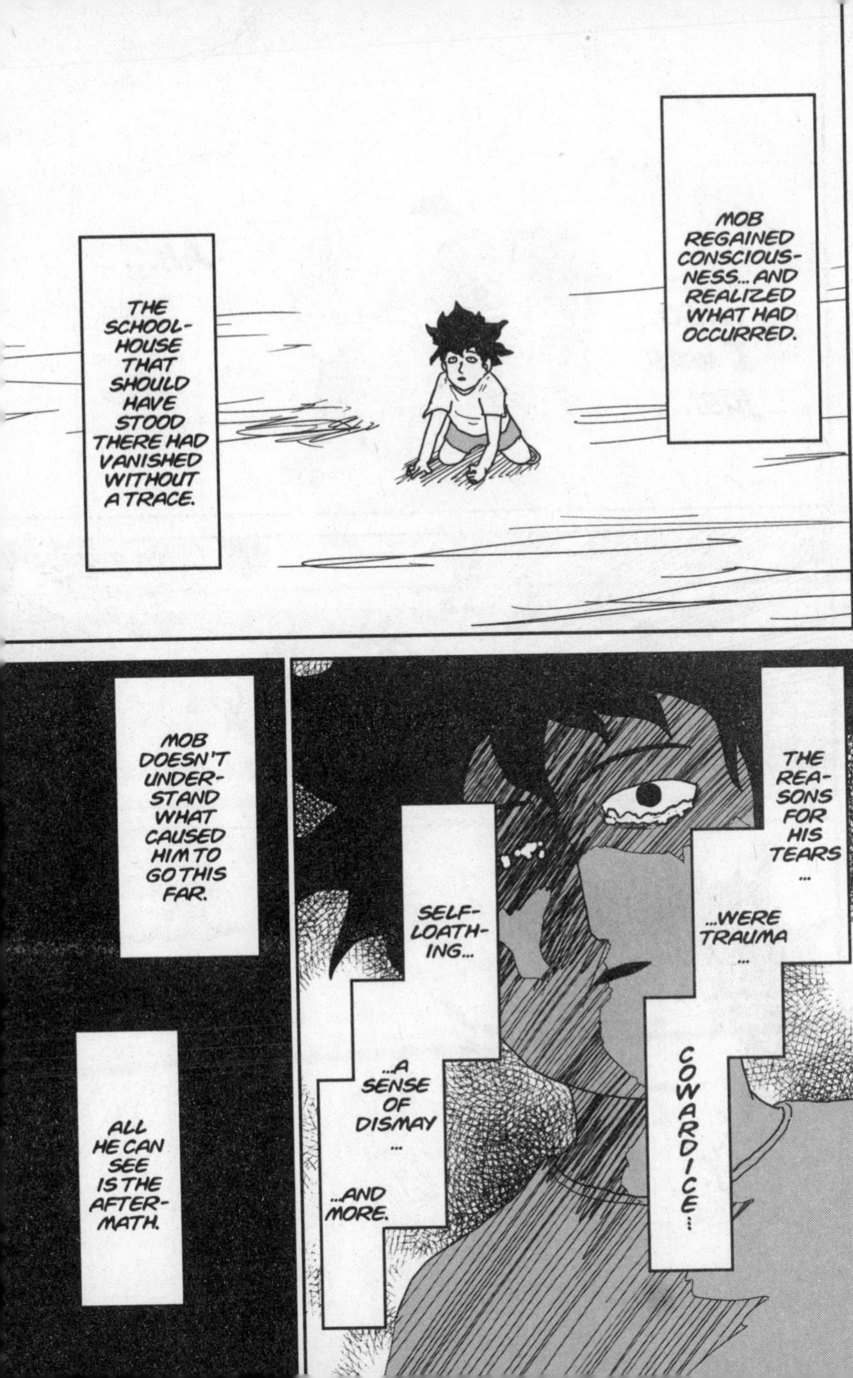
MOB REGAINED CONSCIOUSNESS... AND REALIZED WHAT HAD OCCURRED.
THE SCHOOLHOUSE THAT SHOULD HAVE STOOD THERE HAD VANISHED WITHOUT A TRACE.
THE REASONS FOR HIS TEARS...
...WERE TRAUMA...
COWARDICE...
SELF-LOATHING...
...A SENSE OF DISMAY...
...AND MORE.
MOB DOESN'T UNDERSTAND WHAT CAUSED HIM TO GO THIS FAR.
ALL HE CAN SEE IS THE AFTERMATH.

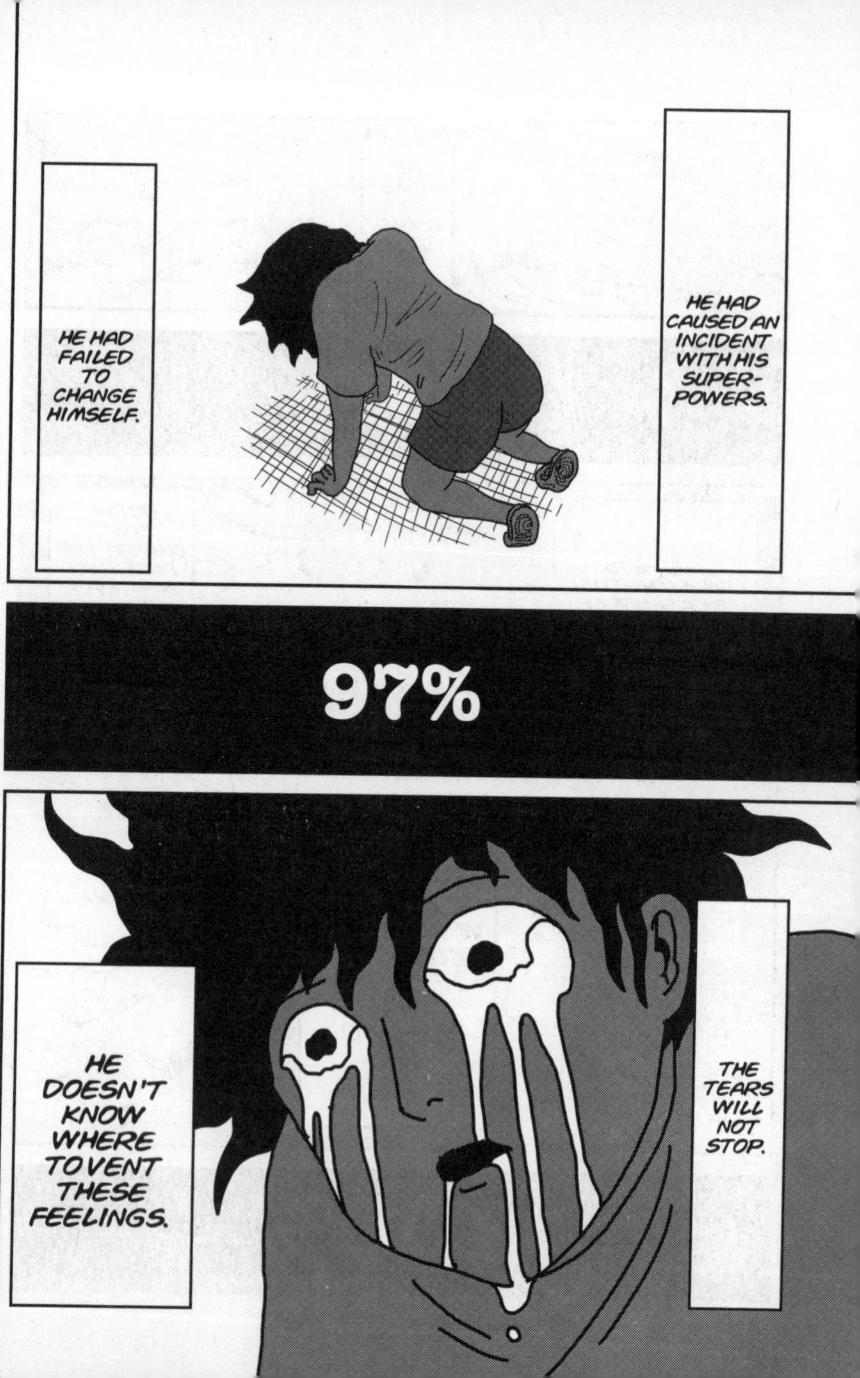
HE HAD CAUSED AN INCIDENT WITH HIS SUPER-POWERS.
HE HAD FAILED TO CHANGE HIMSELF.
97%
THE TEARS WILL NOT STOP.
HE DOESN'T KNOW WHERE TO VENT THESE FEELINGS.

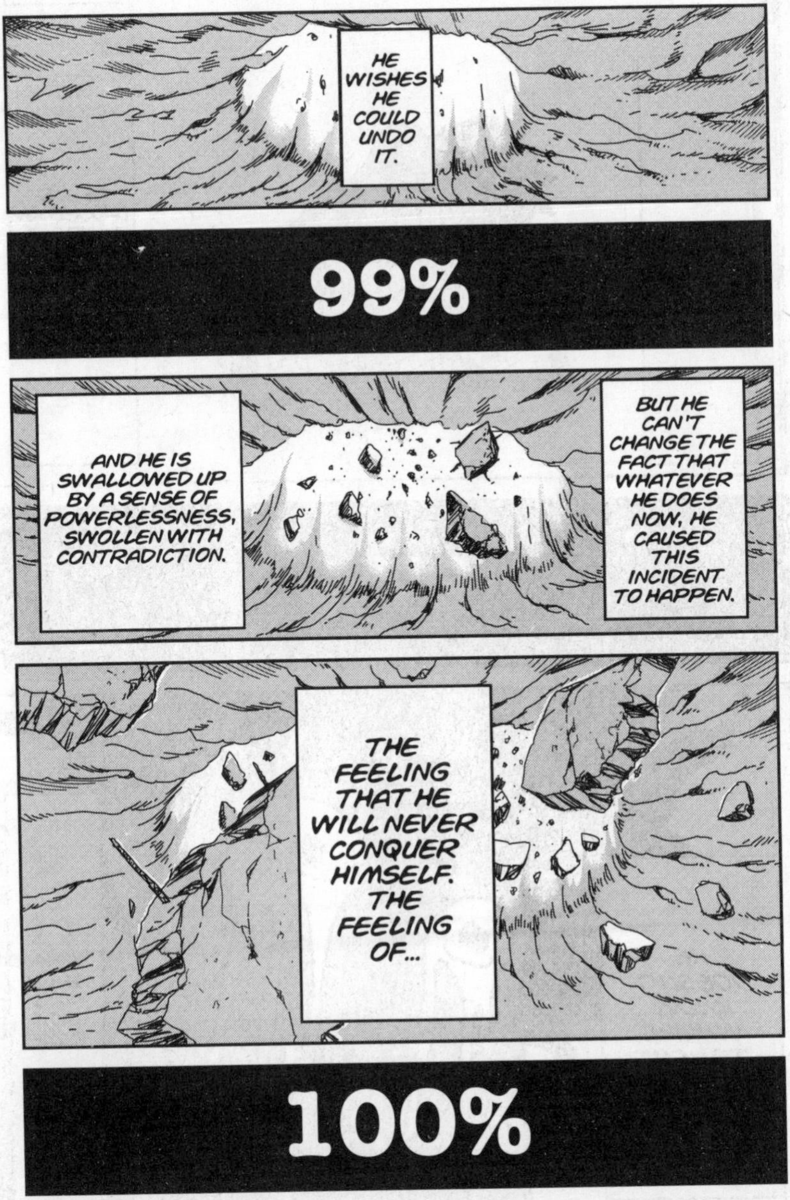
HE WISHES HE COULD UNDO IT.
99%
BUT HE CAN'T CHANGE THE FACT THAT WHATEVER HE DOES NOW, HE CAUSED THIS INCIDENT TO HAPPEN.
AND HE IS SWALLOWED UP BY A SENSE OF POWERLESSNESS, SWOLLEN WITH CONTRADICTION.
THE FEELING THAT HE WILL NEVER CONQUER HIMSELF. THE FEELING OF...
100%

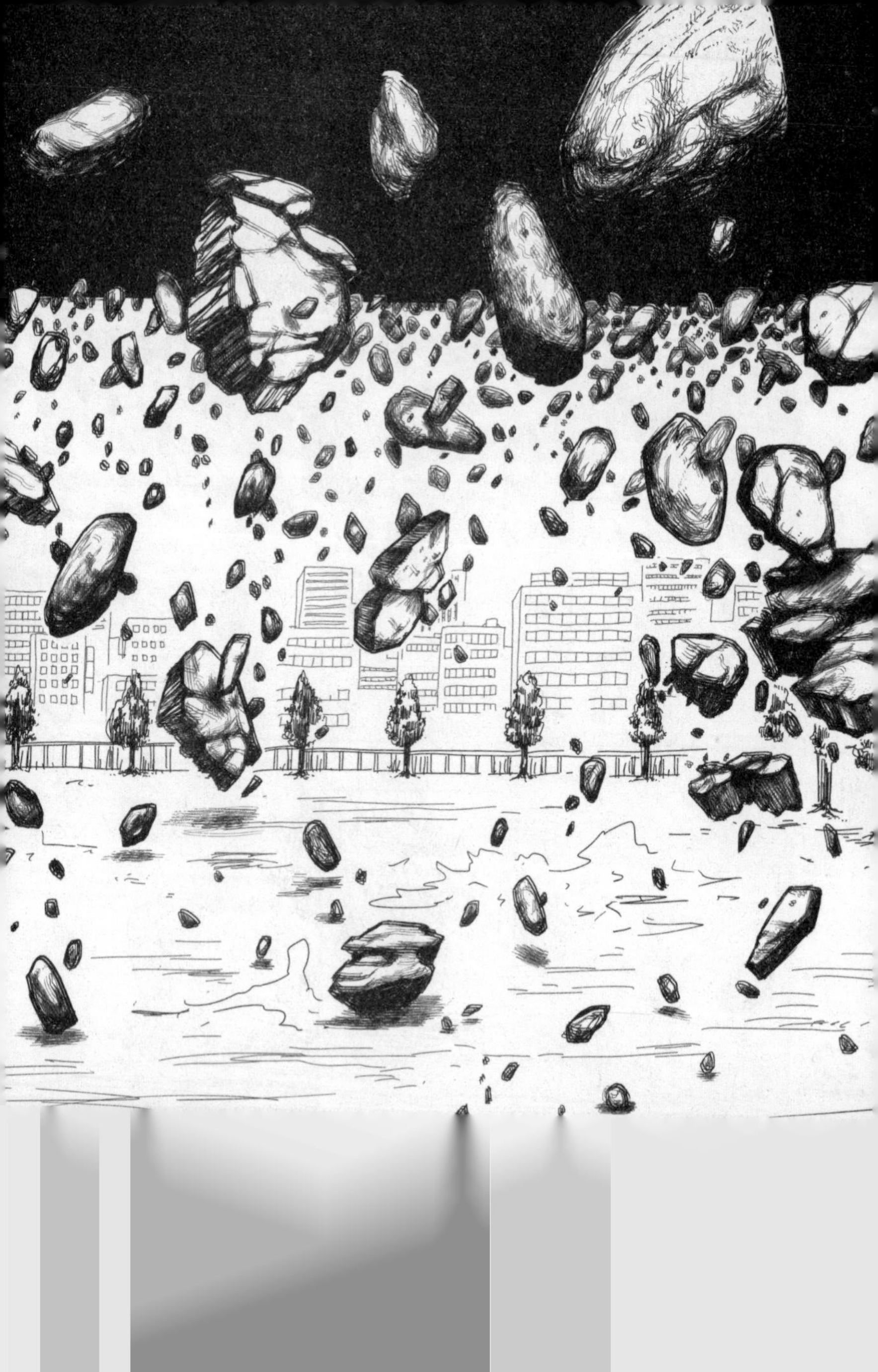

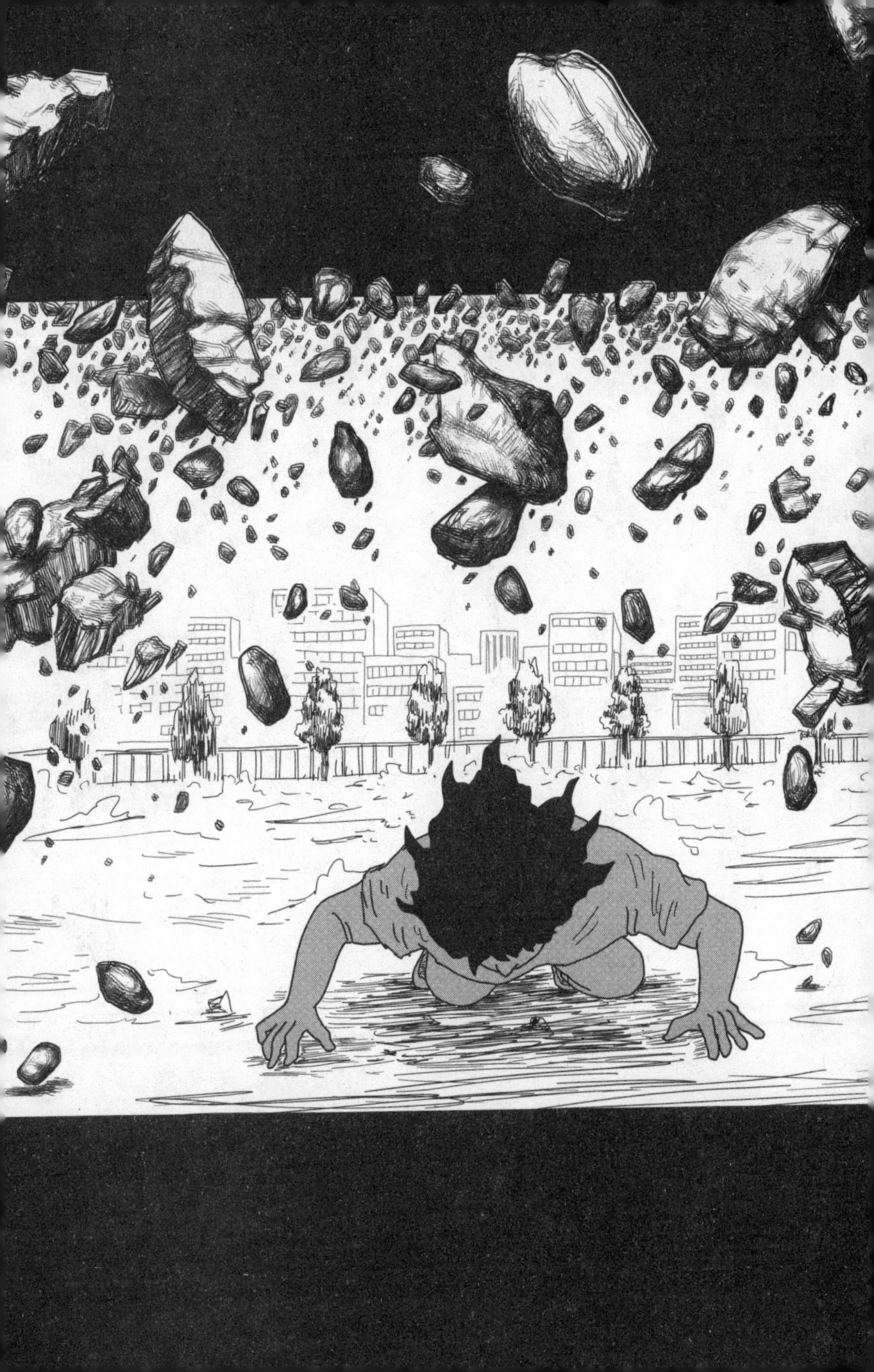

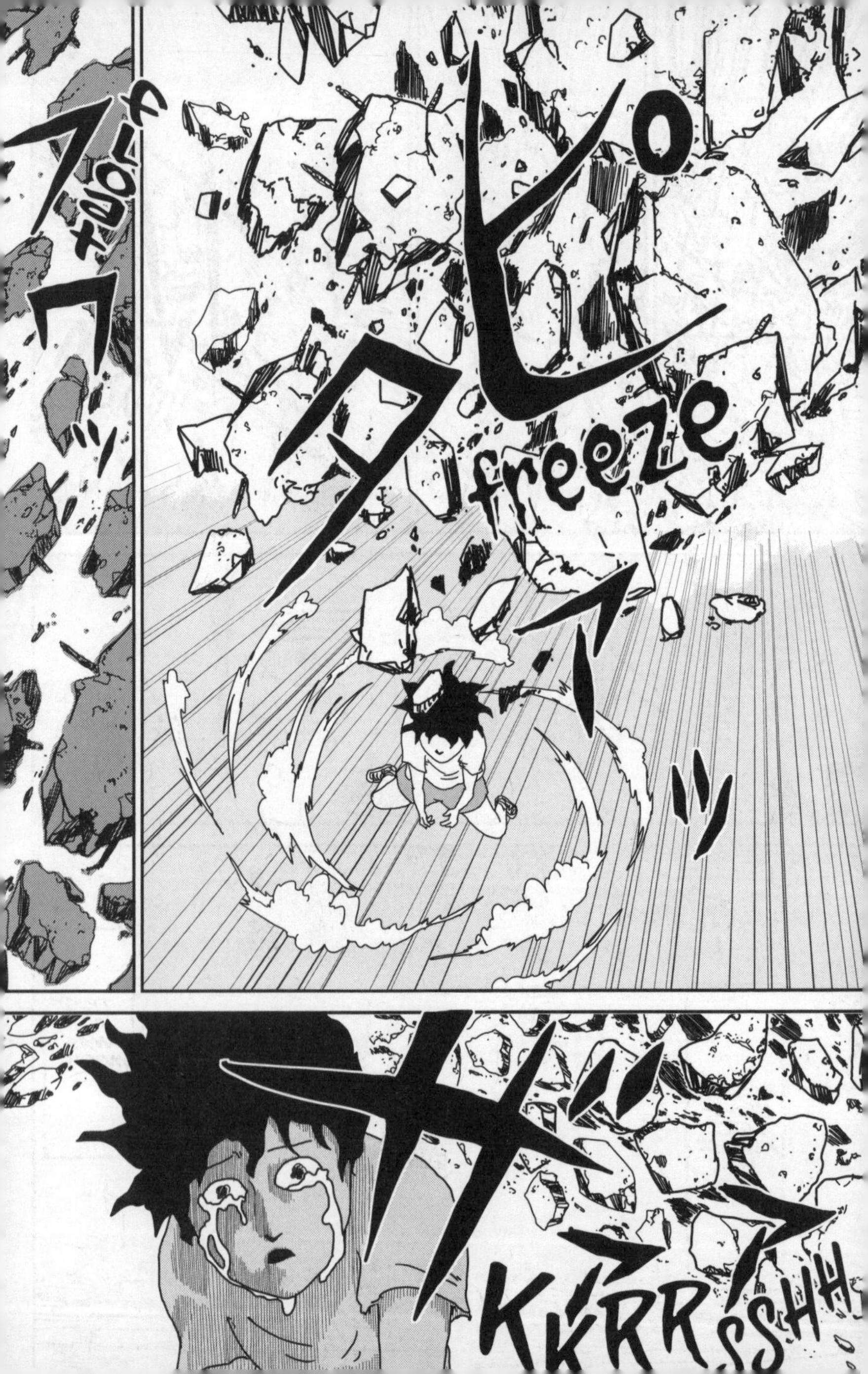
freeze
float
KKRRSSHH

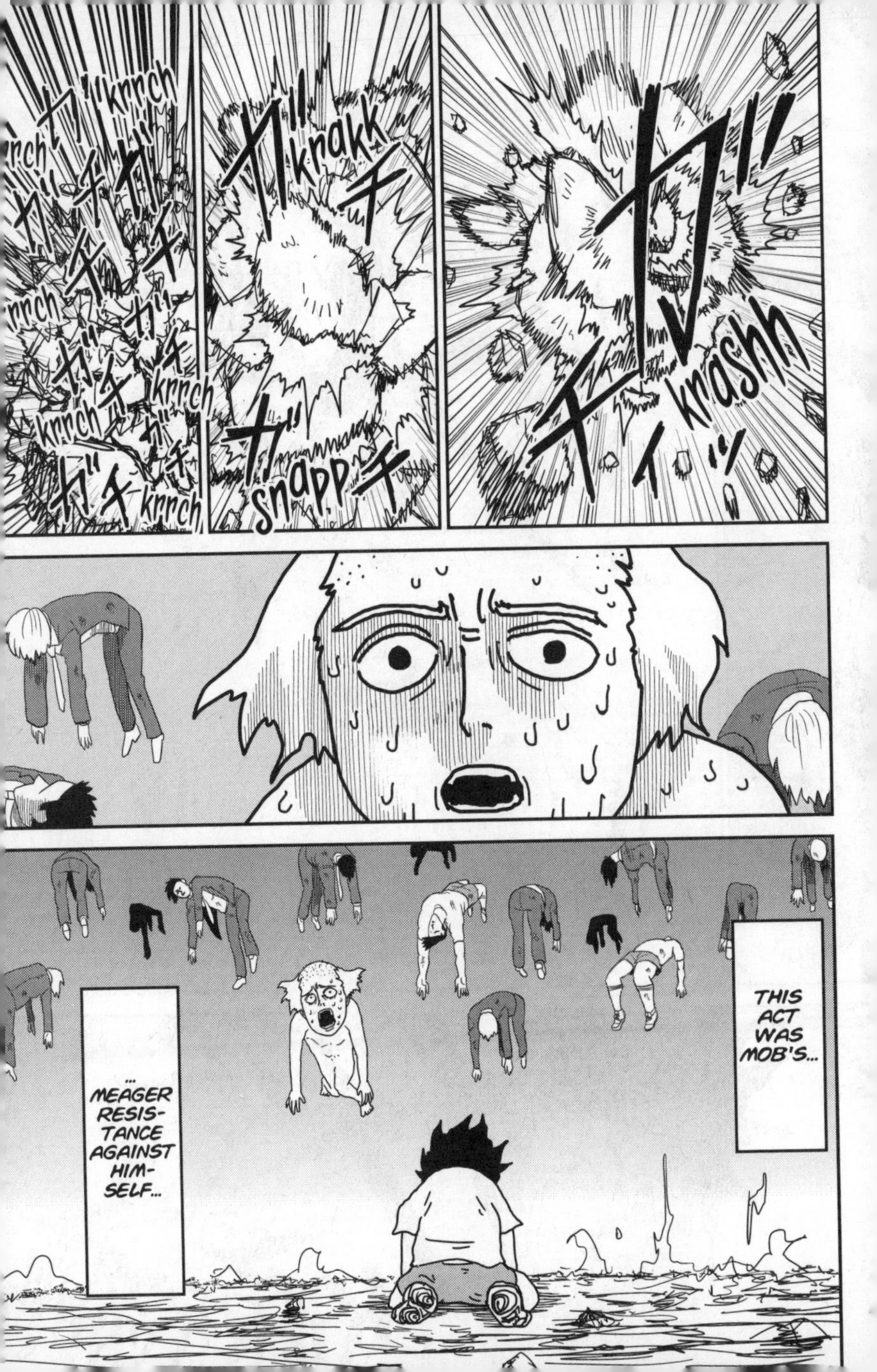
krashh
krakk
snapp
krrch
krrch
krrch
krrch
krrch
THIS ACT WAS MOB'S...
...MEAGER RESIS-TANCE AGAINST HIM-SELF...

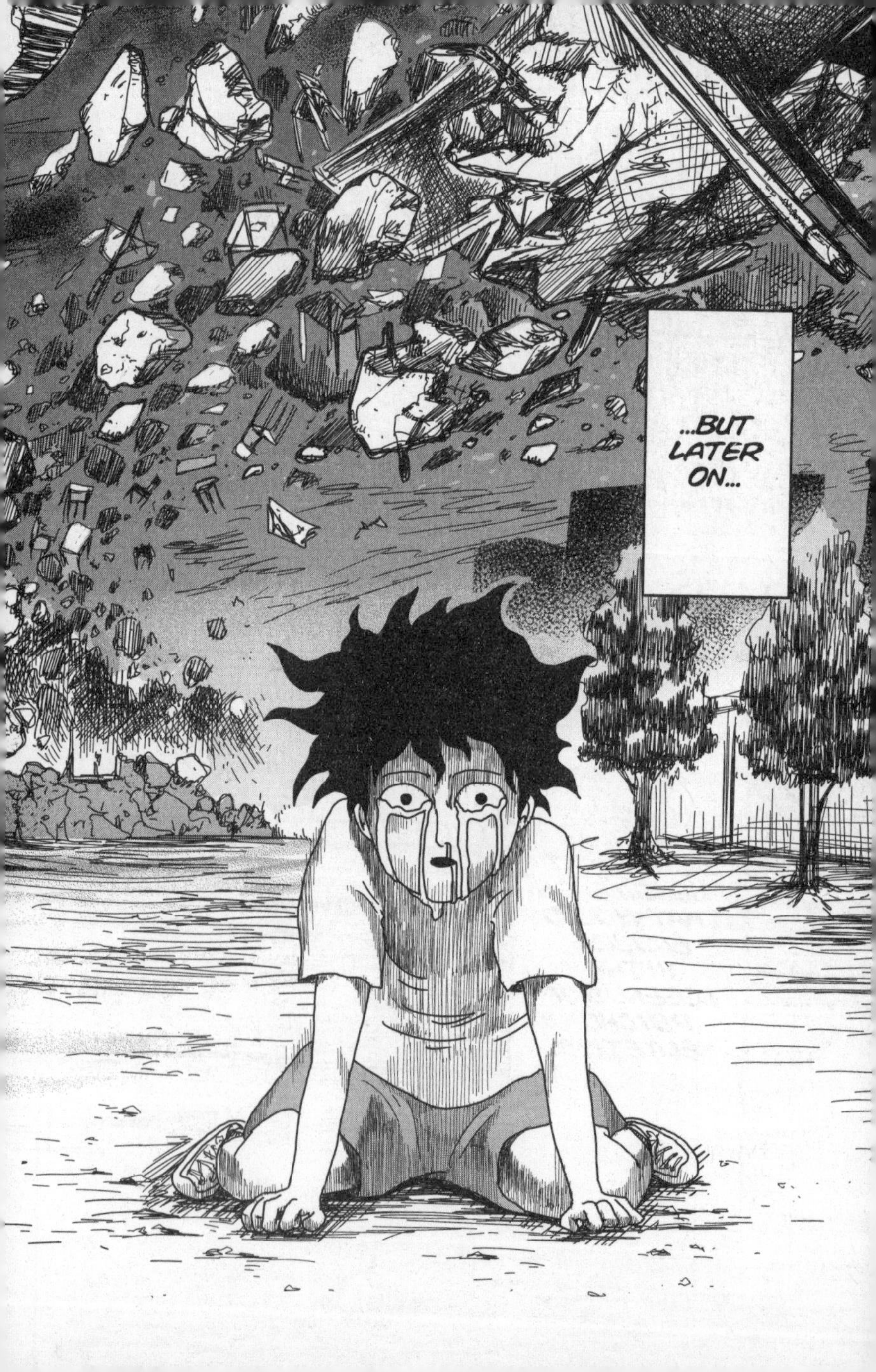
...BUT LATER ON...

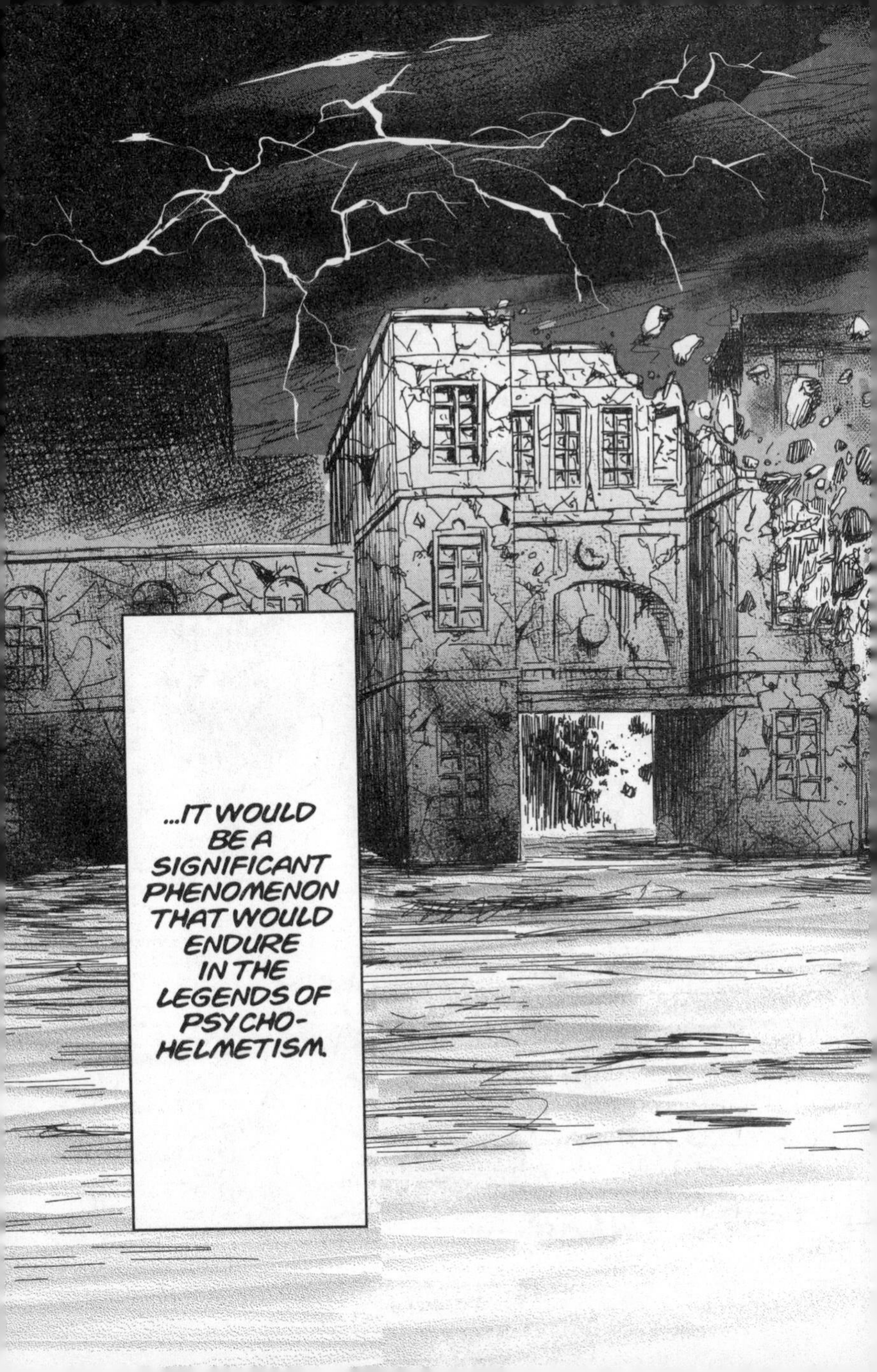
...IT WOULD BE A SIGNIFICANT PHENOMENON THAT WOULD ENDURE IN THE LEGENDS OF PSYCHO-HELMETISM.

Bonus

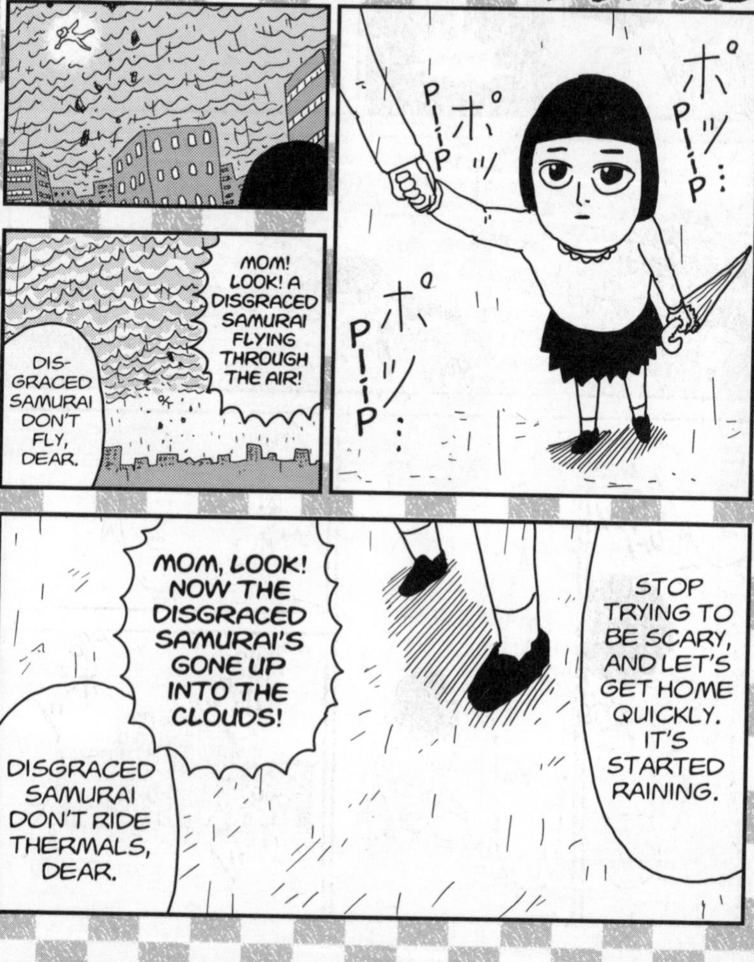
ポッ
P-I-P :
ポッ
P-I-P
ポッ
P-I-P :
MOM! LOOK! A DISGRACED SAMURAI FLYING THROUGH THE AIR!
DIS-GRACED SAMURAI DON'T FLY, DEAR.
MOM, LOOK! NOW THE DISGRACED SAMURAI'S GONE UP INTO THE CLOUDS!
DISGRACED SAMURAI DON'T RIDE THERMALS, DEAR.
STOP TRYING TO BE SCARY, AND LET'S GET HOME QUICKLY. IT'S STARTED RAINING.

CHAPTER 19: CONCLUSION

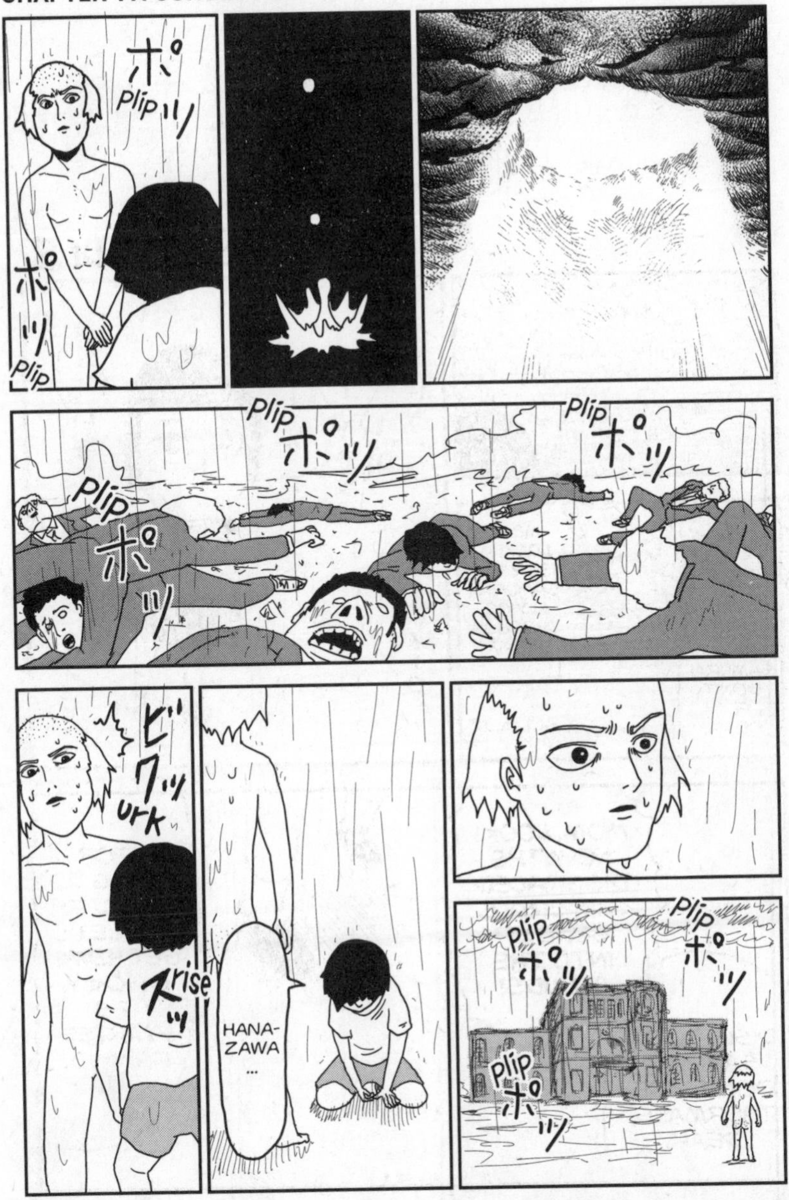

ポツ plip
ポツ plip
plip ポツ
plip ポツ
plip ポツ
plip ポツ
plip ポツ
plip ポツ
HANA-ZAWA ...
ビクッ urk
ズッ rise

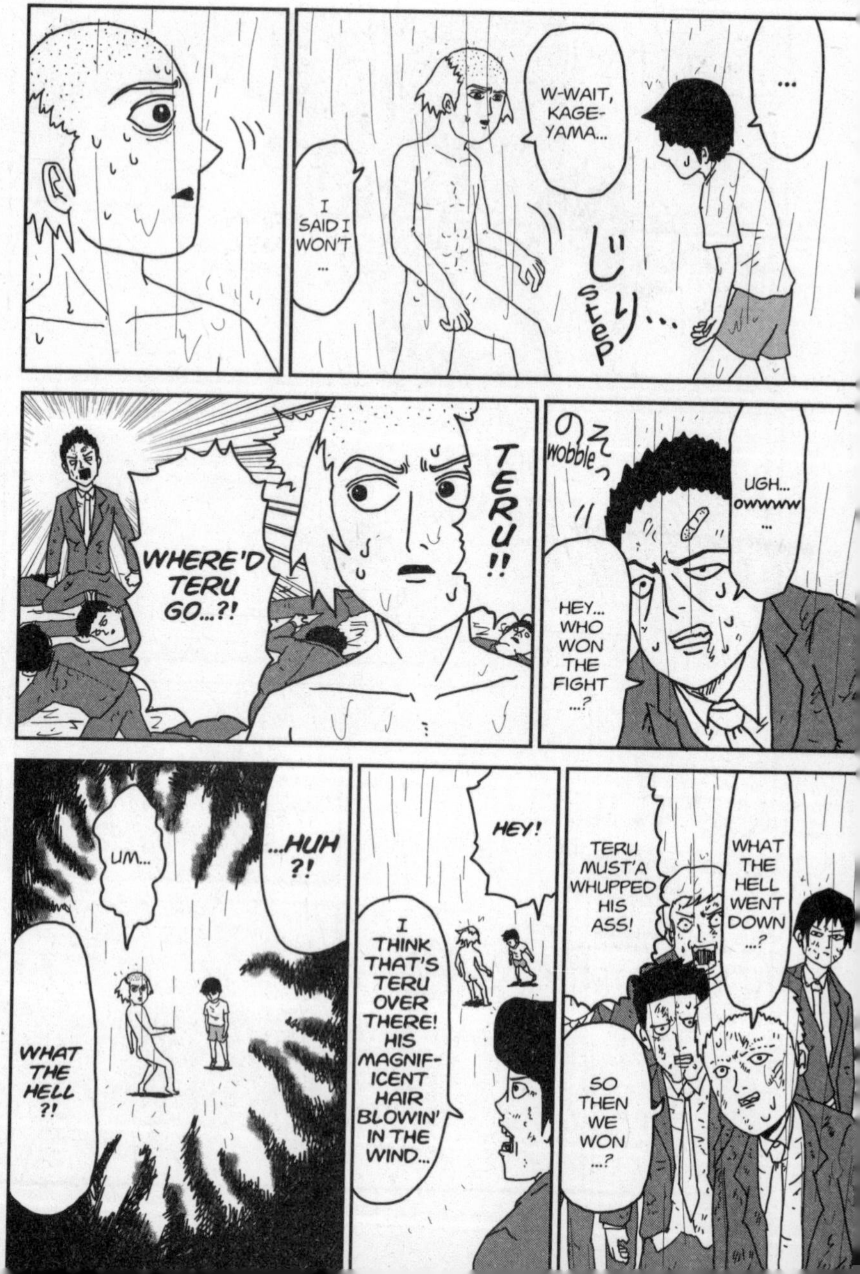
...
W-WAIT, KAGE-YAMA...
じり step...
I SAID I WON'T ...
UGH... OWWWW ...
のそっ wobble
HEY... WHO WON THE FIGHT ...?
TERU!!
WHERE'D TERU GO...?!
WHAT THE HELL WENT DOWN ...?
TERU MUST'A WHUPPED HIS ASS!
SO THEN WE WON ...?
HEY!
I THINK THAT'S TERU OVER THERE! HIS MAGNIFICENT HAIR BLOWIN' IN THE WIND...
...HUH ?!
UM...
WHAT THE HELL ?!

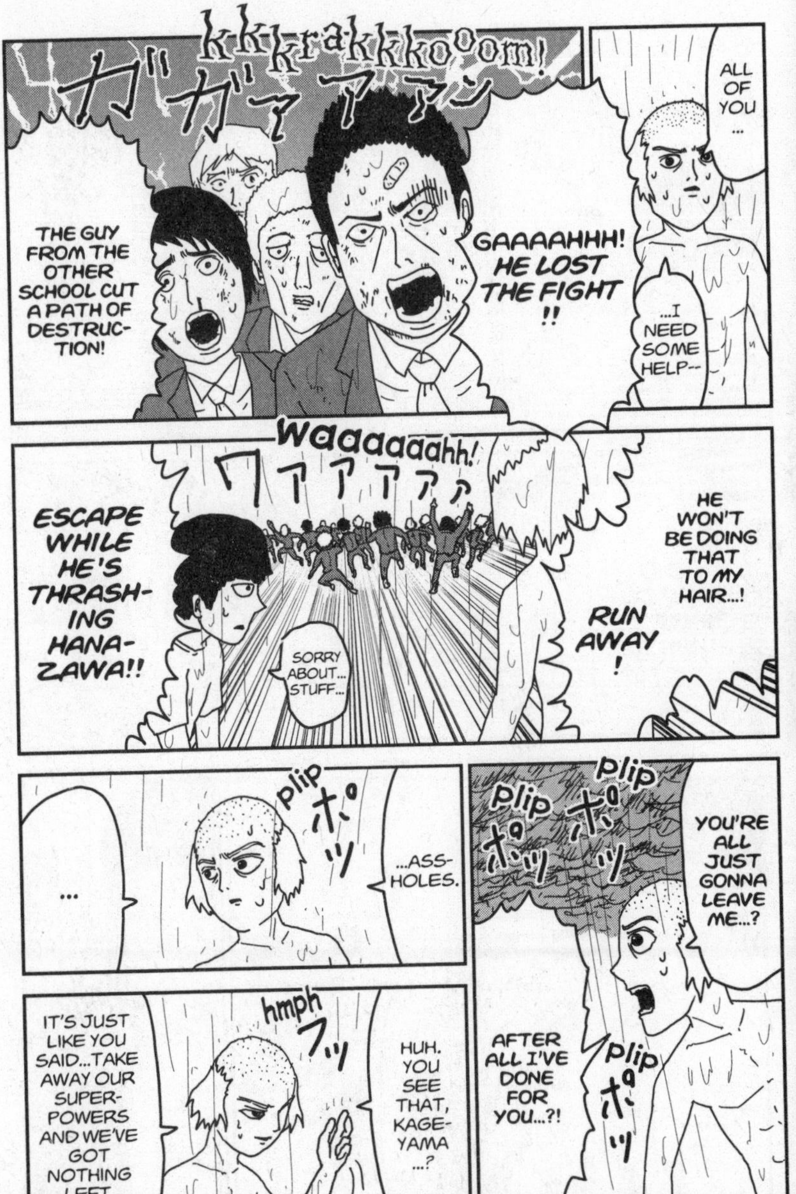
ALL OF YOU ...
...I NEED SOME HELP--
kkkrakkkoooom!
ガガァアァン
GAAAAHHH! HE LOST THE FIGHT!!
THE GUY FROM THE OTHER SCHOOL CUT A PATH OF DESTRUCTION!
Waaaaaahh!
ワァァァァ
HE WON'T BE DOING THAT TO MY HAIR...!
RUN AWAY!
ESCAPE WHILE HE'S THRASHING HANAZAWA!!
SORRY ABOUT... STUFF...
plip plip plip
ポツポツ
YOU'RE ALL JUST GONNA LEAVE ME...?
AFTER ALL I'VE DONE FOR YOU...?!
plip
ポツ
plip
ポツ
...ASSHOLES.
...
hmph
フッ
HUH. YOU SEE THAT, KAGEYAMA...?
IT'S JUST LIKE YOU SAID...TAKE AWAY OUR SUPERPOWERS AND WE'VE GOT NOTHING LEFT.

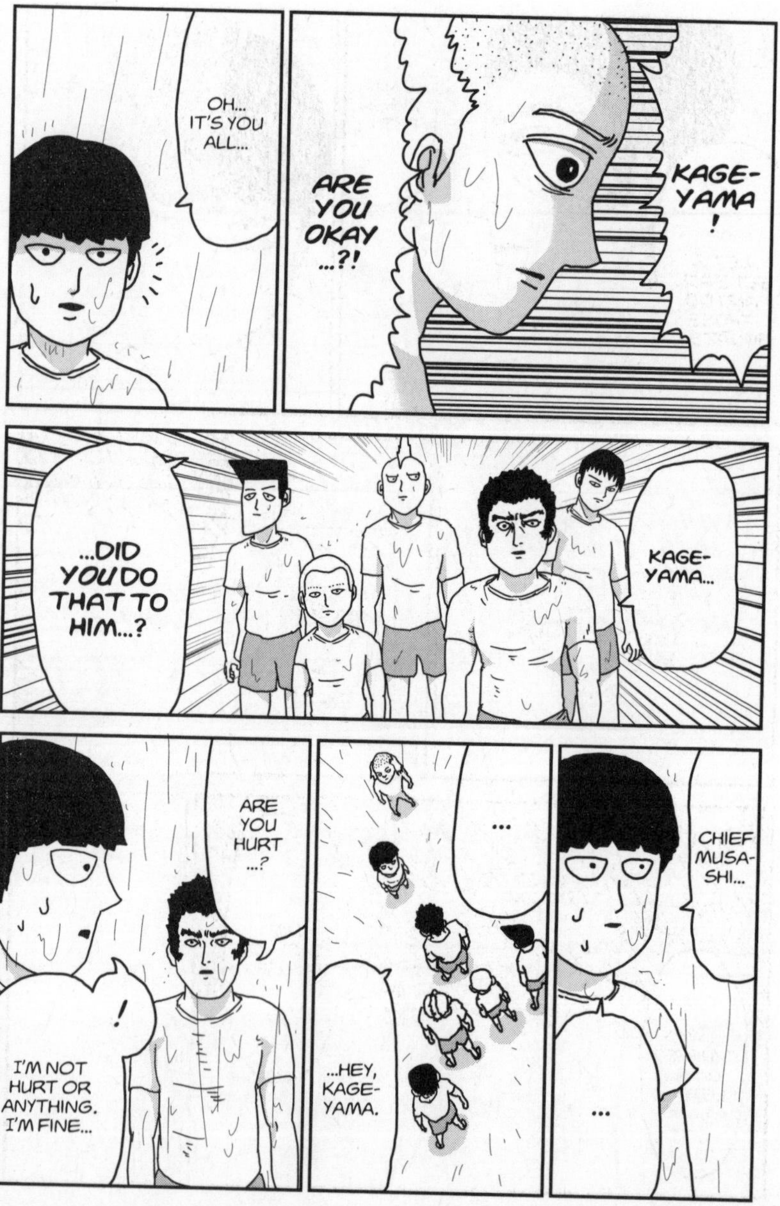
KAGE-YAMA!
ARE YOU OKAY...?!
OH... IT'S YOU ALL...
KAGE-YAMA...
...DID YOU DO THAT TO HIM...?
CHIEF MUSA-SHI...
...
...
...HEY, KAGE-YAMA.
ARE YOU HURT...?
!
I'M NOT HURT OR ANYTHING. I'M FINE...

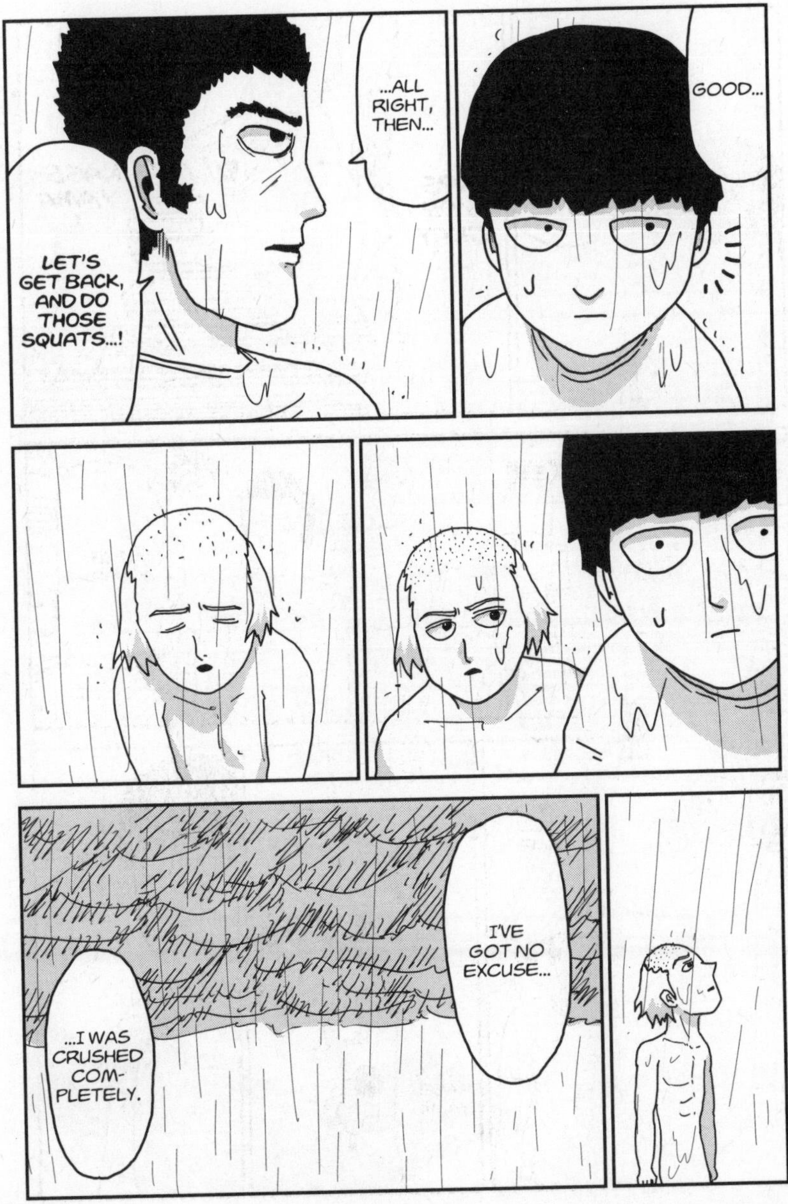
GOOD...
...ALL RIGHT, THEN...
LET'S GET BACK, AND DO THOSE SQUATS...!
I'VE GOT NO EXCUSE...
...I WAS CRUSHED COM-PLETELY.

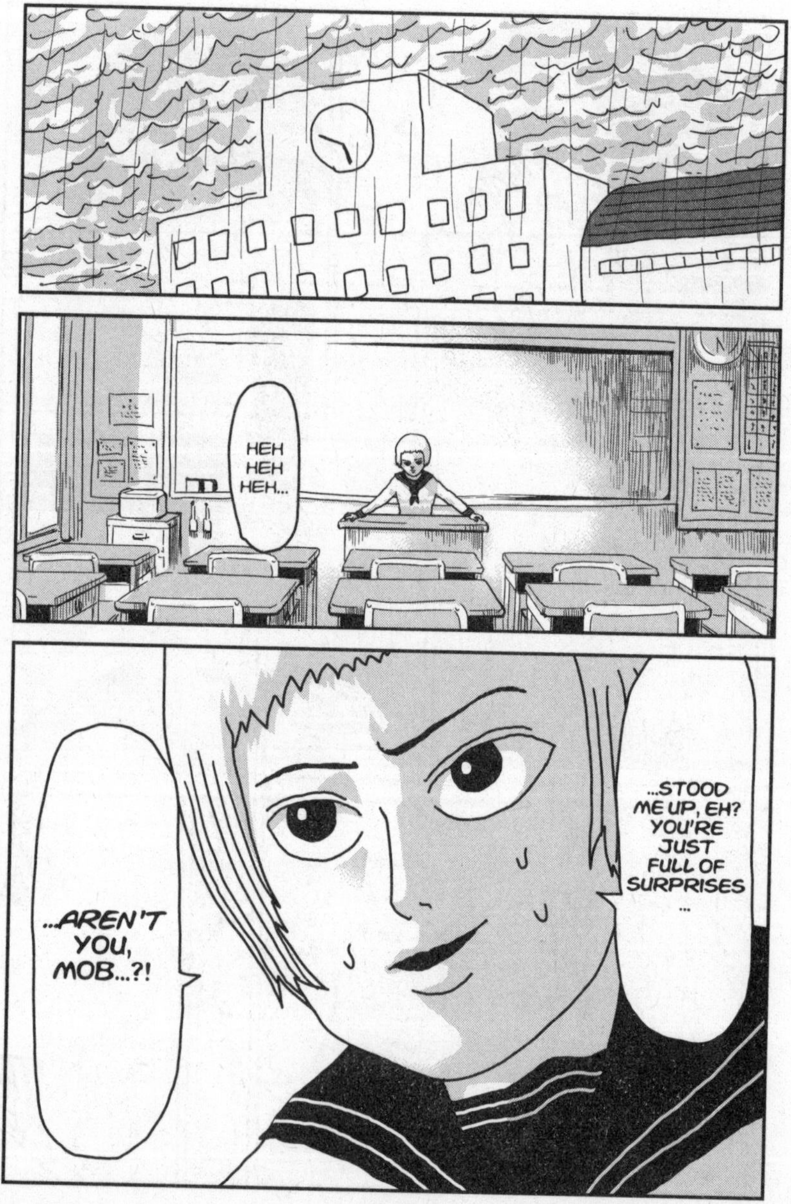
HEH HEH HEH...
...STOOD ME UP, EH? YOU'RE JUST FULL OF SURPRISES ...
...AREN'T YOU, MOB...?!

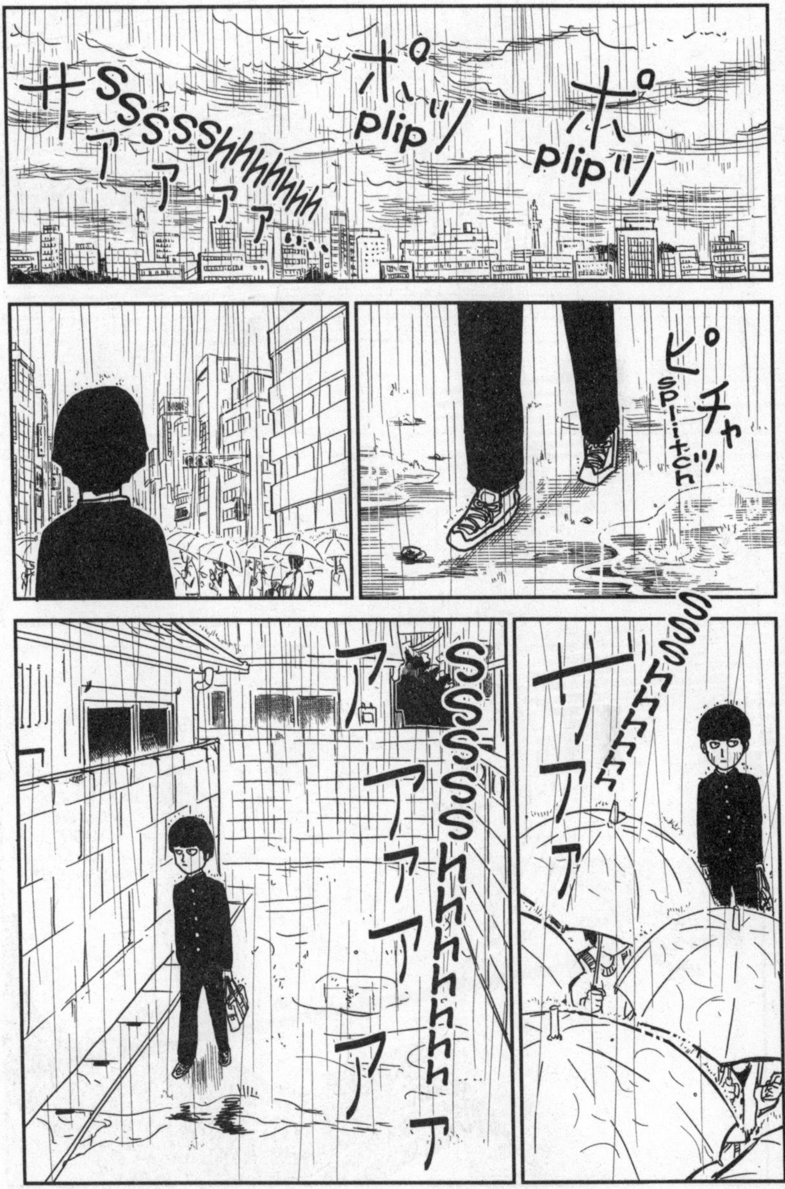

ポッ
plip
ポッ
plip
サアアア…
Sssssshhhhhhhhh...
ピチャッ
splitch
ザアア
Sssshhhhhhh
Ssssssshhhhhhhh

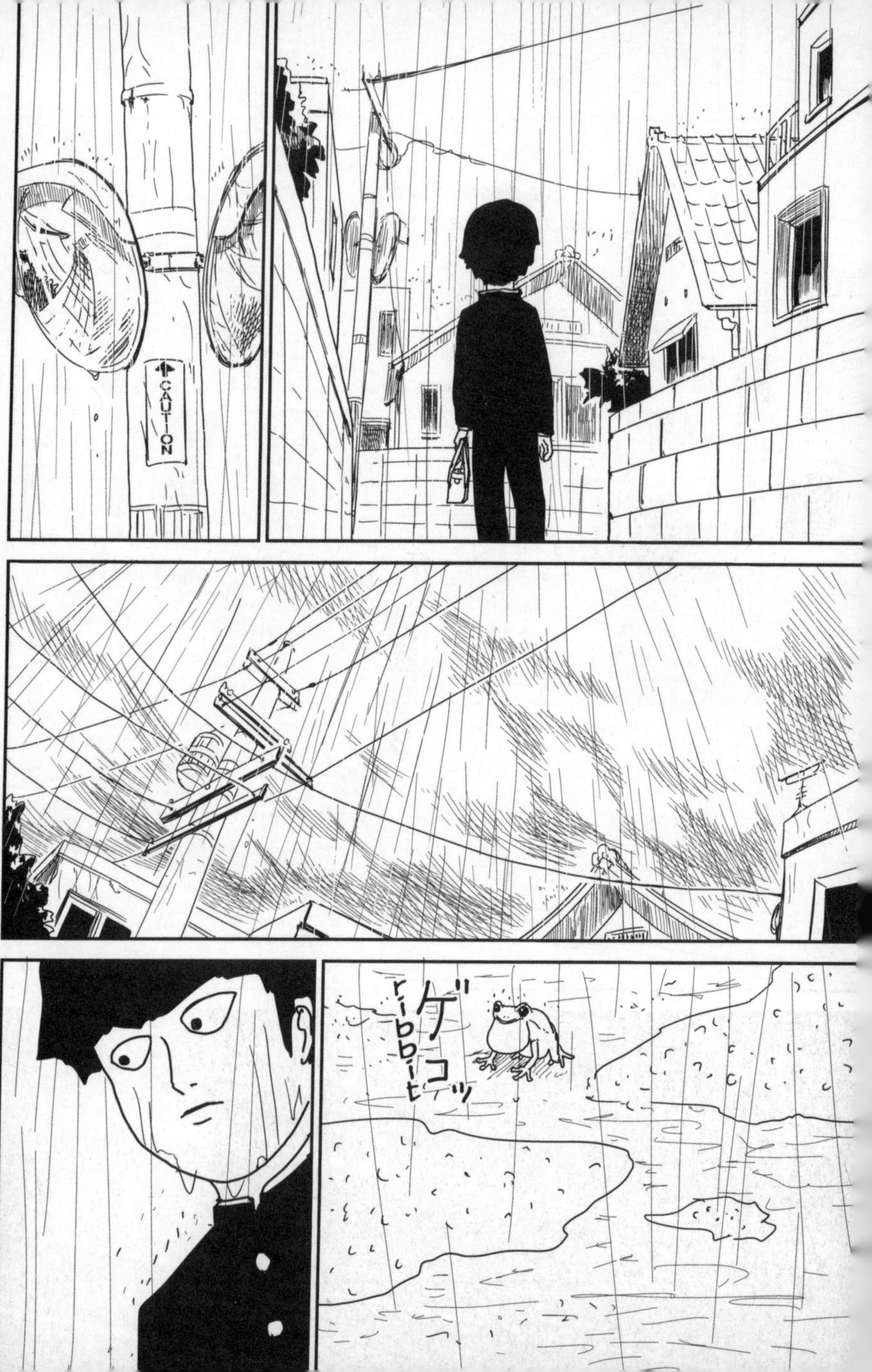
CAUTION
ゲコッ
ribbit

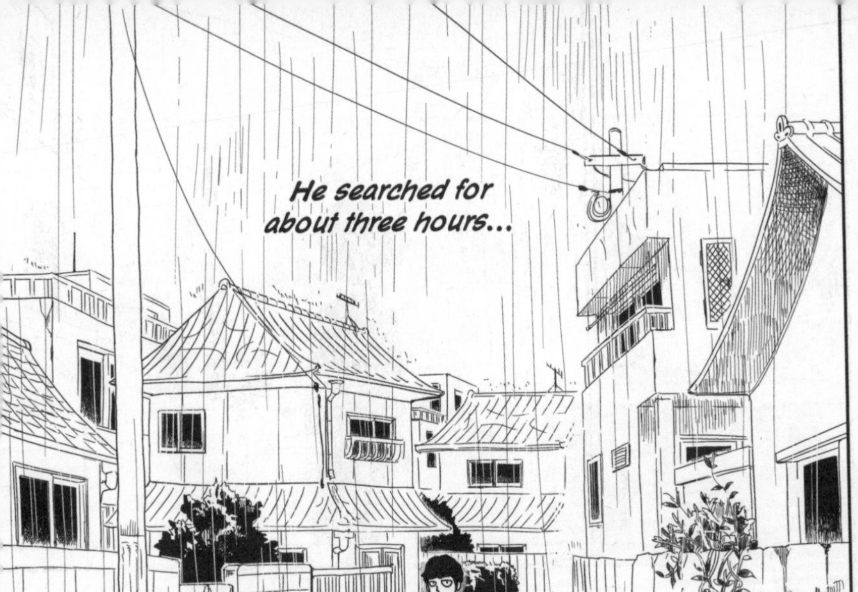
He searched for
about three hours...
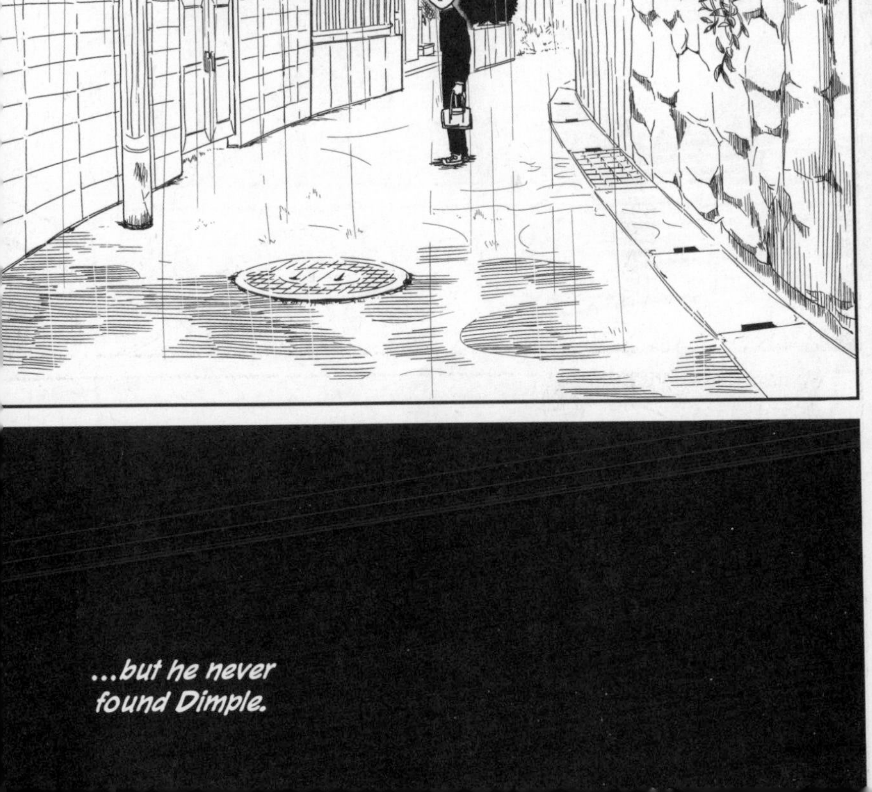
...but he never
found Dimple.

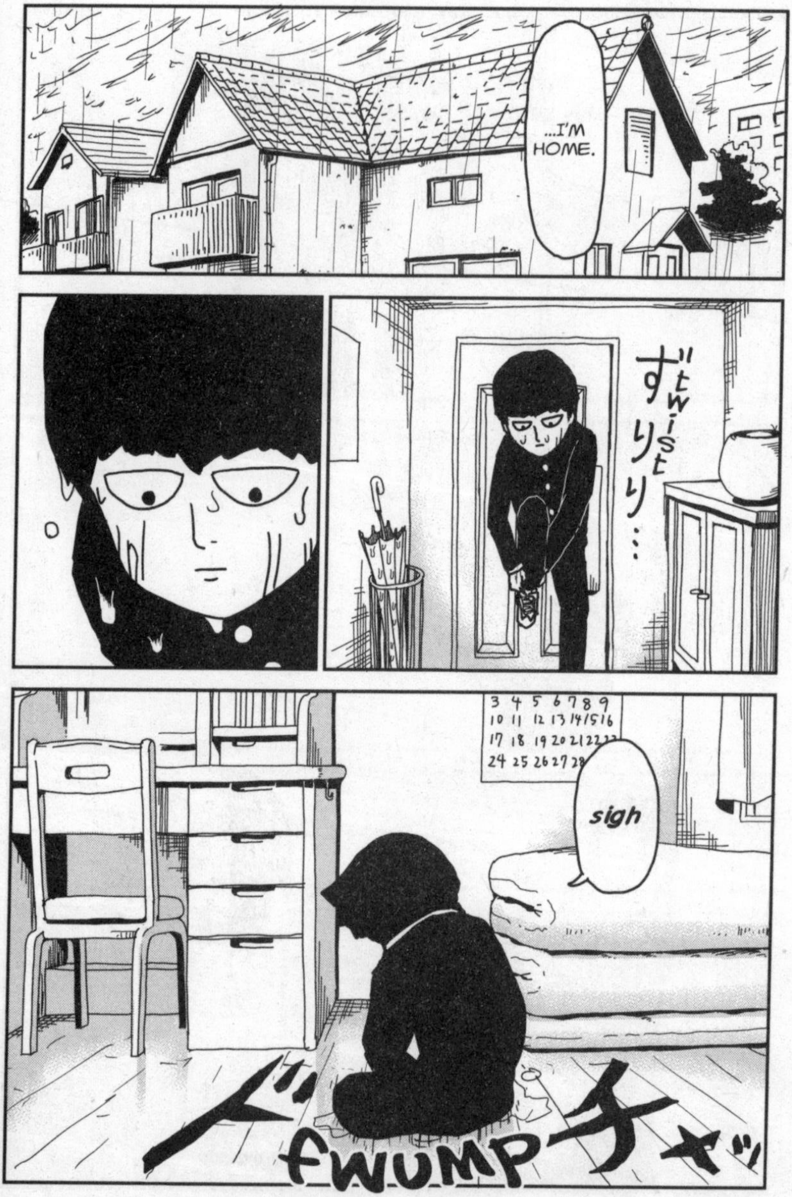
...I'M HOME.
ずりり…
twist
3 4 5 6 7 8 9
10 11 12 13 14 15 16
sigh
ドチャッ
fwump

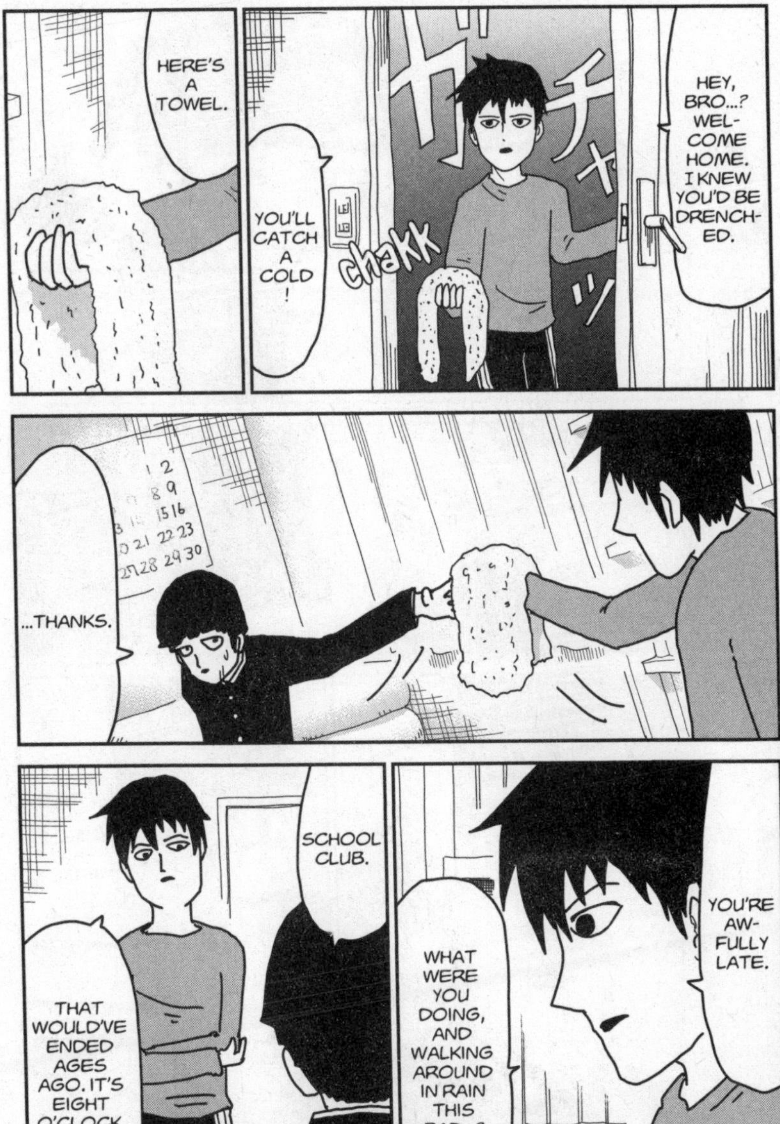
HEY, BRO...? WELCOME HOME. I KNEW YOU'D BE DRENCHED.
ガチャッ
chakk
YOU'LL CATCH A COLD!
HERE'S A TOWEL.
...THANKS.
YOU'RE AWFULLY LATE.
WHAT WERE YOU DOING, AND WALKING AROUND IN RAIN THIS BAD...?
SCHOOL CLUB.
THAT WOULD'VE ENDED AGES AGO. IT'S EIGHT O'CLOCK.

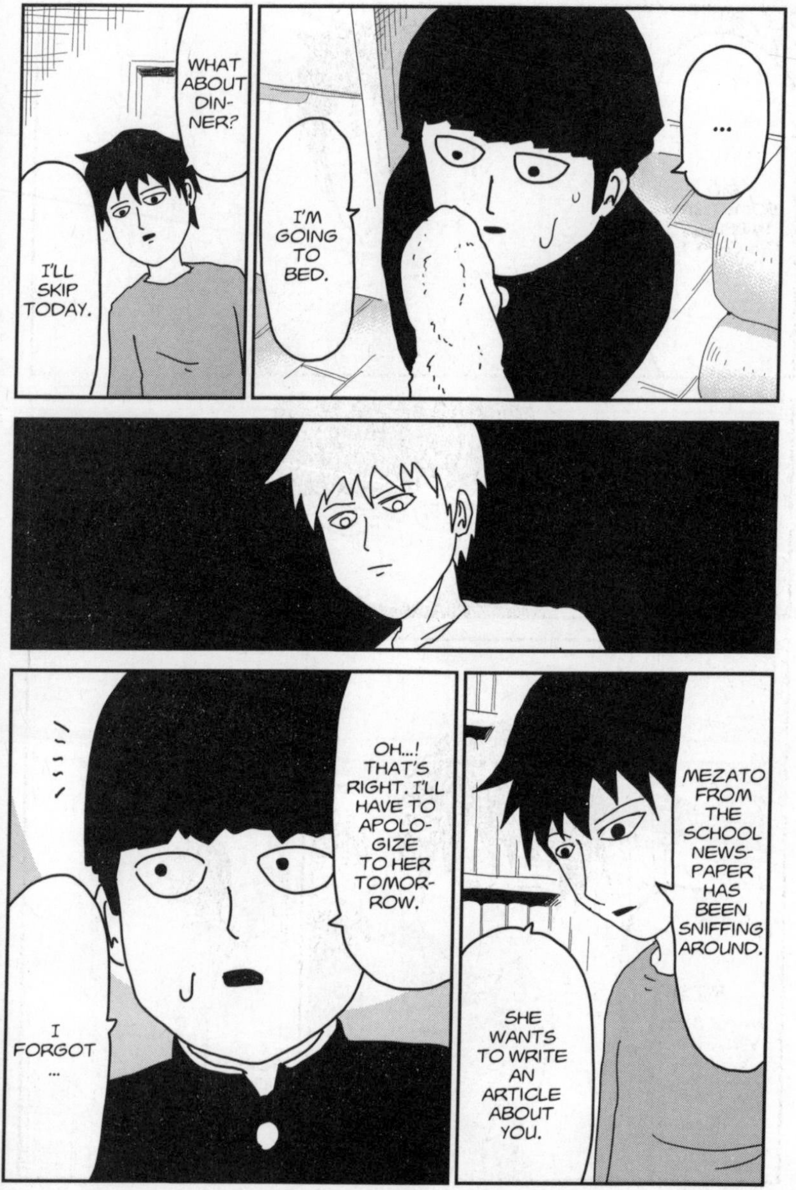
...
I'M GOING TO BED.
WHAT ABOUT DINNER?
I'LL SKIP TODAY.
MEZATO FROM THE SCHOOL NEWSPAPER HAS BEEN SNIFFING AROUND.
SHE WANTS TO WRITE AN ARTICLE ABOUT YOU.
OH...! THAT'S RIGHT. I'LL HAVE TO APOLOGIZE TO HER TOMORROW.
I FORGOT...

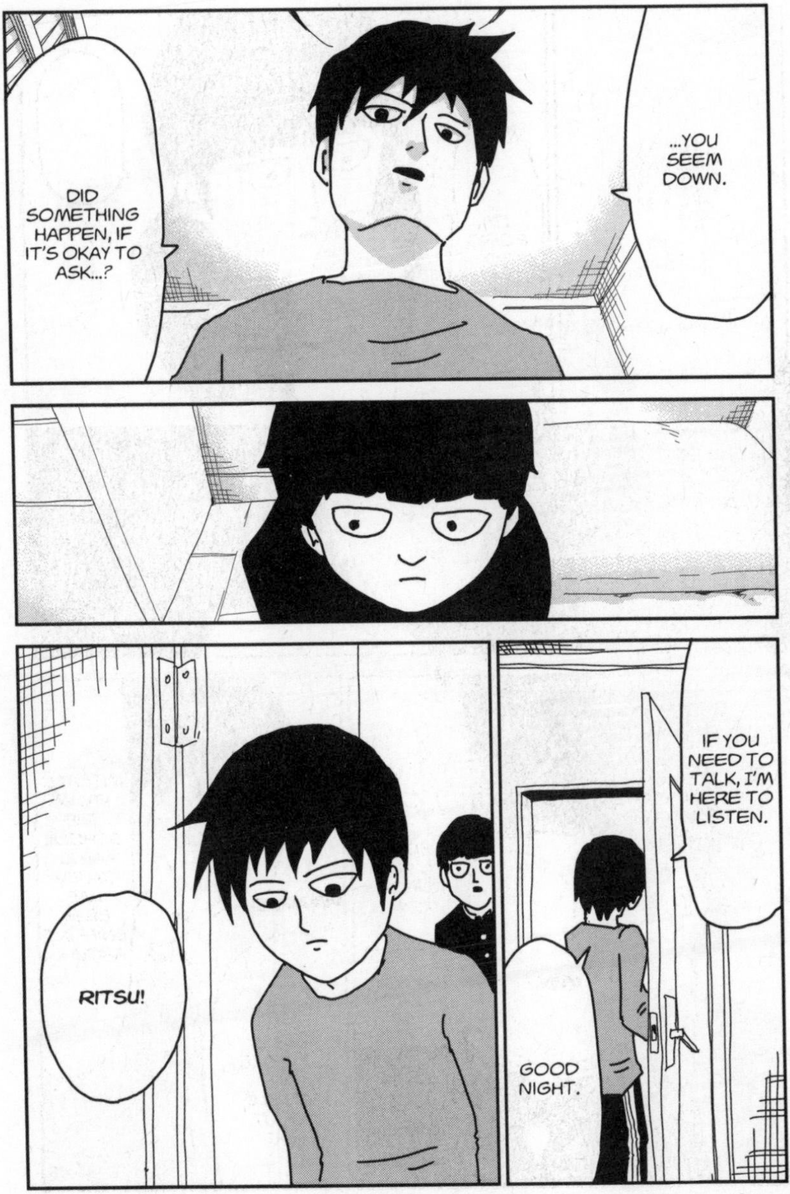
...YOU SEEM DOWN.
DID SOMETHING HAPPEN, IF IT'S OKAY TO ASK...?
IF YOU NEED TO TALK, I'M HERE TO LISTEN.
GOOD NIGHT.
RITSU!

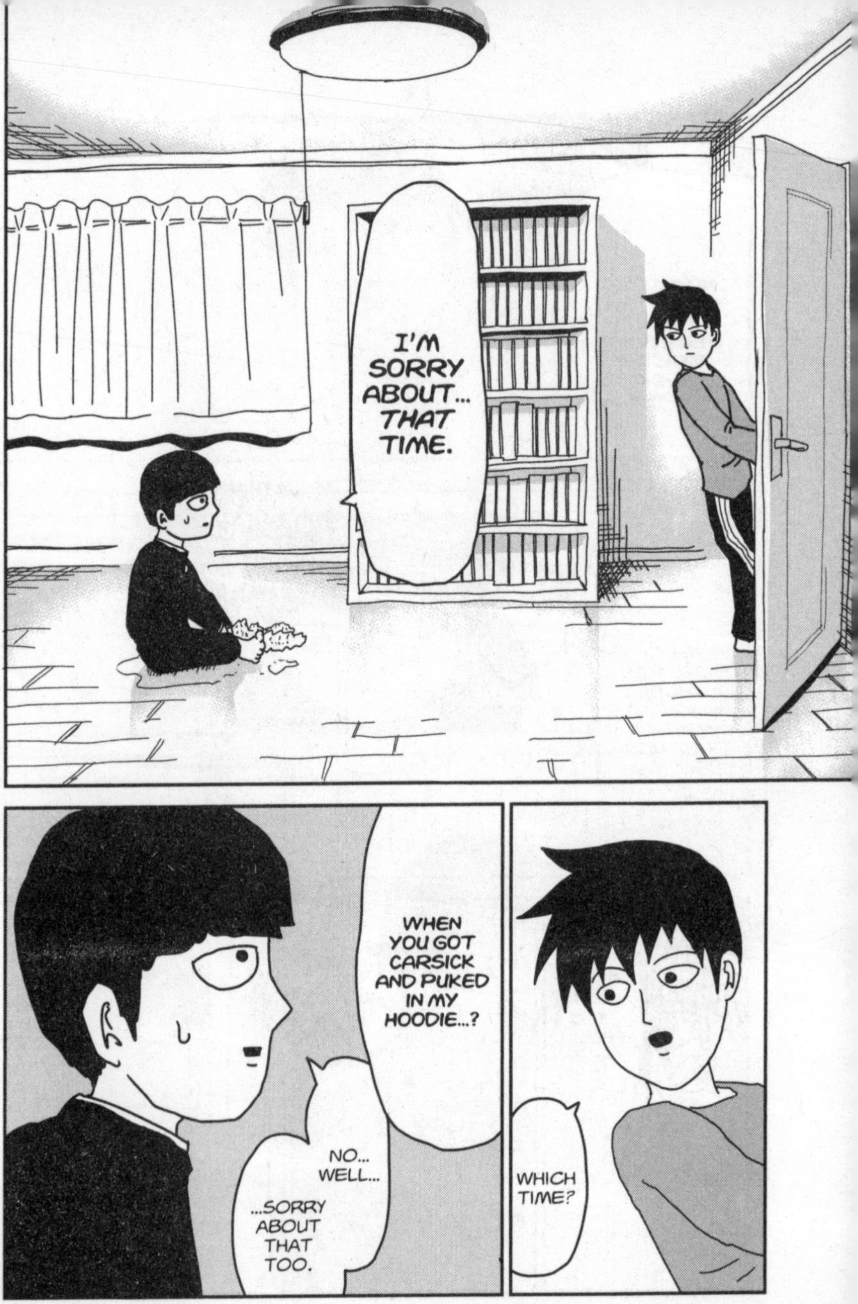
I'M SORRY ABOUT... THAT TIME.
WHICH TIME?
WHEN YOU GOT CARSICK AND PUKED IN MY HOODIE...?
NO... WELL...
...SORRY ABOUT THAT TOO.

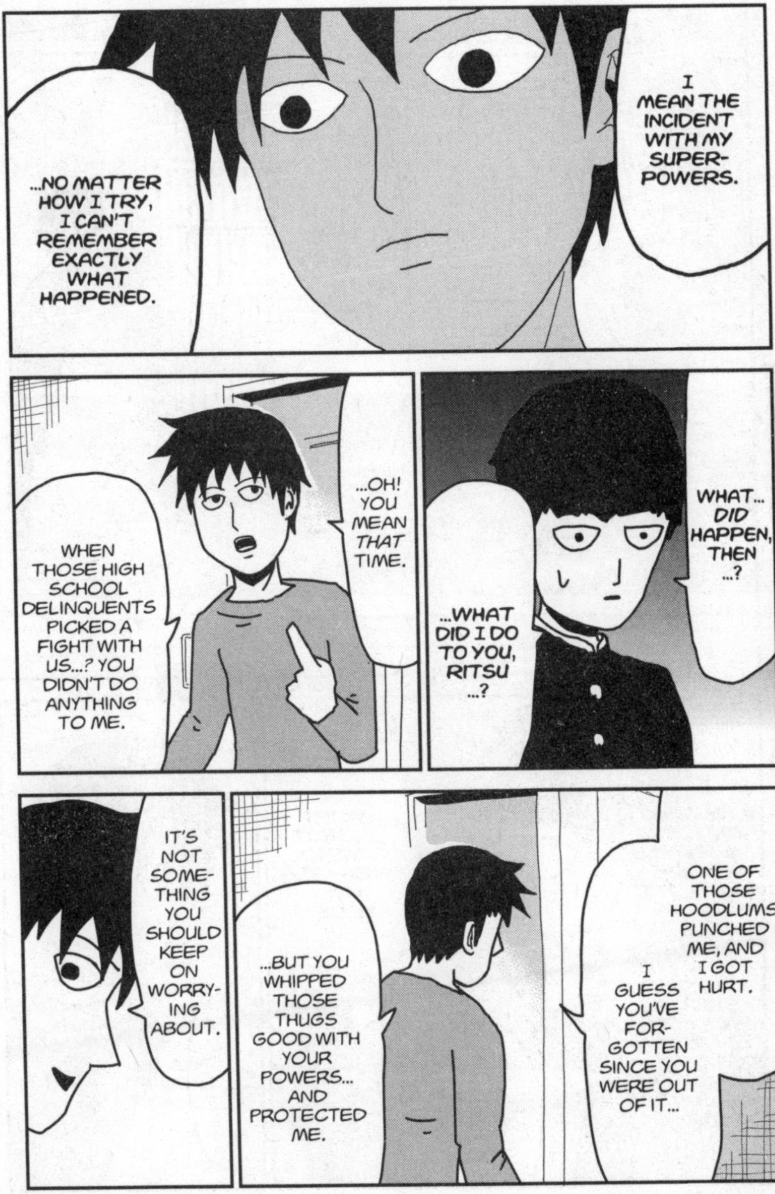
I MEAN THE INCIDENT WITH MY SUPER-POWERS.
...NO MATTER HOW I TRY, I CAN'T REMEMBER EXACTLY WHAT HAPPENED.
WHAT... *DID* HAPPEN, THEN ...?
...WHAT DID I DO TO YOU, RITSU ...?
...OH! YOU MEAN *THAT* TIME.
WHEN THOSE HIGH SCHOOL DELINQUENTS PICKED A FIGHT WITH US...? YOU DIDN'T DO ANYTHING TO ME.
ONE OF THOSE HOODLUMS PUNCHED ME, AND I GOT HURT.
I GUESS YOU'VE FOR-GOTTEN SINCE YOU WERE OUT OF IT...
...BUT YOU WHIPPED THOSE THUGS GOOD WITH YOUR POWERS... AND PROTECTED ME.
IT'S NOT SOME-THING YOU SHOULD KEEP ON WORRY-ING ABOUT.

GOOD NIGHT.

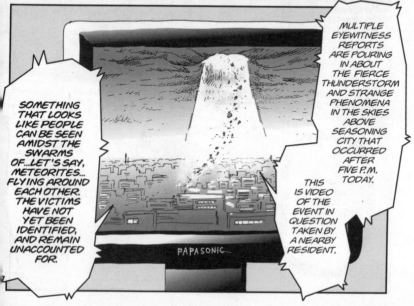

MULTIPLE EYEWITNESS REPORTS ARE POURING IN ABOUT THE FIERCE THUNDERSTORM AND STRANGE PHENOMENA IN THE SKIES ABOVE SEASONING CITY THAT OCCURRED AFTER FIVE P.M. TODAY.

THIS IS VIDEO OF THE EVENT IN QUESTION TAKEN BY A NEARBY RESIDENT.

SOMETHING THAT LOOKS LIKE PEOPLE CAN BE SEEN AMIDST THE SWARMS OF...LET'S SAY, METEORITES... FLYING AROUND EACH OTHER. THE VICTIMS HAVE NOT YET BEEN IDENTIFIED, AND REMAIN UNACCOUNTED FOR.

PAPASONIC

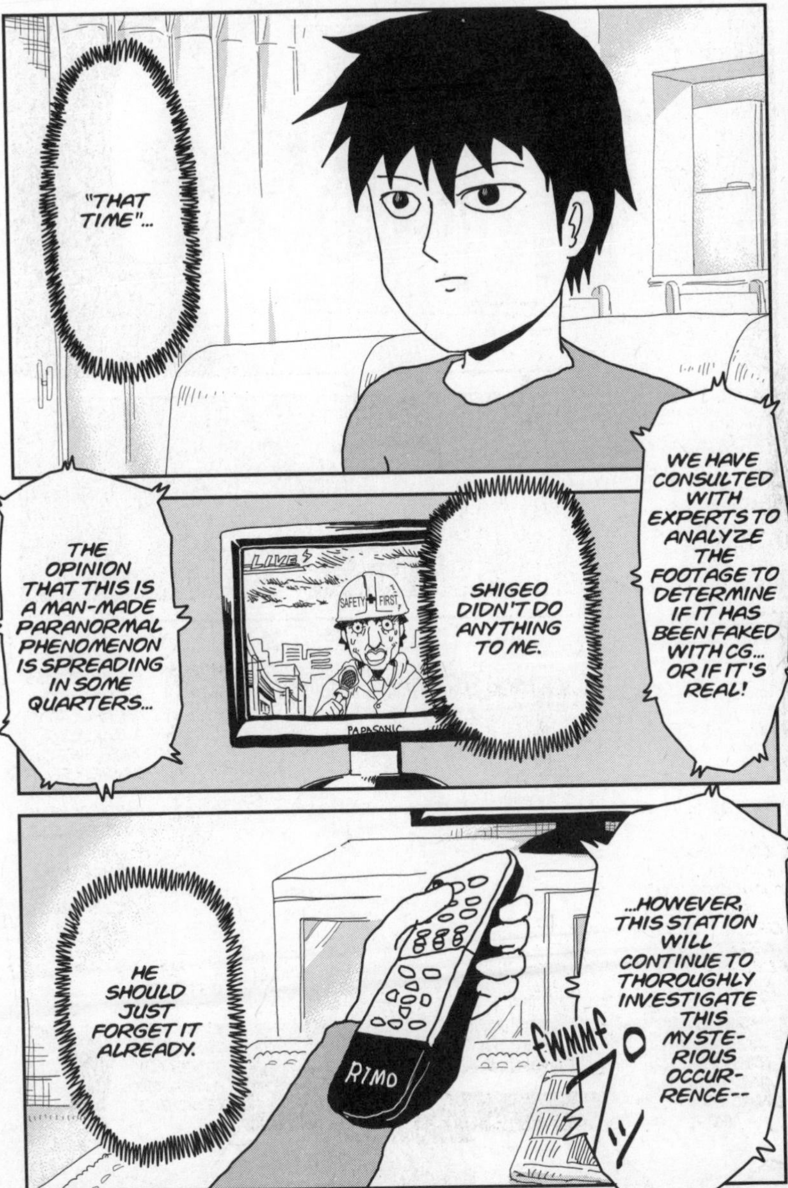
"THAT TIME"...
WE HAVE CONSULTED WITH EXPERTS TO ANALYZE THE FOOTAGE TO DETERMINE IF IT HAS BEEN FAKED WITH CG... OR IF IT'S REAL!
SHIGEO DIDN'T DO ANYTHING TO ME.
LIVE
SAFETY FIRST
PAPASONIC
THE OPINION THAT THIS IS A MAN-MADE PARANORMAL PHENOMENON IS SPREADING IN SOME QUARTERS...
...HOWEVER, THIS STATION WILL CONTINUE TO THOROUGHLY INVESTIGATE THIS MYSTERIOUS OCCURRENCE--
fwmmf
RIMO
HE SHOULD JUST FORGET IT ALREADY.

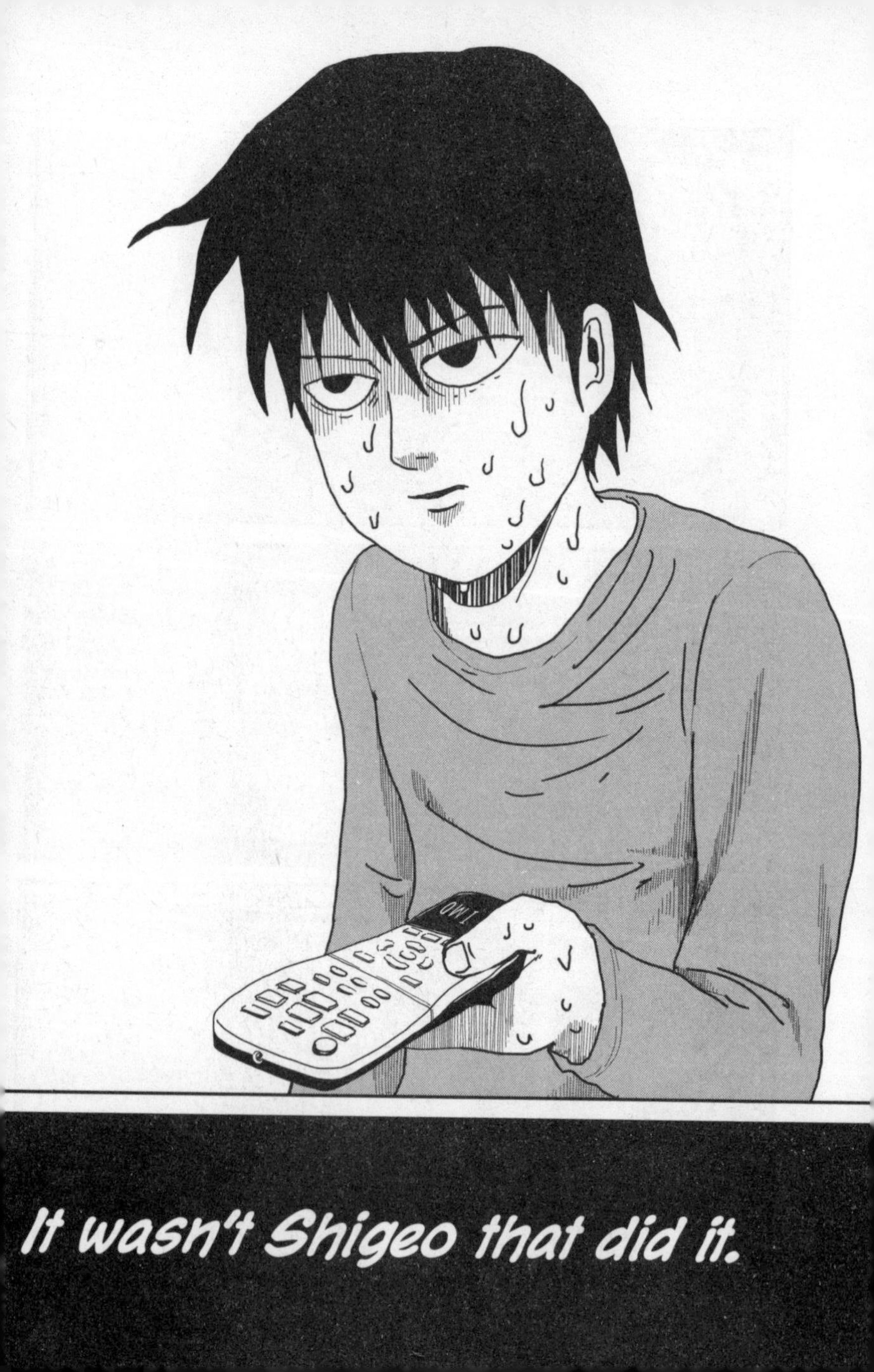
It wasn't Shigeo that did it.

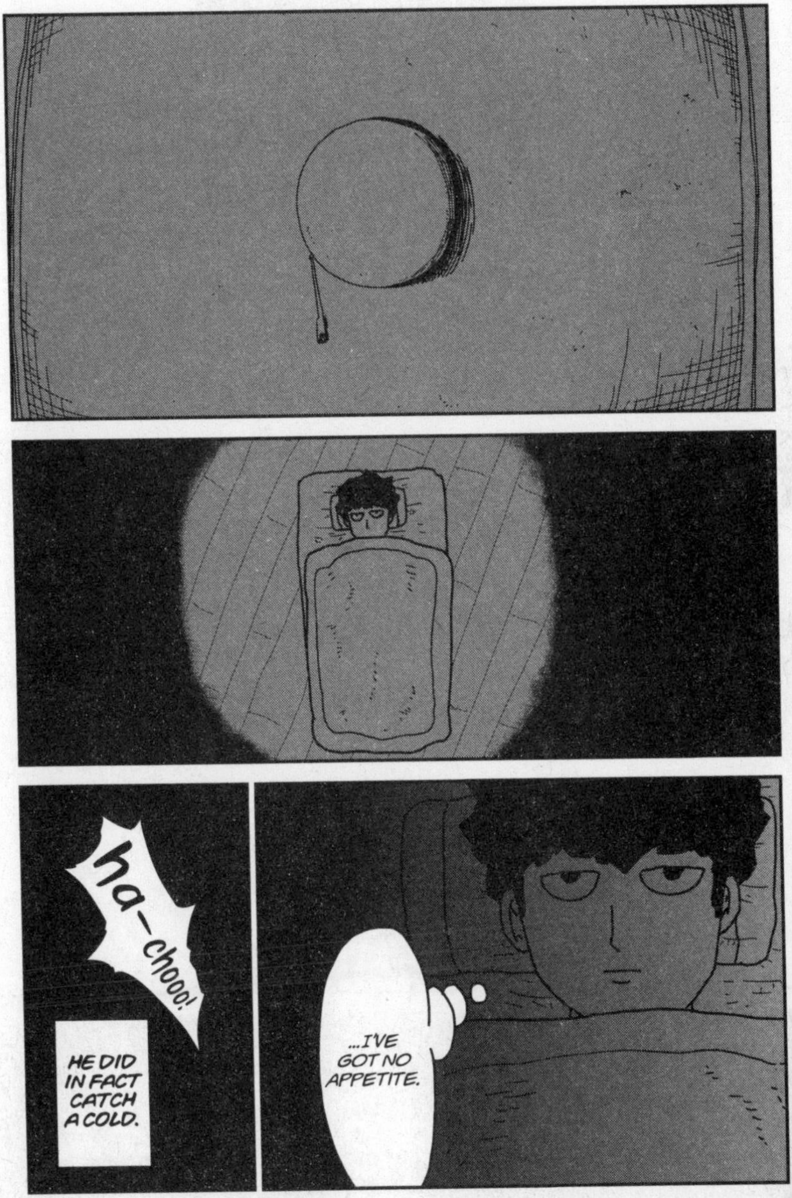
...I'VE GOT NO APPETITE.
ha-chooo!
HE DID IN FACT CATCH A COLD.

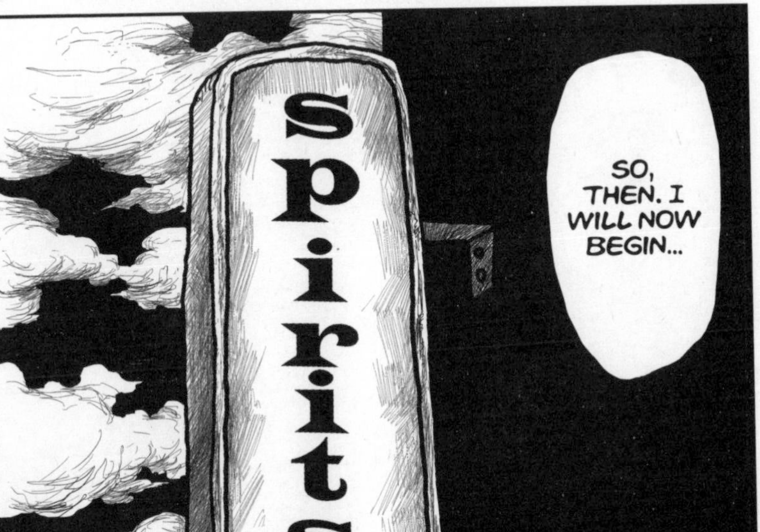
Spirits & such
SO, THEN. I WILL NOW BEGIN...
CHAPTER 20: THE STUDENT COUNCIL

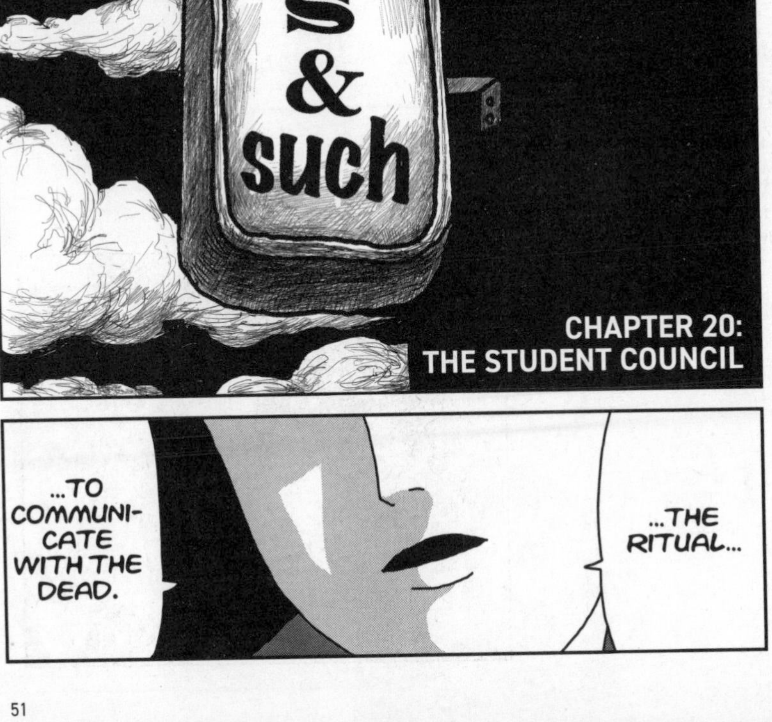
...THE RITUAL...
...TO COMMUNI-CATE WITH THE DEAD.

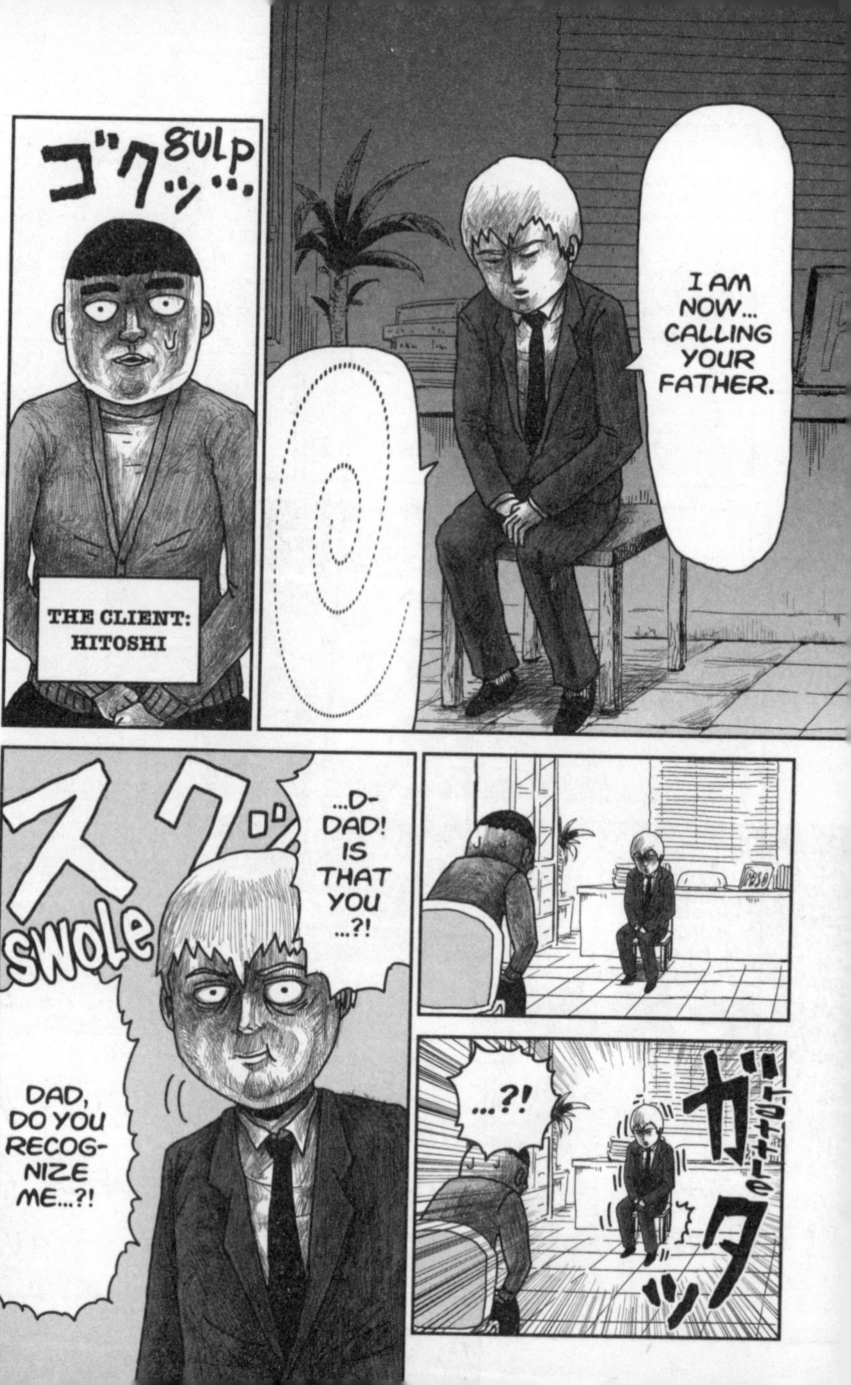
I AM NOW... CALLING YOUR FATHER.
ゴクッ
GULP
THE CLIENT: HITOSHI
...?!
ガタッ
RATTLE
スクッ
SWOLE
...D-DAD! IS THAT YOU ...?!
DAD, DO YOU RECOG-NIZE ME...?!

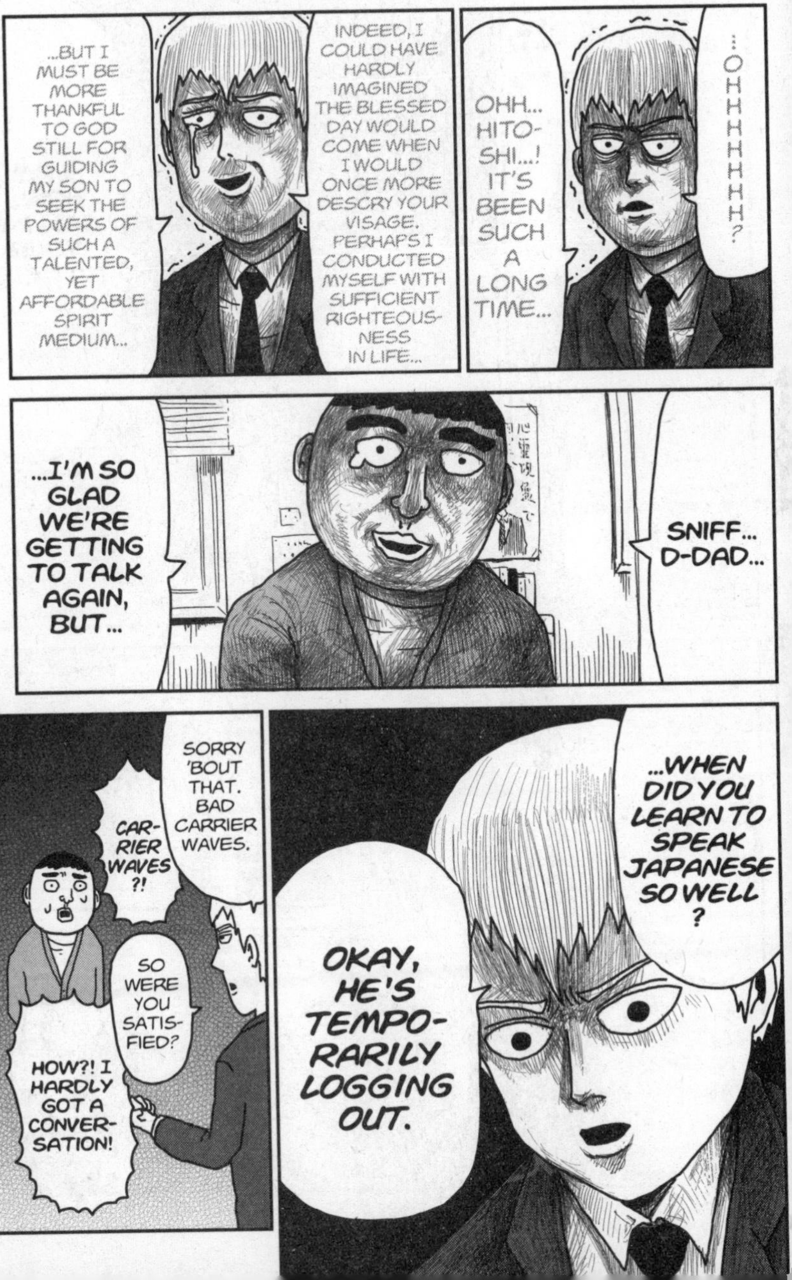
...OHHHHHHH?
OHH... HITOSHI...! IT'S BEEN SUCH A LONG TIME...
INDEED, I COULD HAVE HARDLY IMAGINED THE BLESSED DAY WOULD COME WHEN I WOULD ONCE MORE DESCRY YOUR VISAGE. PERHAPS I CONDUCTED MYSELF WITH SUFFICIENT RIGHTEOUSNESS IN LIFE...
...BUT I MUST BE MORE THANKFUL TO GOD STILL FOR GUIDING MY SON TO SEEK THE POWERS OF SUCH A TALENTED, YET AFFORDABLE SPIRIT MEDIUM...
SNIFF... D-DAD...
...I'M SO GLAD WE'RE GETTING TO TALK AGAIN, BUT...
...WHEN DID YOU LEARN TO SPEAK JAPANESE SO WELL?
OKAY, HE'S TEMPORARILY LOGGING OUT.
SORRY 'BOUT THAT. BAD CARRIER WAVES.
CARRIER WAVES?!
SO WERE YOU SATISFIED?
HOW?! I HARDLY GOT A CONVERSATION!

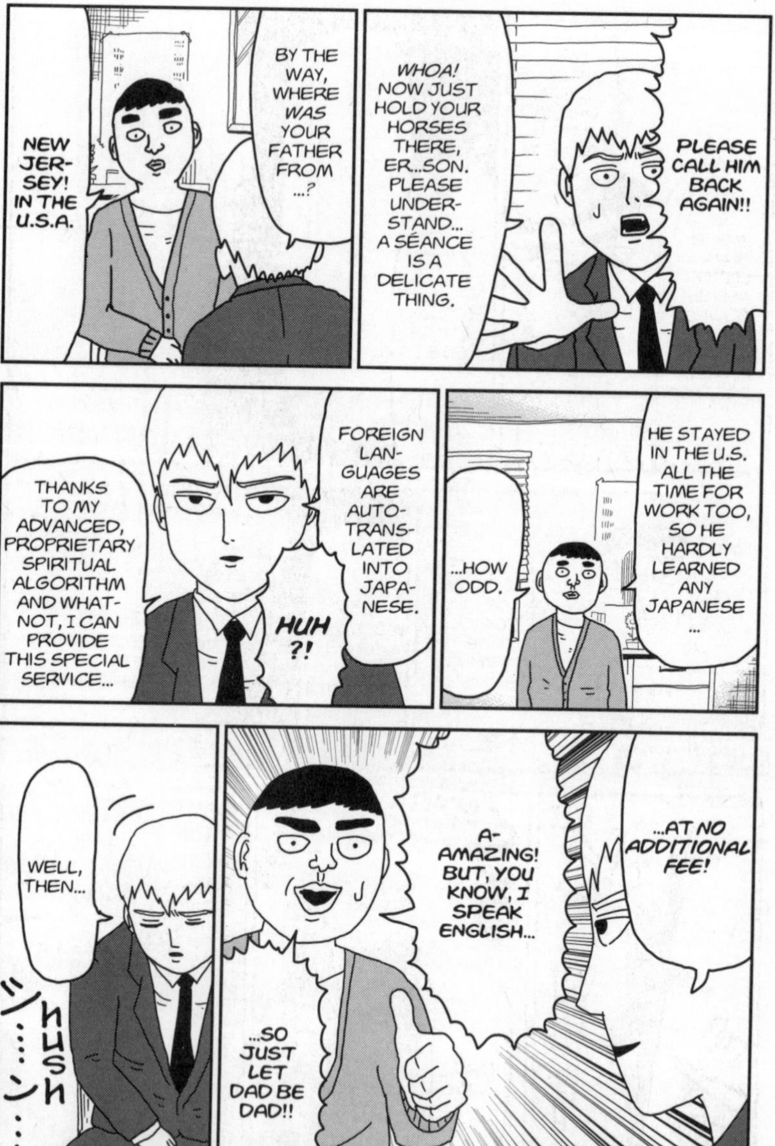
PLEASE CALL HIM BACK AGAIN!!
WHOA! NOW JUST HOLD YOUR HORSES THERE, ER...SON. PLEASE UNDERSTAND... A SÉANCE IS A DELICATE THING.
BY THE WAY, WHERE WAS YOUR FATHER FROM ...?
NEW JERSEY! IN THE U.S.A.
HE STAYED IN THE U.S. ALL THE TIME FOR WORK TOO, SO HE HARDLY LEARNED ANY JAPANESE ...
...HOW ODD.
FOREIGN LANGUAGES ARE AUTO-TRANSLATED INTO JAPANESE.
HUH?!
THANKS TO MY ADVANCED, PROPRIETARY SPIRITUAL ALGORITHM AND WHATNOT, I CAN PROVIDE THIS SPECIAL SERVICE...
...AT NO ADDITIONAL FEE!
A-AMAZING! BUT, YOU KNOW, I SPEAK ENGLISH...
...SO JUST LET DAD BE DAD!!
WELL, THEN...
HUSH

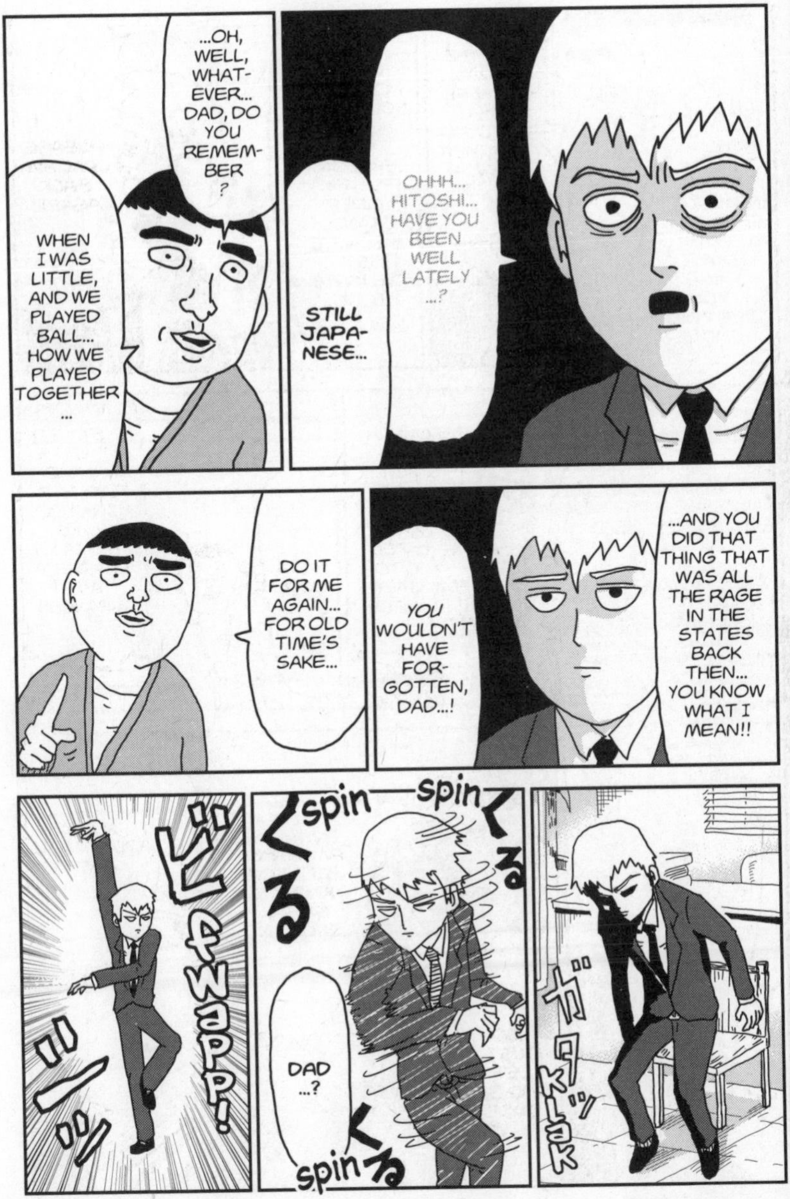
OHHH... HITOSHI... HAVE YOU BEEN WELL LATELY ...?
STILL JAPANESE...
...OH, WELL, WHATEVER... DAD, DO YOU REMEMBER ?
WHEN I WAS LITTLE, AND WE PLAYED BALL... HOW WE PLAYED TOGETHER ...
...AND YOU DID THAT THING THAT WAS ALL THE RAGE IN THE STATES BACK THEN... YOU KNOW WHAT I MEAN!!
YOU WOULDN'T HAVE FORGOTTEN, DAD...!
DO IT FOR ME AGAIN... FOR OLD TIME'S SAKE...
ガタッ
klak
spin
spin
DAD ...?
spin
fwapp!

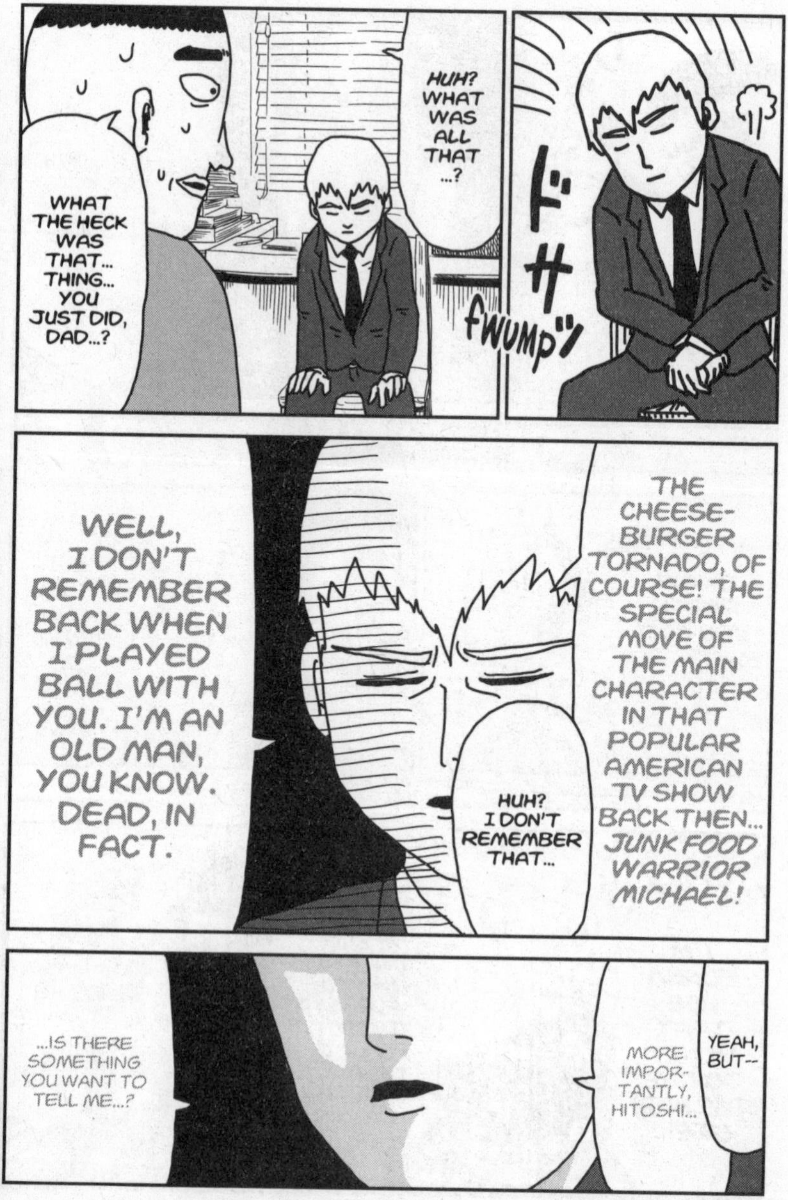
ドサ
fwumpッ
HUH? WHAT WAS ALL THAT ...?
WHAT THE HECK WAS THAT... THING... YOU JUST DID, DAD...?
THE CHEESE-BURGER TORNADO, OF COURSE! THE SPECIAL MOVE OF THE MAIN CHARACTER IN THAT POPULAR AMERICAN TV SHOW BACK THEN... JUNK FOOD WARRIOR MICHAEL!
HUH? I DON'T REMEMBER THAT...
WELL, I DON'T REMEMBER BACK WHEN I PLAYED BALL WITH YOU. I'M AN OLD MAN, YOU KNOW. DEAD, IN FACT.
YEAH, BUT--
MORE IMPOR-TANTLY, HITOSHI...
...IS THERE SOMETHING YOU WANT TO TELL ME...?

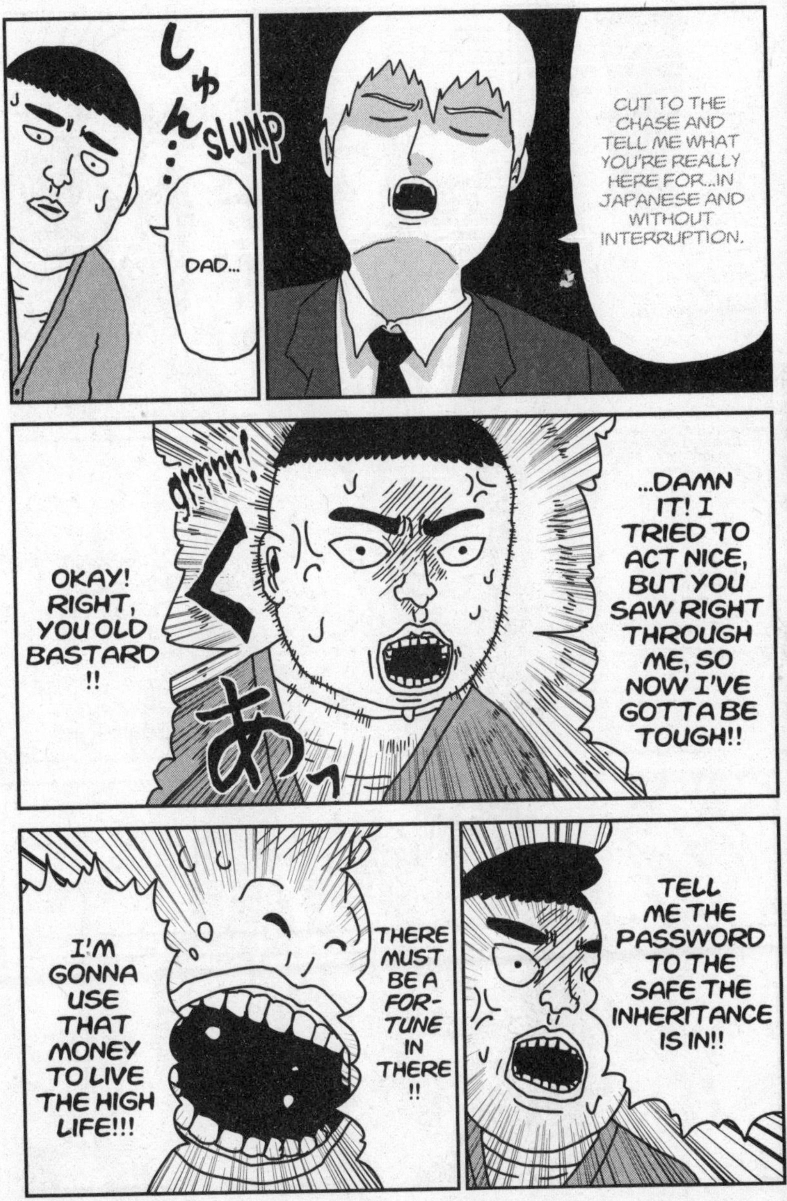
CUT TO THE CHASE AND TELL ME WHAT YOU'RE REALLY HERE FOR...IN JAPANESE AND WITHOUT INTERRUPTION.
しゅん…
SLUMP
DAD...
...DAMN IT! I TRIED TO ACT NICE, BUT YOU SAW RIGHT THROUGH ME, SO NOW I'VE GOTTA BE TOUGH!!
grrrr!
くあっ
OKAY! RIGHT, YOU OLD BASTARD !!
TELL ME THE PASSWORD TO THE SAFE THE INHERITANCE IS IN!!
THERE MUST BE A FOR-TUNE IN THERE !!
I'M GONNA USE THAT MONEY TO LIVE THE HIGH LIFE!!!

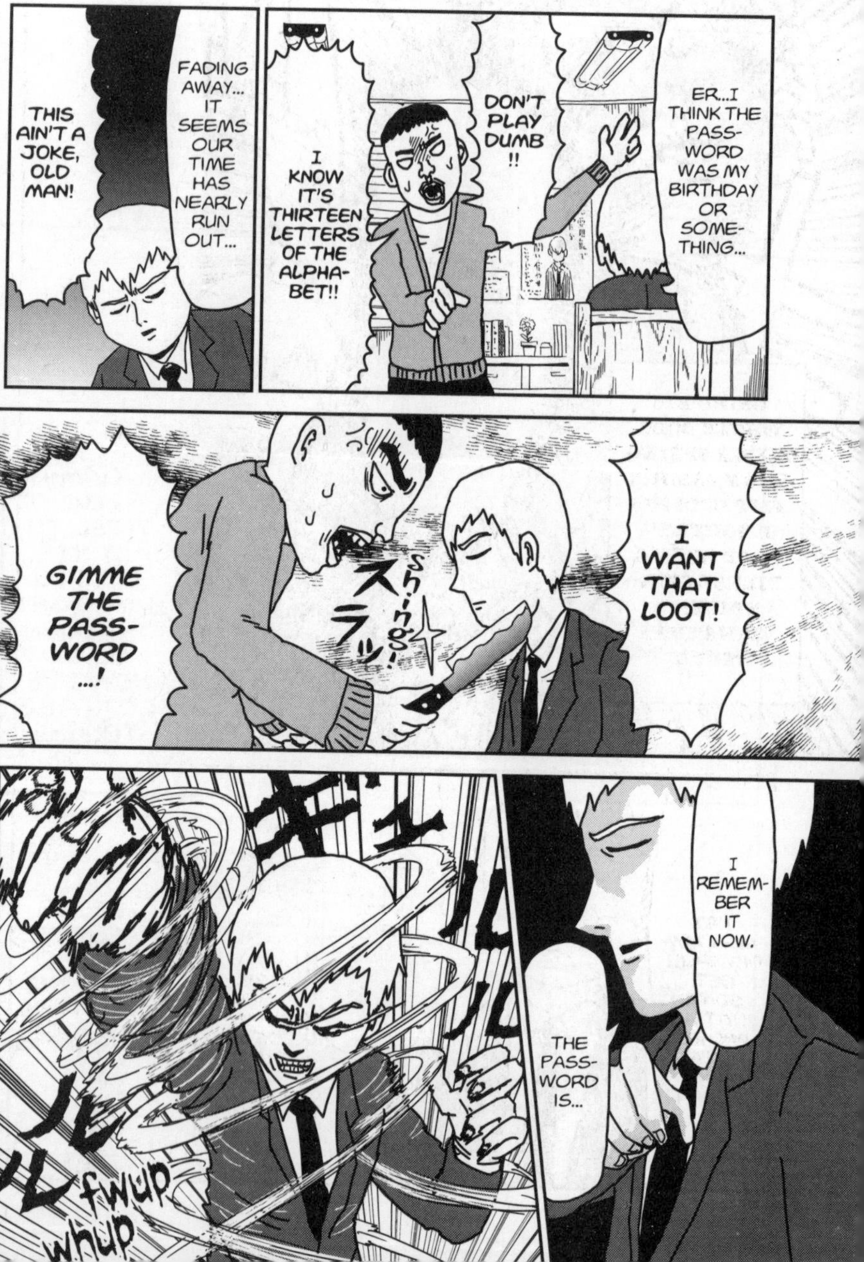
ER...I THINK THE PASS-WORD WAS MY BIRTHDAY OR SOME-THING...
DON'T PLAY DUMB!!
I KNOW IT'S THIRTEEN LETTERS OF THE ALPHA-BET!!
FADING AWAY... IT SEEMS OUR TIME HAS NEARLY RUN OUT...
THIS AIN'T A JOKE, OLD MAN!
I WANT THAT LOOT!
スラッ
shing!
GIMME THE PASS-WORD ...!
I REMEM-BER IT NOW.
THE PASS-WORD IS...
fwup
whup

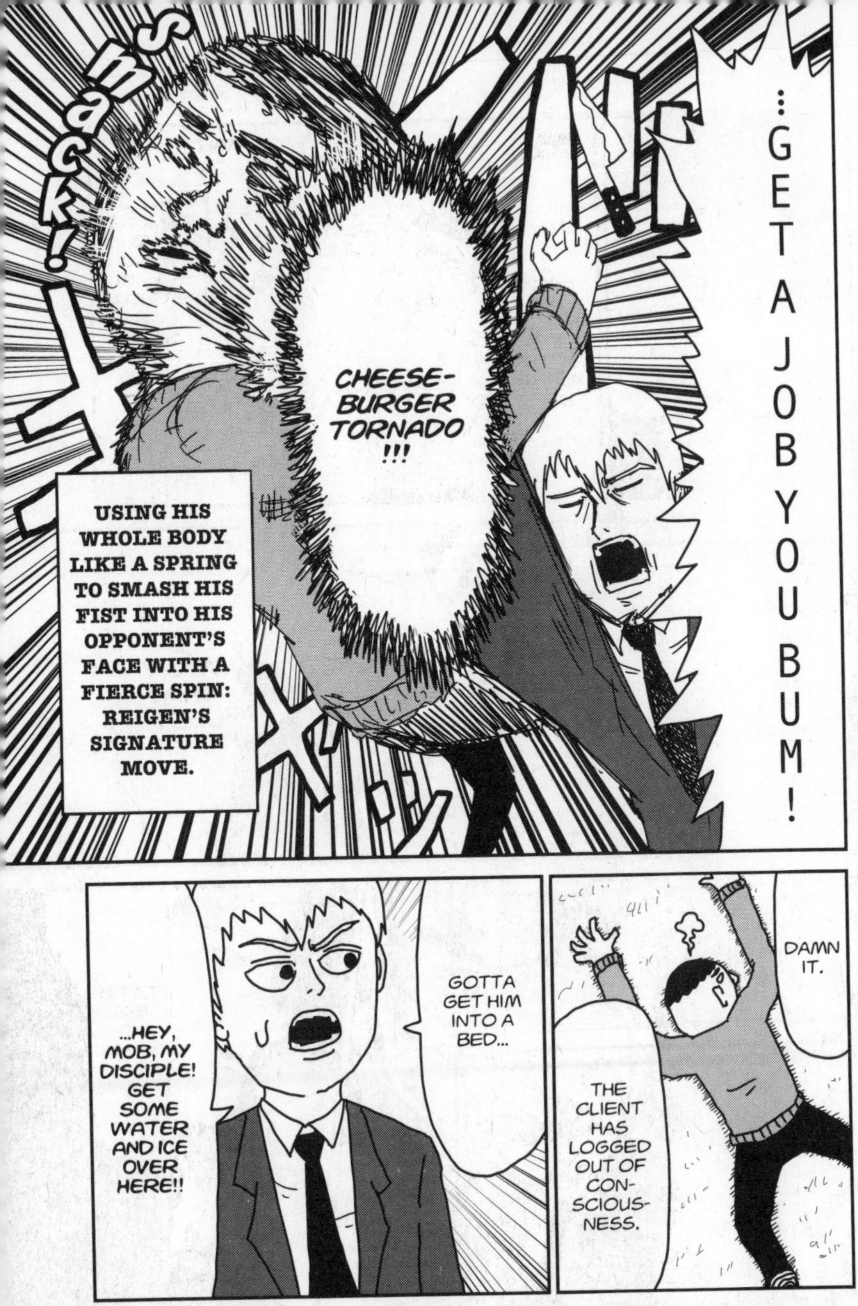

...GET A JOB YOU BUM!
Smack!
CHEESE-BURGER TORNADO!!!
USING HIS WHOLE BODY LIKE A SPRING TO SMASH HIS FIST INTO HIS OPPONENT'S FACE WITH A FIERCE SPIN: REIGEN'S SIGNATURE MOVE.
DAMN IT.
THE CLIENT HAS LOGGED OUT OF CON-SCIOUS-NESS.
GOTTA GET HIM INTO A BED...
...HEY, MOB, MY DISCIPLE! GET SOME WATER AND ICE OVER HERE!!

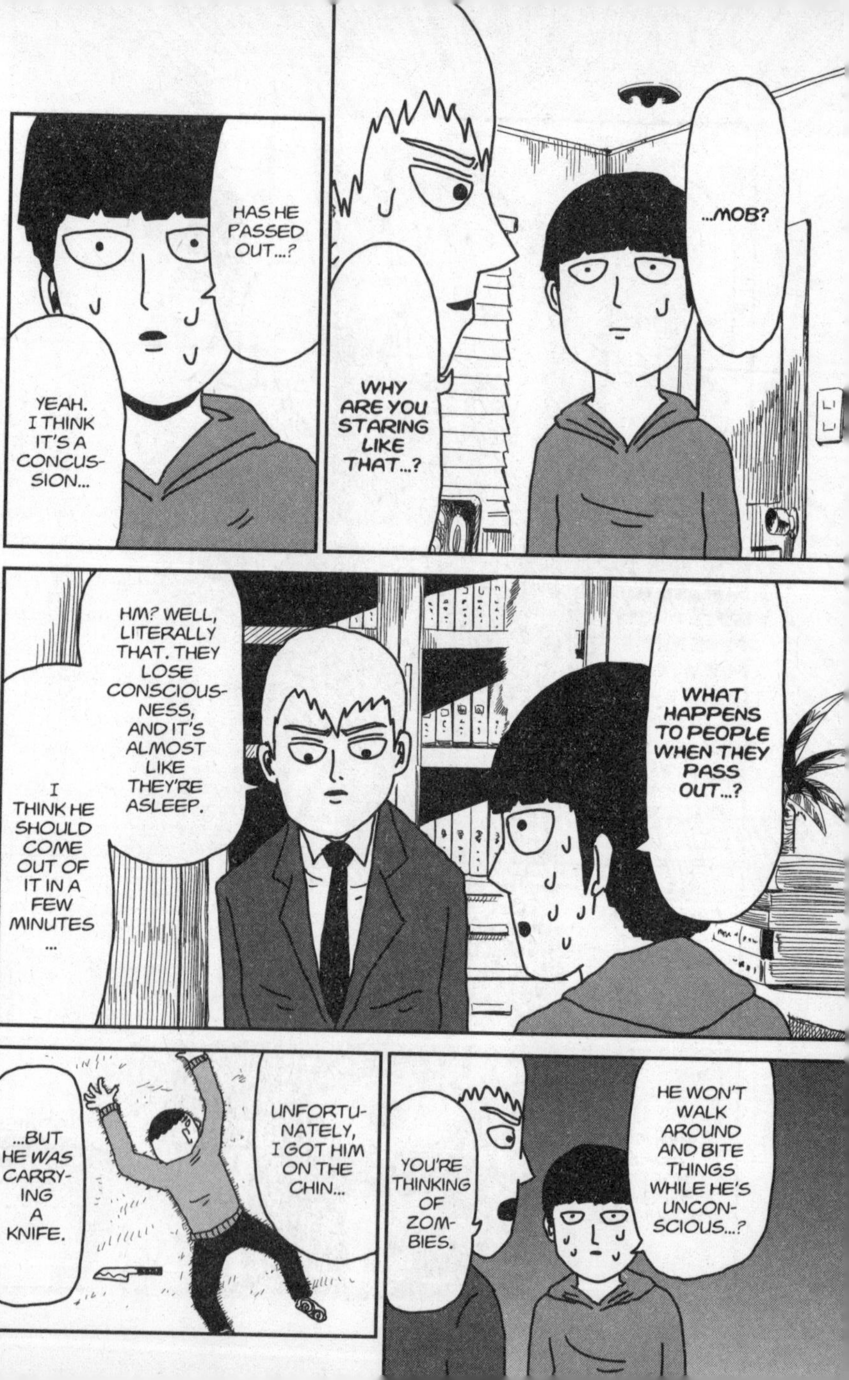
...MOB?
WHY ARE YOU STARING LIKE THAT...?
HAS HE PASSED OUT...?
YEAH. I THINK IT'S A CONCUSSION...
WHAT HAPPENS TO PEOPLE WHEN THEY PASS OUT...?
HM? WELL, LITERALLY THAT. THEY LOSE CONSCIOUSNESS, AND IT'S ALMOST LIKE THEY'RE ASLEEP.
I THINK HE SHOULD COME OUT OF IT IN A FEW MINUTES ...
HE WON'T WALK AROUND AND BITE THINGS WHILE HE'S UNCONSCIOUS...?
YOU'RE THINKING OF ZOMBIES.
UNFORTUNATELY, I GOT HIM ON THE CHIN...
...BUT HE *WAS* CARRYING A KNIFE.

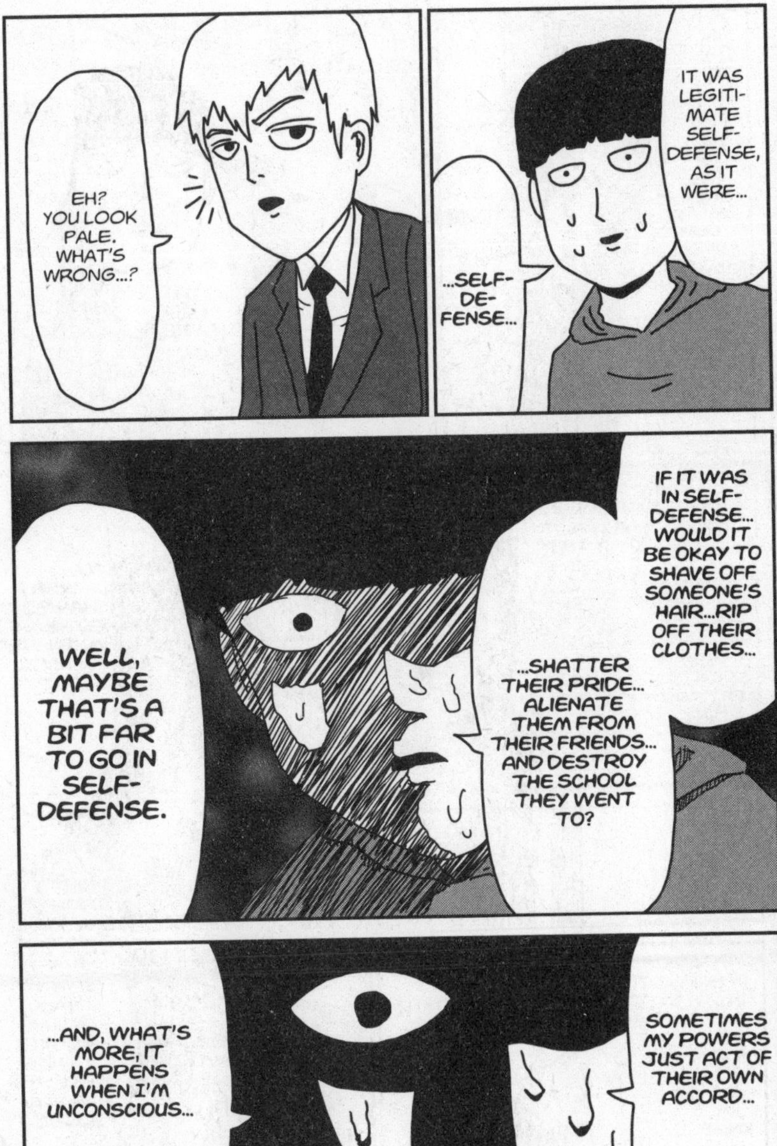
IT WAS LEGITIMATE SELF-DEFENSE, AS IT WERE...
...SELF-DEFENSE...
EH? YOU LOOK PALE. WHAT'S WRONG...?
IF IT WAS IN SELF-DEFENSE... WOULD IT BE OKAY TO SHAVE OFF SOMEONE'S HAIR...RIP OFF THEIR CLOTHES...
...SHATTER THEIR PRIDE... ALIENATE THEM FROM THEIR FRIENDS... AND DESTROY THE SCHOOL THEY WENT TO?
WELL, MAYBE THAT'S A BIT FAR TO GO IN SELF-DEFENSE.
SOMETIMES MY POWERS JUST ACT OF THEIR OWN ACCORD...
...AND, WHAT'S MORE, IT HAPPENS WHEN I'M UNCONSCIOUS...

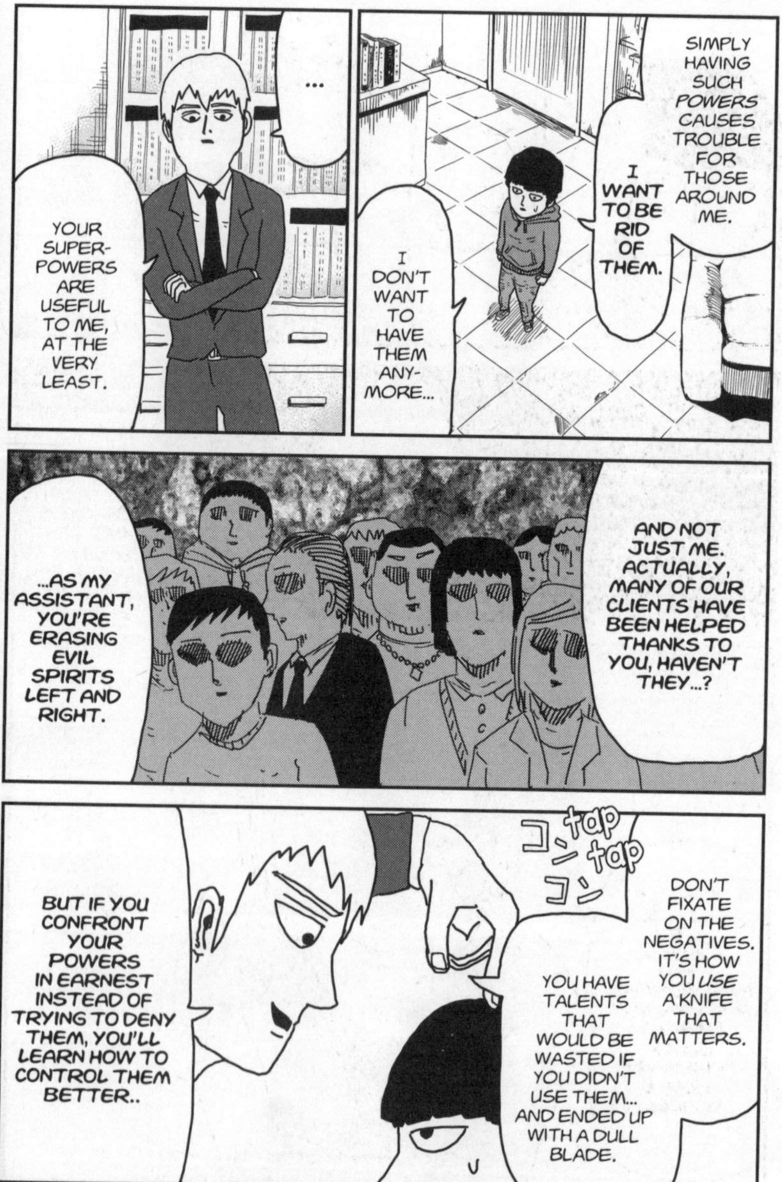
SIMPLY HAVING SUCH POWERS CAUSES TROUBLE FOR THOSE AROUND ME.
I WANT TO BE RID OF THEM.
I DON'T WANT TO HAVE THEM ANY-MORE...
...
YOUR SUPER-POWERS ARE USEFUL TO ME, AT THE VERY LEAST.
AND NOT JUST ME. ACTUALLY, MANY OF OUR CLIENTS HAVE BEEN HELPED THANKS TO YOU, HAVEN'T THEY...?
...AS MY ASSISTANT, YOU'RE ERASING EVIL SPIRITS LEFT AND RIGHT.
コン tap
コン tap
DON'T FIXATE ON THE NEGATIVES. IT'S HOW YOU *USE* A KNIFE THAT MATTERS.
YOU HAVE TALENTS THAT WOULD BE WASTED IF YOU DIDN'T USE THEM... AND ENDED UP WITH A DULL BLADE.
BUT IF YOU CONFRONT YOUR POWERS IN EARNEST INSTEAD OF TRYING TO DENY THEM, YOU'LL LEARN HOW TO CONTROL THEM BETTER..

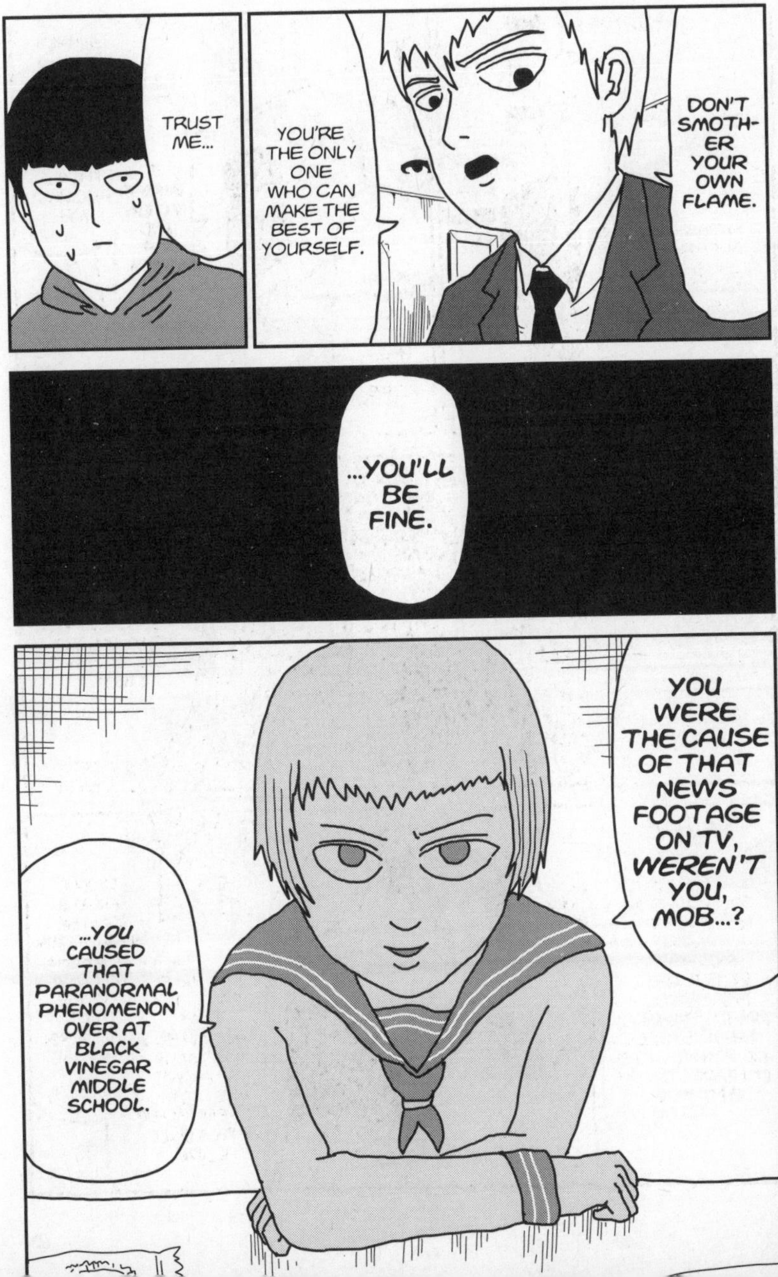
DON'T SMOTH-ER YOUR OWN FLAME.
YOU'RE THE ONLY ONE WHO CAN MAKE THE BEST OF YOURSELF.
TRUST ME...
...YOU'LL BE FINE.
YOU WERE THE CAUSE OF THAT NEWS FOOTAGE ON TV, WEREN'T YOU, MOB...?
...YOU CAUSED THAT PARANORMAL PHENOMENON OVER AT BLACK VINEGAR MIDDLE SCHOOL.

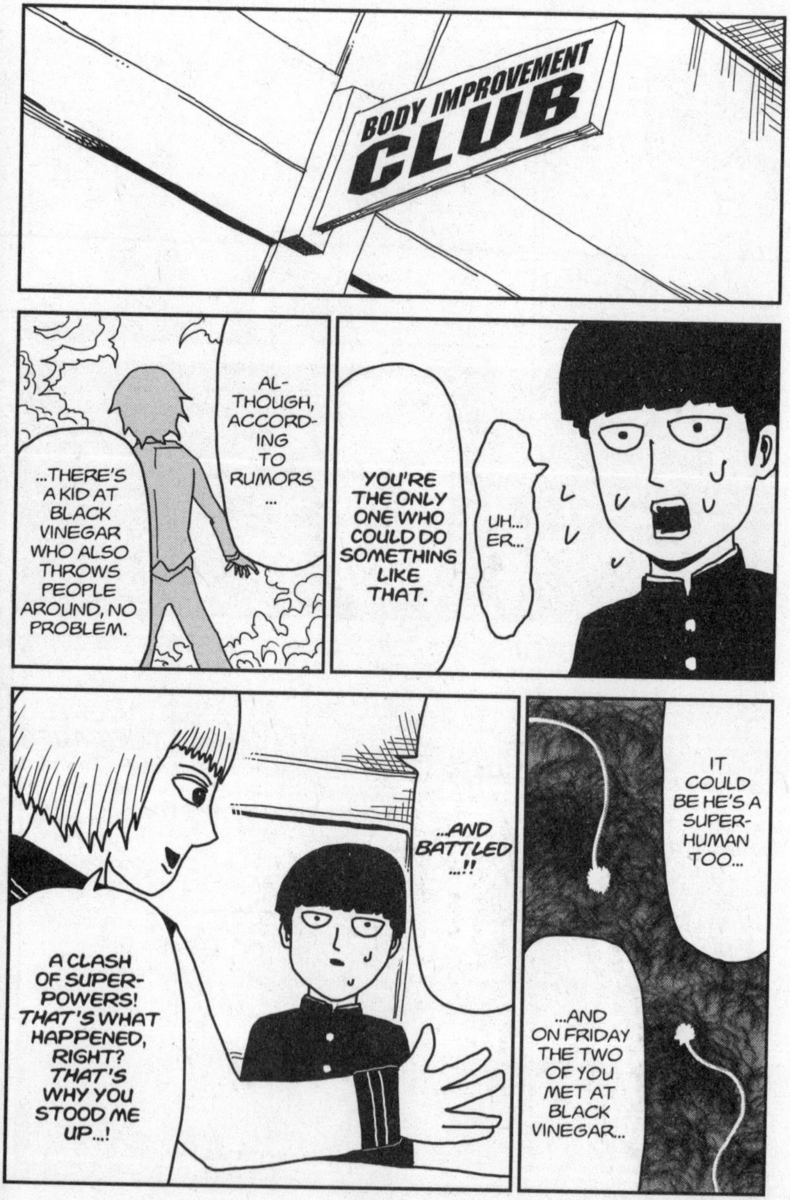
BODY IMPROVEMENT CLUB
YOU'RE THE ONLY ONE WHO COULD DO SOMETHING LIKE THAT.
UH... ER...
ALTHOUGH, ACCORDING TO RUMORS...
...THERE'S A KID AT BLACK VINEGAR WHO ALSO THROWS PEOPLE AROUND, NO PROBLEM.
IT COULD BE HE'S A SUPERHUMAN TOO...
...AND ON FRIDAY THE TWO OF YOU MET AT BLACK VINEGAR...
...AND BATTLED ...!!
A CLASH OF SUPERPOWERS! THAT'S WHAT HAPPENED, RIGHT? THAT'S WHY YOU STOOD ME UP...!

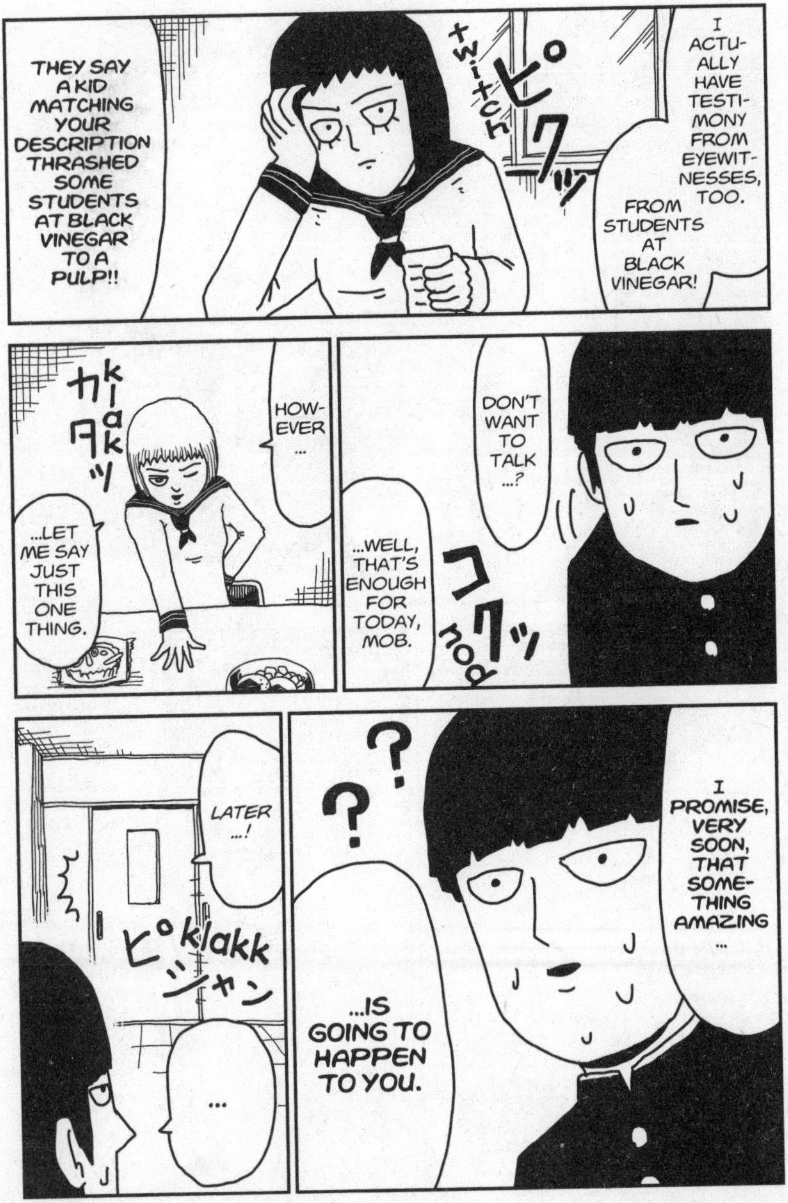
I ACTUALLY HAVE TESTIMONY FROM EYEWITNESSES, TOO.
FROM STUDENTS AT BLACK VINEGAR!
twitch
THEY SAY A KID MATCHING YOUR DESCRIPTION THRASHED SOME STUDENTS AT BLACK VINEGAR TO A PULP!!
DON'T WANT TO TALK...?
nod
...WELL, THAT'S ENOUGH FOR TODAY, MOB.
HOWEVER...
klak
...LET ME SAY JUST THIS ONE THING.
I PROMISE, VERY SOON, THAT SOMETHING AMAZING...
...IS GOING TO HAPPEN TO YOU.
LATER...!
klakk
...

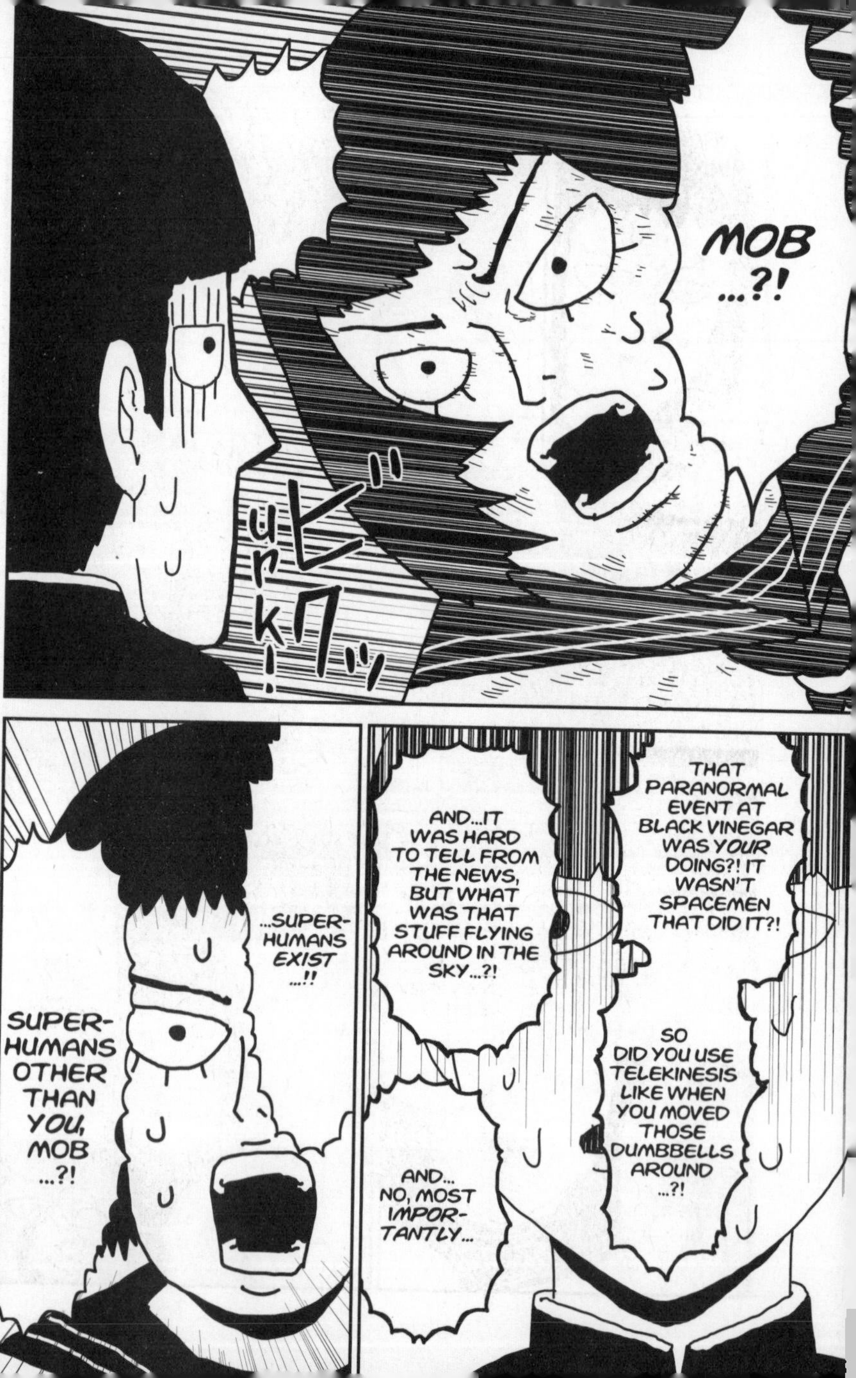
MOB ...?!
ビクッ
urk!!
THAT PARANORMAL EVENT AT BLACK VINEGAR WAS YOUR DOING?! IT WASN'T SPACEMEN THAT DID IT?!
SO DID YOU USE TELEKINESIS LIKE WHEN YOU MOVED THOSE DUMBBELLS AROUND ...?!
AND...IT WAS HARD TO TELL FROM THE NEWS, BUT WHAT WAS THAT STUFF FLYING AROUND IN THE SKY...?!
AND... NO, MOST IMPORTANTLY...
...SUPER-HUMANS EXIST ...!!
SUPER-HUMANS OTHER THAN YOU, MOB ...?!

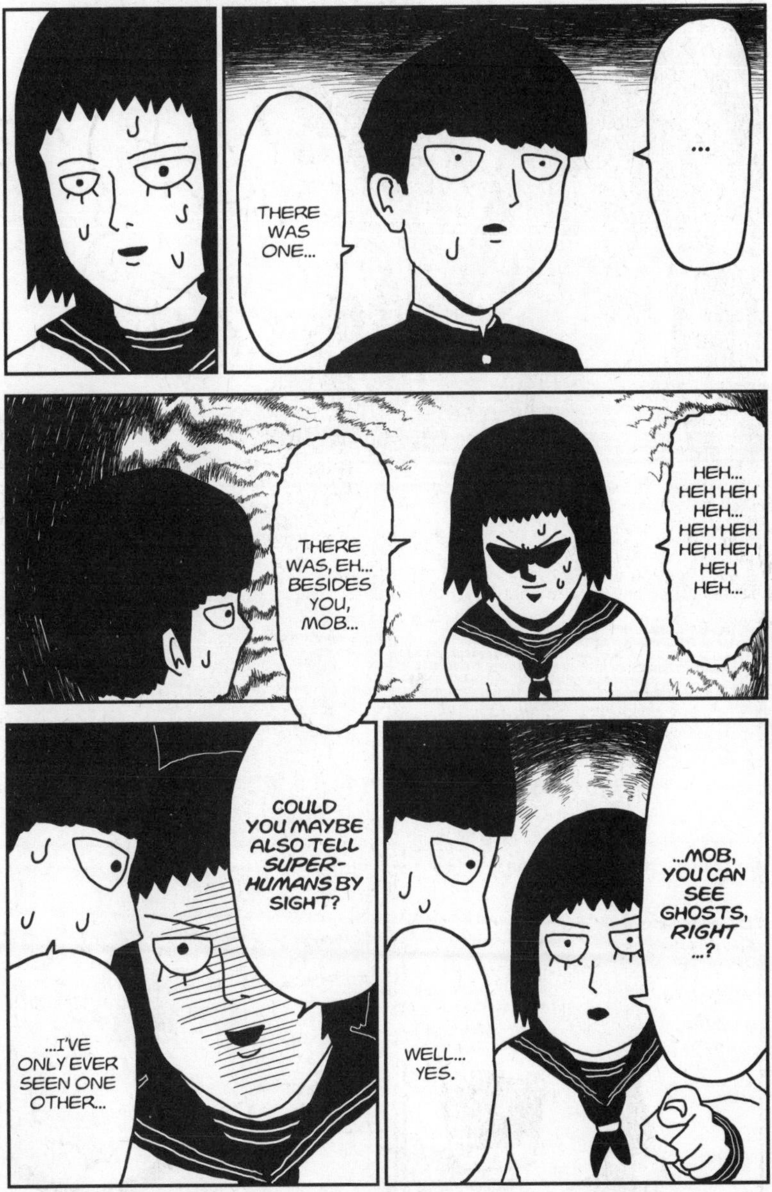
...
THERE WAS ONE...
HEH... HEH HEH HEH... HEH HEH HEH HEH HEH HEH...
THERE WAS, EH... BESIDES YOU, MOB...
...MOB, YOU CAN SEE GHOSTS, *RIGHT* ...?
WELL... YES.
COULD YOU MAYBE ALSO TELL *SUPER-HUMANS* BY SIGHT?
...I'VE ONLY EVER SEEN ONE OTHER...

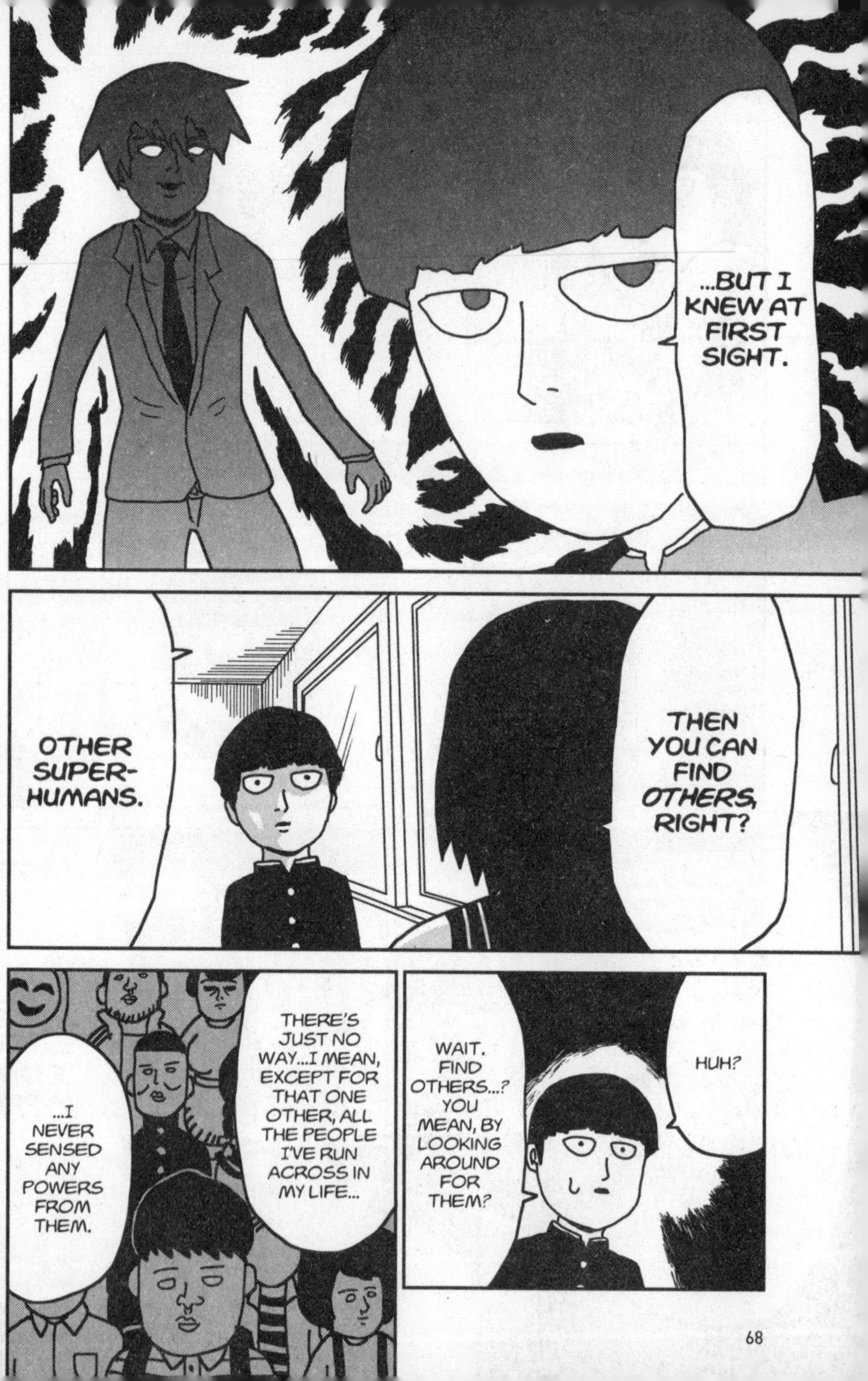
...BUT I KNEW AT FIRST SIGHT.
THEN YOU CAN FIND OTHERS, RIGHT?
OTHER SUPER-HUMANS.
HUH?
WAIT. FIND OTHERS...? YOU MEAN, BY LOOKING AROUND FOR THEM?
THERE'S JUST NO WAY...I MEAN, EXCEPT FOR THAT ONE OTHER, ALL THE PEOPLE I'VE RUN ACROSS IN MY LIFE...
...I NEVER SENSED ANY POWERS FROM THEM.

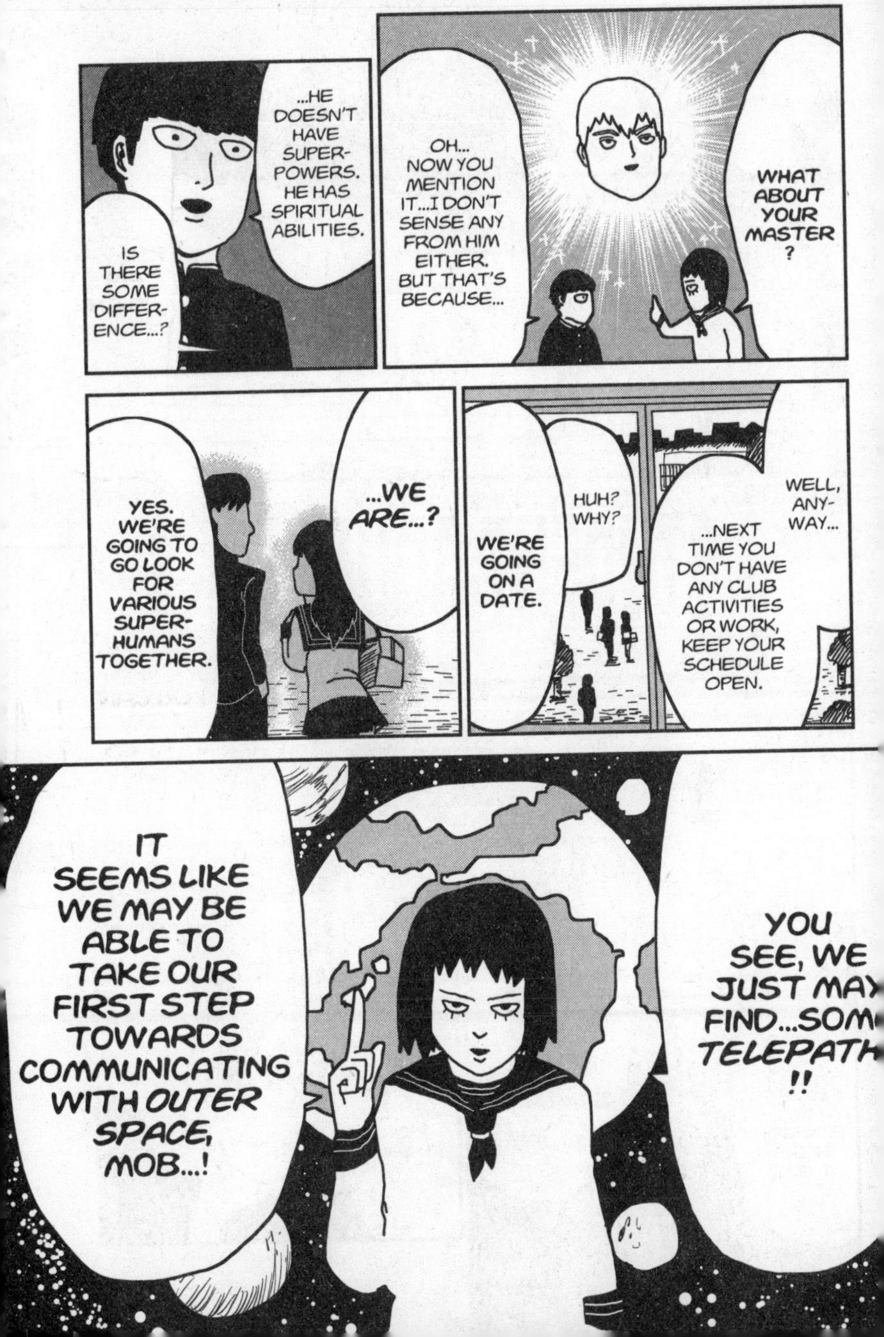
WHAT ABOUT YOUR MASTER?
OH... NOW YOU MENTION IT...I DON'T SENSE ANY FROM HIM EITHER. BUT THAT'S BECAUSE...
...HE DOESN'T HAVE SUPER-POWERS. HE HAS SPIRITUAL ABILITIES.
IS THERE SOME DIFFERENCE...?
WELL, ANYWAY...
...NEXT TIME YOU DON'T HAVE ANY CLUB ACTIVITIES OR WORK, KEEP YOUR SCHEDULE OPEN.
HUH? WHY?
WE'RE GOING ON A DATE.
...WE ARE...?
YES. WE'RE GOING TO GO LOOK FOR VARIOUS SUPER-HUMANS TOGETHER.
YOU SEE, WE JUST MAY FIND...SOME TELEPATH!!
IT SEEMS LIKE WE MAY BE ABLE TO TAKE OUR FIRST STEP TOWARDS COMMUNICATING WITH OUTER SPACE, MOB...!

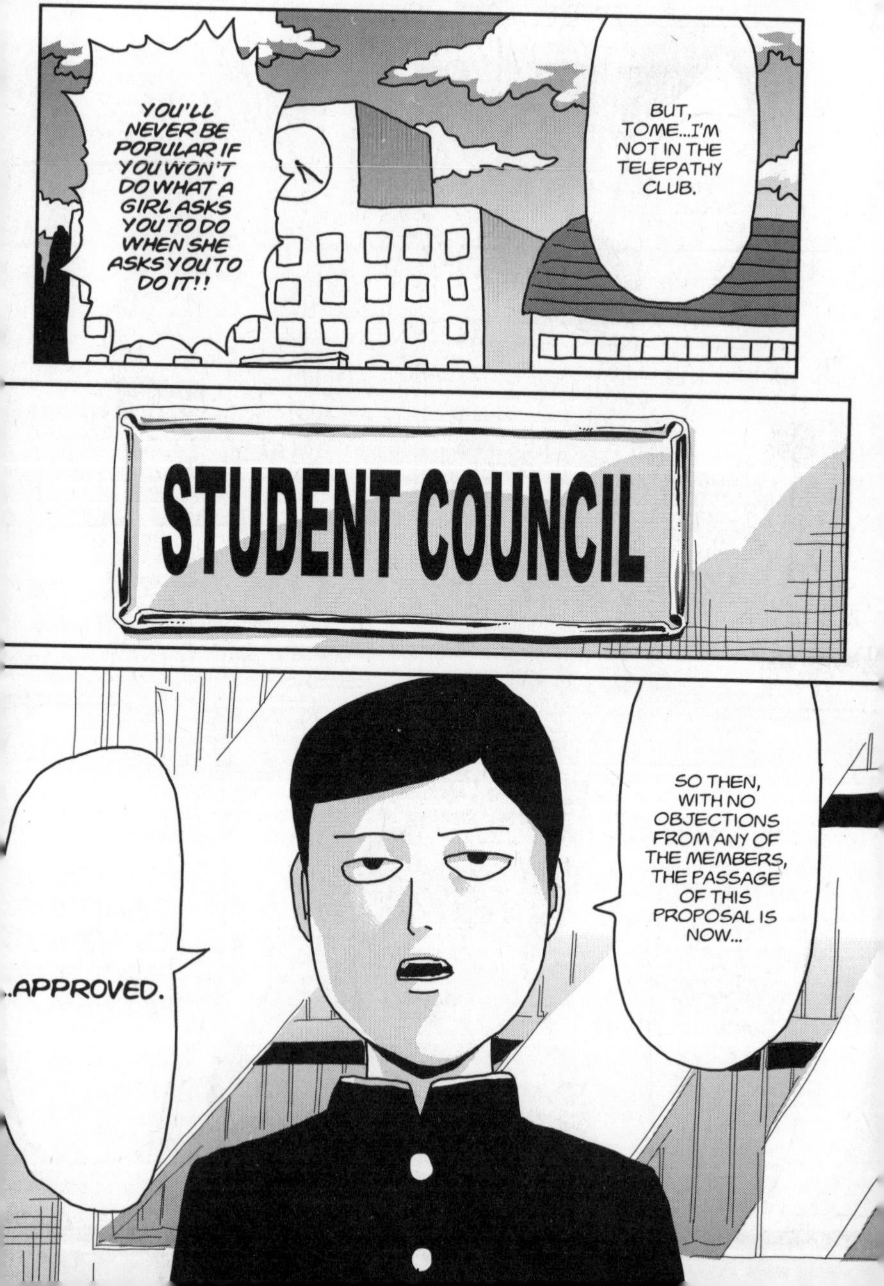
BUT, TOME...I'M NOT IN THE TELEPATHY CLUB.
YOU'LL NEVER BE POPULAR IF YOU WON'T DO WHAT A GIRL ASKS YOU TO DO WHEN SHE ASKS YOU TO DO IT!!
STUDENT COUNCIL
SO THEN, WITH NO OBJECTIONS FROM ANY OF THE MEMBERS, THE PASSAGE OF THIS PROPOSAL IS NOW...
..APPROVED.

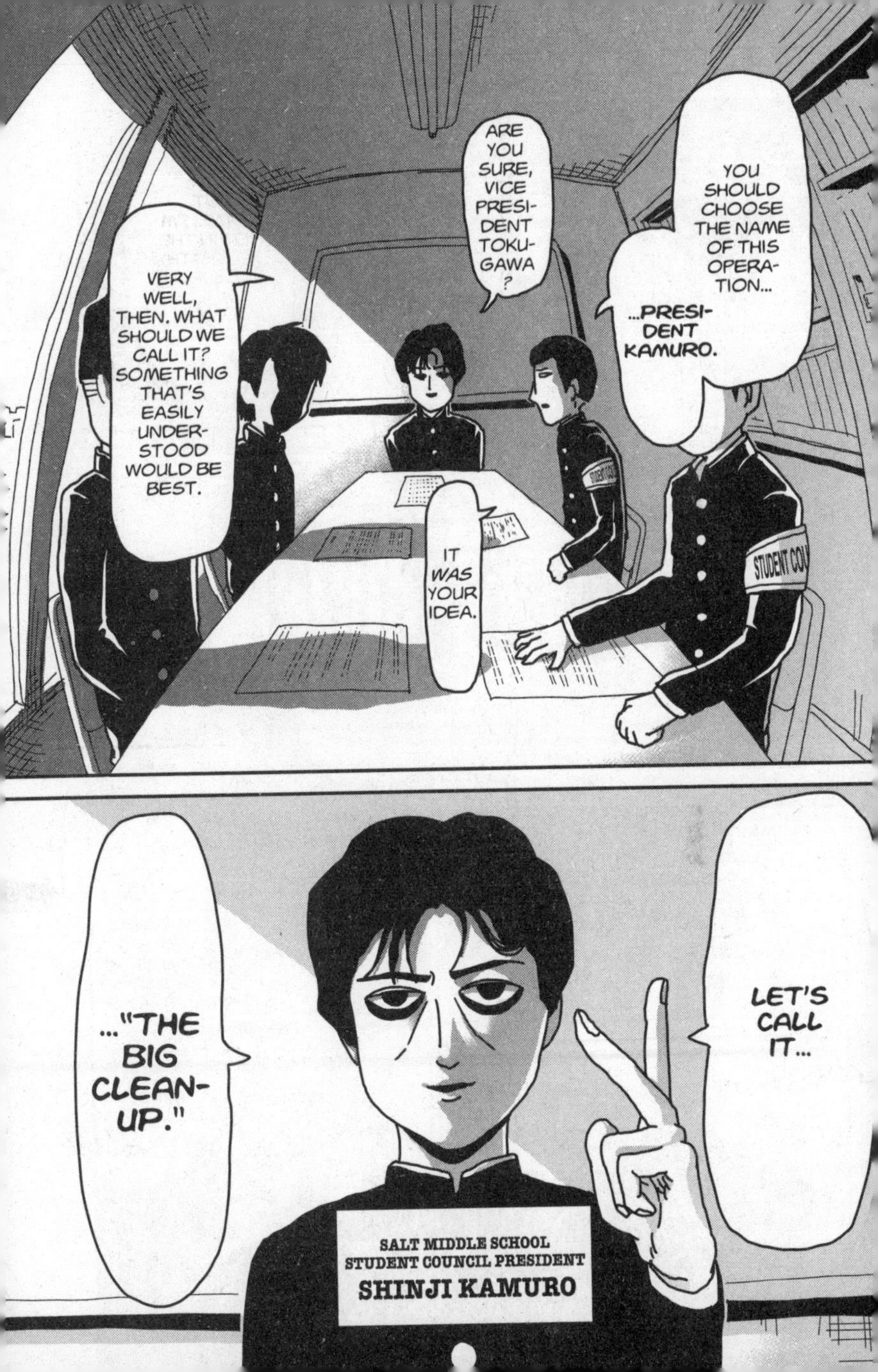
YOU SHOULD CHOOSE THE NAME OF THIS OPERATION...
...PRESIDENT KAMURO.
ARE YOU SURE, VICE PRESIDENT TOKUGAWA?
IT WAS YOUR IDEA.
VERY WELL, THEN. WHAT SHOULD WE CALL IT? SOMETHING THAT'S EASILY UNDERSTOOD WOULD BE BEST.
LET'S CALL IT...
..."THE BIG CLEAN-UP."
SALT MIDDLE SCHOOL
STUDENT COUNCIL PRESIDENT
SHINJI KAMURO

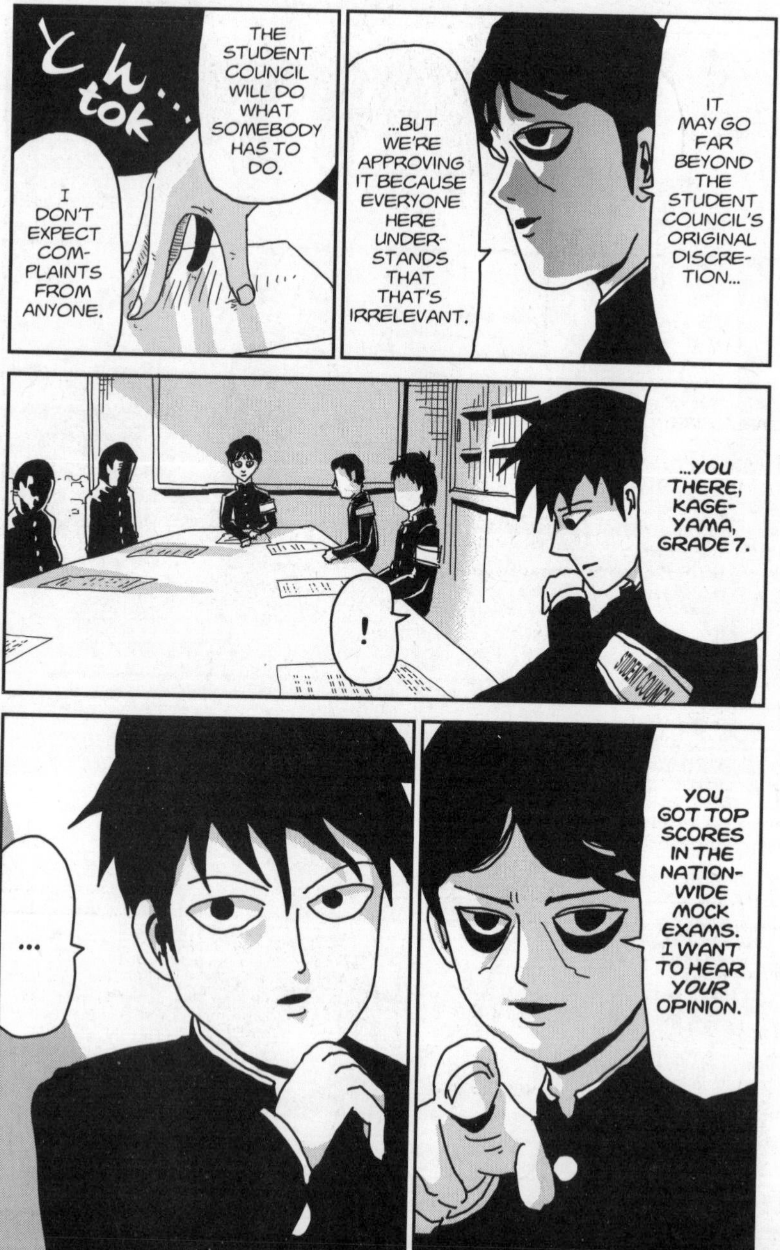
IT MAY GO FAR BEYOND THE STUDENT COUNCIL'S ORIGINAL DISCRETION...
...BUT WE'RE APPROVING IT BECAUSE EVERYONE HERE UNDERSTANDS THAT THAT'S IRRELEVANT.
THE STUDENT COUNCIL WILL DO WHAT SOMEBODY HAS TO DO.
とん…
tok
I DON'T EXPECT COMPLAINTS FROM ANYONE.
...YOU THERE, KAGEYAMA, GRADE 7.
STUDENT COUNCIL
!
YOU GOT TOP SCORES IN THE NATIONWIDE MOCK EXAMS. I WANT TO HEAR *YOUR* OPINION.
...

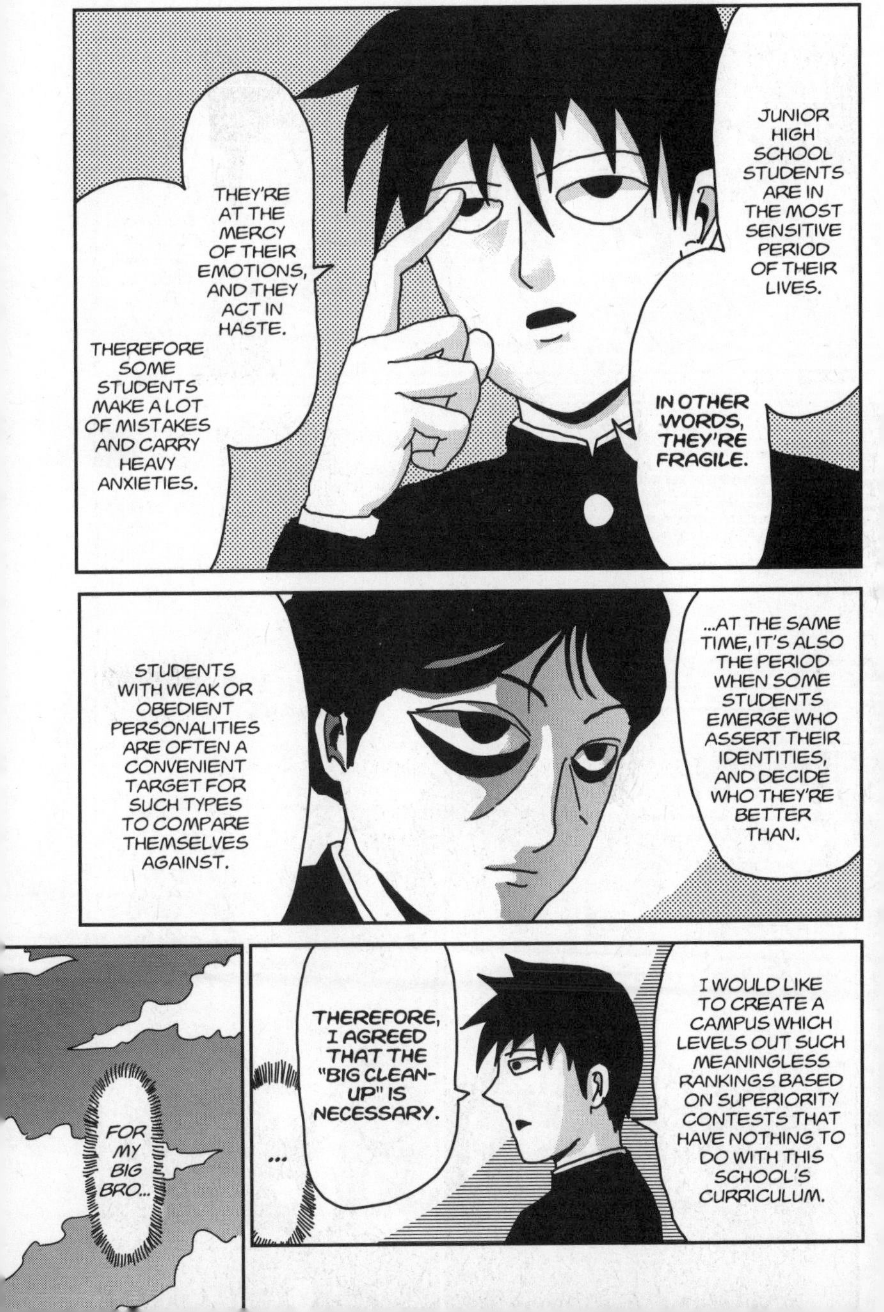
JUNIOR HIGH SCHOOL STUDENTS ARE IN THE MOST SENSITIVE PERIOD OF THEIR LIVES.
IN OTHER WORDS, THEY'RE FRAGILE.
THEY'RE AT THE MERCY OF THEIR EMOTIONS, AND THEY ACT IN HASTE.
THEREFORE SOME STUDENTS MAKE A LOT OF MISTAKES AND CARRY HEAVY ANXIETIES.
...AT THE SAME TIME, IT'S ALSO THE PERIOD WHEN SOME STUDENTS EMERGE WHO ASSERT THEIR IDENTITIES, AND DECIDE WHO THEY'RE BETTER THAN.
STUDENTS WITH WEAK OR OBEDIENT PERSONALITIES ARE OFTEN A CONVENIENT TARGET FOR SUCH TYPES TO COMPARE THEMSELVES AGAINST.
I WOULD LIKE TO CREATE A CAMPUS WHICH LEVELS OUT SUCH MEANINGLESS RANKINGS BASED ON SUPERIORITY CONTESTS THAT HAVE NOTHING TO DO WITH THIS SCHOOL'S CURRICULUM.
THEREFORE, I AGREED THAT THE "BIG CLEAN-UP" IS NECESSARY.
...
FOR MY BIG BRO...

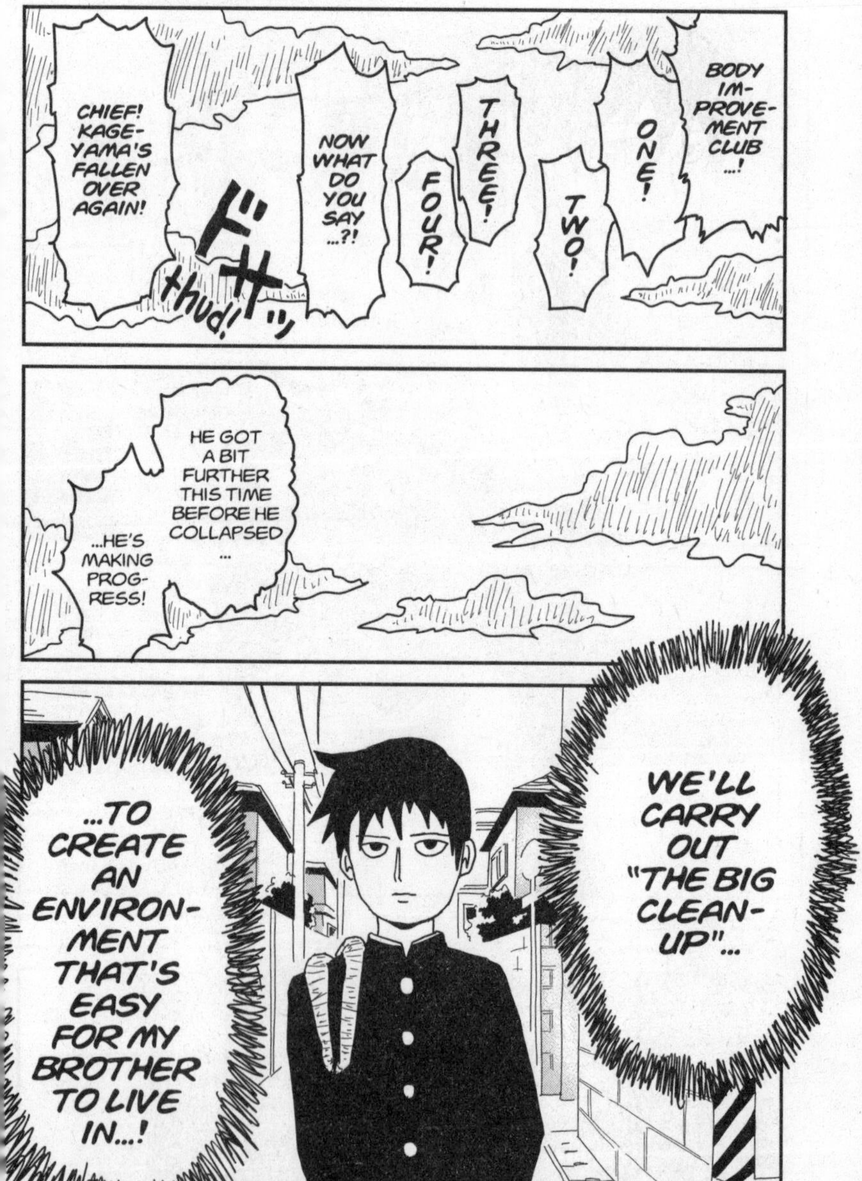
BODY IMPROVEMENT CLUB...!
ONE!
TWO!
THREE!
FOUR!
NOW WHAT DO YOU SAY...?!
ドサッ
thud!
CHIEF! KAGEYAMA'S FALLEN OVER AGAIN!
HE GOT A BIT FURTHER THIS TIME BEFORE HE COLLAPSED...
...HE'S MAKING PROGRESS!
WE'LL CARRY OUT "THE BIG CLEAN-UP"...
...TO CREATE AN ENVIRONMENT THAT'S EASY FOR MY BROTHER TO LIVE IN...!

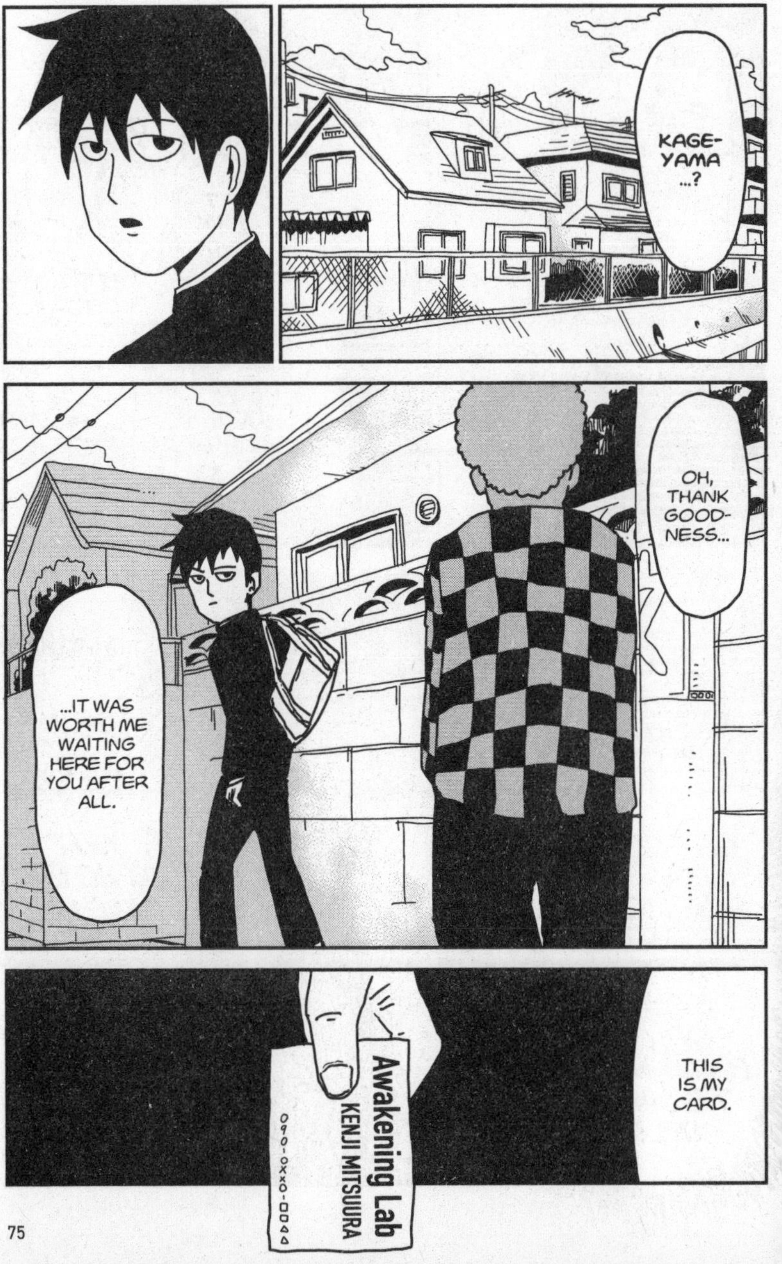
KAGE-YAMA ...?
OH, THANK GOOD-NESS...
...IT WAS WORTH ME WAITING HERE FOR YOU AFTER ALL.
THIS IS MY CARD.
Awakening Lab
KENJI MITSUURA
090-0X0-□□△△

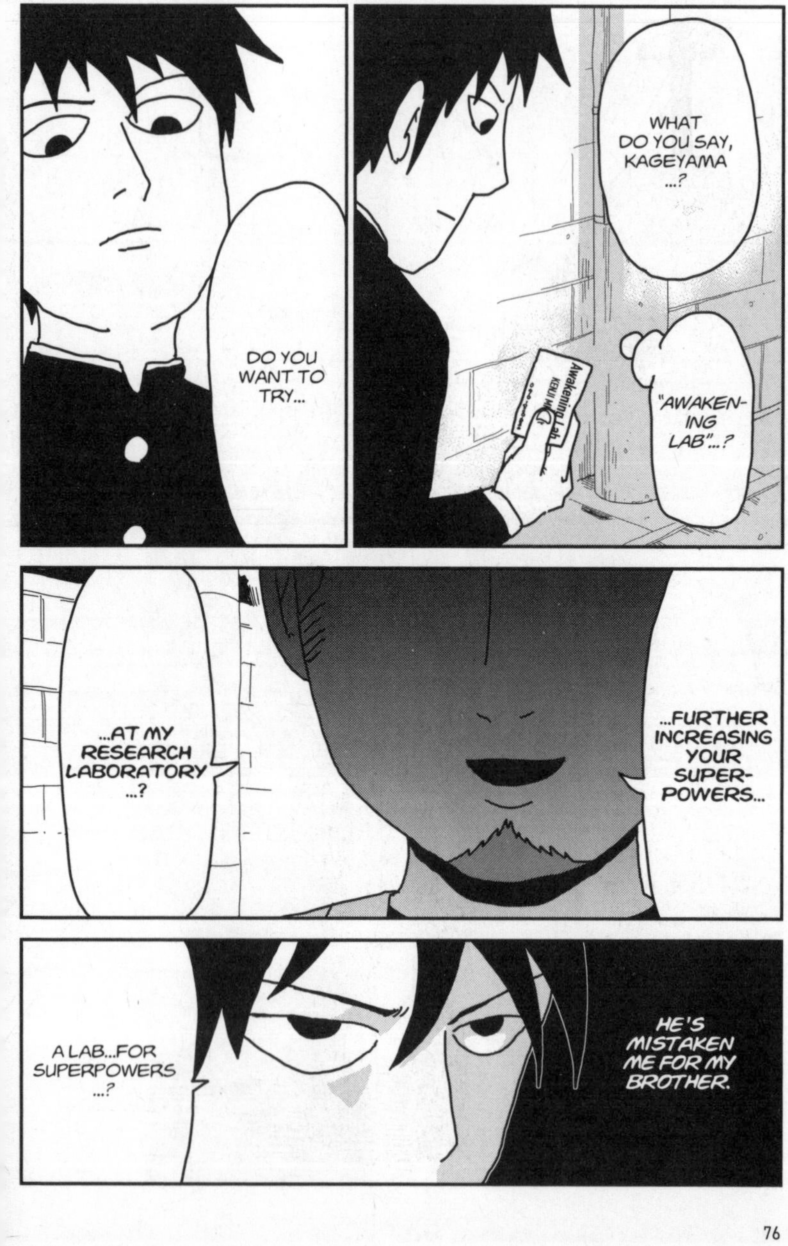
WHAT DO YOU SAY, KAGEYAMA ...?
Awakening Lab
"AWAKEN-ING LAB"...?
DO YOU WANT TO TRY...
...FURTHER INCREASING YOUR SUPER-POWERS...
...AT MY RESEARCH LABORATORY ...?
HE'S MISTAKEN ME FOR MY BROTHER.
A LAB...FOR SUPERPOWERS ...?

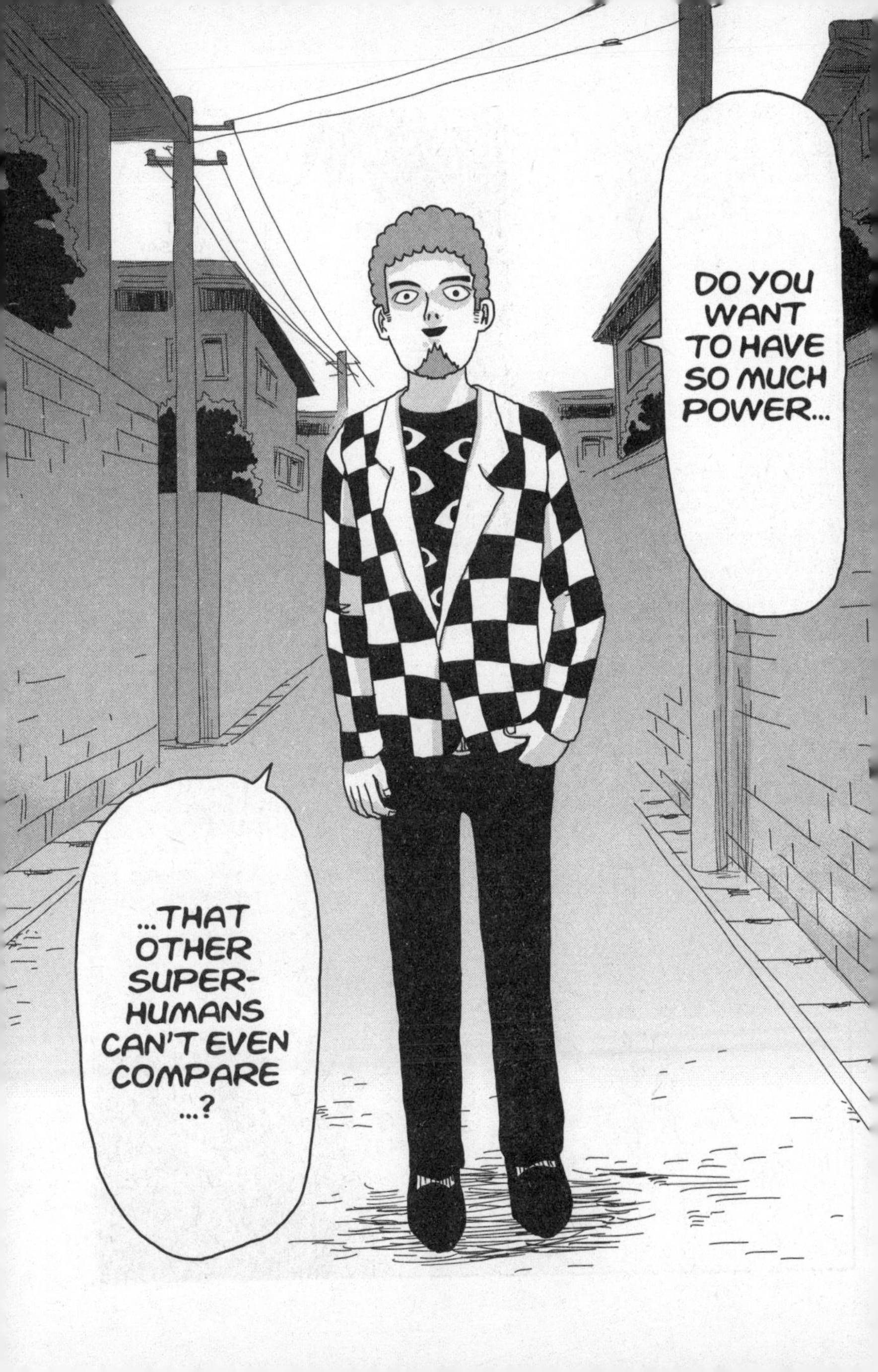
DO YOU WANT TO HAVE SO MUCH POWER...
...THAT OTHER SUPER-HUMANS CAN'T EVEN COMPARE ...?

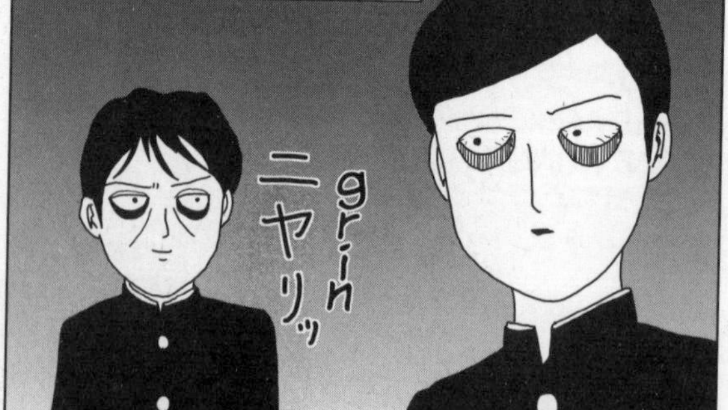
BEFORE A TEST
ニヤリッ
grin

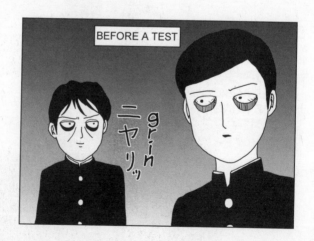

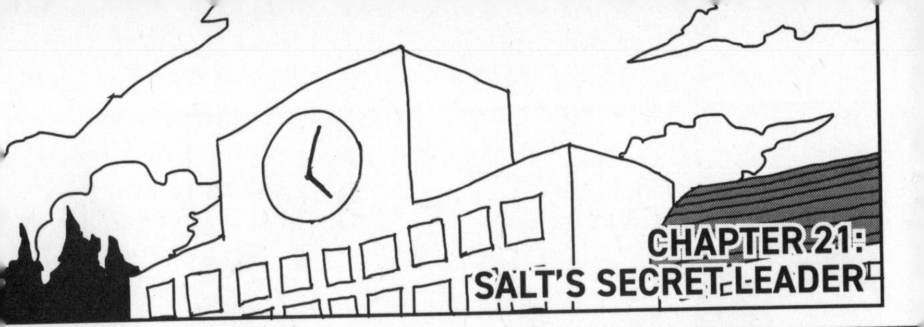
CHAPTER 21:
SALT'S SECRET LEADER

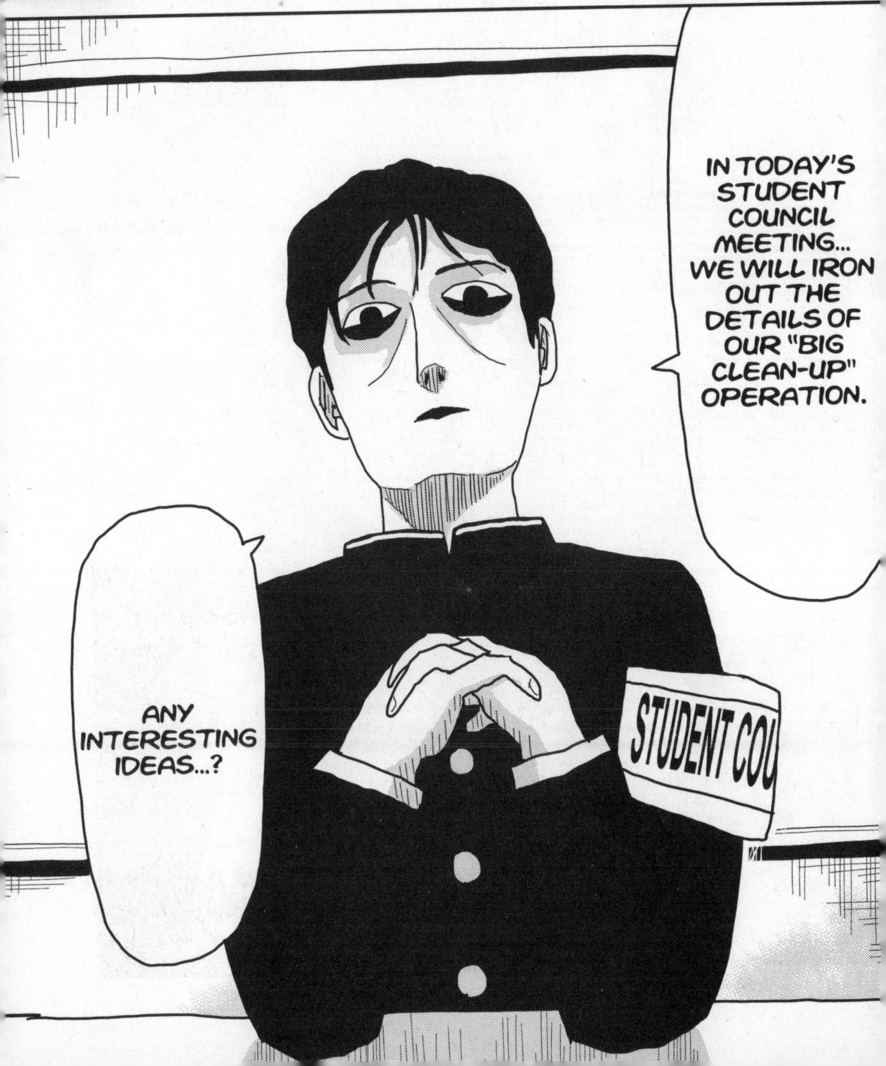
IN TODAY'S STUDENT COUNCIL MEETING... WE WILL IRON OUT THE DETAILS OF OUR "BIG CLEAN-UP" OPERATION.
STUDENT COU
ANY INTERESTING IDEAS...?

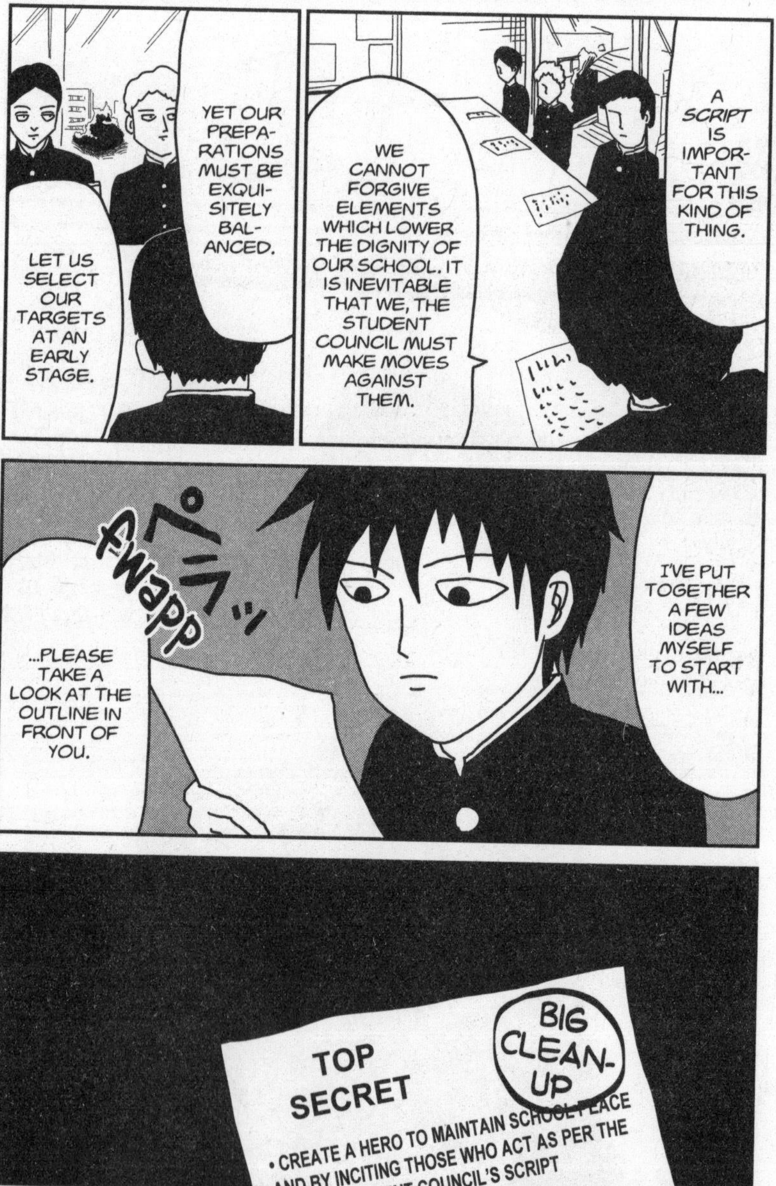
A SCRIPT IS IMPORTANT FOR THIS KIND OF THING.
WE CANNOT FORGIVE ELEMENTS WHICH LOWER THE DIGNITY OF OUR SCHOOL. IT IS INEVITABLE THAT WE, THE STUDENT COUNCIL MUST MAKE MOVES AGAINST THEM.
YET OUR PREPARATIONS MUST BE EXQUISITELY BALANCED.
LET US SELECT OUR TARGETS AT AN EARLY STAGE.
I'VE PUT TOGETHER A FEW IDEAS MYSELF TO START WITH...
パラッ
FWAPP
...PLEASE TAKE A LOOK AT THE OUTLINE IN FRONT OF YOU.
BIG CLEAN-UP
TOP SECRET
• CREATE A HERO TO MAINTAIN SCHOOL PEACE
BY INCITING THOSE WHO ACT AS PER THE
COUNCIL'S SCRIPT

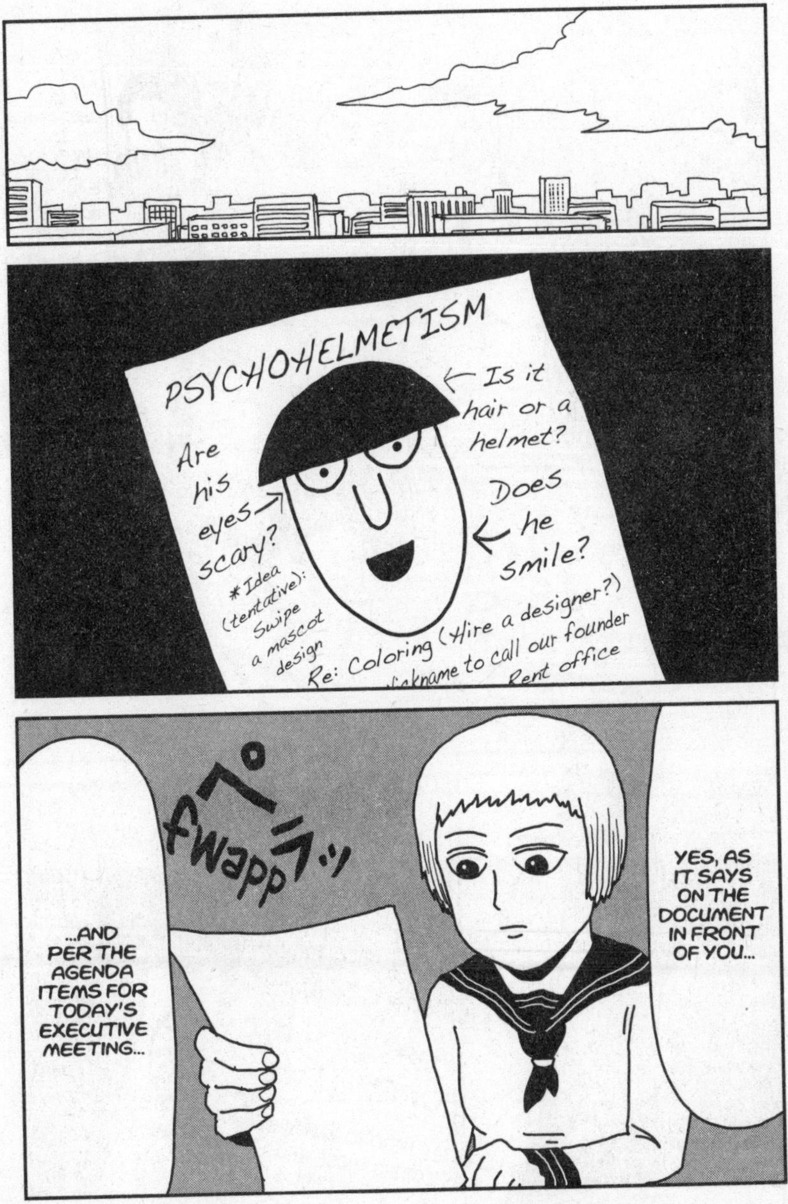
PSYCHOHELMETISM
Is it hair or a helmet?
Are his eyes scary?
Does he smile?
*Idea (tentative): Swipe a mascot design
Re: Coloring (Hire a designer?)
ickname to call our founder
Rent office
YES, AS IT SAYS ON THE DOCUMENT IN FRONT OF YOU...
ぺ fwapp ラッ
...AND PER THE AGENDA ITEMS FOR TODAY'S EXECUTIVE MEETING...

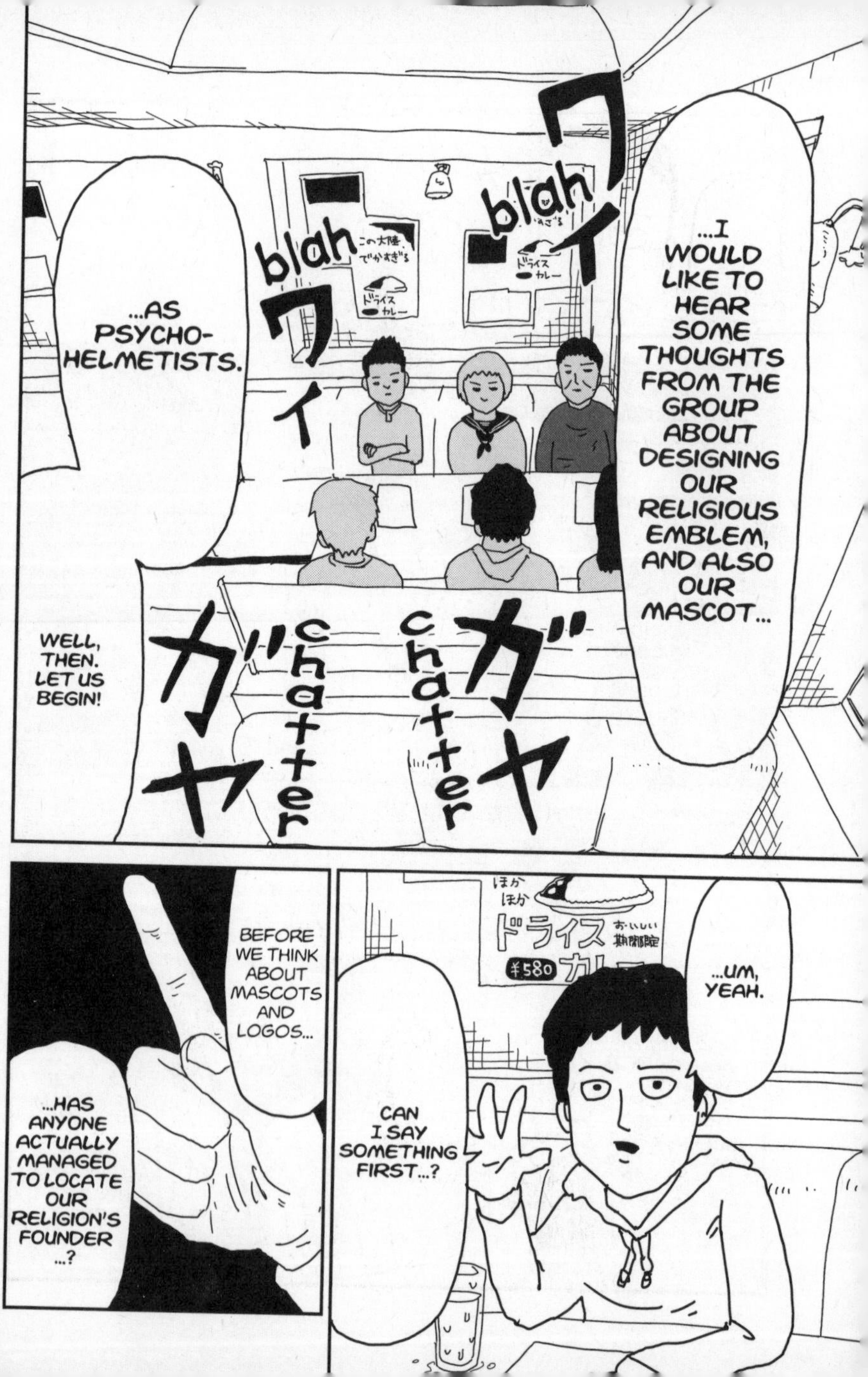

ワイ
blah
ワイ
blah
この大陸、でかすぎる
ドライス カレー
...I WOULD LIKE TO HEAR SOME THOUGHTS FROM THE GROUP ABOUT DESIGNING OUR RELIGIOUS EMBLEM, AND ALSO OUR MASCOT...
...AS PSYCHO-HELMETISTS.
ガヤ
chatter
ガヤ
chatter
WELL, THEN. LET US BEGIN!
ほか ほか
ドライス
おいしい 期間限定
¥580
...UM, YEAH.
CAN I SAY SOMETHING FIRST...?
BEFORE WE THINK ABOUT MASCOTS AND LOGOS...
...HAS ANYONE ACTUALLY MANAGED TO LOCATE OUR RELIGION'S FOUNDER ...?

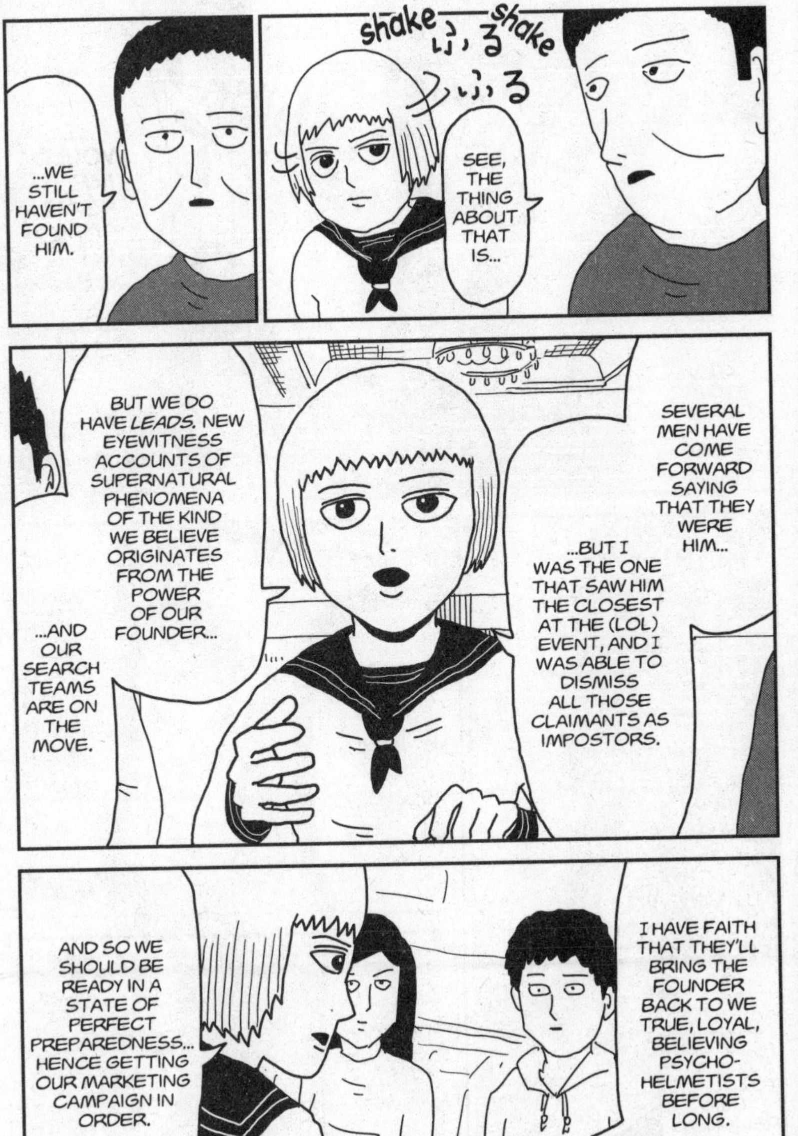
shake shake
ふるふる
SEE, THE THING ABOUT THAT IS...
...WE STILL HAVEN'T FOUND HIM.
SEVERAL MEN HAVE COME FORWARD SAYING THAT THEY WERE HIM...
...BUT I WAS THE ONE THAT SAW HIM THE CLOSEST AT THE (LOL) EVENT, AND I WAS ABLE TO DISMISS ALL THOSE CLAIMANTS AS IMPOSTORS.
BUT WE DO HAVE *LEADS*. NEW EYEWITNESS ACCOUNTS OF SUPERNATURAL PHENOMENA OF THE KIND WE BELIEVE ORIGINATES FROM THE POWER OF OUR FOUNDER...
...AND OUR SEARCH TEAMS ARE ON THE MOVE.
I HAVE FAITH THAT THEY'LL BRING THE FOUNDER BACK TO WE TRUE, LOYAL, BELIEVING PSYCHO-HELMETISTS BEFORE LONG.
AND SO WE SHOULD BE READY IN A STATE OF PERFECT PREPAREDNESS... HENCE GETTING OUR MARKETING CAMPAIGN IN ORDER.

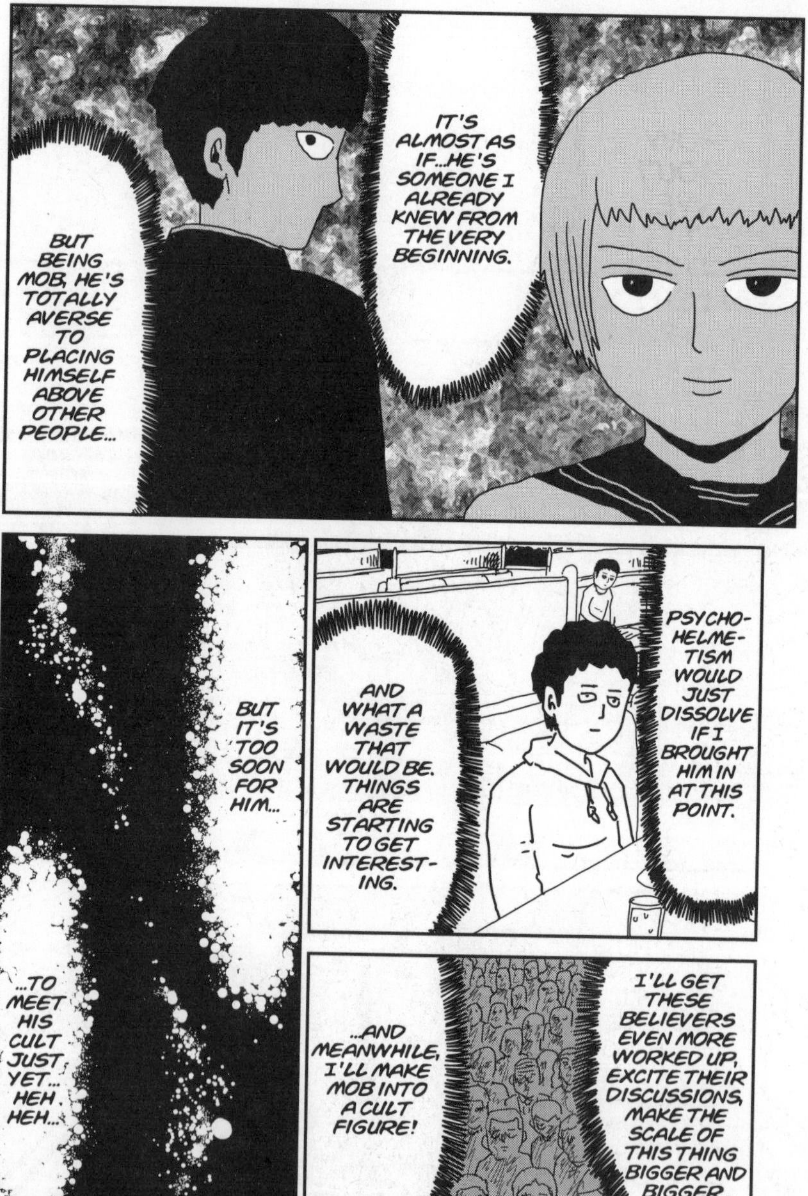
IT'S ALMOST AS IF...HE'S SOMEONE I ALREADY KNEW FROM THE VERY BEGINNING.
BUT BEING MOB, HE'S TOTALLY AVERSE TO PLACING HIMSELF ABOVE OTHER PEOPLE...
PSYCHO-HELME-TISM WOULD JUST DISSOLVE IF I BROUGHT HIM IN AT THIS POINT.
AND WHAT A WASTE THAT WOULD BE. THINGS ARE STARTING TO GET INTEREST-ING.
I'LL GET THESE BELIEVERS EVEN MORE WORKED UP, EXCITE THEIR DISCUSSIONS, MAKE THE SCALE OF THIS THING BIGGER AND BIGGER...
...AND MEANWHILE, I'LL MAKE MOB INTO A CULT FIGURE!
BUT IT'S TOO SOON FOR HIM...
...TO MEET HIS CULT JUST YET... HEH HEH...

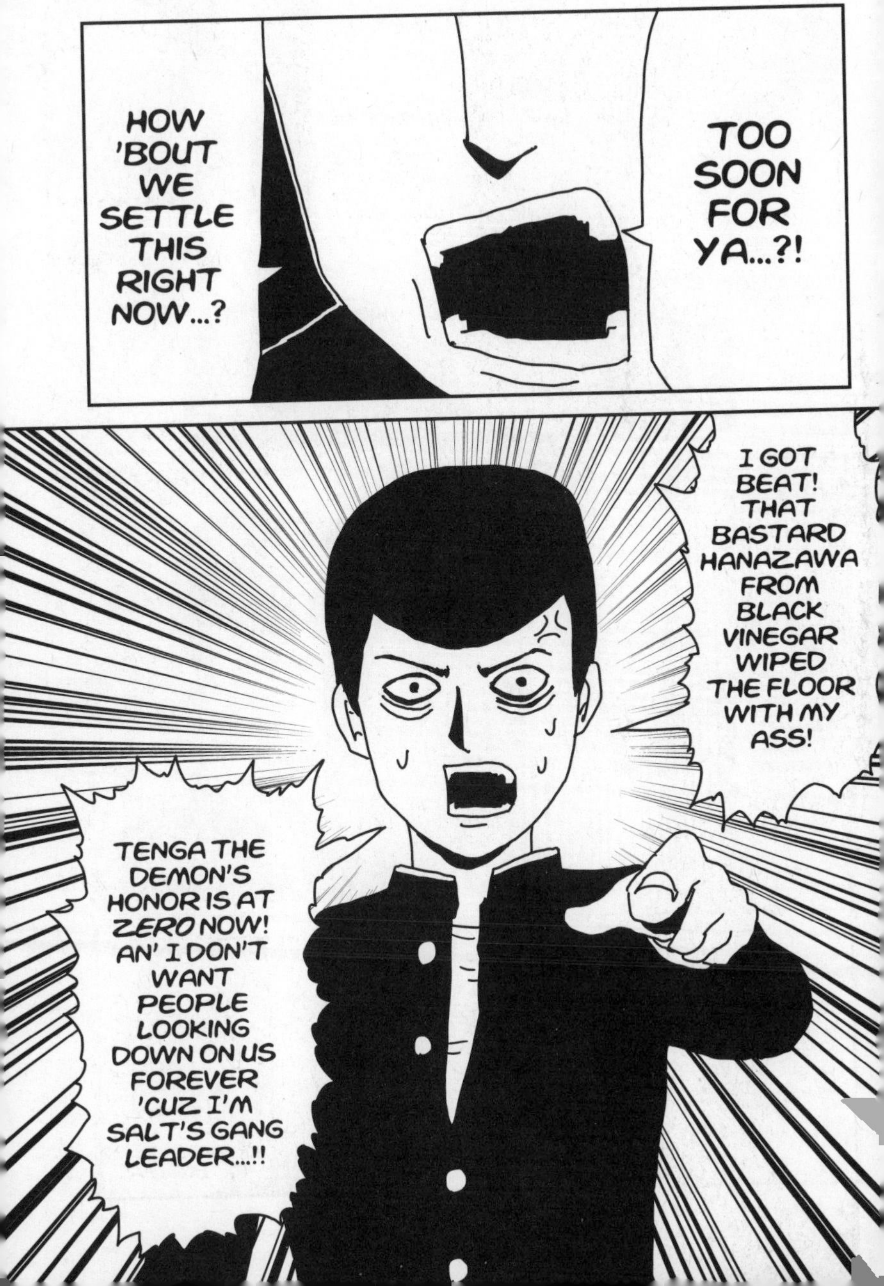
TOO SOON FOR YA...?!
HOW 'BOUT WE SETTLE THIS RIGHT NOW...?
I GOT BEAT! THAT BASTARD HANAZAWA FROM BLACK VINEGAR WIPED THE FLOOR WITH MY ASS!
TENGA THE DEMON'S HONOR IS AT *ZERO* NOW! AN' I DON'T WANT PEOPLE LOOKING DOWN ON US FOREVER 'CUZ I'M SALT'S GANG LEADER...!!

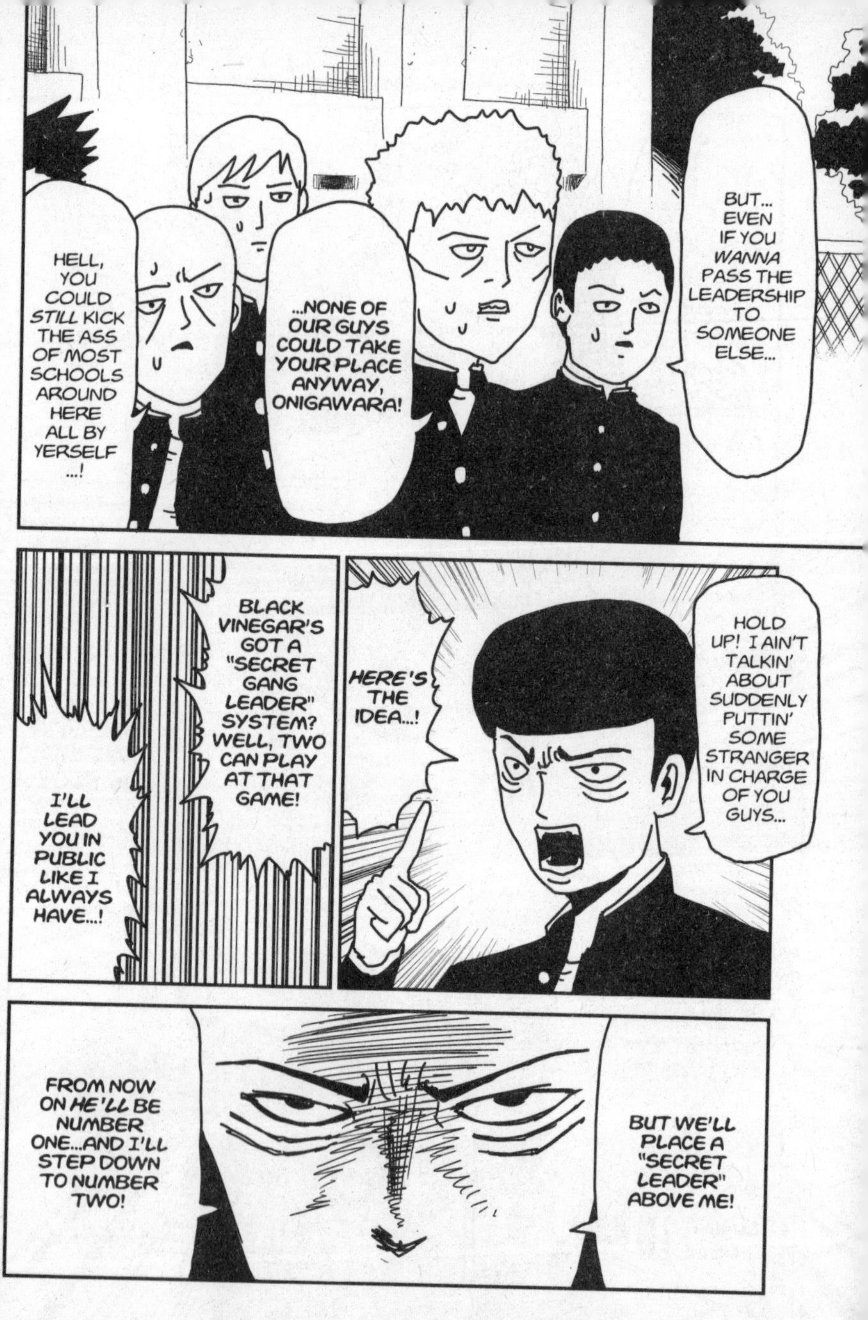
BUT... EVEN IF YOU WANNA PASS THE LEADERSHIP TO SOMEONE ELSE...
...NONE OF OUR GUYS COULD TAKE YOUR PLACE ANYWAY, ONIGAWARA!
HELL, YOU COULD STILL KICK THE ASS OF MOST SCHOOLS AROUND HERE ALL BY YERSELF ...!
HOLD UP! I AIN'T TALKIN' ABOUT SUDDENLY PUTTIN' SOME STRANGER IN CHARGE OF YOU GUYS...
HERE'S THE IDEA...!
BLACK VINEGAR'S GOT A "SECRET GANG LEADER" SYSTEM? WELL, TWO CAN PLAY AT THAT GAME!
I'LL LEAD YOU IN PUBLIC LIKE I ALWAYS HAVE...!
BUT WE'LL PLACE A "SECRET LEADER" ABOVE ME!
FROM NOW ON HE'LL BE NUMBER ONE...AND I'LL STEP DOWN TO NUMBER TWO!

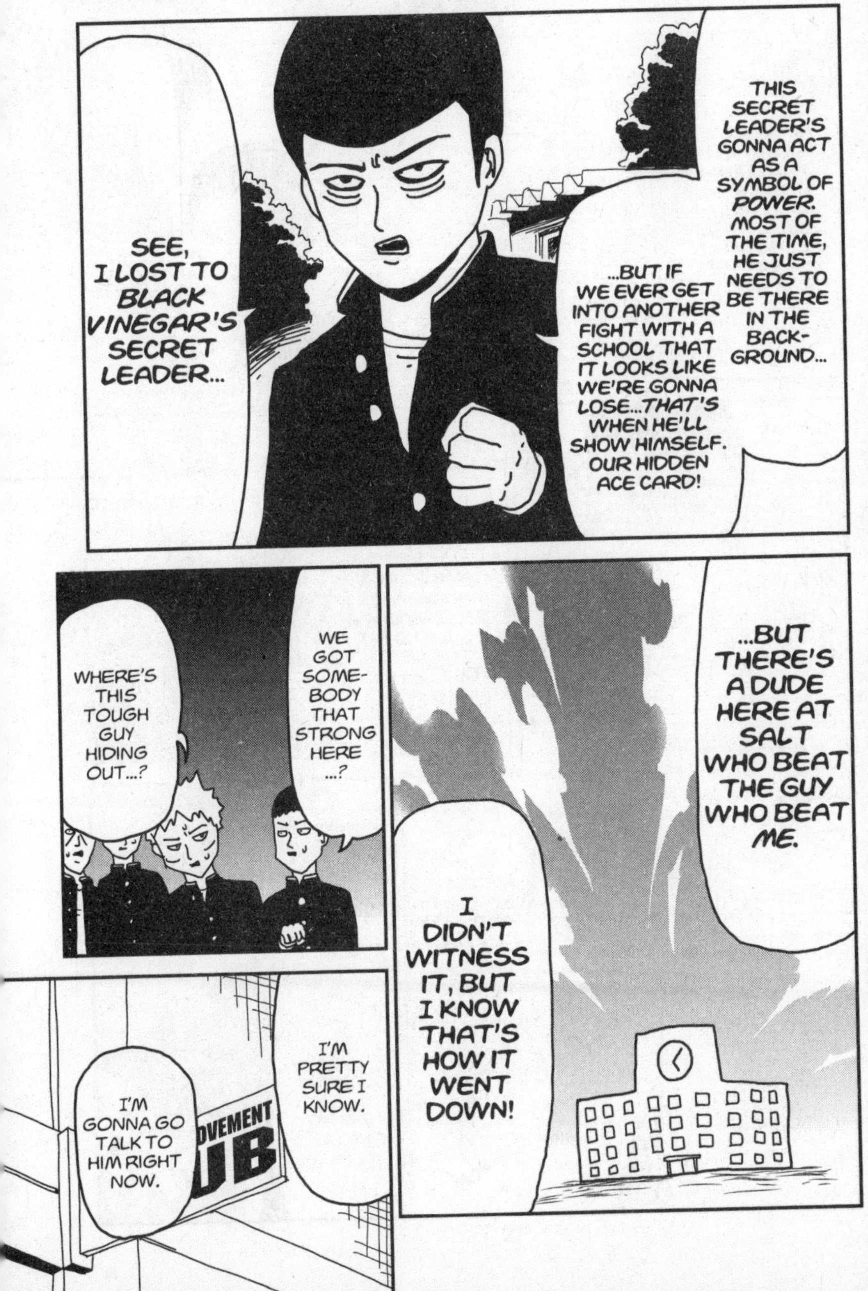
THIS SECRET LEADER'S GONNA ACT AS A SYMBOL OF POWER. MOST OF THE TIME, HE JUST NEEDS TO BE THERE IN THE BACKGROUND...
...BUT IF WE EVER GET INTO ANOTHER FIGHT WITH A SCHOOL THAT IT LOOKS LIKE WE'RE GONNA LOSE...THAT'S WHEN HE'LL SHOW HIMSELF. OUR HIDDEN ACE CARD!
SEE, I LOST TO BLACK VINEGAR'S SECRET LEADER...
...BUT THERE'S A DUDE HERE AT SALT WHO BEAT THE GUY WHO BEAT ME.
I DIDN'T WITNESS IT, BUT I KNOW THAT'S HOW IT WENT DOWN!
WE GOT SOMEBODY THAT STRONG HERE ...?
WHERE'S THIS TOUGH GUY HIDING OUT...?
I'M PRETTY SURE I KNOW.
I'M GONNA GO TALK TO HIM RIGHT NOW.

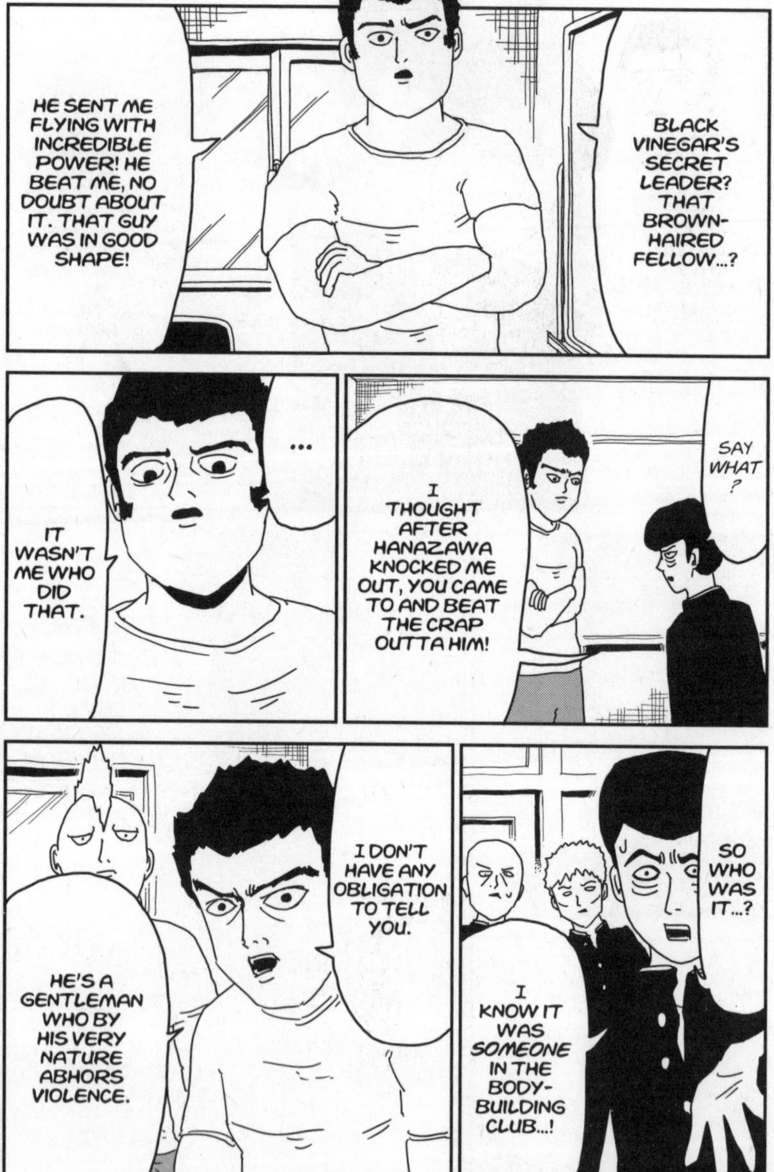
BLACK VINEGAR'S SECRET LEADER? THAT BROWN-HAIRED FELLOW...?
HE SENT ME FLYING WITH INCREDIBLE POWER! HE BEAT ME, NO DOUBT ABOUT IT. THAT GUY WAS IN GOOD SHAPE!
SAY WHAT?
I THOUGHT AFTER HANAZAWA KNOCKED ME OUT, YOU CAME TO AND BEAT THE CRAP OUTTA HIM!
...
IT WASN'T ME WHO DID THAT.
SO WHO WAS IT...?
I KNOW IT WAS SOMEONE IN THE BODY-BUILDING CLUB...!
I DON'T HAVE ANY OBLIGATION TO TELL YOU.
HE'S A GENTLEMAN WHO BY HIS VERY NATURE ABHORS VIOLENCE.

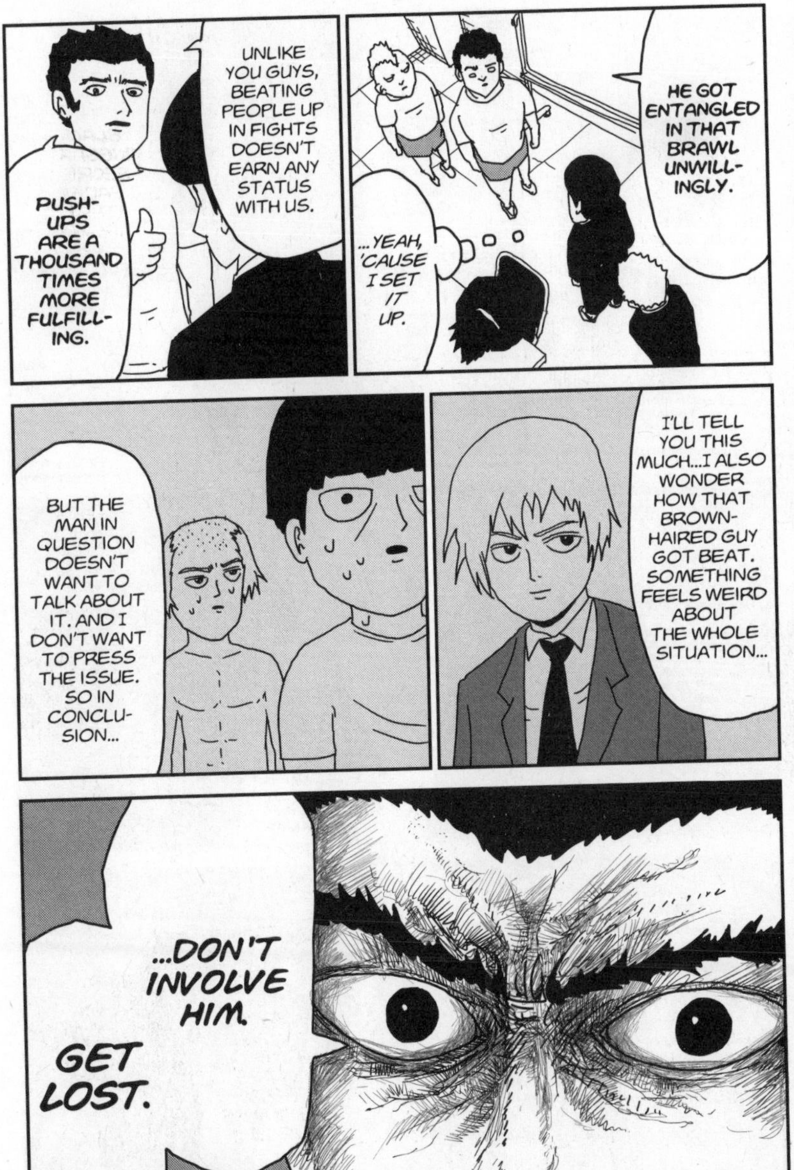
HE GOT ENTANGLED IN THAT BRAWL UNWILLINGLY.
...YEAH, 'CAUSE I SET IT UP.
UNLIKE YOU GUYS, BEATING PEOPLE UP IN FIGHTS DOESN'T EARN ANY STATUS WITH US.
PUSH-UPS ARE A THOUSAND TIMES MORE FULFILLING.
I'LL TELL YOU THIS MUCH...I ALSO WONDER HOW THAT BROWN-HAIRED GUY GOT BEAT. SOMETHING FEELS WEIRD ABOUT THE WHOLE SITUATION...
BUT THE MAN IN QUESTION DOESN'T WANT TO TALK ABOUT IT. AND I DON'T WANT TO PRESS THE ISSUE. SO IN CONCLUSION...
...DON'T INVOLVE HIM.
GET LOST.

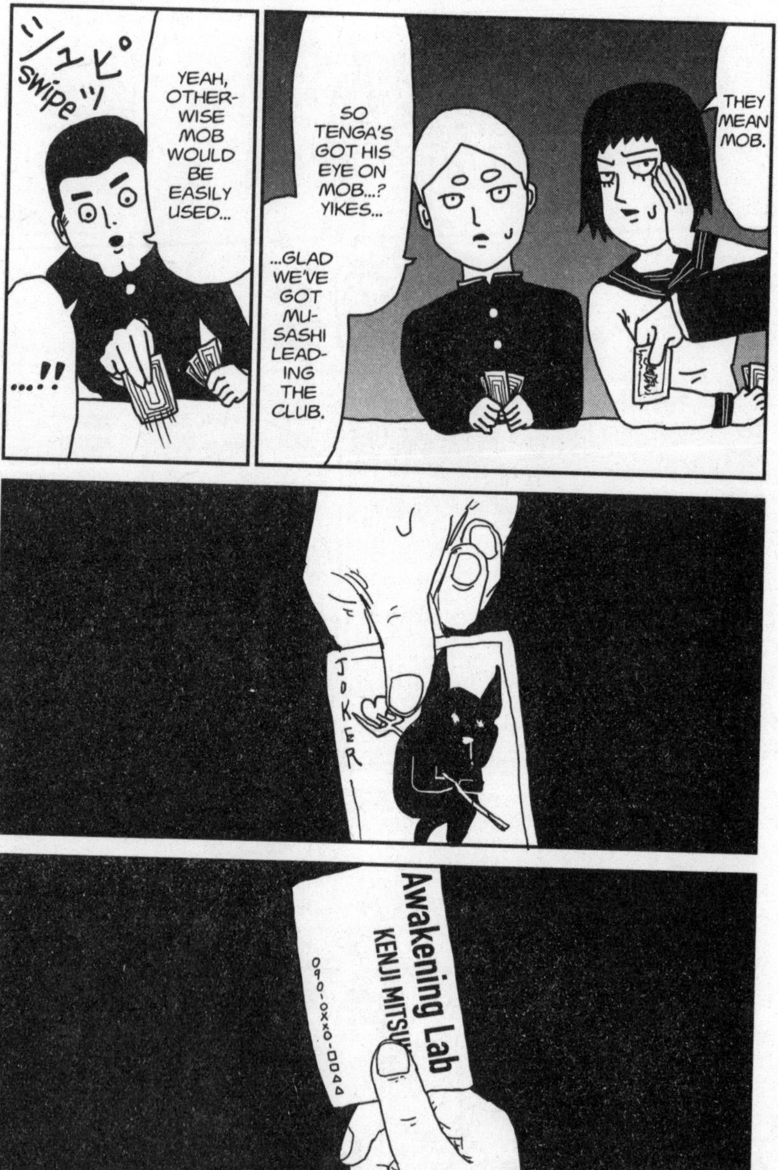
THEY MEAN MOB.
SO TENGA'S GOT HIS EYE ON MOB...? YIKES...
...GLAD WE'VE GOT MU-SASHI LEAD-ING THE CLUB.
YEAH, OTHER-WISE MOB WOULD BE EASILY USED...
シュピッ
swipe
...!!
JOKER
Awakening Lab
KENJI MITSU

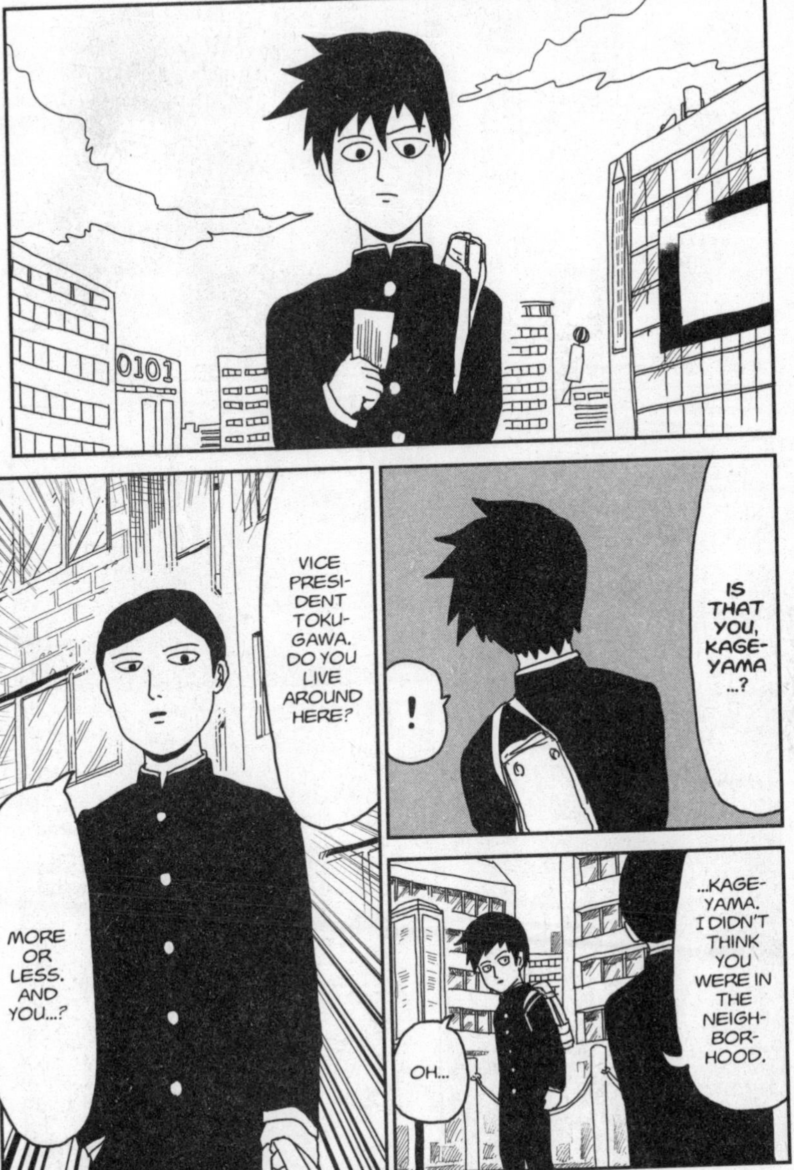
IS THAT YOU, KAGE-YAMA ...?
!
...KAGE-YAMA. I DIDN'T THINK YOU WERE IN THE NEIGH-BOR-HOOD.
OH...
VICE PRESI-DENT TOKU-GAWA. DO YOU LIVE AROUND HERE?
MORE OR LESS. AND YOU...?

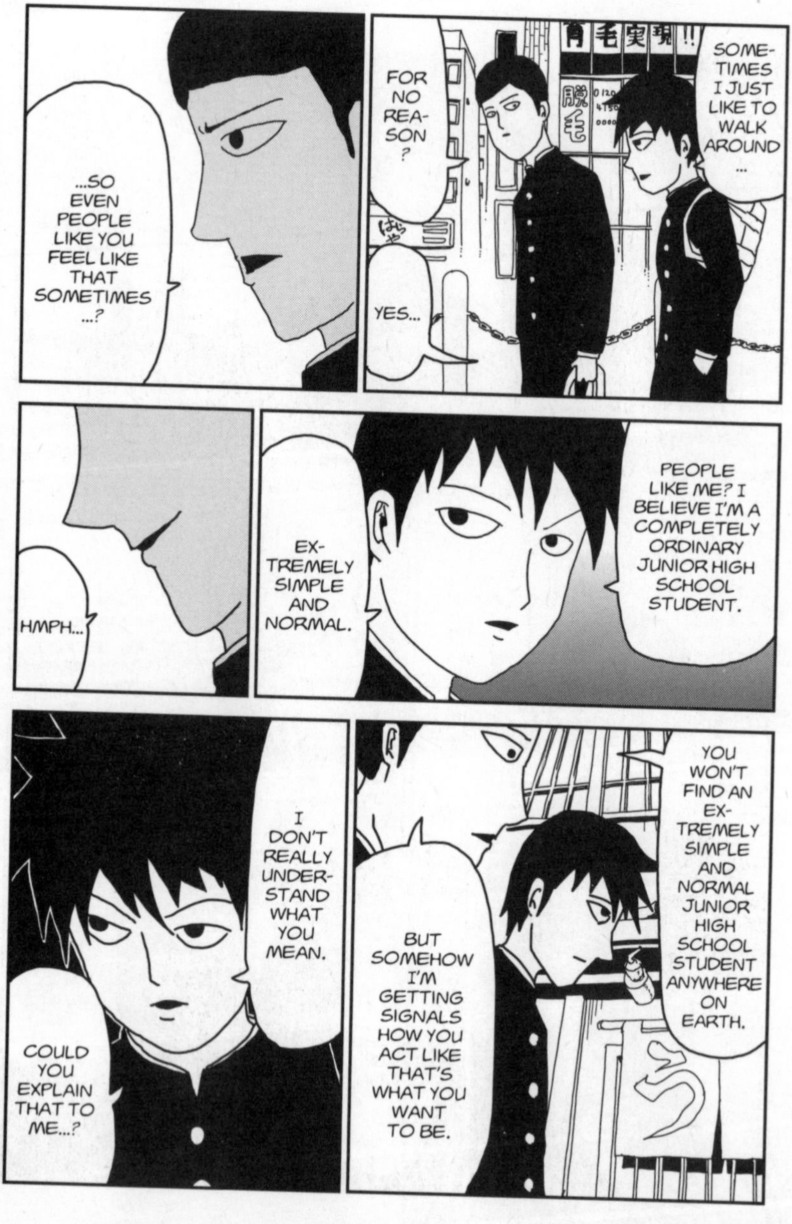
育毛実現!!
SOMETIMES I JUST LIKE TO WALK AROUND ...
FOR NO REASON?
YES...
...SO EVEN PEOPLE LIKE YOU FEEL LIKE THAT SOMETIMES ...?
PEOPLE LIKE ME? I BELIEVE I'M A COMPLETELY ORDINARY JUNIOR HIGH SCHOOL STUDENT.
EXTREMELY SIMPLE AND NORMAL.
HMPH...
YOU WON'T FIND AN EXTREMELY SIMPLE AND NORMAL JUNIOR HIGH SCHOOL STUDENT ANYWHERE ON EARTH.
BUT SOMEHOW I'M GETTING SIGNALS HOW YOU ACT LIKE THAT'S WHAT YOU WANT TO BE.
I DON'T REALLY UNDERSTAND WHAT YOU MEAN.
COULD YOU EXPLAIN THAT TO ME...?

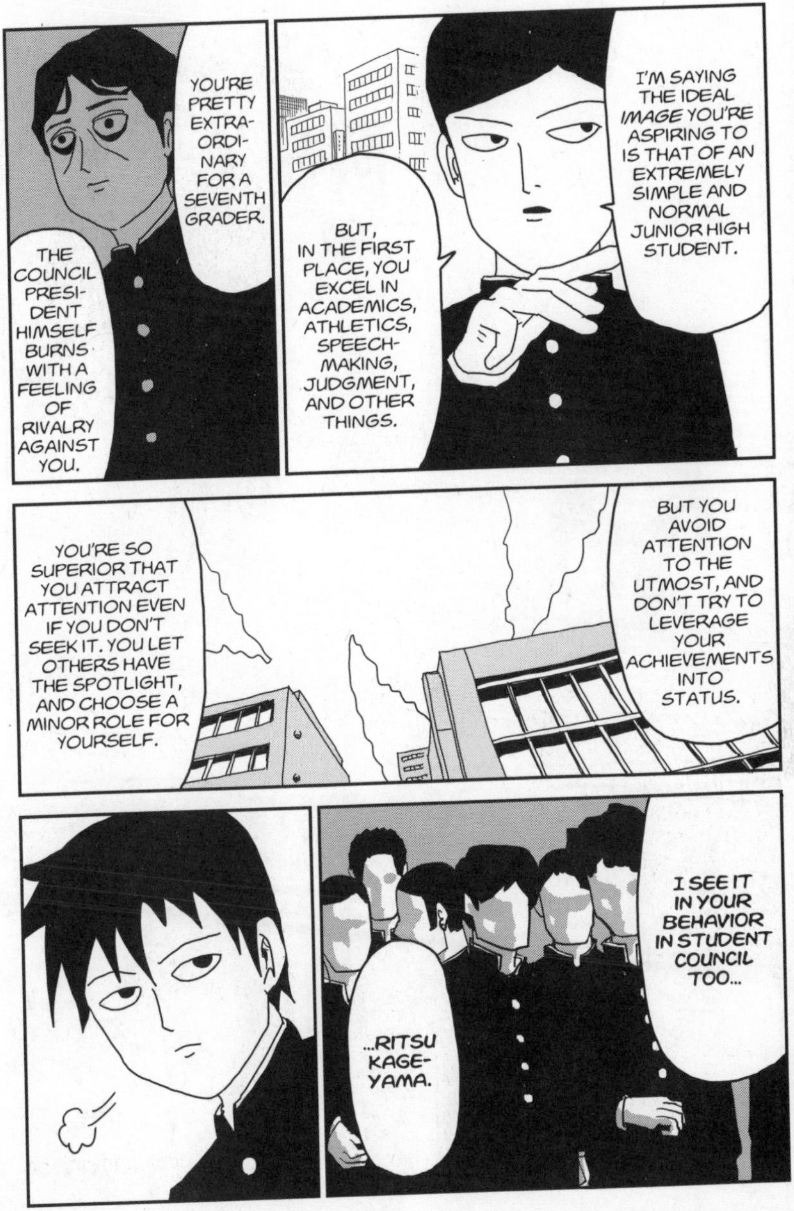
I'M SAYING THE IDEAL *IMAGE* YOU'RE ASPIRING TO IS THAT OF AN EXTREMELY SIMPLE AND NORMAL JUNIOR HIGH STUDENT.
BUT, IN THE FIRST PLACE, YOU EXCEL IN ACADEMICS, ATHLETICS, SPEECH-MAKING, JUDGMENT, AND OTHER THINGS.
YOU'RE PRETTY EXTRA-ORDI-NARY FOR A SEVENTH GRADER.
THE COUNCIL PRESI-DENT HIMSELF BURNS WITH A FEELING OF RIVALRY AGAINST YOU.
BUT YOU AVOID ATTENTION TO THE UTMOST, AND DON'T TRY TO LEVERAGE YOUR ACHIEVEMENTS INTO STATUS.
YOU'RE SO SUPERIOR THAT YOU ATTRACT ATTENTION EVEN IF YOU DON'T SEEK IT. YOU LET OTHERS HAVE THE SPOTLIGHT, AND CHOOSE A MINOR ROLE FOR YOURSELF.
I SEE IT IN YOUR BEHAVIOR IN STUDENT COUNCIL TOO...
...RITSU KAGE-YAMA.

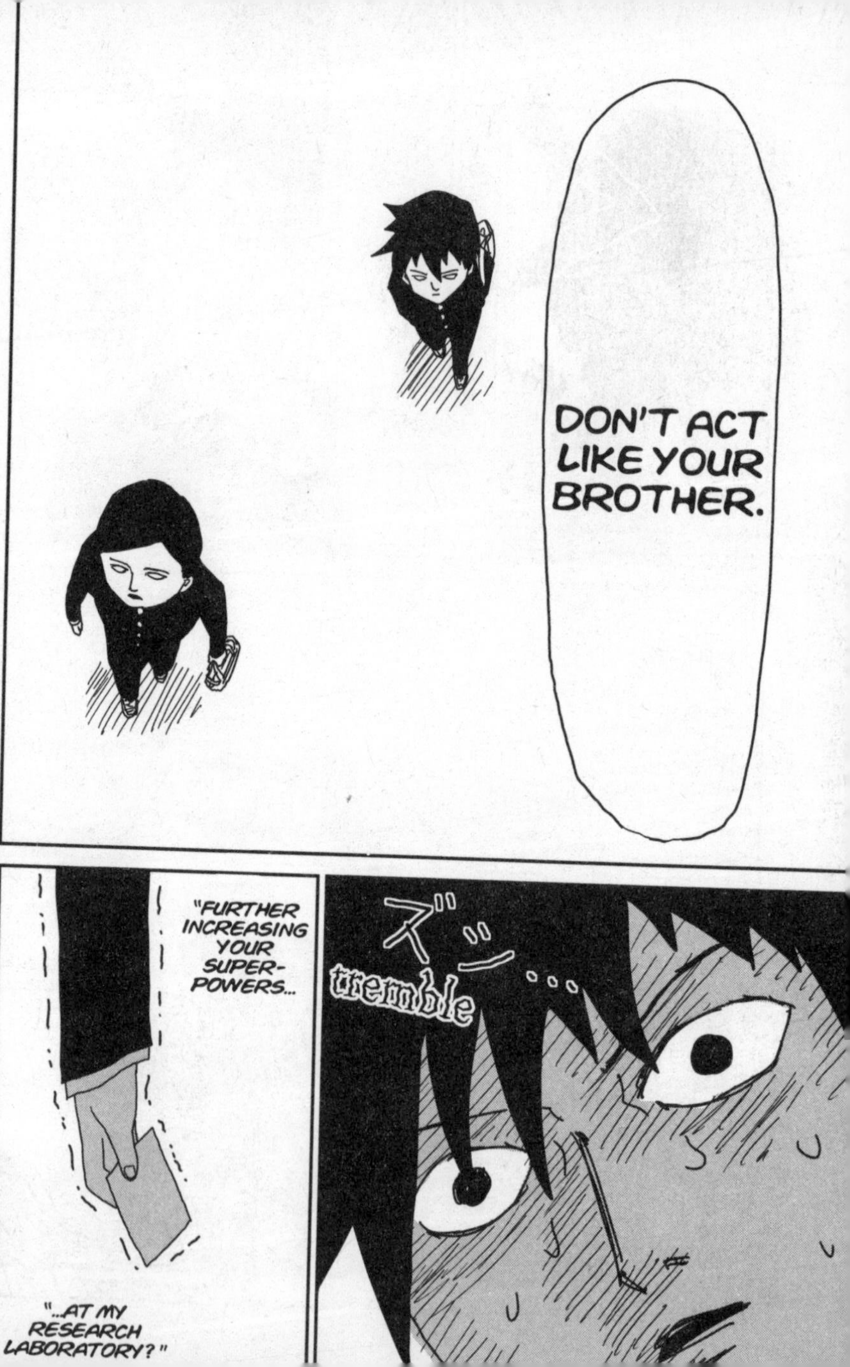
DON'T ACT LIKE YOUR BROTHER.
ズー
tremble
...
"FURTHER INCREASING YOUR SUPER-POWERS...
"...AT MY RESEARCH LABORATORY?"

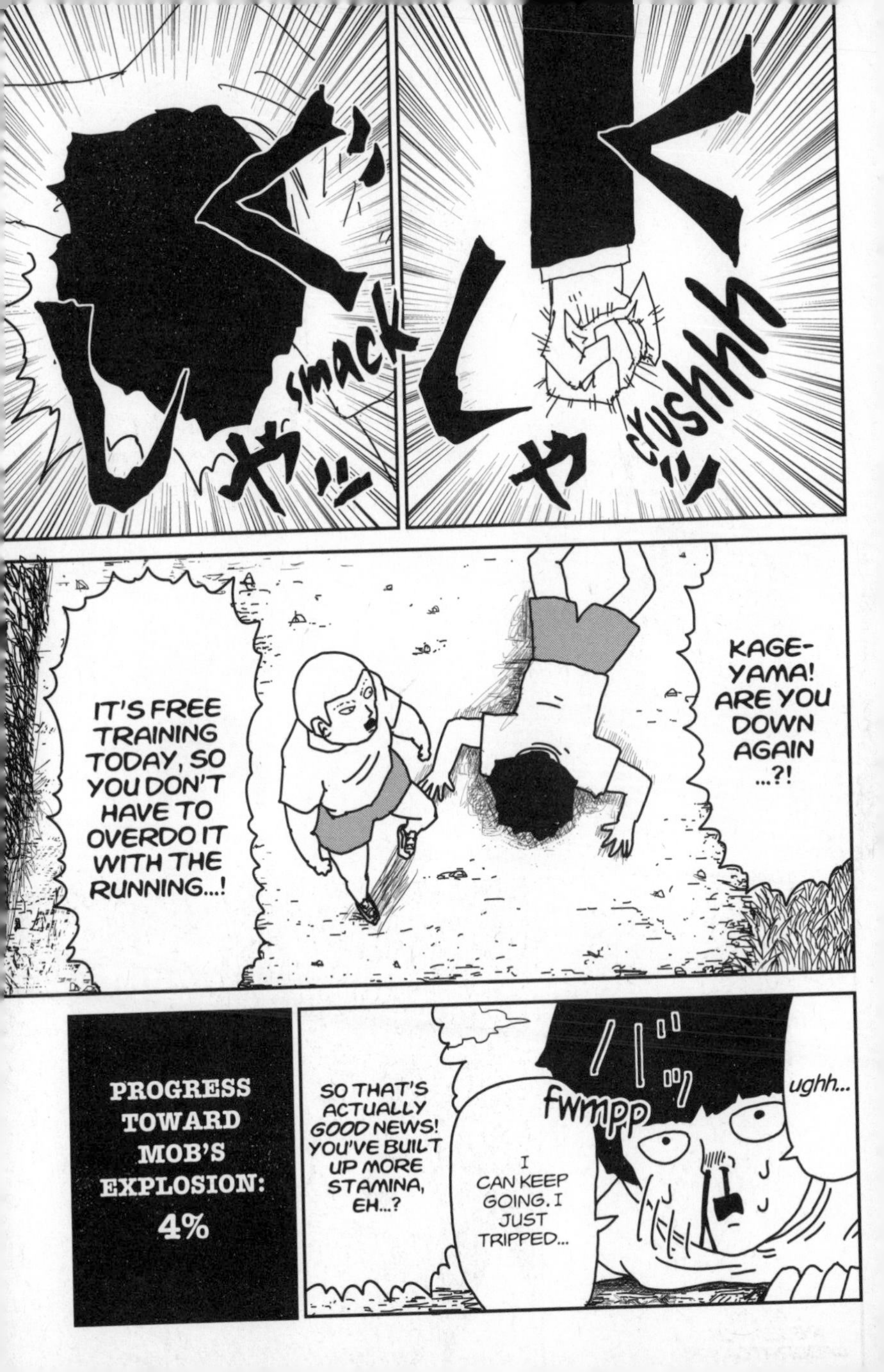
crushhh
smack
KAGE-YAMA! ARE YOU DOWN AGAIN ...?!
IT'S FREE TRAINING TODAY, SO YOU DON'T HAVE TO OVERDO IT WITH THE RUNNING...!
ughh...
fwmpp
I CAN KEEP GOING. I JUST TRIPPED...
SO THAT'S ACTUALLY GOOD NEWS! YOU'VE BUILT UP MORE STAMINA, EH...?
PROGRESS TOWARD MOB'S EXPLOSION: 4%

CHAPTER 22: AWAKENING LAB

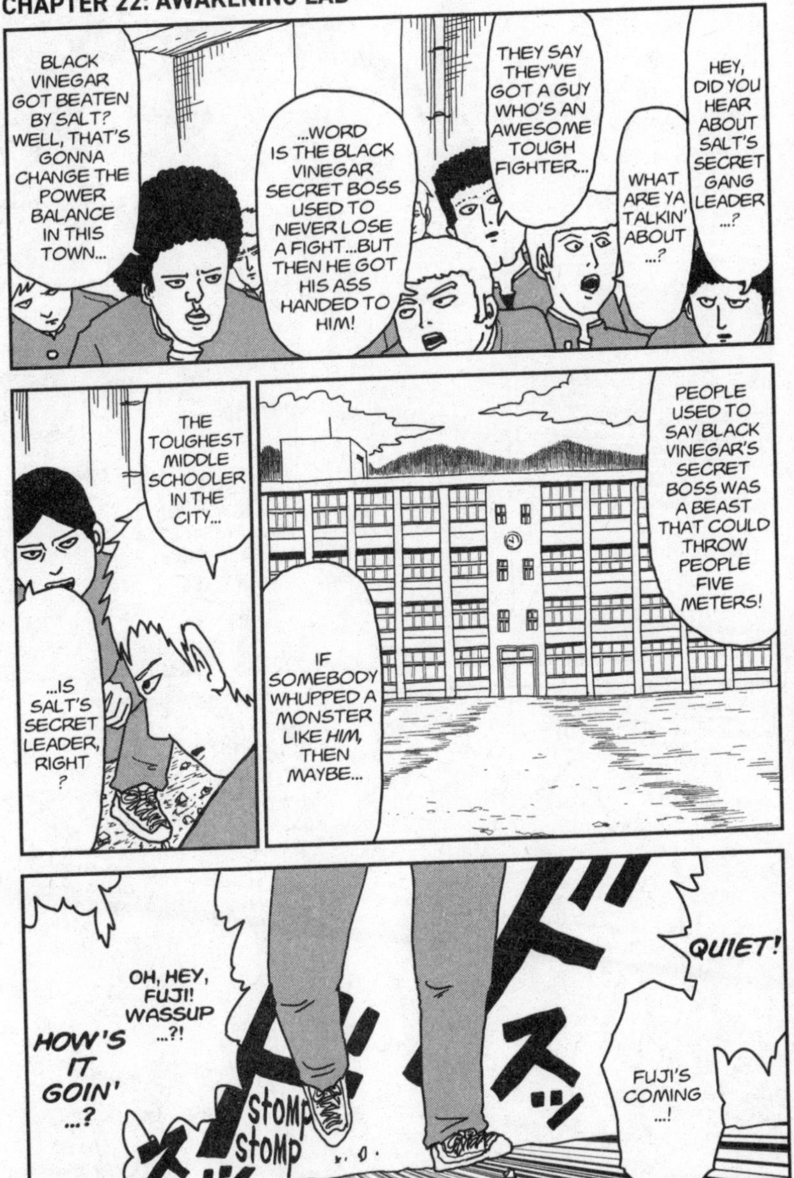
HEY, DID YOU HEAR ABOUT SALT'S SECRET GANG LEADER ...?
WHAT ARE YA TALKIN' ABOUT ...?
THEY SAY THEY'VE GOT A GUY WHO'S AN AWESOME TOUGH FIGHTER...
...WORD IS THE BLACK VINEGAR SECRET BOSS USED TO NEVER LOSE A FIGHT...BUT THEN HE GOT HIS ASS HANDED TO HIM!
BLACK VINEGAR GOT BEATEN BY SALT? WELL, THAT'S GONNA CHANGE THE POWER BALANCE IN THIS TOWN...
PEOPLE USED TO SAY BLACK VINEGAR'S SECRET BOSS WAS A BEAST THAT COULD THROW PEOPLE FIVE METERS!
IF SOMEBODY WHUPPED A MONSTER LIKE *HIM*, THEN MAYBE...
THE TOUGHEST MIDDLE SCHOOLER IN THE CITY...
...IS SALT'S SECRET LEADER, RIGHT?
QUIET!
FUJI'S COMING ...!
OH, HEY, FUJI! WASSUP ...?!
stomp stomp
HOW'S IT GOIN' ...?

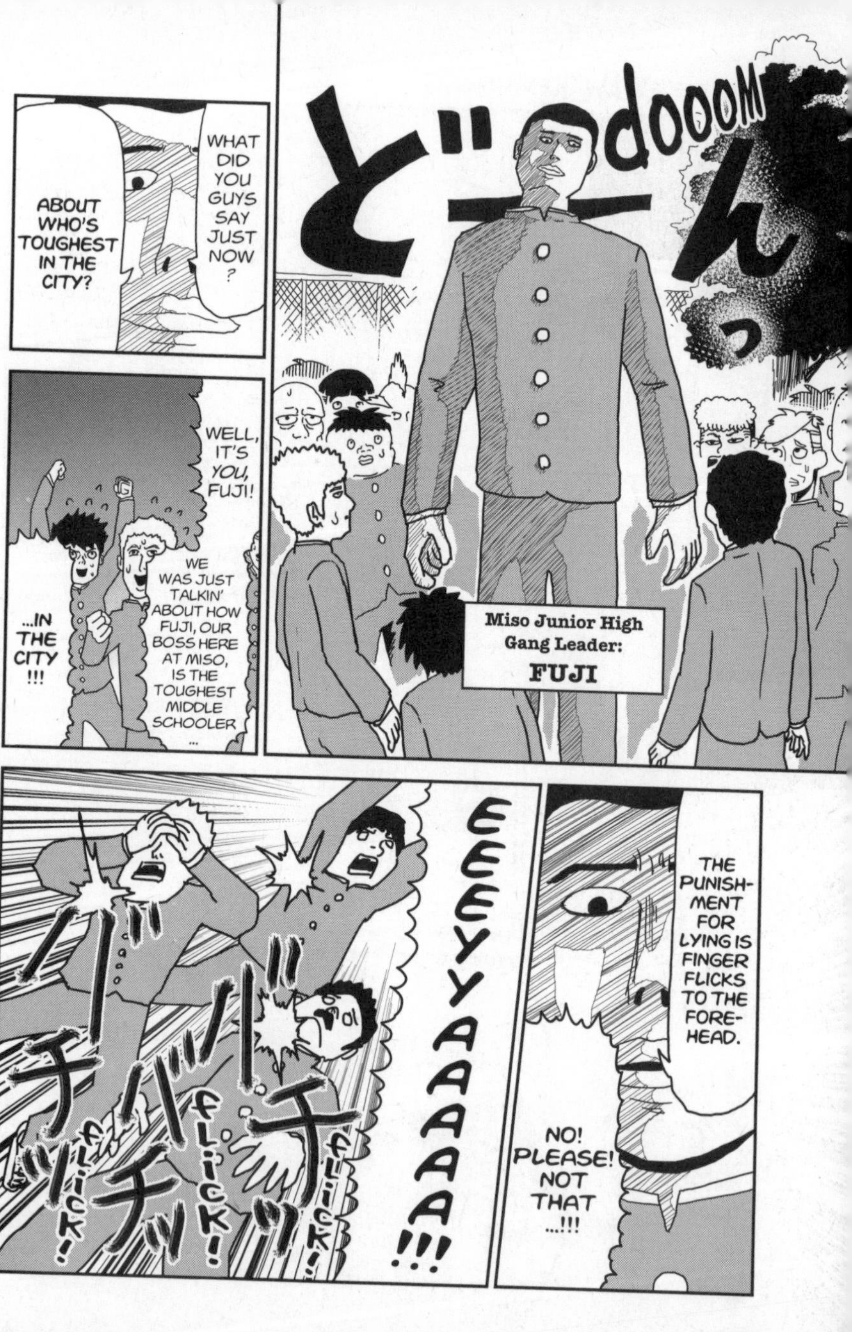
ど
dooom
ん
Miso Junior High Gang Leader:
FUJI
WHAT DID YOU GUYS SAY JUST NOW?
ABOUT WHO'S TOUGHEST IN THE CITY?
WELL, IT'S *YOU*, FUJI!
WE WAS JUST TALKIN' ABOUT HOW FUJI, OUR BOSS HERE AT MISO, IS THE TOUGHEST MIDDLE SCHOOLER...
...IN THE CITY!!!
THE PUNISHMENT FOR LYING IS FINGER FLICKS TO THE FOREHEAD.
NO! PLEASE! NOT THAT...!!!
EEEYYAAAAAA!!!
FLICK!
FLICK!
FLICK!

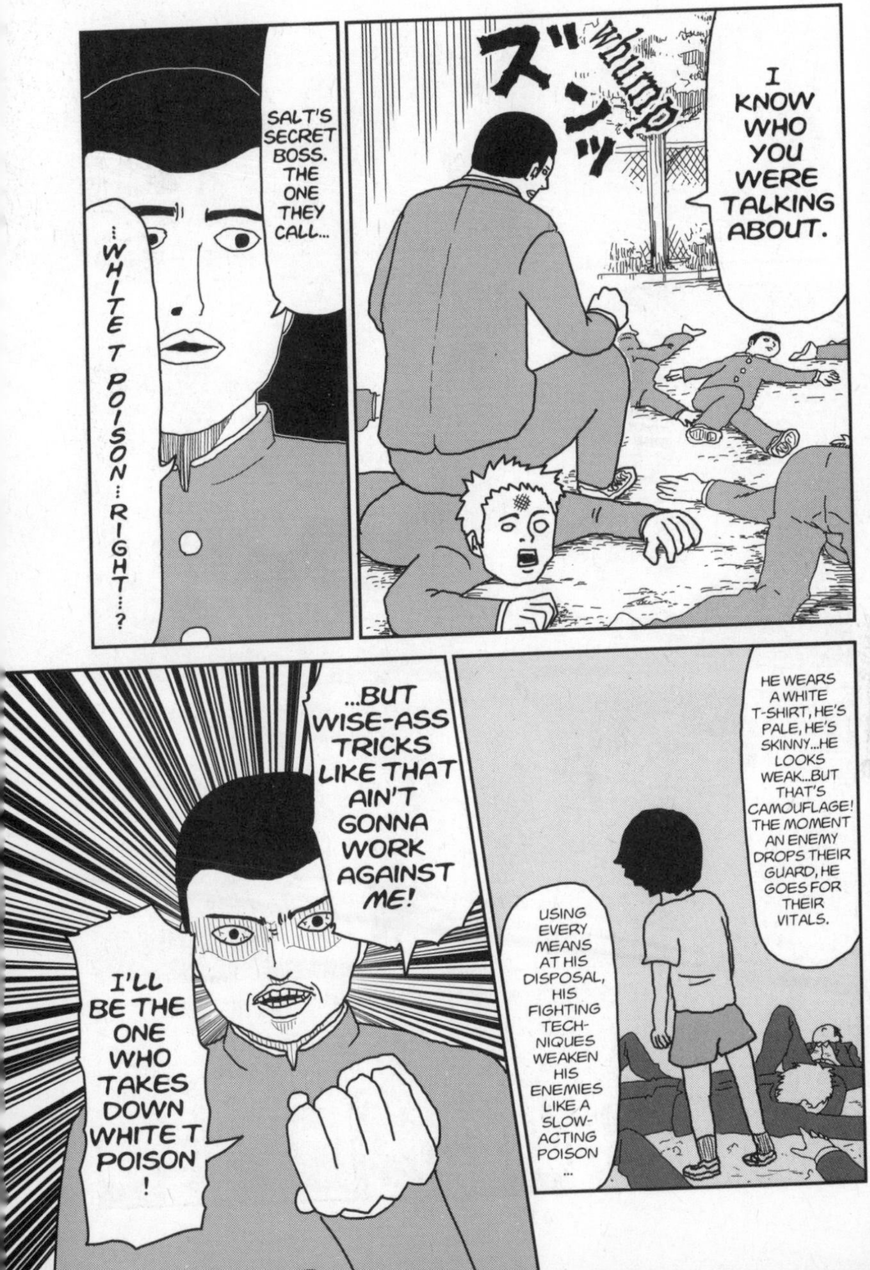
I KNOW WHO YOU WERE TALKING ABOUT.
ズンッ
whump
SALT'S SECRET BOSS. THE ONE THEY CALL...
...WHITE T POISON...RIGHT...?
HE WEARS A WHITE T-SHIRT, HE'S PALE, HE'S SKINNY...HE LOOKS WEAK...BUT THAT'S CAMOUFLAGE! THE MOMENT AN ENEMY DROPS THEIR GUARD, HE GOES FOR THEIR VITALS.
USING EVERY MEANS AT HIS DISPOSAL, HIS FIGHTING TECH-NIQUES WEAKEN HIS ENEMIES LIKE A SLOW-ACTING POISON...
...BUT WISE-ASS TRICKS LIKE THAT AIN'T GONNA WORK AGAINST ME!
I'LL BE THE ONE WHO TAKES DOWN WHITE T POISON!

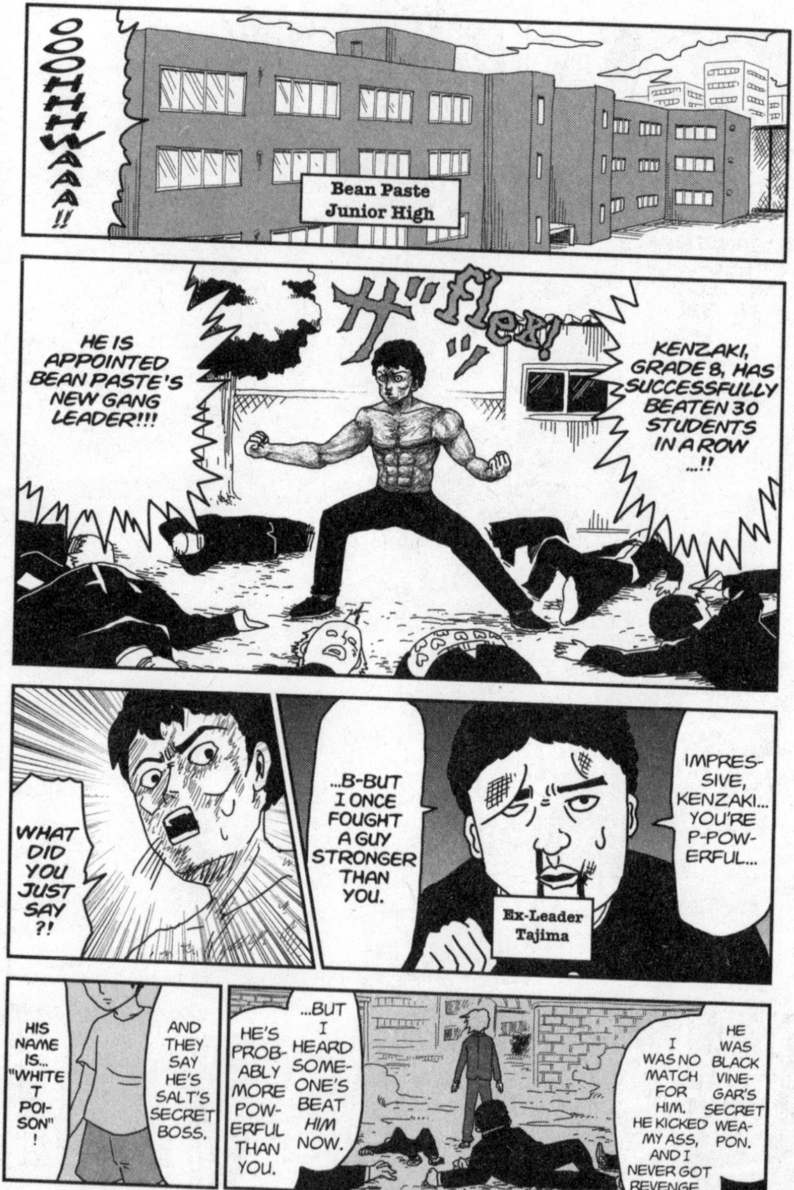
OOOHHHWAAA!!
Bean Paste Junior High
KENZAKI, GRADE 8, HAS SUCCESSFULLY BEATEN 30 STUDENTS IN A ROW ...!!
ザッ flex!
HE IS APPOINTED BEAN PASTE'S NEW GANG LEADER!!!
IMPRES-SIVE, KENZAKI... YOU'RE P-POW-ERFUL...
...B-BUT I ONCE FOUGHT A GUY STRONGER THAN YOU.
Ex-Leader Tajima
WHAT DID YOU JUST SAY?!
HE WAS BLACK VINE-GAR'S SECRET WEA-PON.
I WAS NO MATCH FOR HIM. HE KICKED MY ASS, AND I NEVER GOT REVENGE...
...BUT I HEARD SOME-ONE'S BEAT HIM NOW.
HE'S PROB-ABLY MORE POW-ERFUL THAN YOU.
AND THEY SAY HE'S SALT'S SECRET BOSS.
HIS NAME IS... "WHITE T POI-SON"!

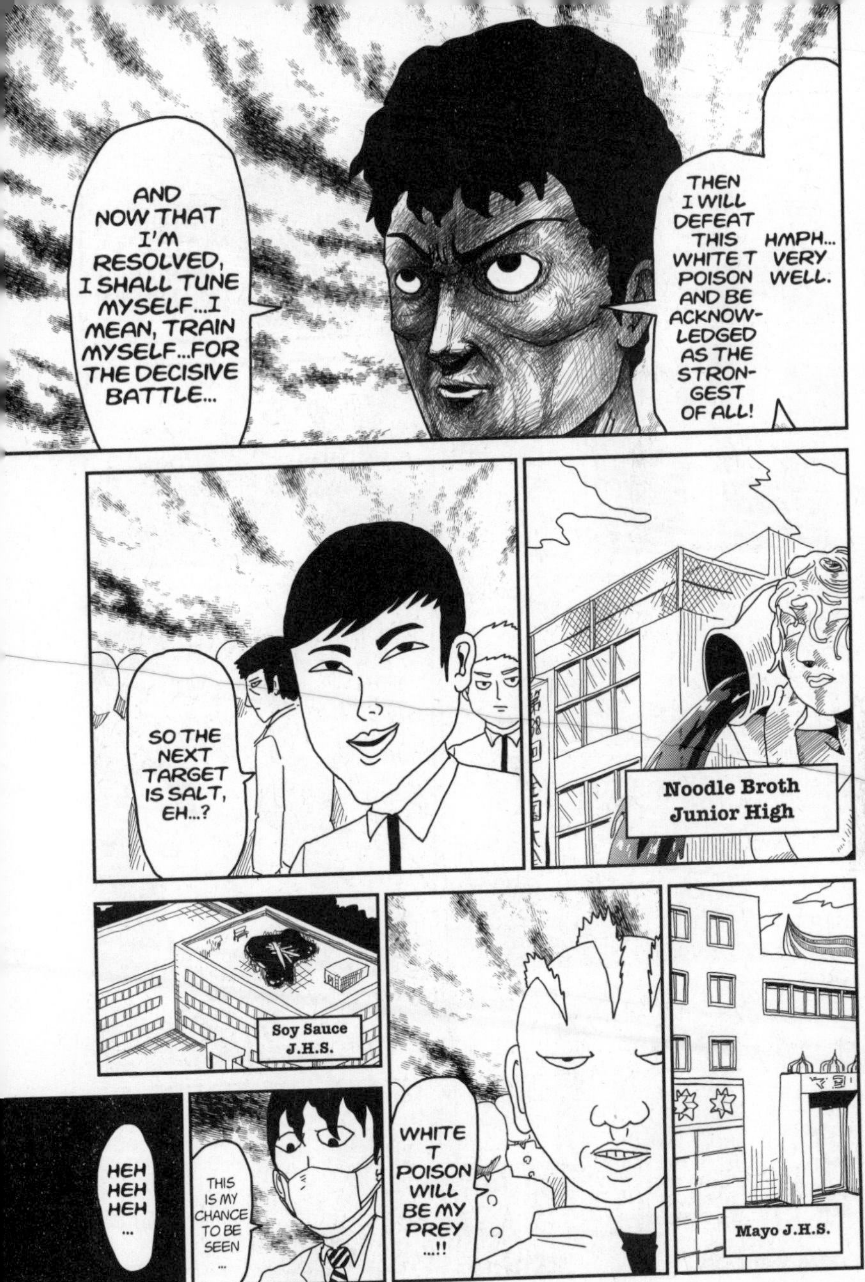
HMPH... VERY WELL.
THEN I WILL DEFEAT THIS WHITE T POISON AND BE ACKNOW-LEDGED AS THE STRON-GEST OF ALL!
AND NOW THAT I'M RESOLVED, I SHALL TUNE MYSELF...I MEAN, TRAIN MYSELF...FOR THE DECISIVE BATTLE...
Noodle Broth Junior High
SO THE NEXT TARGET IS SALT, EH...?
Mayo J.H.S.
WHITE T POISON WILL BE MY PREY ...!!
Soy Sauce J.H.S.
THIS IS MY CHANCE TO BE SEEN ...
HEH HEH HEH ...

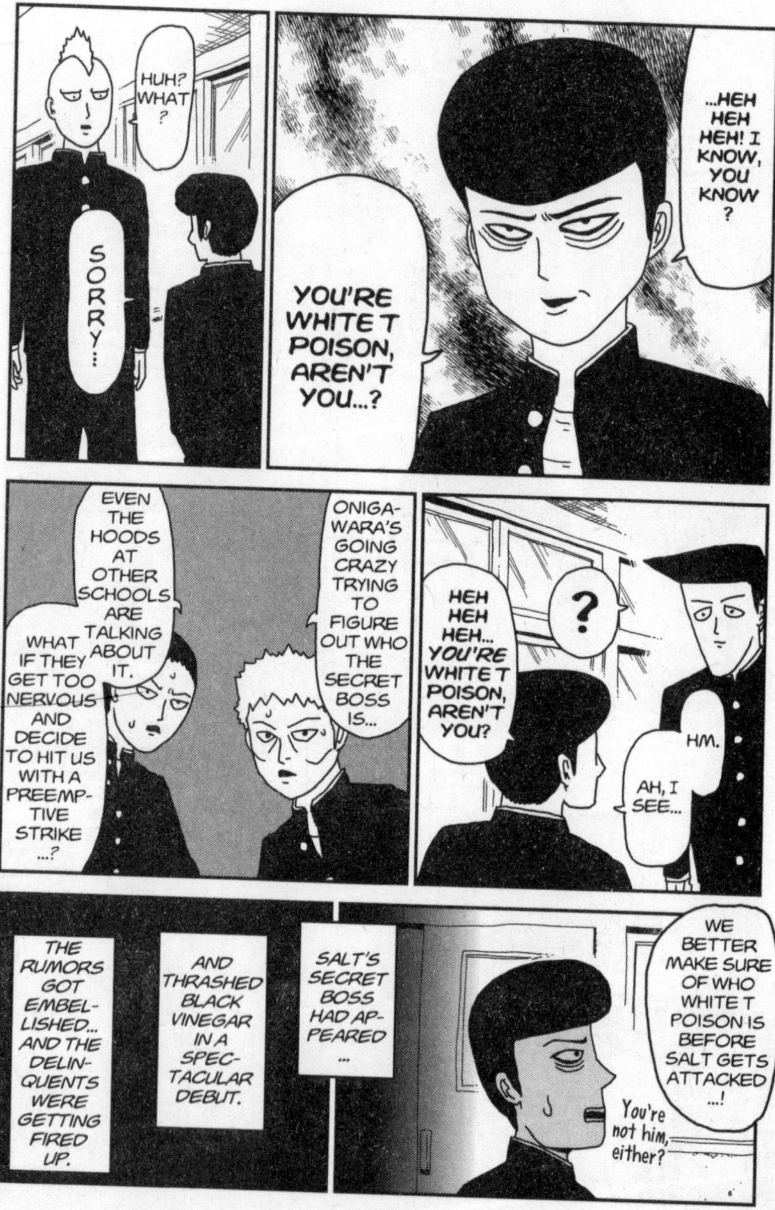
...HEH HEH HEH! I KNOW, YOU KNOW?
YOU'RE WHITE T POISON, AREN'T YOU...?
HUH? WHAT?
SORRY...
HEH HEH HEH... YOU'RE WHITE T POISON, AREN'T YOU?
?
HM.
AH, I SEE...
ONIGA-WARA'S GOING CRAZY TRYING TO FIGURE OUT WHO THE SECRET BOSS IS...
EVEN THE HOODS AT OTHER SCHOOLS ARE TALKING ABOUT IT.
WHAT IF THEY GET TOO NERVOUS AND DECIDE TO HIT US WITH A PREEMPTIVE STRIKE...?
WE BETTER MAKE SURE OF WHO WHITE T POISON IS BEFORE SALT GETS ATTACKED...!
You're not him, either?
SALT'S SECRET BOSS HAD APPEARED...
AND THRASHED BLACK VINEGAR IN A SPECTACULAR DEBUT.
THE RUMORS GOT EMBELLISHED... AND THE DELINQUENTS WERE GETTING FIRED UP.

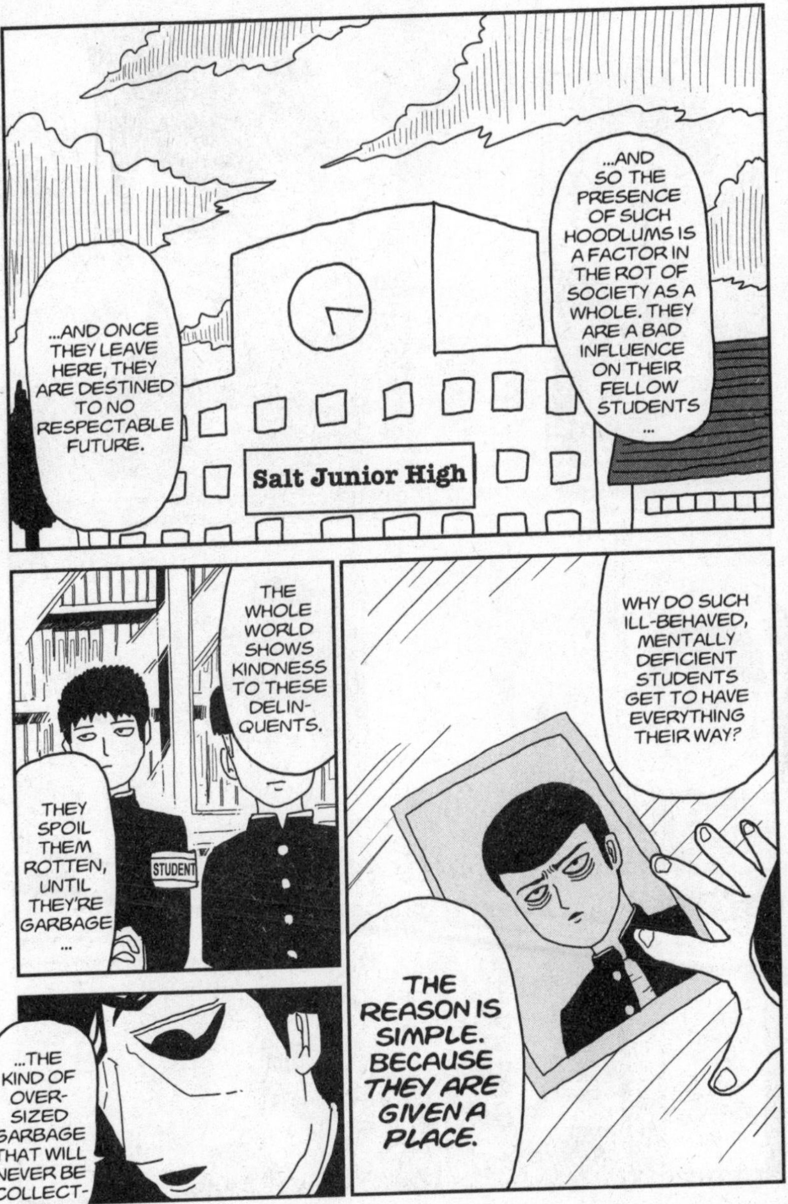
...AND SO THE PRESENCE OF SUCH HOODLUMS IS A FACTOR IN THE ROT OF SOCIETY AS A WHOLE. THEY ARE A BAD INFLUENCE ON THEIR FELLOW STUDENTS ...
...AND ONCE THEY LEAVE HERE, THEY ARE DESTINED TO NO RESPECTABLE FUTURE.
Salt Junior High
WHY DO SUCH ILL-BEHAVED, MENTALLY DEFICIENT STUDENTS GET TO HAVE EVERYTHING THEIR WAY?
THE REASON IS SIMPLE. BECAUSE *THEY ARE GIVEN A PLACE.*
THE WHOLE WORLD SHOWS KINDNESS TO THESE DELIN- QUENTS.
THEY SPOIL THEM ROTTEN, UNTIL THEY'RE GARBAGE ...
STUDENT
...THE KIND OF OVER- SIZED GARBAGE THAT WILL NEVER BE COLLECT- ED.

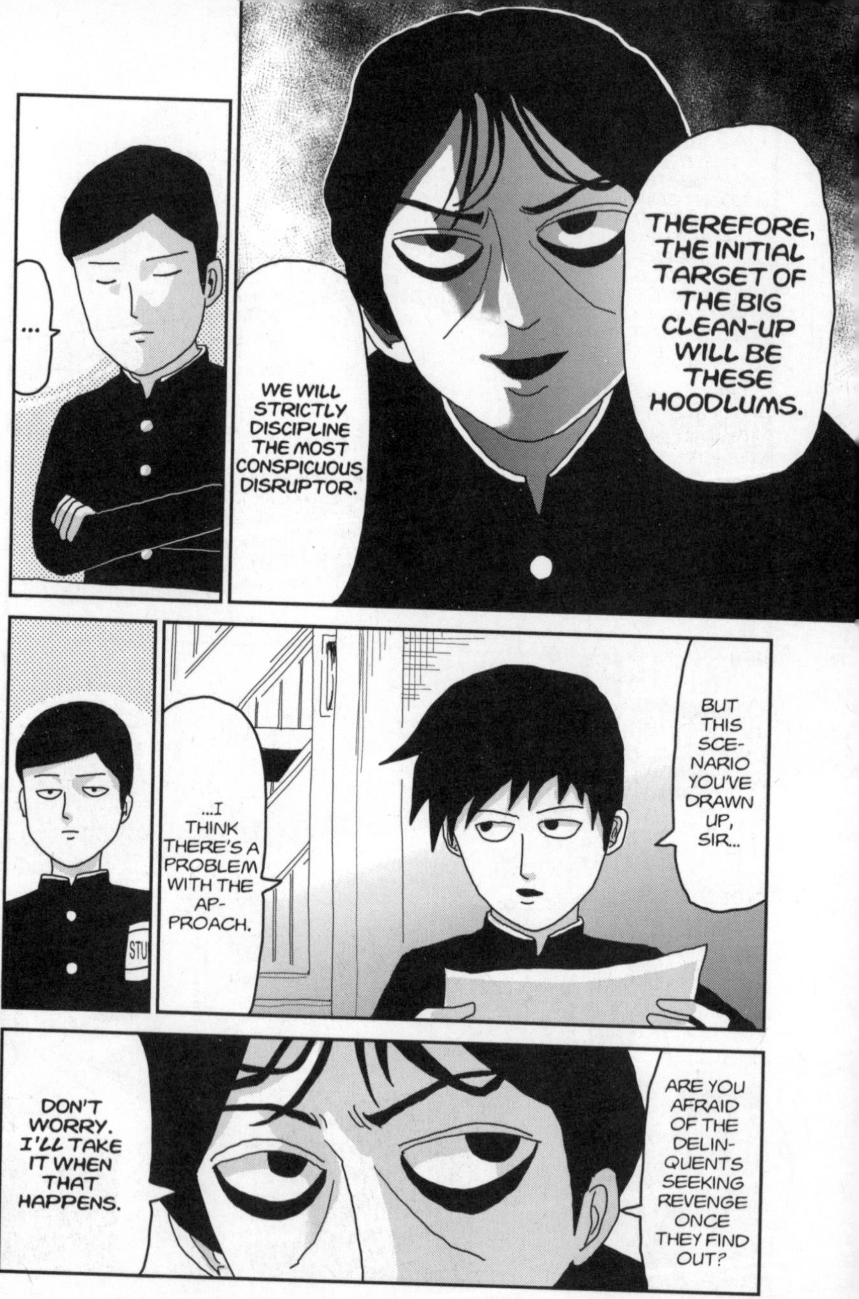
THEREFORE, THE INITIAL TARGET OF THE BIG CLEAN-UP WILL BE THESE HOODLUMS.
WE WILL STRICTLY DISCIPLINE THE MOST CONSPICUOUS DISRUPTOR.
...
BUT THIS SCE-NARIO YOU'VE DRAWN UP, SIR...
...I THINK THERE'S A PROBLEM WITH THE AP-PROACH.
STU
ARE YOU AFRAID OF THE DELIN-QUENTS SEEKING REVENGE ONCE THEY FIND OUT?
DON'T WORRY. I'LL TAKE IT WHEN THAT HAPPENS.

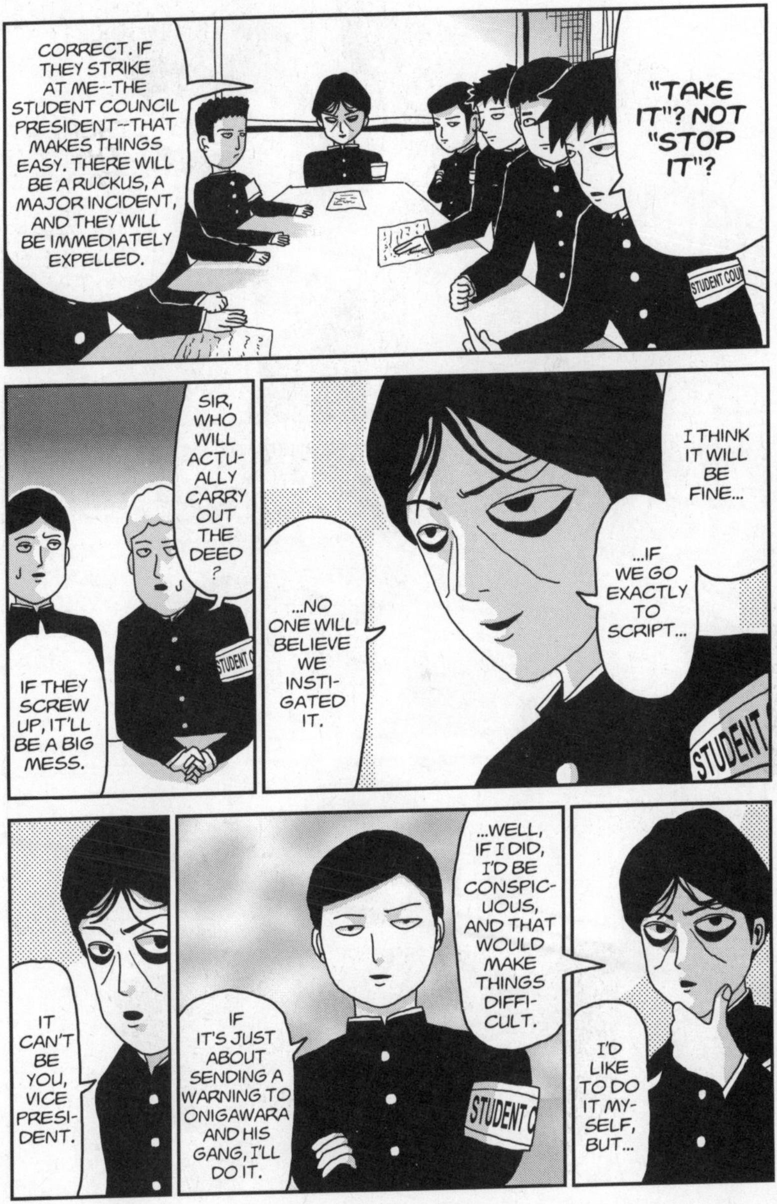
"TAKE IT"? NOT "STOP IT"?
CORRECT. IF THEY STRIKE AT ME--THE STUDENT COUNCIL PRESIDENT--THAT MAKES THINGS EASY. THERE WILL BE A RUCKUS, A MAJOR INCIDENT, AND THEY WILL BE IMMEDIATELY EXPELLED.
I THINK IT WILL BE FINE...
...IF WE GO EXACTLY TO SCRIPT...
...NO ONE WILL BELIEVE WE INSTIGATED IT.
SIR, WHO WILL ACTUALLY CARRY OUT THE DEED?
IF THEY SCREW UP, IT'LL BE A BIG MESS.
I'D LIKE TO DO IT MYSELF, BUT...
...WELL, IF I DID, I'D BE CONSPICUOUS, AND THAT WOULD MAKE THINGS DIFFICULT.
IF IT'S JUST ABOUT SENDING A WARNING TO ONIGAWARA AND HIS GANG, I'LL DO IT.
IT CAN'T BE YOU, VICE PRESIDENT.

HOW CAN I PUT IT...? TOKU- GAWA, YOU'RE TOO FORCE- FUL.

IF SOME- THING HAP- PENED, AND THERE WAS A BRAWL WITH THE DELIN- QUENTS, IT WOULD ALL BE FOR NOTH- ING.

DIR- ECT CON- FRON- TATION ISN'T THE BEST TACTIC.

Ethwap

...HOW ABOUT YOU, KAGE- YAMA?

STUDE STUDE STUDE

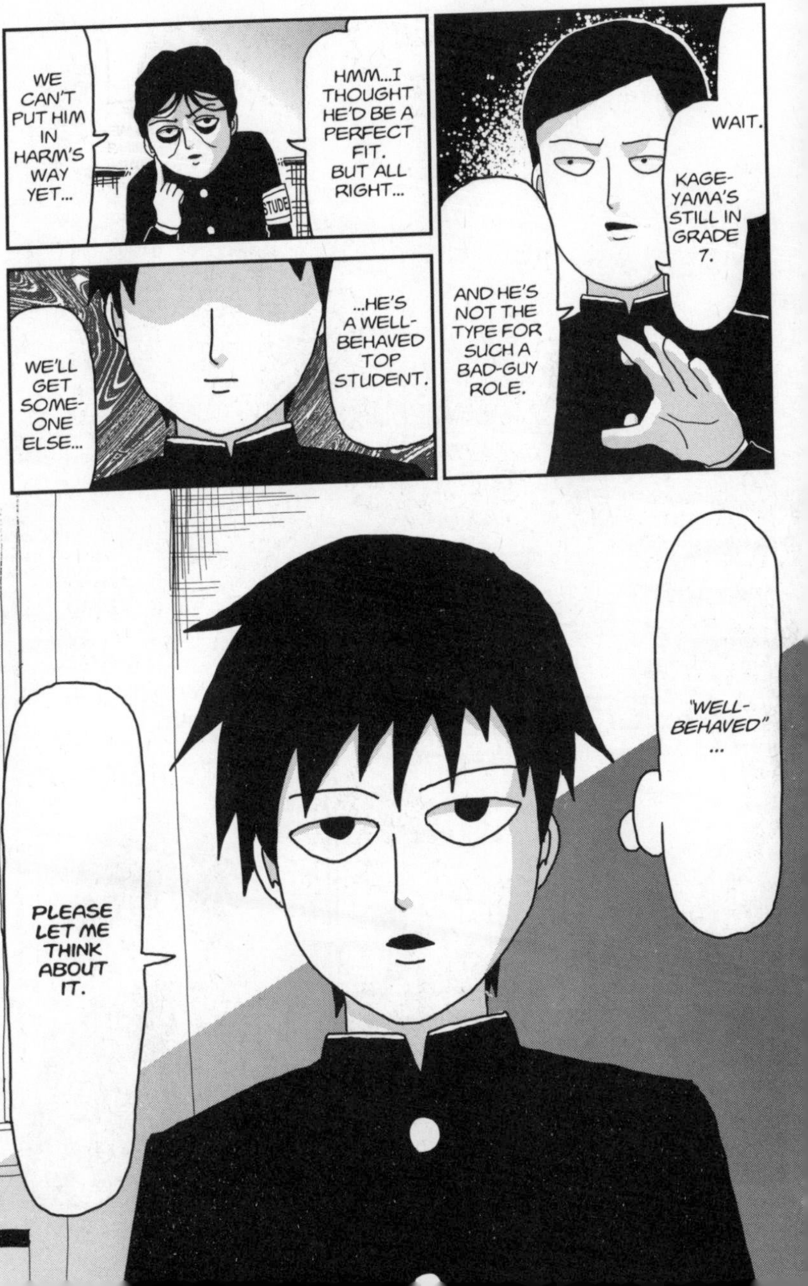
WAIT.
KAGE-YAMA'S STILL IN GRADE 7.
AND HE'S NOT THE TYPE FOR SUCH A BAD-GUY ROLE.
HMM...I THOUGHT HE'D BE A PERFECT FIT. BUT ALL RIGHT...
WE CAN'T PUT HIM IN HARM'S WAY YET...
...HE'S A WELL-BEHAVED TOP STUDENT.
WE'LL GET SOME-ONE ELSE...
"WELL-BEHAVED" ...
PLEASE LET ME THINK ABOUT IT.

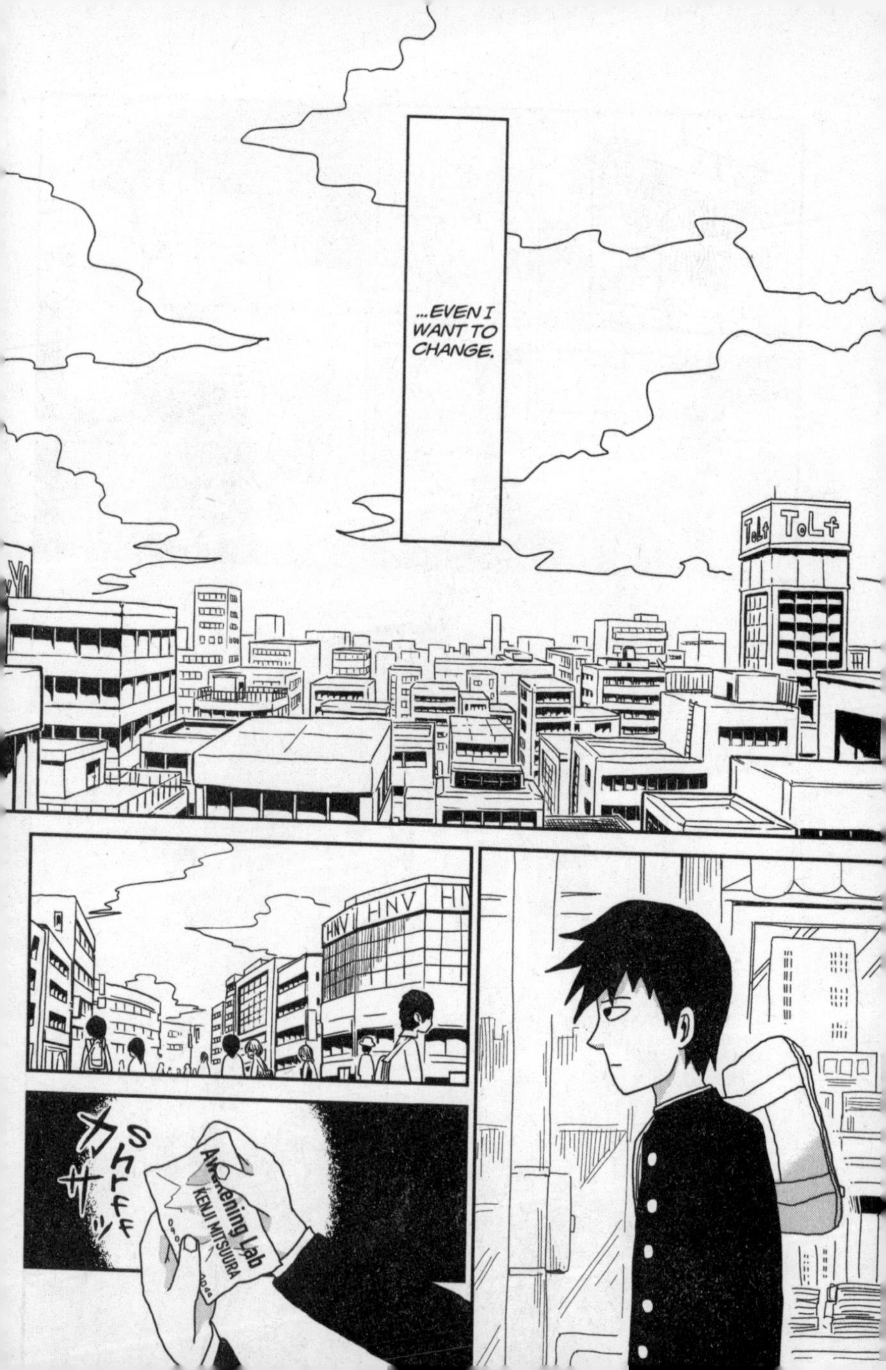
...EVEN I WANT TO CHANGE.
SHFFF
KENJI MITSUURA

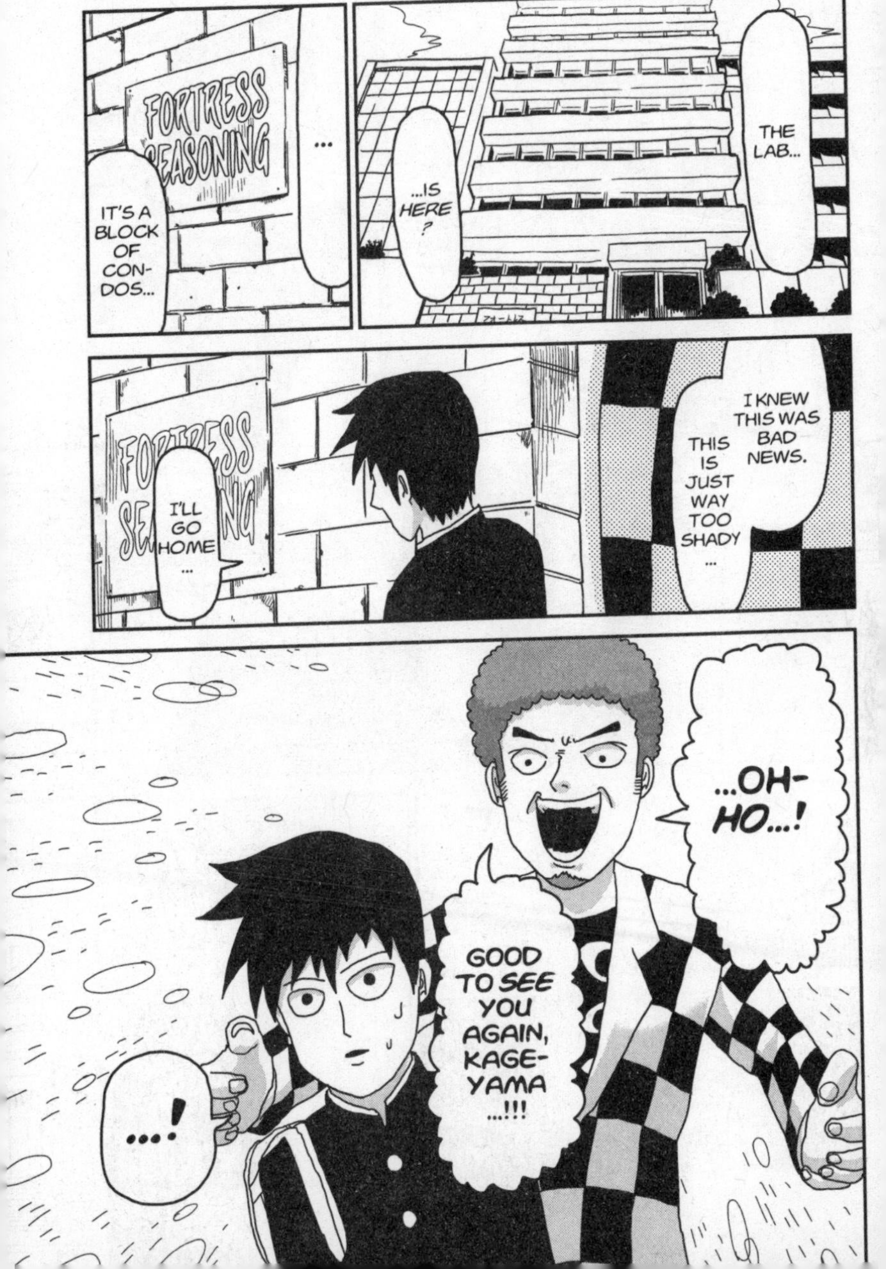
THE LAB...
...IS HERE?
...
FORTRESS SEASONING
IT'S A BLOCK OF CON-DOS...
I KNEW THIS WAS BAD NEWS.
THIS IS JUST WAY TOO SHADY...
FORTRESS SEASONING
I'LL GO HOME...
...OH-HO...!
GOOD TO SEE YOU AGAIN, KAGE-YAMA...!!!
...!

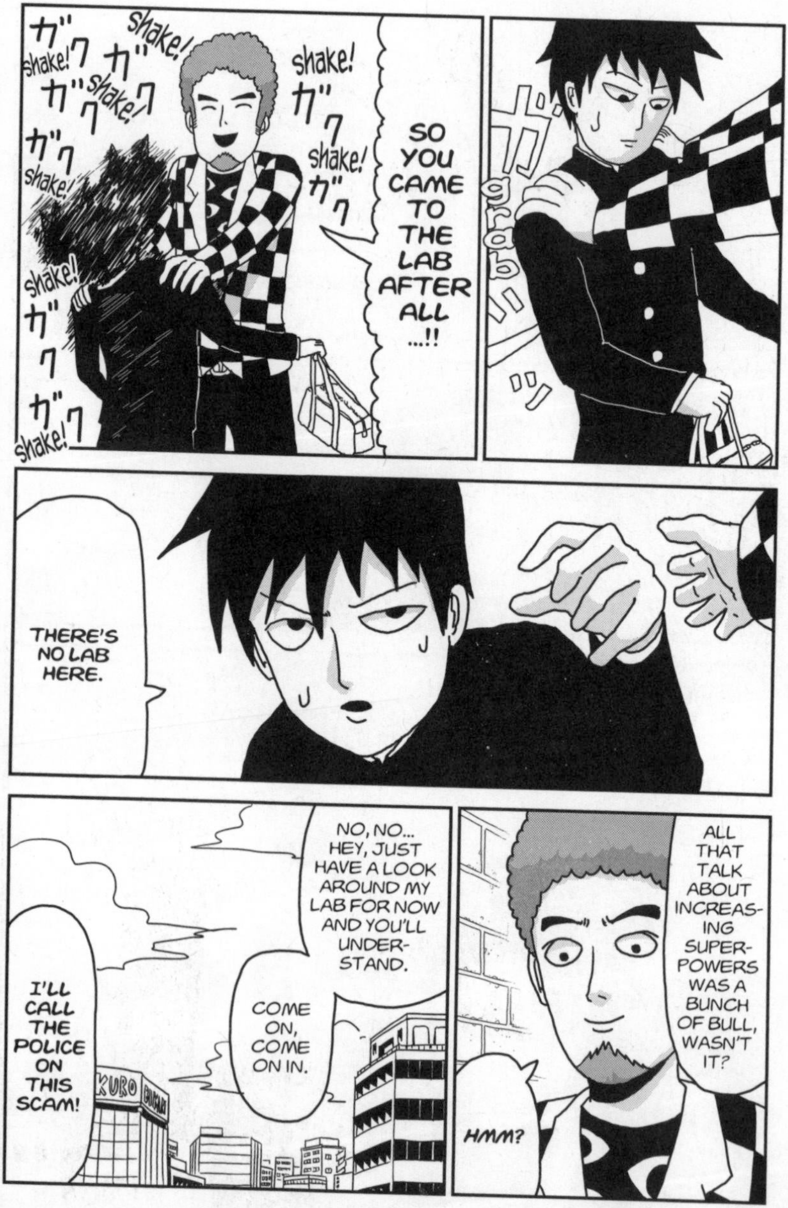
ガッ
grab
SO YOU CAME TO THE LAB AFTER ALL...!!
shake!
shake!
shake!
shake!
shake!
shake!
shake!
THERE'S NO LAB HERE.
ALL THAT TALK ABOUT INCREASING SUPERPOWERS WAS A BUNCH OF BULL, WASN'T IT?
HMM?
NO, NO... HEY, JUST HAVE A LOOK AROUND MY LAB FOR NOW AND YOU'LL UNDERSTAND.
COME ON, COME ON IN.
I'LL CALL THE POLICE ON THIS SCAM!
KURO

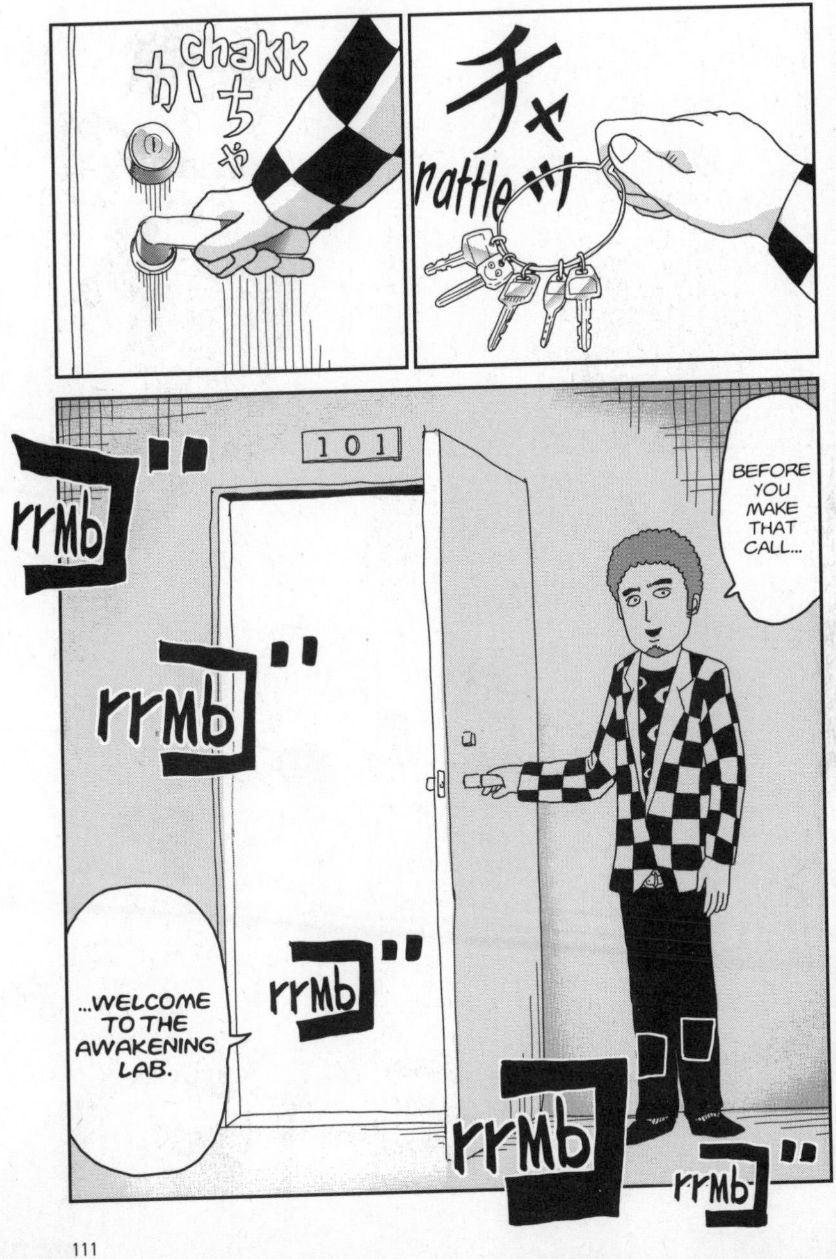
チャッ
rattle
かちゃ
chakk
BEFORE YOU MAKE THAT CALL...
...WELCOME TO THE AWAKENING LAB.
rrmb
rrmb
rrmb
rrmb
rrmb

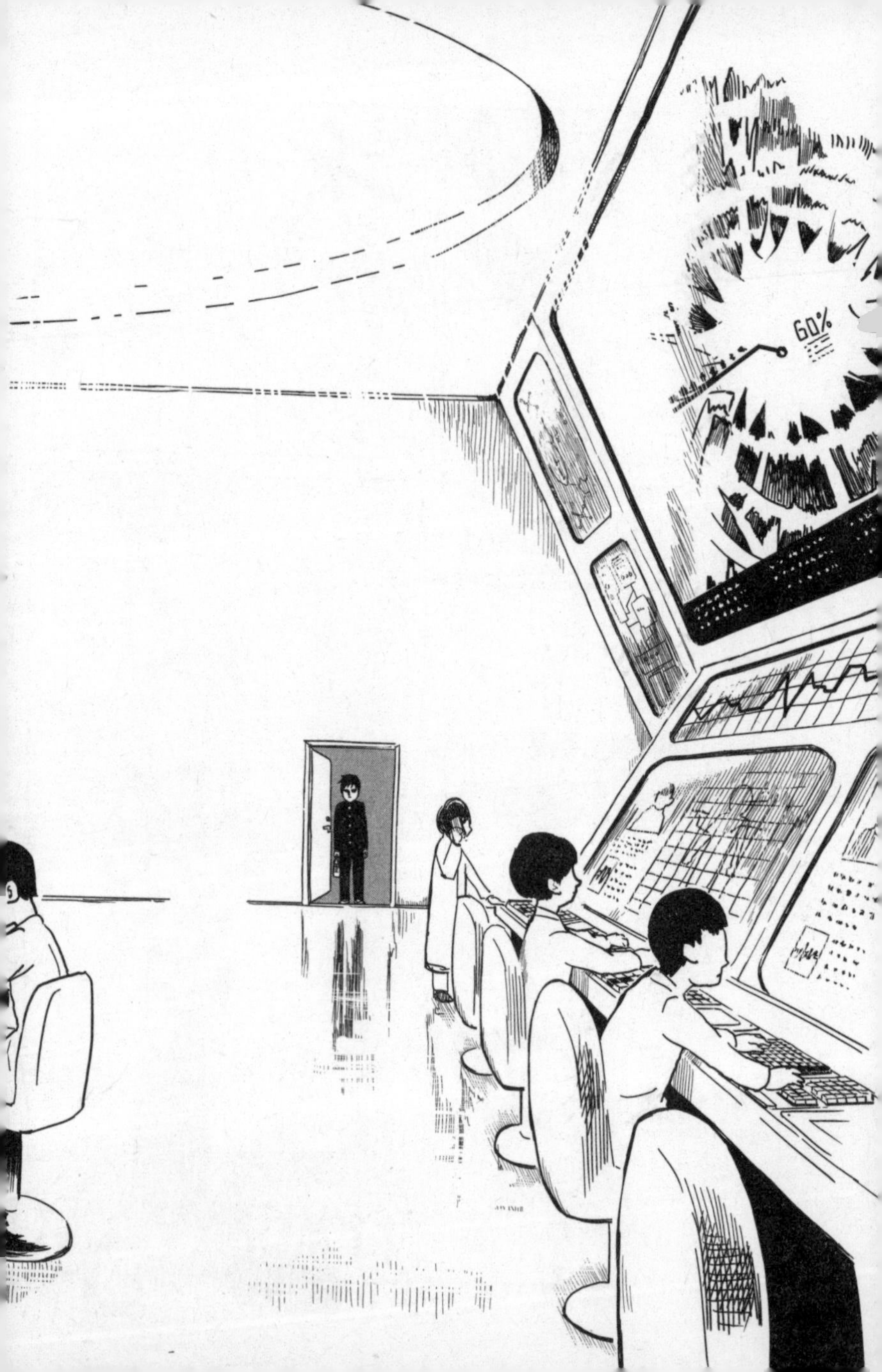
60%

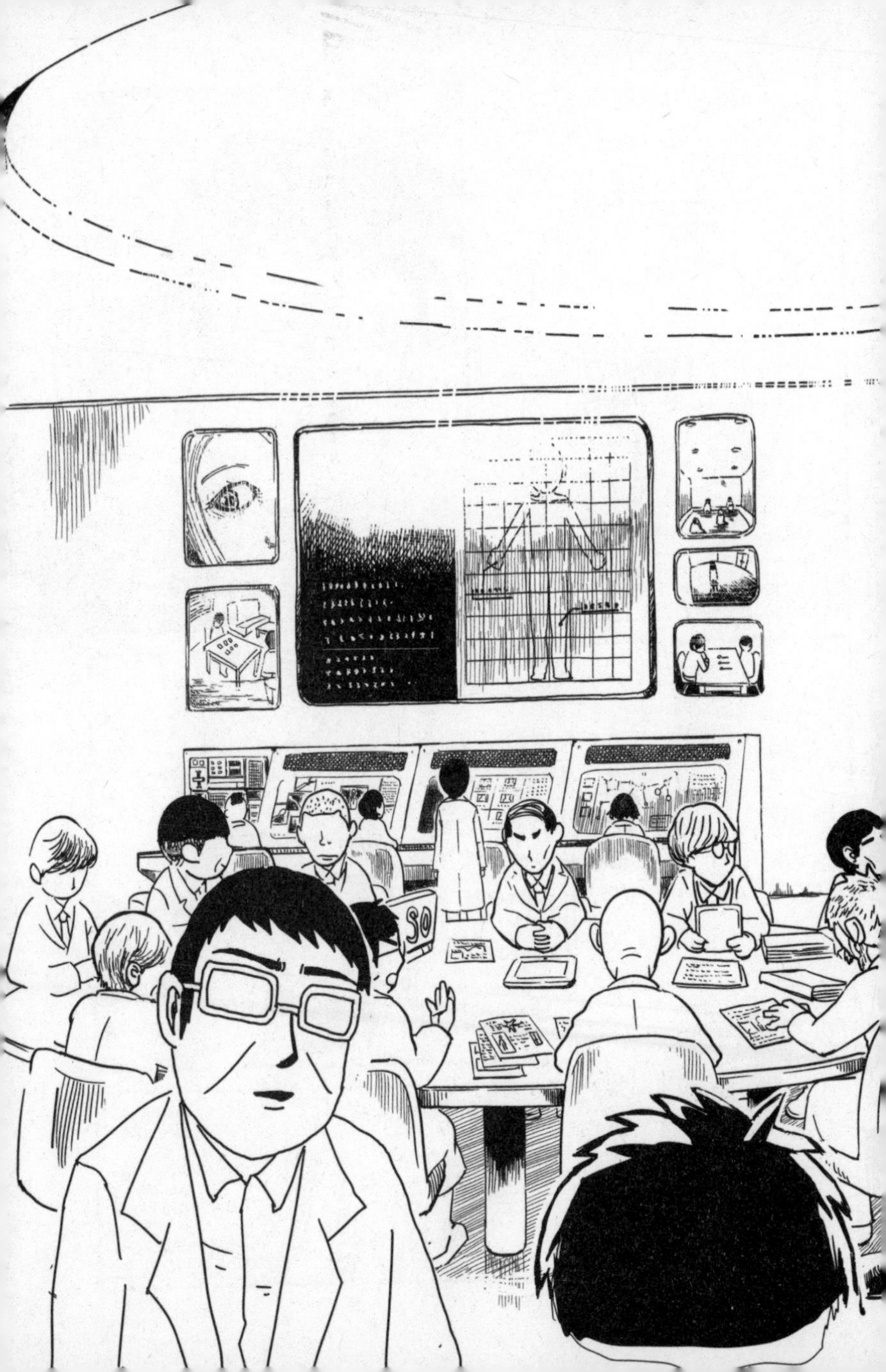

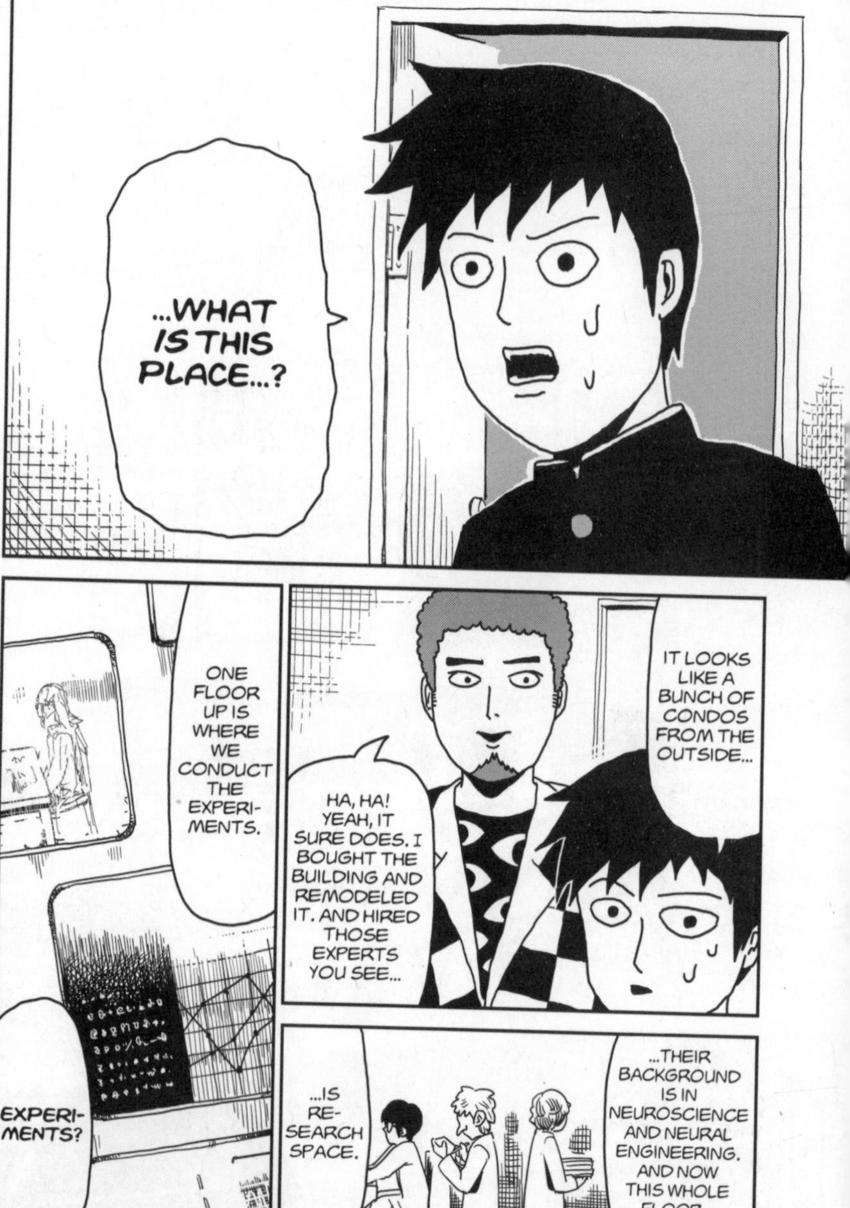
...WHAT IS THIS PLACE...?
IT LOOKS LIKE A BUNCH OF CONDOS FROM THE OUTSIDE...
HA, HA! YEAH, IT SURE DOES. I BOUGHT THE BUILDING AND REMODELED IT. AND HIRED THOSE EXPERTS YOU SEE...
...THEIR BACKGROUND IS IN NEUROSCIENCE AND NEURAL ENGINEERING. AND NOW THIS WHOLE FLOOR...
...IS RE-SEARCH SPACE.
ONE FLOOR UP IS WHERE WE CONDUCT THE EXPERI-MENTS.
EXPERI-MENTS?

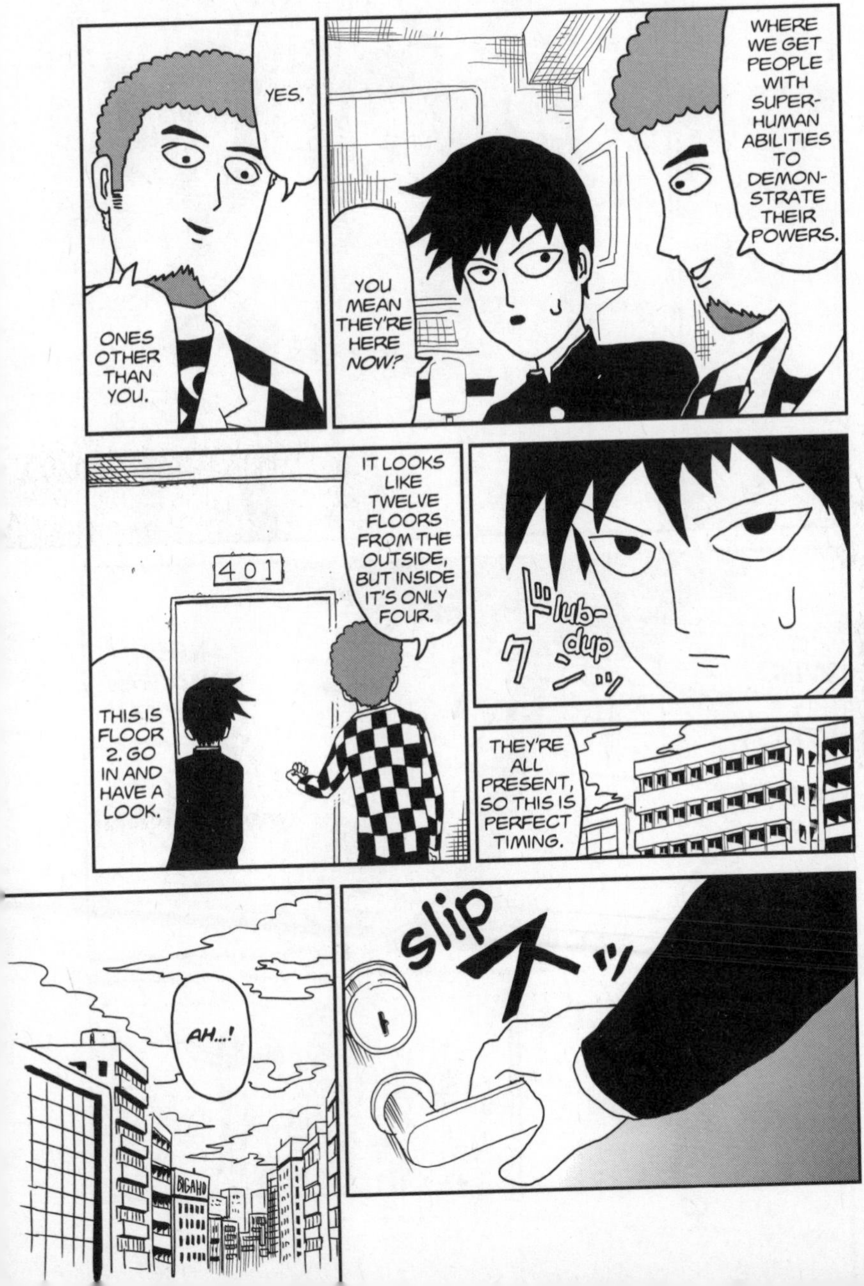
WHERE WE GET PEOPLE WITH SUPER-HUMAN ABILITIES TO DEMON-STRATE THEIR POWERS.
YOU MEAN THEY'RE HERE *NOW?*
YES.
ONES OTHER THAN YOU.
ドクンッ
lub-dup
THEY'RE ALL PRESENT, SO THIS IS PERFECT TIMING.
401
IT LOOKS LIKE TWELVE FLOORS FROM THE OUTSIDE, BUT INSIDE IT'S ONLY FOUR.
THIS IS FLOOR 2. GO IN AND HAVE A LOOK.
slip
スッ
AH...!
BIGAHO

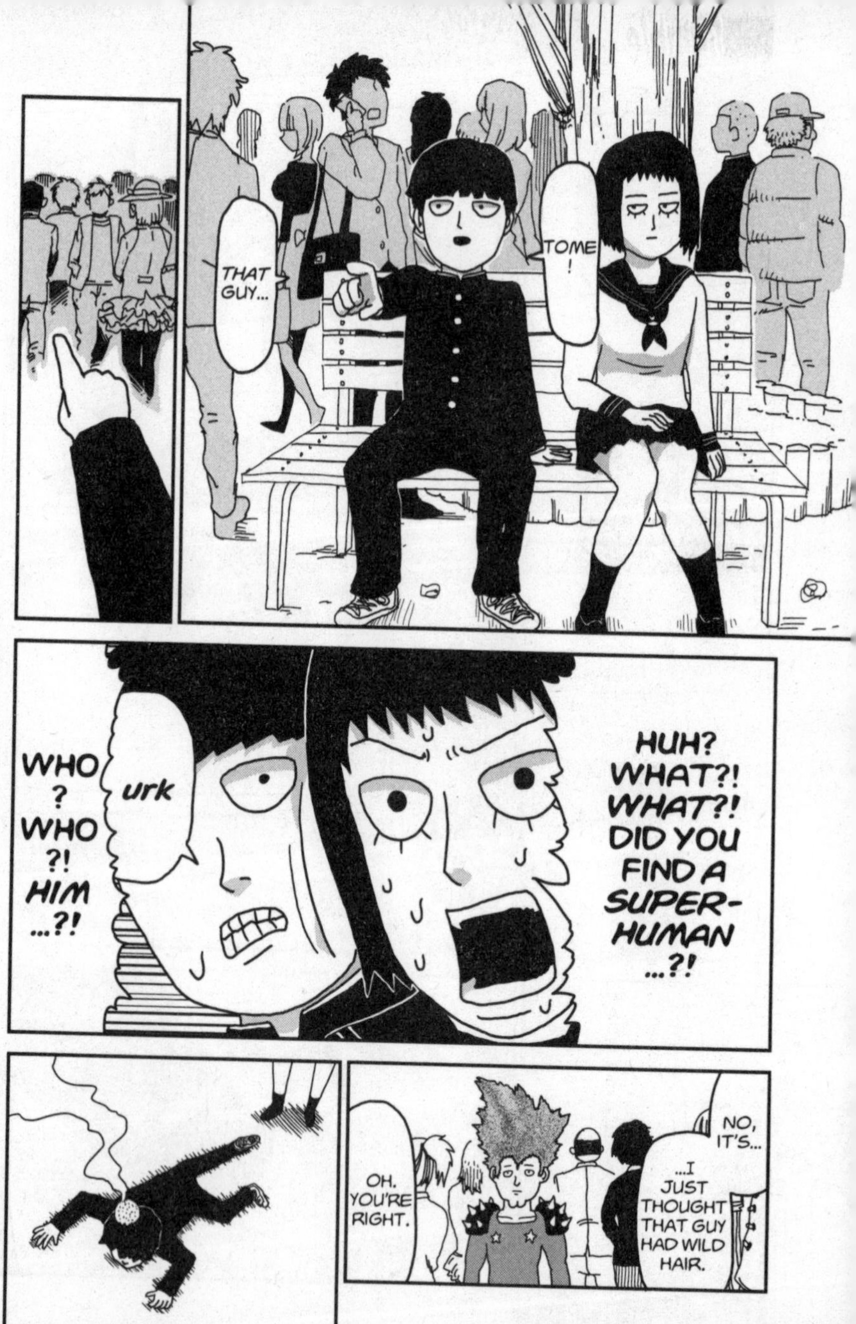

TOME !
THAT GUY...
HUH? WHAT?! WHAT?! DID YOU FIND A SUPER-HUMAN ...?!
urk
WHO ? WHO ?! HIM ...?!
NO, IT'S...
...I JUST THOUGHT THAT GUY HAD WILD HAIR.
OH. YOU'RE RIGHT.

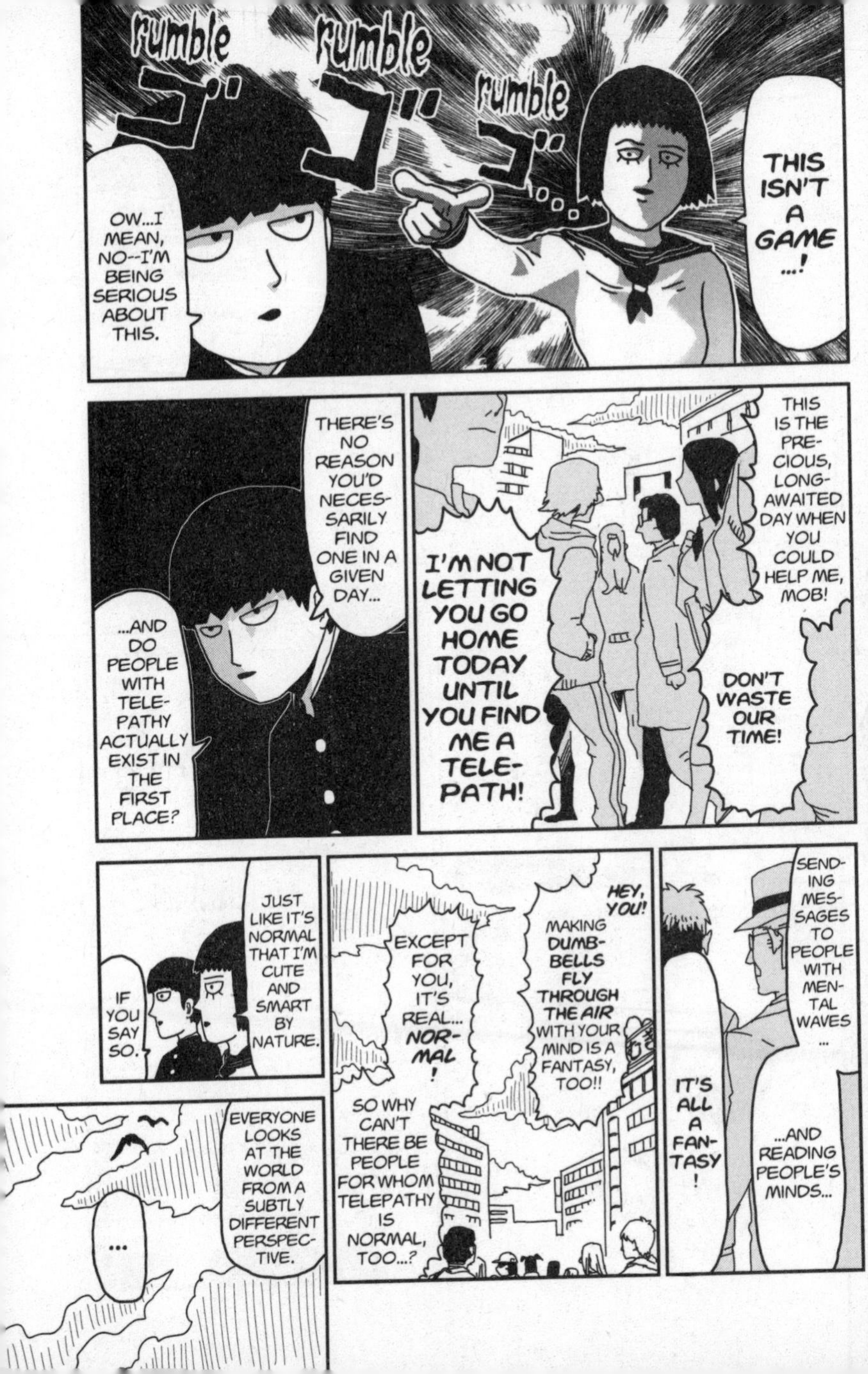
THIS ISN'T A GAME...!
rumble
ゴ
rumble
ゴ
rumble
ゴ...
OW...I MEAN, NO--I'M BEING SERIOUS ABOUT THIS.
THIS IS THE PRECIOUS, LONG-AWAITED DAY WHEN YOU COULD HELP ME, MOB!
DON'T WASTE OUR TIME!
I'M NOT LETTING YOU GO HOME TODAY UNTIL YOU FIND ME A TELEPATH!
THERE'S NO REASON YOU'D NECESSARILY FIND ONE IN A GIVEN DAY...
...AND DO PEOPLE WITH TELEPATHY ACTUALLY EXIST IN THE FIRST PLACE?
SENDING MESSAGES TO PEOPLE WITH MENTAL WAVES...
...AND READING PEOPLE'S MINDS...
IT'S ALL A FANTASY!
HEY, YOU!
MAKING DUMBBELLS FLY THROUGH THE AIR WITH YOUR MIND IS A FANTASY, TOO!!
EXCEPT FOR YOU, IT'S REAL... NORMAL!
SO WHY CAN'T THERE BE PEOPLE FOR WHOM TELEPATHY IS NORMAL, TOO...?
JUST LIKE IT'S NORMAL THAT I'M CUTE AND SMART BY NATURE.
IF YOU SAY SO.
EVERYONE LOOKS AT THE WORLD FROM A SUBTLY DIFFERENT PERSPECTIVE.
...

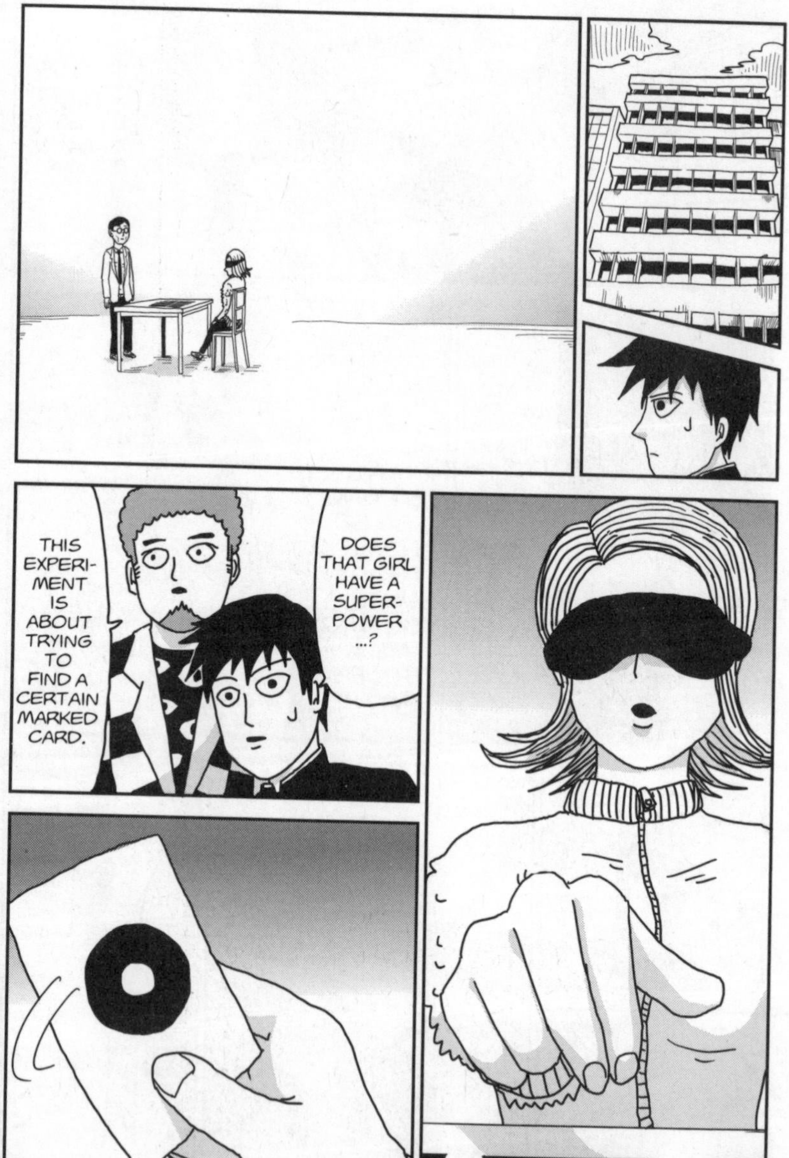
DOES THAT GIRL HAVE A SUPER-POWER ...?
THIS EXPERIMENT IS ABOUT TRYING TO FIND A CERTAIN MARKED CARD.

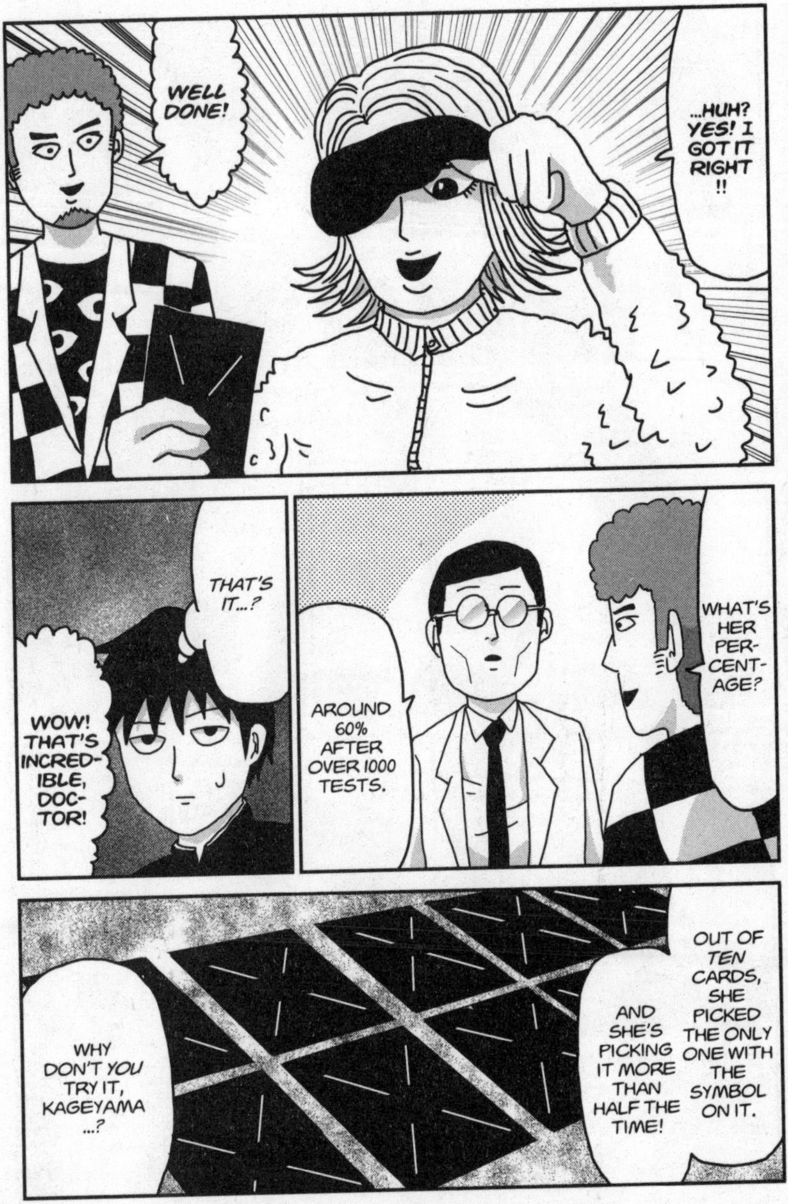
...HUH? YES! I GOT IT RIGHT !!
WELL DONE!
WHAT'S HER PERCENTAGE?
AROUND 60% AFTER OVER 1000 TESTS.
THAT'S IT...?
WOW! THAT'S INCREDIBLE, DOCTOR!
OUT OF TEN CARDS, SHE PICKED THE ONLY ONE WITH THE SYMBOL ON IT.
AND SHE'S PICKING IT MORE THAN HALF THE TIME!
WHY DON'T YOU TRY IT, KAGEYAMA ...?

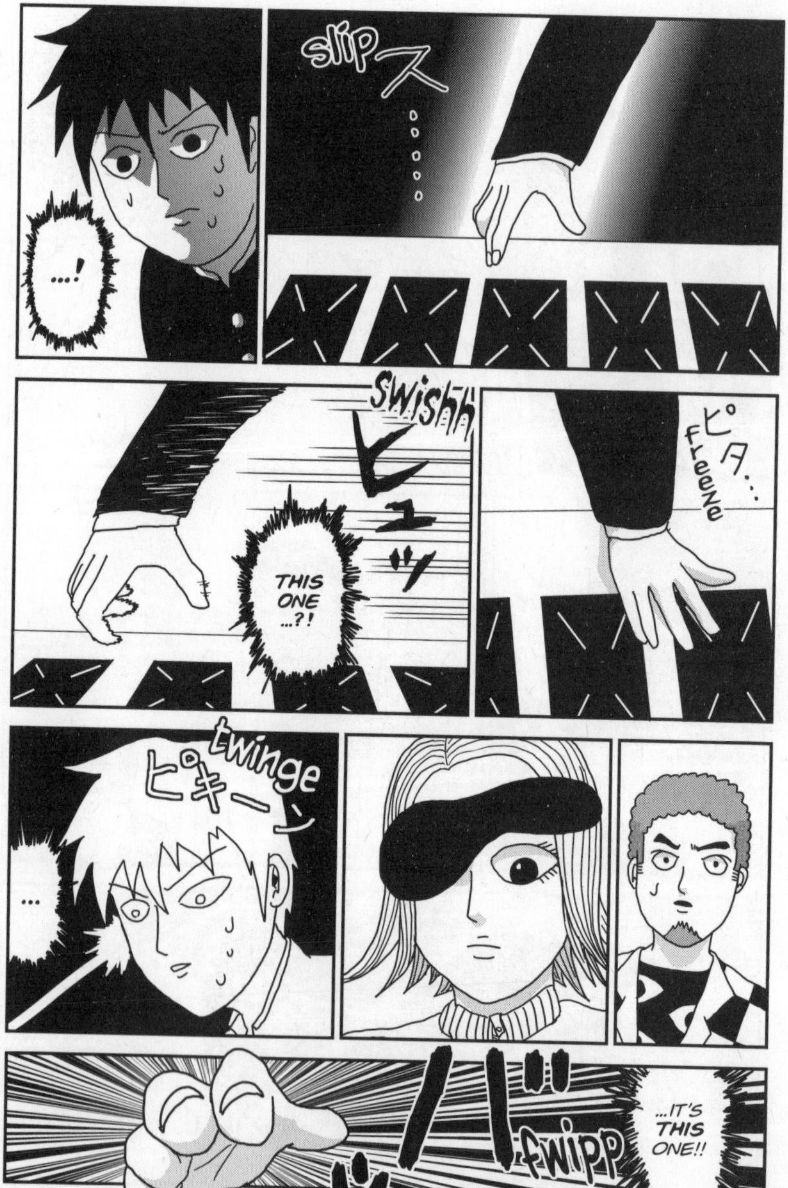

slip
ス
....!
ピタ…
freeze
swishh
ヒュッ
THIS ONE ...?!
twinge
ピキーン
...
fwipp
...IT'S THIS ONE!!

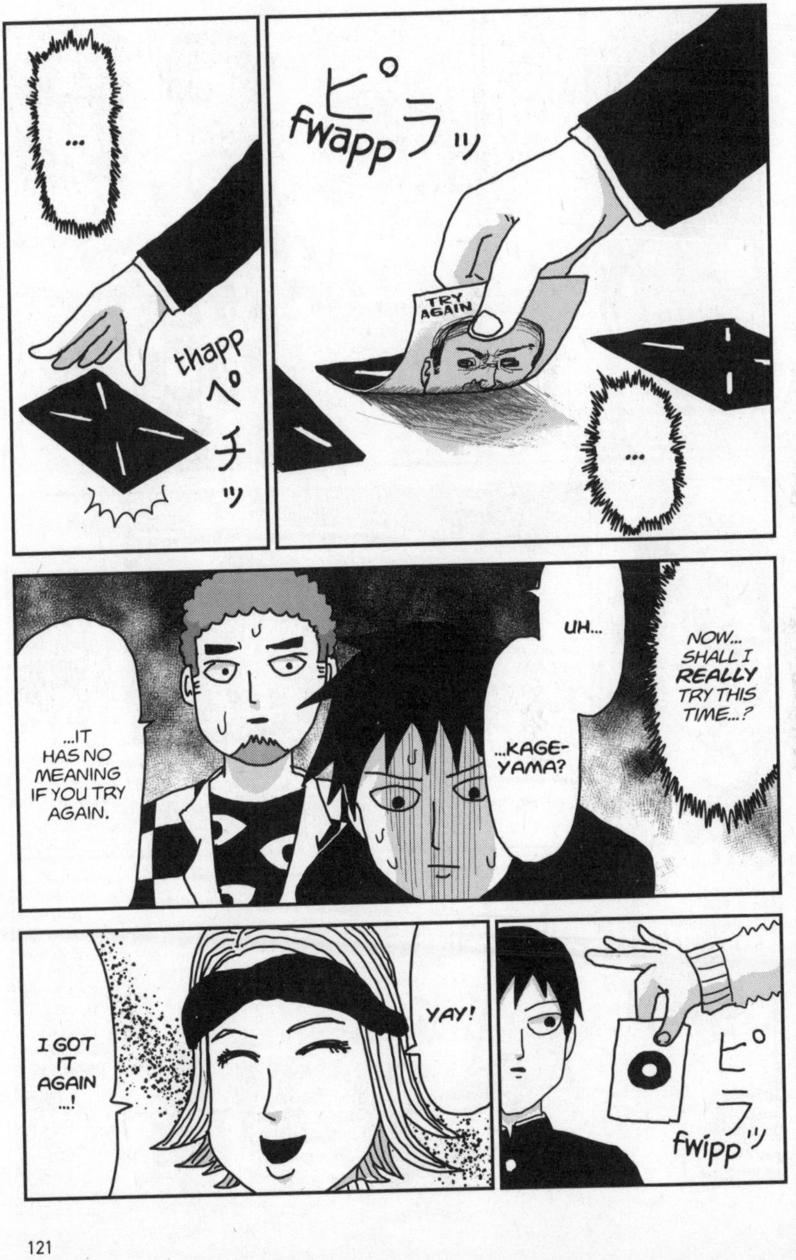
ピラッ
fwapp
TRY AGAIN
...
...
thapp
ペチッ
NOW... SHALL I **REALLY** TRY THIS TIME...?
UH...
...KAGE-YAMA?
...IT HAS NO MEANING IF YOU TRY AGAIN.
ピラッ
fwipp
YAY!
I GOT IT AGAIN ...!

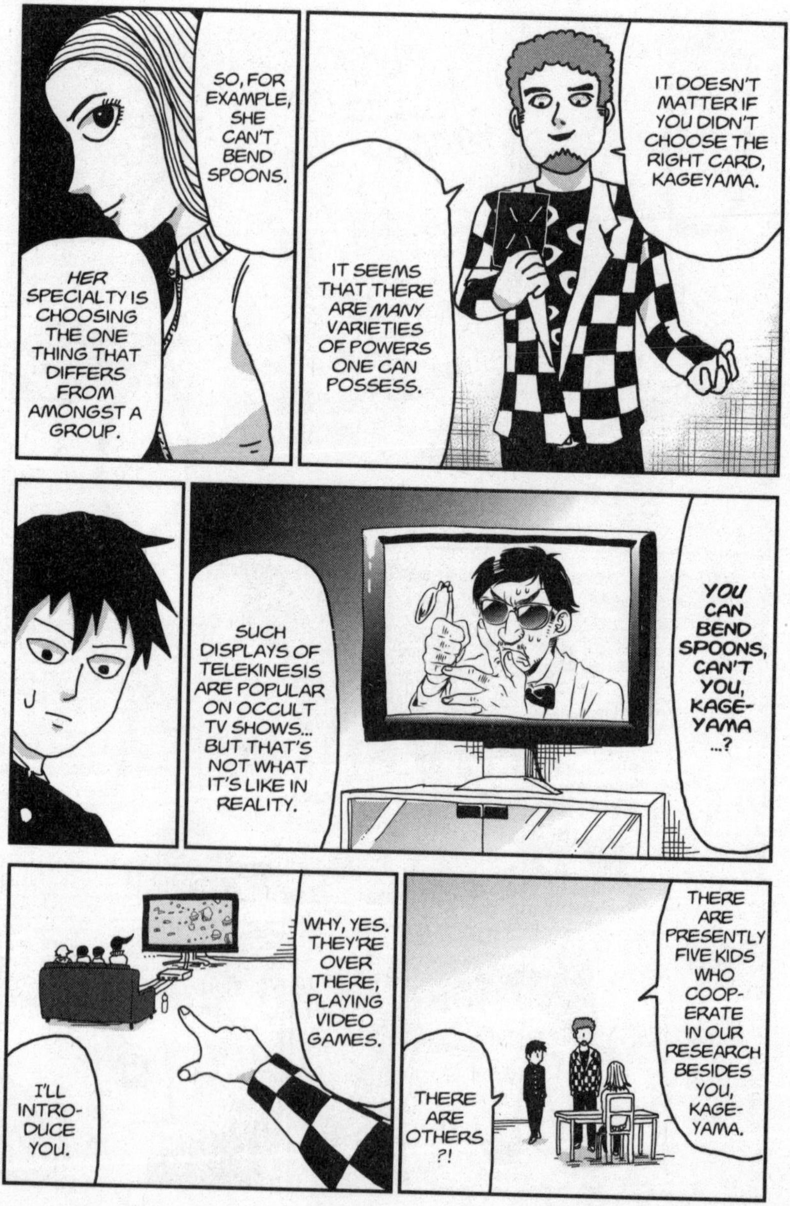
IT DOESN'T MATTER IF YOU DIDN'T CHOOSE THE RIGHT CARD, KAGEYAMA.
IT SEEMS THAT THERE ARE *MANY* VARIETIES OF POWERS ONE CAN POSSESS.
SO, FOR EXAMPLE, SHE CAN'T BEND SPOONS.
HER SPECIALTY IS CHOOSING THE ONE THING THAT DIFFERS FROM AMONGST A GROUP.
YOU CAN BEND SPOONS, CAN'T YOU, KAGE-YAMA ...?
SUCH DISPLAYS OF TELEKINESIS ARE POPULAR ON OCCULT TV SHOWS... BUT THAT'S NOT WHAT IT'S LIKE IN REALITY.
THERE ARE PRESENTLY FIVE KIDS WHO COOP-ERATE IN OUR RESEARCH BESIDES YOU, KAGE-YAMA.
THERE ARE OTHERS ?!
WHY, YES. THEY'RE OVER THERE, PLAYING VIDEO GAMES.
I'LL INTRO-DUCE YOU.

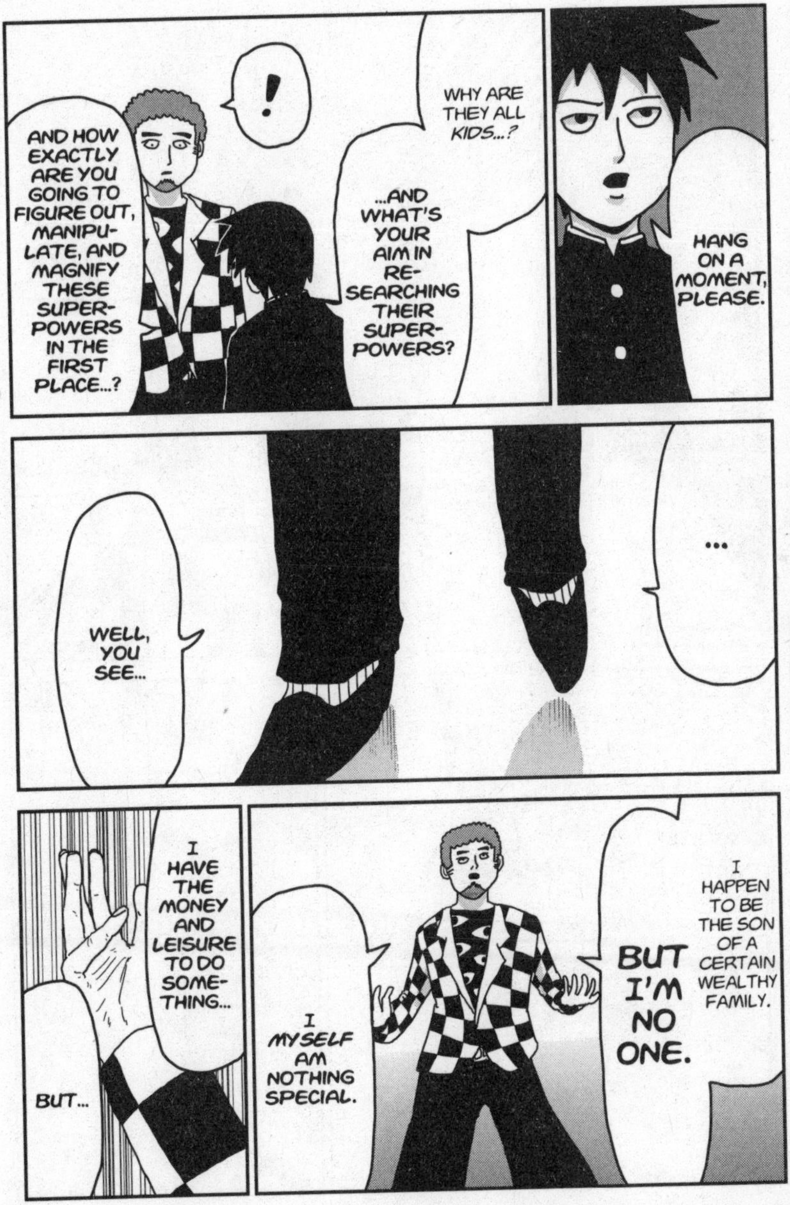
HANG ON A MOMENT, PLEASE.
WHY ARE THEY ALL KIDS...?
...AND WHAT'S YOUR AIM IN RE-SEARCHING THEIR SUPER-POWERS?
!
AND HOW EXACTLY ARE YOU GOING TO FIGURE OUT, MANIPU-LATE, AND MAGNIFY THESE SUPER-POWERS IN THE FIRST PLACE...?
...
WELL, YOU SEE...
I HAPPEN TO BE THE SON OF A CERTAIN WEALTHY FAMILY.
BUT I'M NO ONE.
I MYSELF AM NOTHING SPECIAL.
I HAVE THE MONEY AND LEISURE TO DO SOME-THING...
BUT...

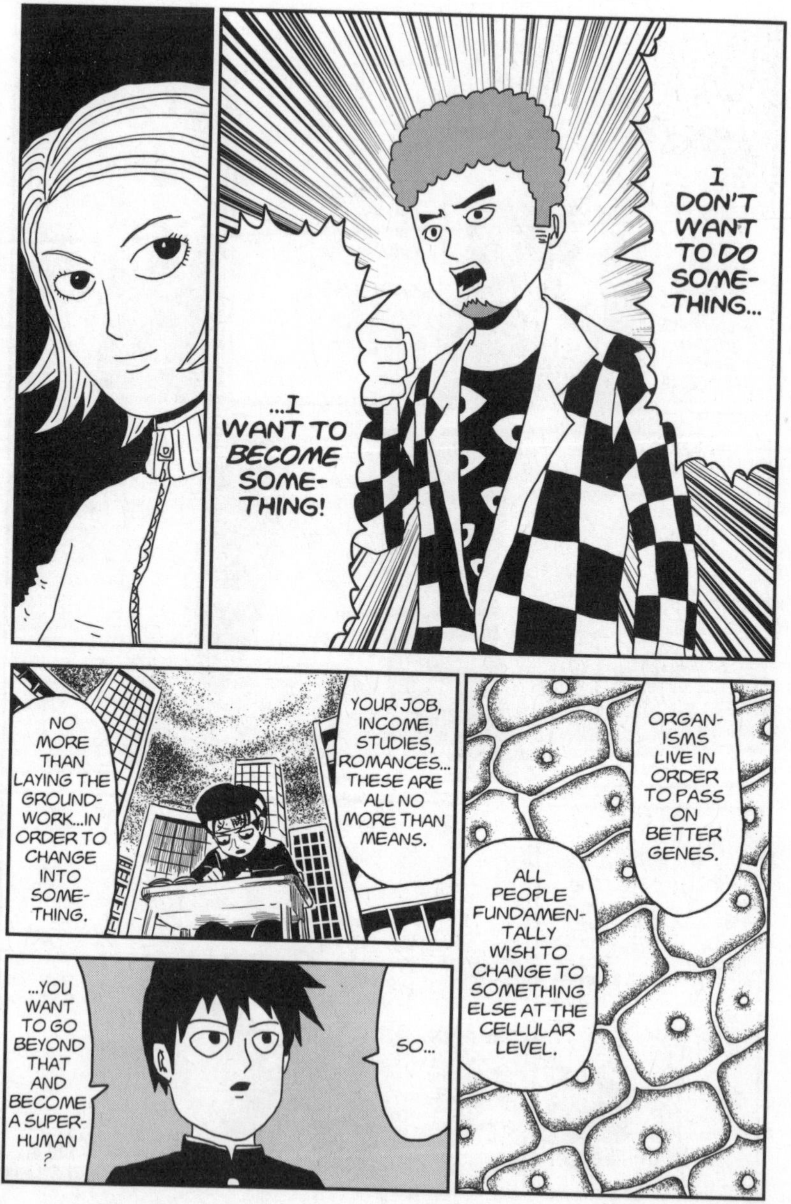
I DON'T WANT TO DO SOMETHING...
...I WANT TO *BECOME* SOMETHING!
ORGANISMS LIVE IN ORDER TO PASS ON BETTER GENES.
ALL PEOPLE FUNDAMENTALLY WISH TO CHANGE TO SOMETHING ELSE AT THE CELLULAR LEVEL.
YOUR JOB, INCOME, STUDIES, ROMANCES... THESE ARE ALL NO MORE THAN MEANS.
NO MORE THAN LAYING THE GROUNDWORK...IN ORDER TO CHANGE INTO SOMETHING.
SO...
...YOU WANT TO GO BEYOND THAT AND BECOME A SUPERHUMAN?

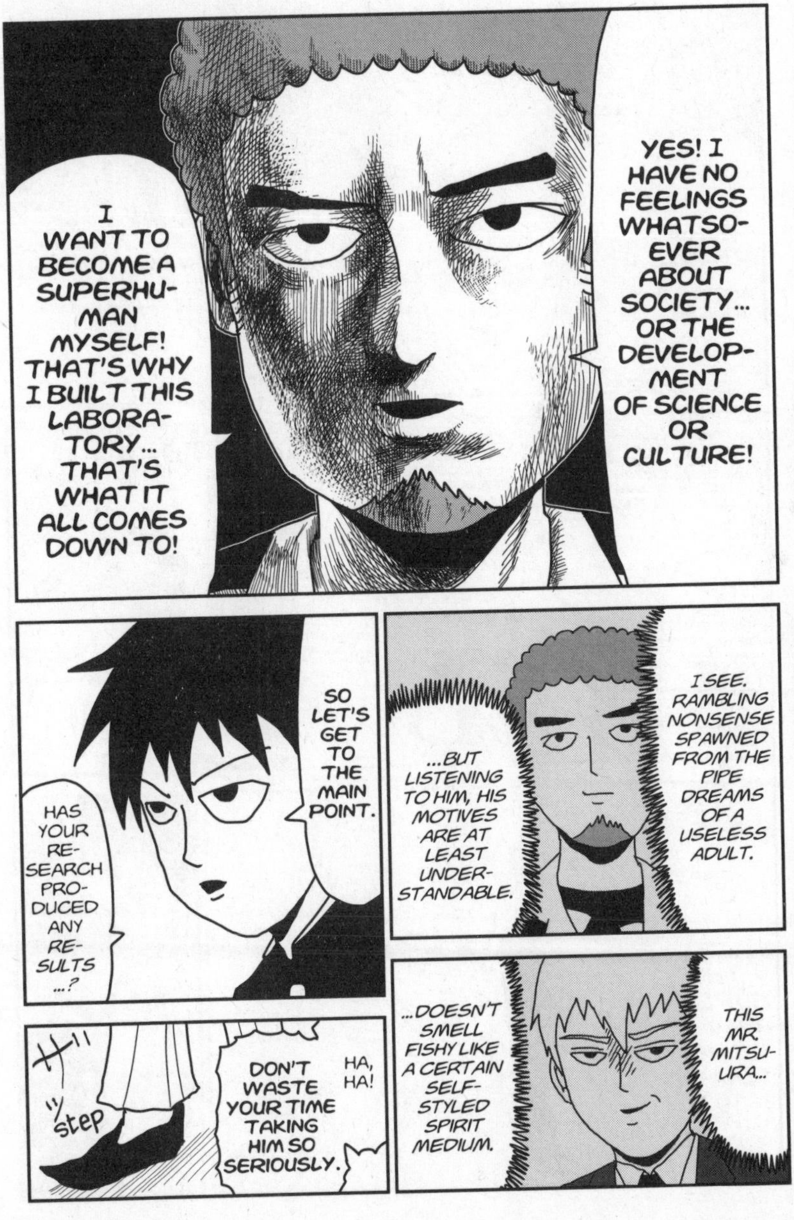
YES! I HAVE NO FEELINGS WHATSO-EVER ABOUT SOCIETY... OR THE DEVELOP-MENT OF SCIENCE OR CULTURE!
I WANT TO BECOME A SUPERHU-MAN MYSELF! THAT'S WHY I BUILT THIS LABORA-TORY... THAT'S WHAT IT ALL COMES DOWN TO!
I SEE. RAMBLING NONSENSE SPAWNED FROM THE PIPE DREAMS OF A USELESS ADULT.
...BUT LISTENING TO HIM, HIS MOTIVES ARE AT LEAST UNDER-STANDABLE.
SO LET'S GET TO THE MAIN POINT.
HAS YOUR RE-SEARCH PRO-DUCED ANY RE-SULTS ...?
THIS MR. MITSU-URA...
...DOESN'T SMELL FISHY LIKE A CERTAIN SELF-STYLED SPIRIT MEDIUM.
HA, HA!
DON'T WASTE YOUR TIME TAKING HIM SO SERIOUSLY.
step

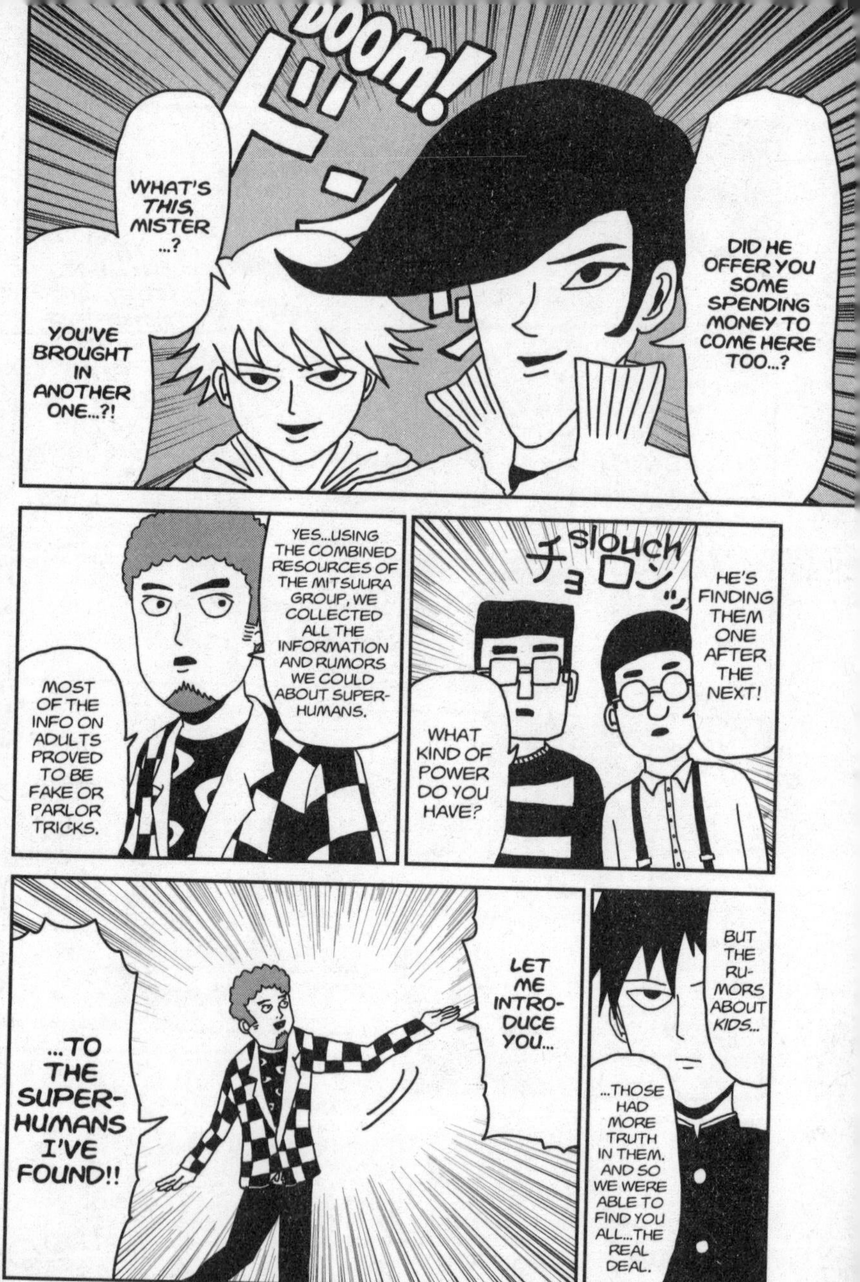
DOOM!
DID HE OFFER YOU SOME SPENDING MONEY TO COME HERE TOO...?
WHAT'S THIS, MISTER ...?
YOU'VE BROUGHT IN ANOTHER ONE...?!
slouch
チョロンッ
HE'S FINDING THEM ONE AFTER THE NEXT!
WHAT KIND OF POWER DO YOU HAVE?
YES...USING THE COMBINED RESOURCES OF THE MITSUURA GROUP, WE COLLECTED ALL THE INFORMATION AND RUMORS WE COULD ABOUT SUPER-HUMANS.
MOST OF THE INFO ON ADULTS PROVED TO BE FAKE OR PARLOR TRICKS.
BUT THE RU-MORS ABOUT KIDS...
...THOSE HAD MORE TRUTH IN THEM. AND SO WE WERE ABLE TO FIND YOU ALL...THE REAL DEAL.
LET ME INTRO-DUCE YOU...
...TO THE SUPER-HUMANS I'VE FOUND!!

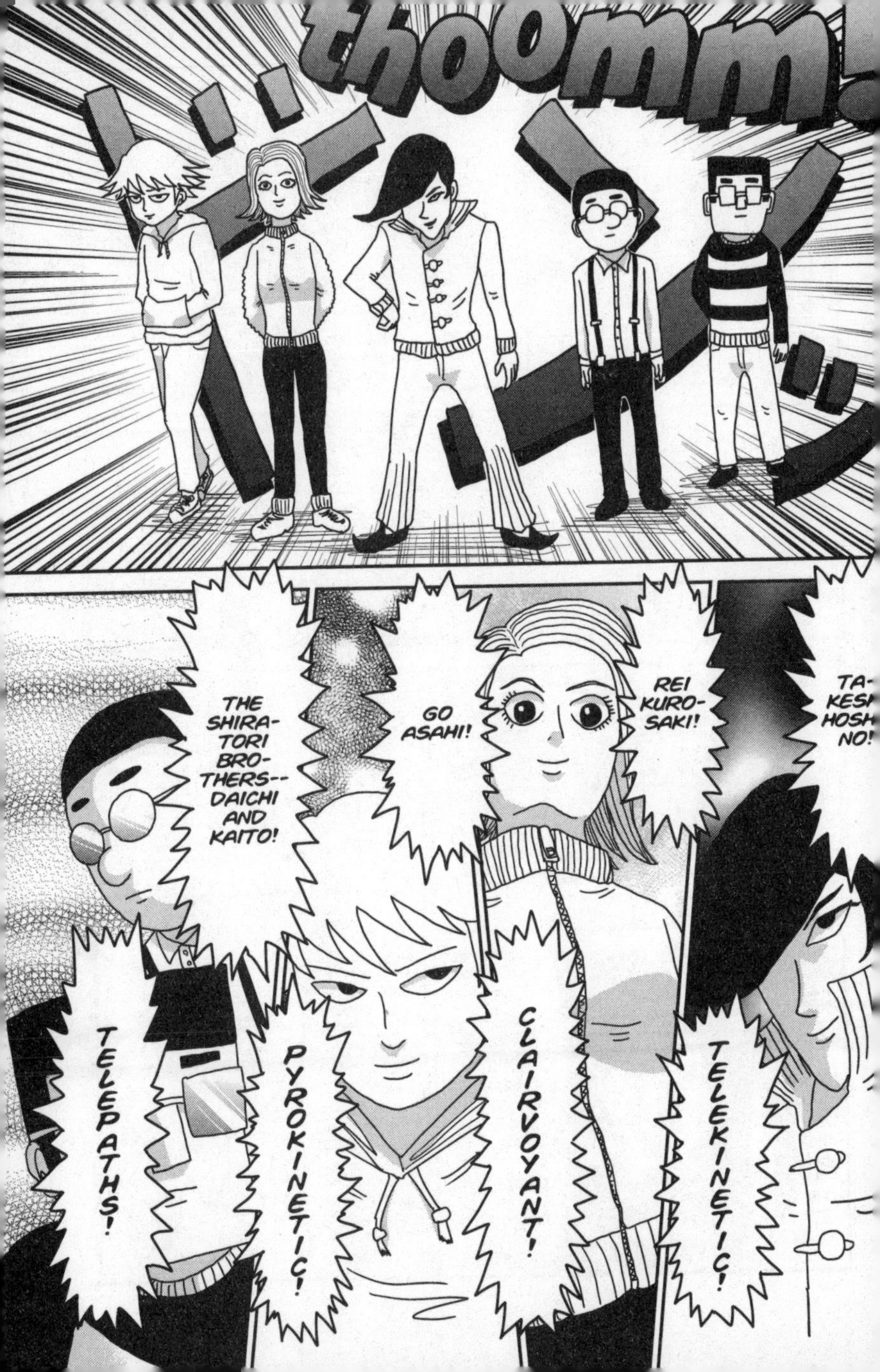
thoomm!
TA-KESH HOSH NO!
TELEKINETIC!
REI KURO-SAKI!
CLAIRVOYANT!
GO ASAHI!
PYROKINETIC!
THE SHIRA-TORI BRO-THERS--DAICHI AND KAITO!
TELEPATHS!

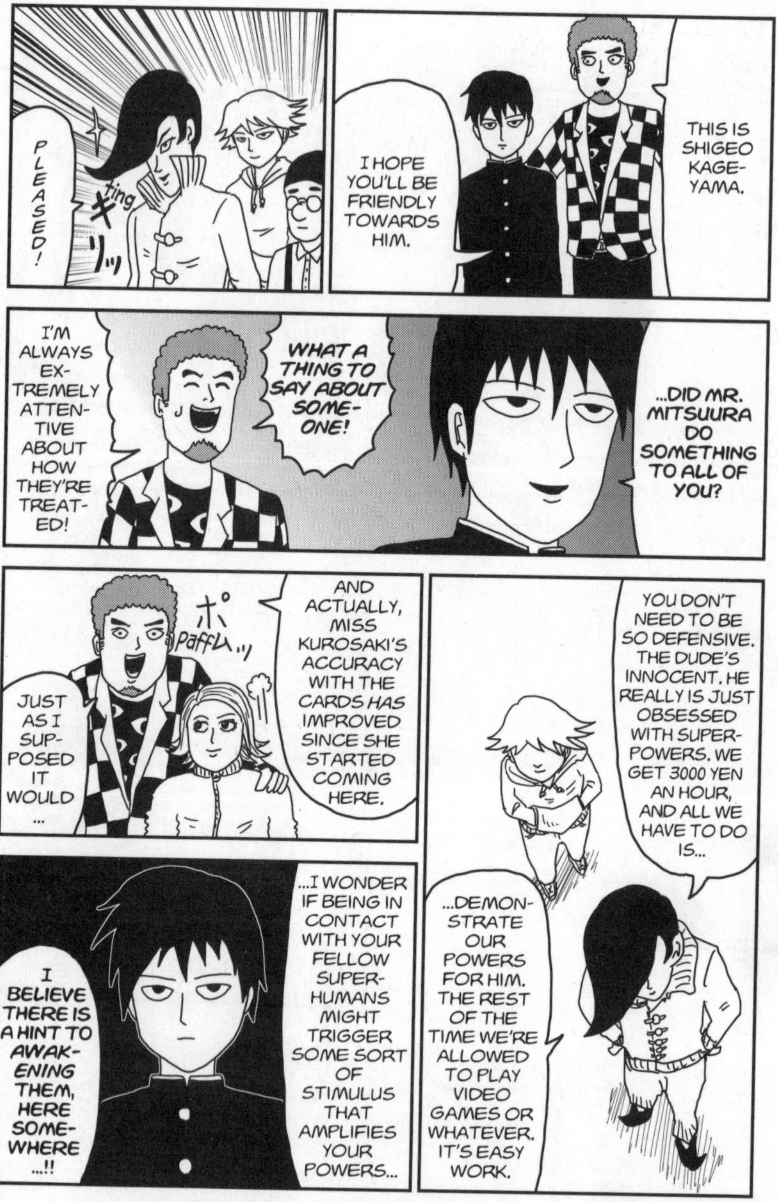
THIS IS SHIGEO KAGE-YAMA.
I HOPE YOU'LL BE FRIENDLY TOWARDS HIM.
PLEASED!
ting
...DID MR. MITSUURA DO SOMETHING TO ALL OF YOU?
WHAT A THING TO SAY ABOUT SOME-ONE!
I'M ALWAYS EX-TREMELY ATTEN-TIVE ABOUT HOW THEY'RE TREAT-ED!
YOU DON'T NEED TO BE SO DEFENSIVE. THE DUDE'S INNOCENT. HE REALLY IS JUST OBSESSED WITH SUPER-POWERS. WE GET 3000 YEN AN HOUR, AND ALL WE HAVE TO DO IS...
...DEMON-STRATE OUR POWERS FOR HIM. THE REST OF THE TIME WE'RE ALLOWED TO PLAY VIDEO GAMES OR WHATEVER. IT'S EASY WORK.
AND ACTUALLY, MISS KUROSAKI'S ACCURACY WITH THE CARDS HAS IMPROVED SINCE SHE STARTED COMING HERE.
paff
JUST AS I SUP-POSED IT WOULD ...
...I WONDER IF BEING IN CONTACT WITH YOUR FELLOW SUPER-HUMANS MIGHT TRIGGER SOME SORT OF STIMULUS THAT AMPLIFIES YOUR POWERS...
I BELIEVE THERE IS A HINT TO AWAK-ENING THEM, HERE SOME-WHERE ...!!

...UNLIKE THEM, I'M NOT A SUPER-HUMAN.

BUT IF THE PURPOSE OF THIS RESEARCH IS TO MAKE MR. MITSUURA'S PIPE DREAMS A REALITY... THEN I'M INTERESTED. AFTER ALL, MY WHOLE GOAL...MY WHOLE LIFE...

...HAS ALWAYS BEEN TO REACH THAT STAN-DARD.

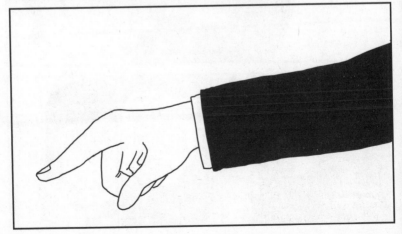

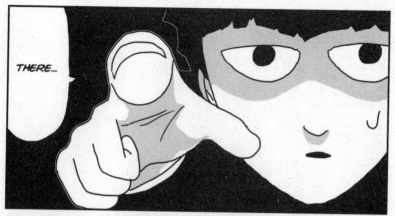

THERE...

A SUPER-HUMAN...

SOME-ONE WITH WEIRD HAIR?

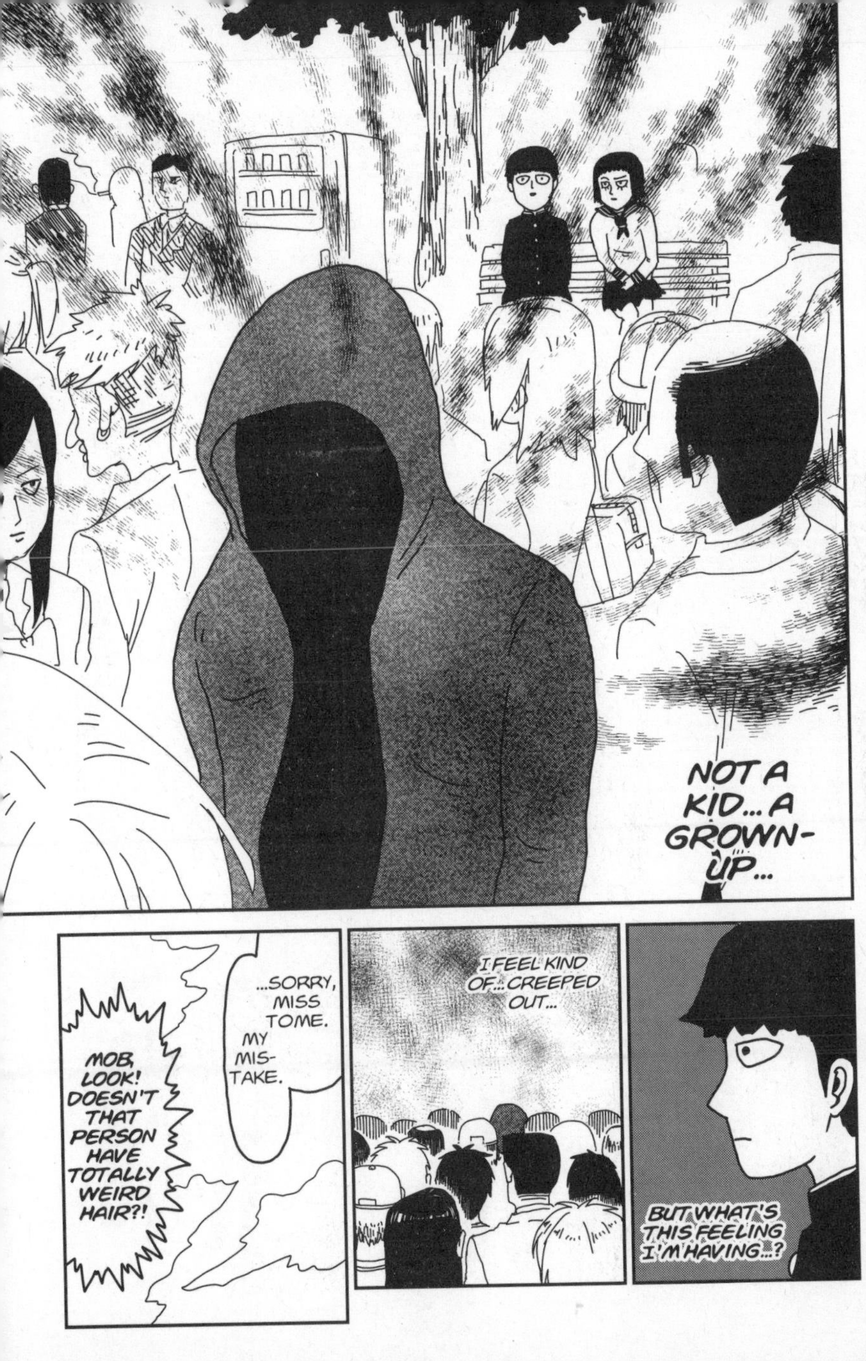
NOT A KID... A GROWN-UP...
BUT WHAT'S THIS FEELING I'M HAVING...?
I FEEL KIND OF... CREEPED OUT...
...SORRY, MISS TOME. MY MISTAKE.
MOB, LOOK! DOESN'T THAT PERSON HAVE TOTALLY WEIRD HAIR?!

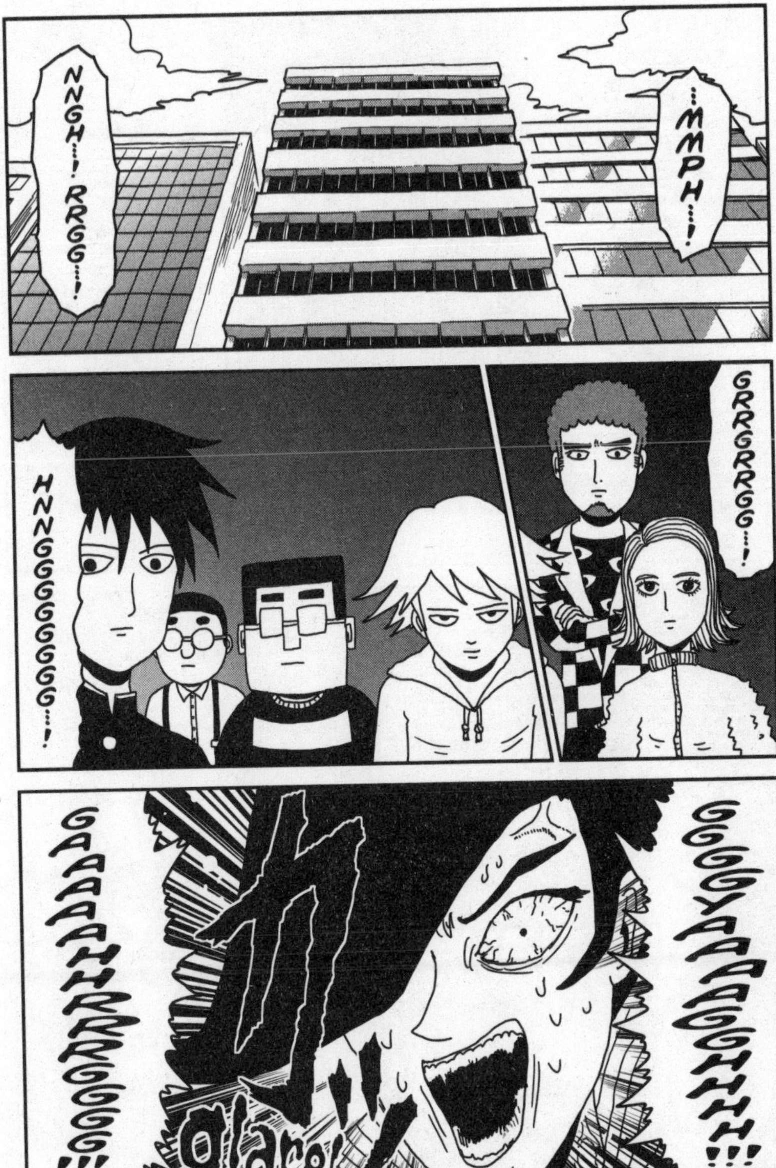
...MMPH...!
NNGH...! RRGG...!
GRRGRRGG...!
HNNGGGGGGGGG...!
GGGYAAAAAGGHHHH!!
glare!
GAAAAAHHRRRRGGGG!!

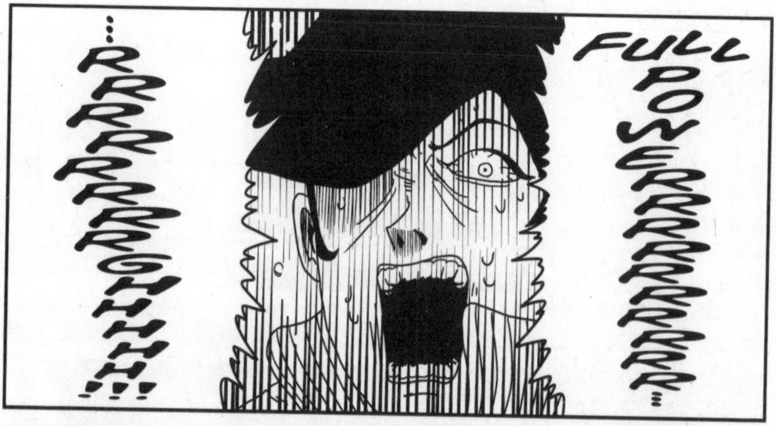
FULL POWERRRRRRRRRR...
...RRRRRRRRRGHHHH!!!

CHAPTER 23: IN ORDER TO BECOME

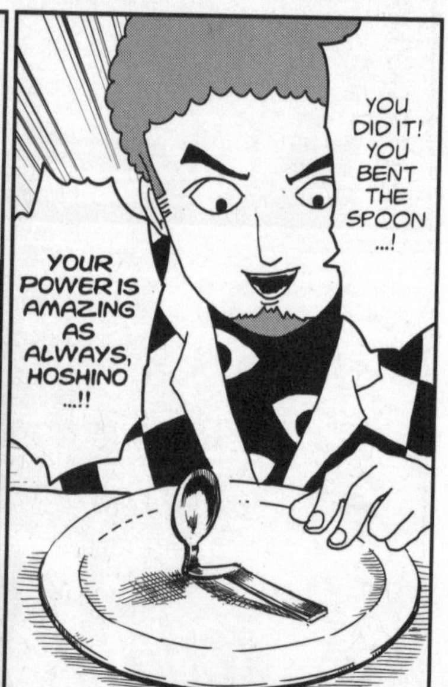
YOU DID IT! YOU BENT THE SPOON ...!
YOUR POWER IS AMAZING AS ALWAYS, HOSHINO ...!!

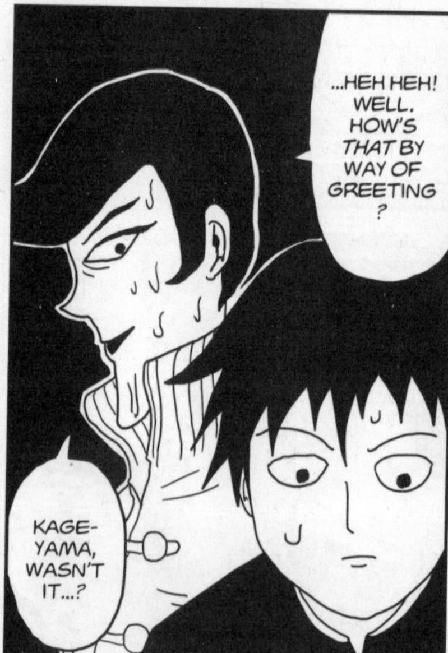
...HEH HEH! WELL. HOW'S *THAT* BY WAY OF GREETING ?
KAGE-YAMA, WASN'T IT...?

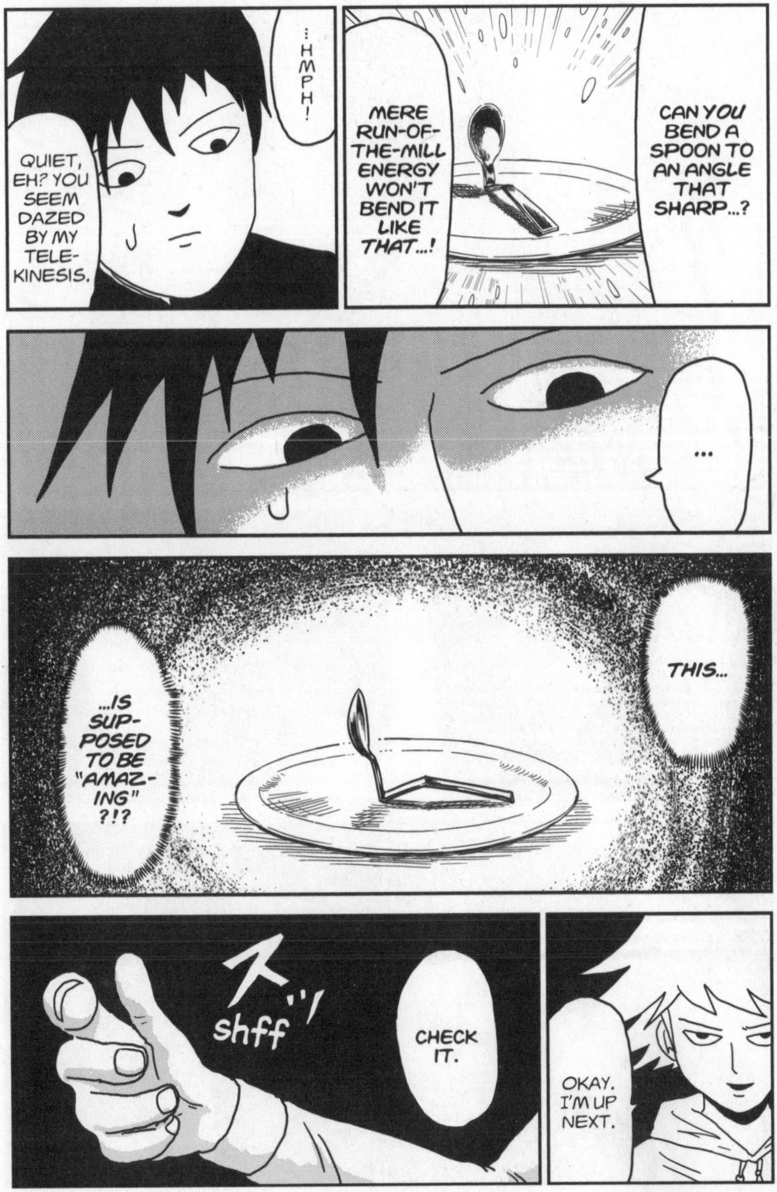
CAN YOU BEND A SPOON TO AN ANGLE THAT SHARP...?
MERE RUN-OF-THE-MILL ENERGY WON'T BEND IT LIKE THAT...!
...HMPH!
QUIET, EH? YOU SEEM DAZED BY MY TELE-KINESIS.
...
THIS...
...IS SUP-POSED TO BE "AMAZ-ING"?!?
OKAY. I'M UP NEXT.
CHECK IT.
スッ
shff

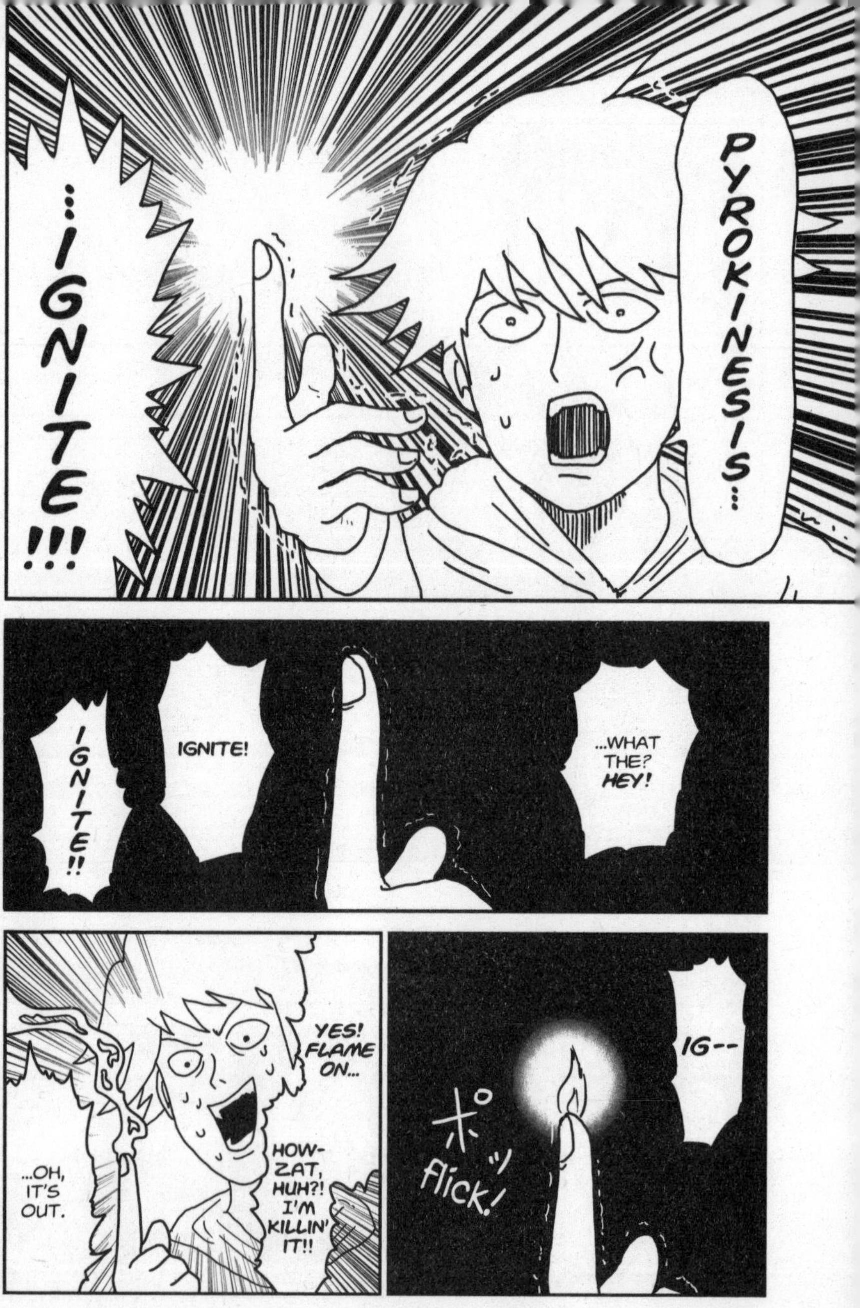
PYROKINESIS...
...IGNITE!!!
...WHAT THE? HEY!
IGNITE!
IGNITE!!
IG--
ポッ
flick!
YES! FLAME ON...
HOW-ZAT, HUH?! I'M KILLIN' IT!!
...OH, IT'S OUT.

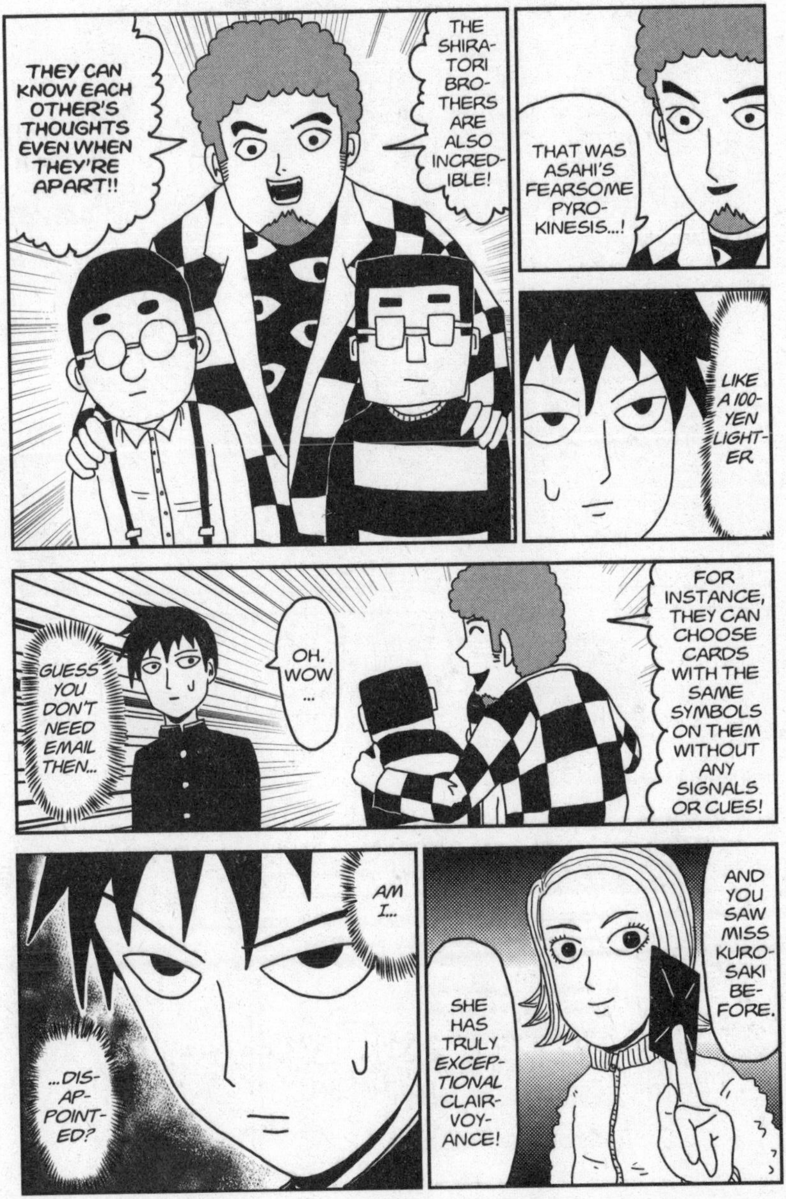

THAT WAS ASAHI'S FEARSOME PYROKINESIS...!
LIKE A 100-YEN LIGHTER
THE SHIRATORI BROTHERS ARE ALSO INCREDIBLE!
THEY CAN KNOW EACH OTHER'S THOUGHTS EVEN WHEN THEY'RE APART!!
FOR INSTANCE, THEY CAN CHOOSE CARDS WITH THE SAME SYMBOLS ON THEM WITHOUT ANY SIGNALS OR CUES!
OH. WOW ...
GUESS YOU DON'T NEED EMAIL THEN...
AND YOU SAW MISS KUROSAKI BEFORE.
SHE HAS TRULY EXCEPTIONAL CLAIRVOYANCE!
AM I...
...DISAPPOINTED?

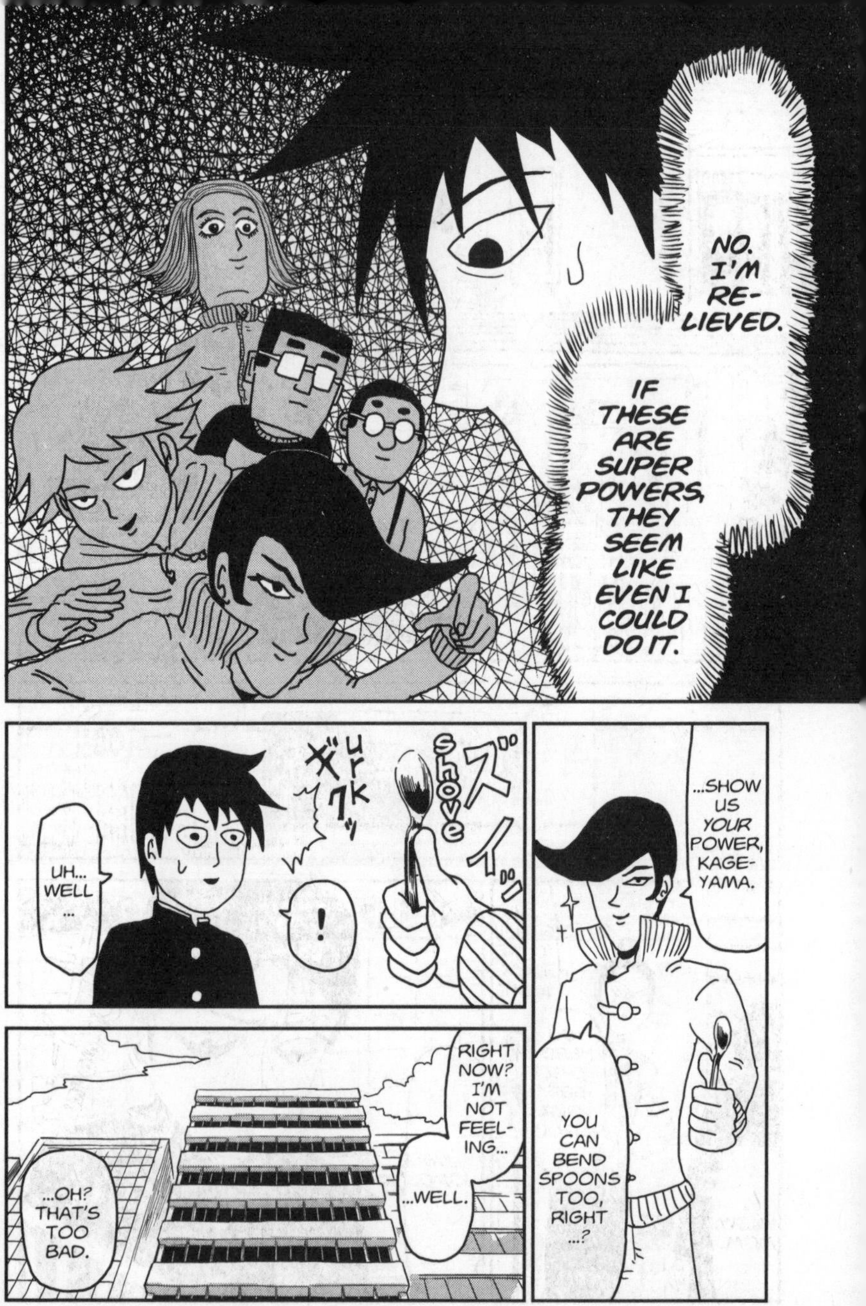
NO. I'M RE-LIEVED.
IF THESE ARE SUPER POWERS, THEY SEEM LIKE EVEN I COULD DO IT.
...SHOW US YOUR POWER, KAGE-YAMA.
YOU CAN BEND SPOONS TOO, RIGHT ...?
ズイ
shove
ギクッ
urk
!
UH... WELL ...
RIGHT NOW? I'M NOT FEELING...
...WELL.
...OH? THAT'S TOO BAD.

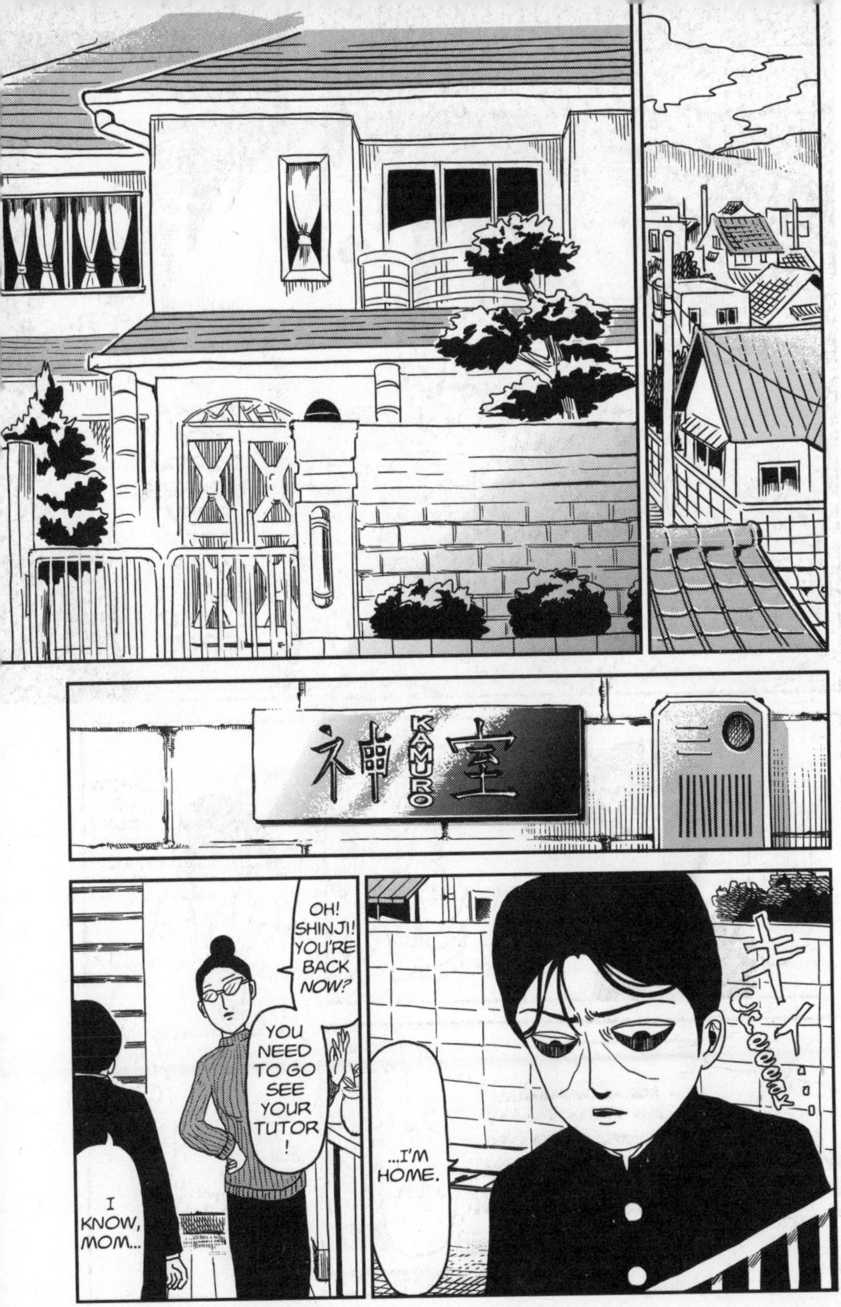
神室
KAMURO
キイ
Creeeeak
...I'M HOME.
OH! SHINJI! YOU'RE BACK NOW?
YOU NEED TO GO SEE YOUR TUTOR!
I KNOW, MOM...

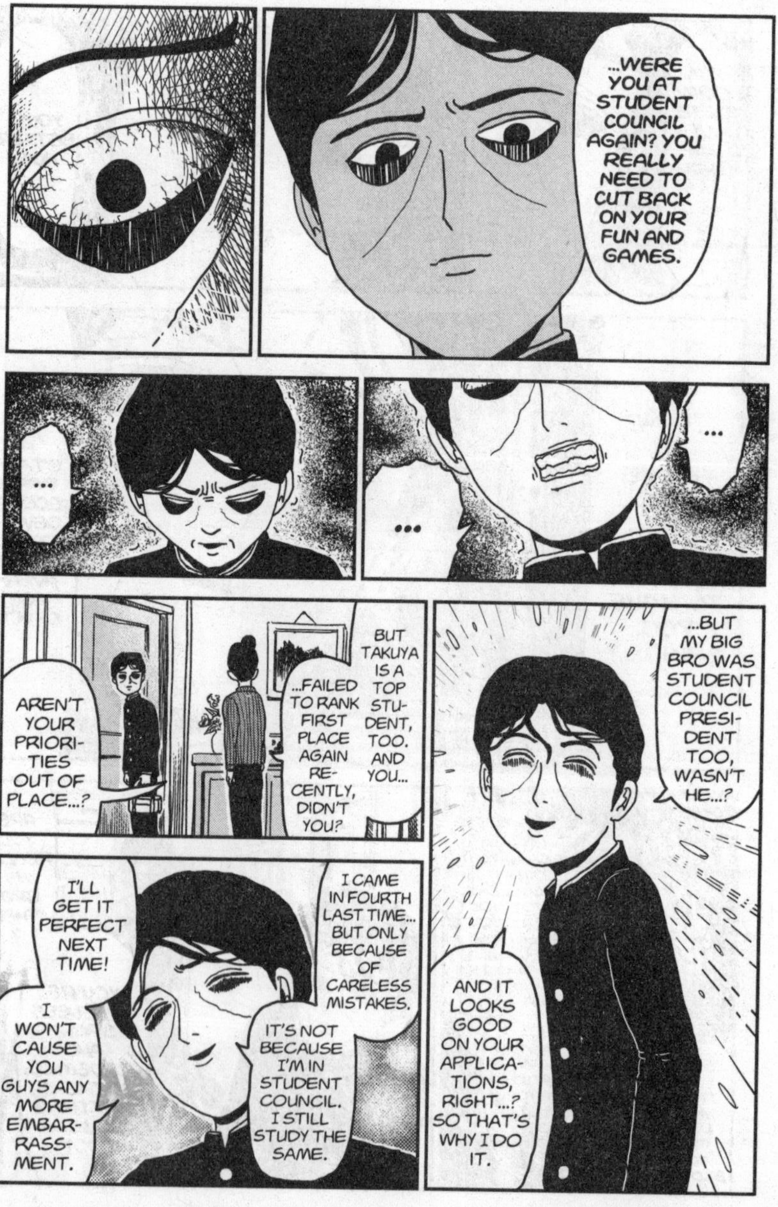
...WERE YOU AT STUDENT COUNCIL AGAIN? YOU REALLY NEED TO CUT BACK ON YOUR FUN AND GAMES.
...
...
...
...BUT MY BIG BRO WAS STUDENT COUNCIL PRESI-DENT TOO, WASN'T HE...?
AND IT LOOKS GOOD ON YOUR APPLICA-TIONS, RIGHT...? SO THAT'S WHY I DO IT.
BUT TAKUYA IS A TOP STU-DENT, TOO. AND YOU...
...FAILED TO RANK FIRST PLACE AGAIN RE-CENTLY, DIDN'T YOU?
AREN'T YOUR PRIORI-TIES OUT OF PLACE...?
I CAME IN FOURTH LAST TIME... BUT ONLY BECAUSE OF CARELESS MISTAKES.
IT'S NOT BECAUSE I'M IN STUDENT COUNCIL. I STILL STUDY THE SAME.
I'LL GET IT PERFECT NEXT TIME!
I WON'T CAUSE YOU GUYS ANY MORE EMBAR-RASS-MENT.

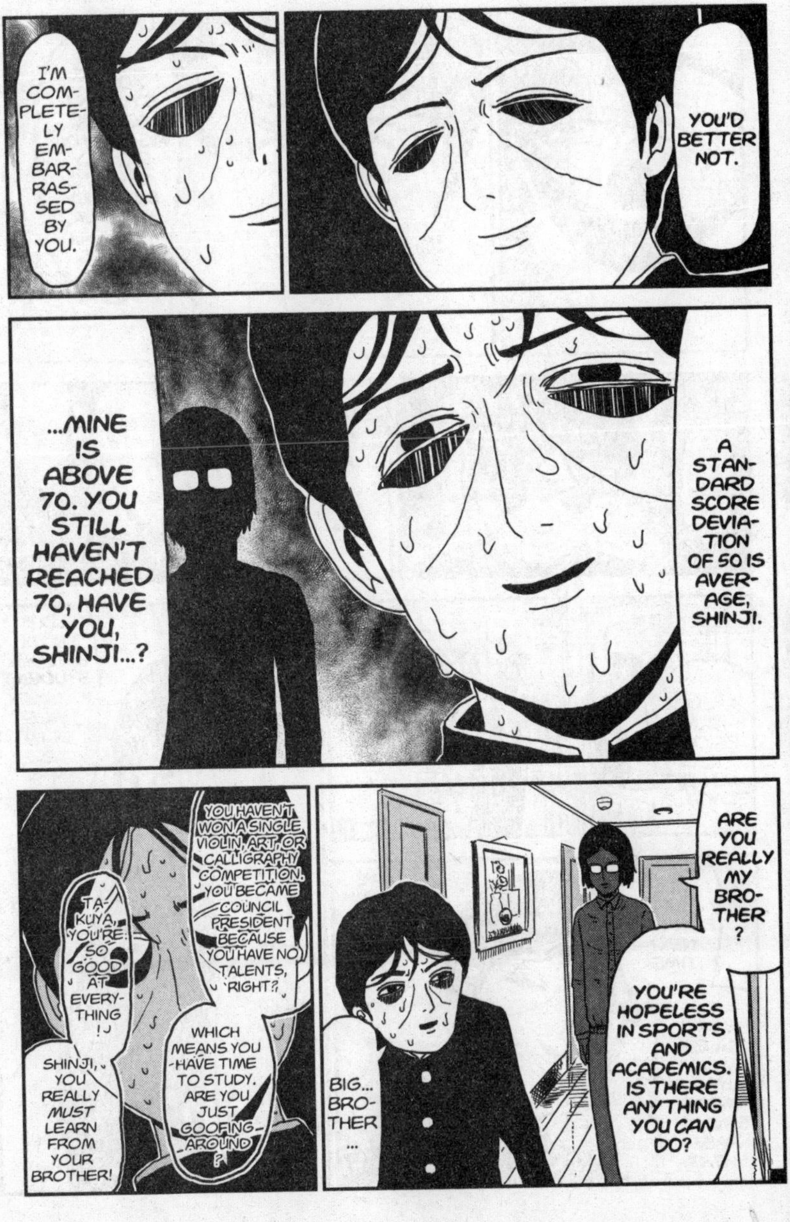
YOU'D BETTER NOT.
I'M COMPLETELY EMBARRASSED BY YOU.
A STANDARD SCORE DEVIATION OF 50 IS AVERAGE, SHINJI.
...MINE IS ABOVE 70. YOU STILL HAVEN'T REACHED 70, HAVE YOU, SHINJI...?
ARE YOU REALLY MY BROTHER?
YOU'RE HOPELESS IN SPORTS AND ACADEMICS. IS THERE ANYTHING YOU CAN DO?
BIG... BROTHER...
YOU HAVEN'T WON A SINGLE VIOLIN, ART, OR CALLIGRAPHY COMPETITION. YOU BECAME COUNCIL PRESIDENT BECAUSE YOU HAVE NO TALENTS, RIGHT?
TAKUYA, YOU'RE SO GOOD AT EVERYTHING!
WHICH MEANS YOU HAVE TIME TO STUDY. ARE YOU JUST GOOFING AROUND?
SHINJI, YOU REALLY MUST LEARN FROM YOUR BROTHER!

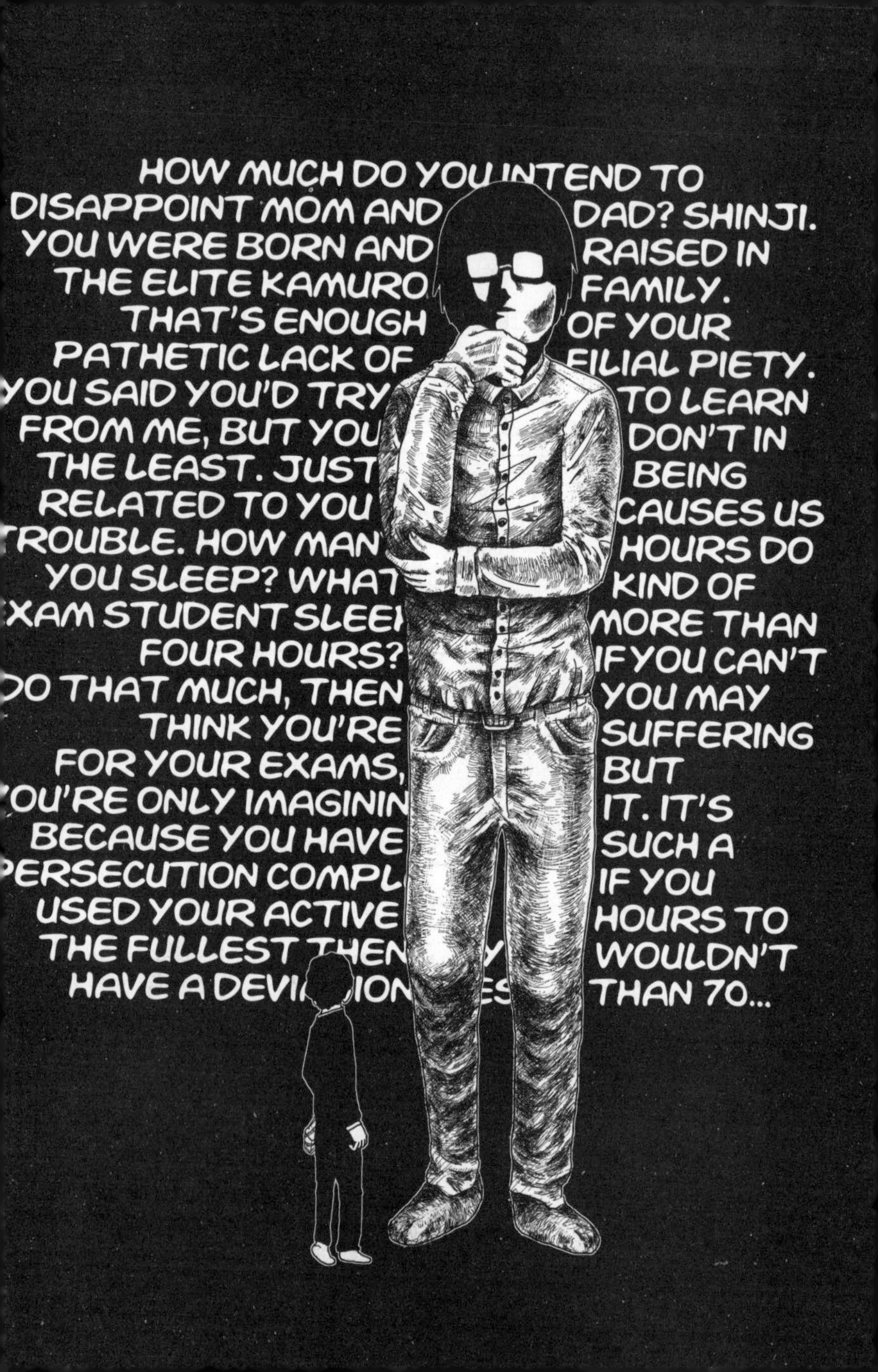
HOW MUCH DO YOU INTEND TO DISAPPOINT MOM AND DAD? SHINJI. YOU WERE BORN AND RAISED IN THE ELITE KAMURO FAMILY. THAT'S ENOUGH OF YOUR PATHETIC LACK OF FILIAL PIETY. YOU SAID YOU'D TRY TO LEARN FROM ME, BUT YOU DON'T IN THE LEAST. JUST BEING RELATED TO YOU CAUSES US TROUBLE. HOW MANY HOURS DO YOU SLEEP? WHAT KIND OF EXAM STUDENT SLEEPS MORE THAN FOUR HOURS? IF YOU CAN'T DO THAT MUCH, THEN YOU MAY THINK YOU'RE SUFFERING FOR YOUR EXAMS, BUT YOU'RE ONLY IMAGINING IT. IT'S BECAUSE YOU HAVE SUCH A PERSECUTION COMPLEX. IF YOU USED YOUR ACTIVE HOURS TO THE FULLEST THEN YOU WOULDN'T HAVE A DEVIATION LESS THAN 70...

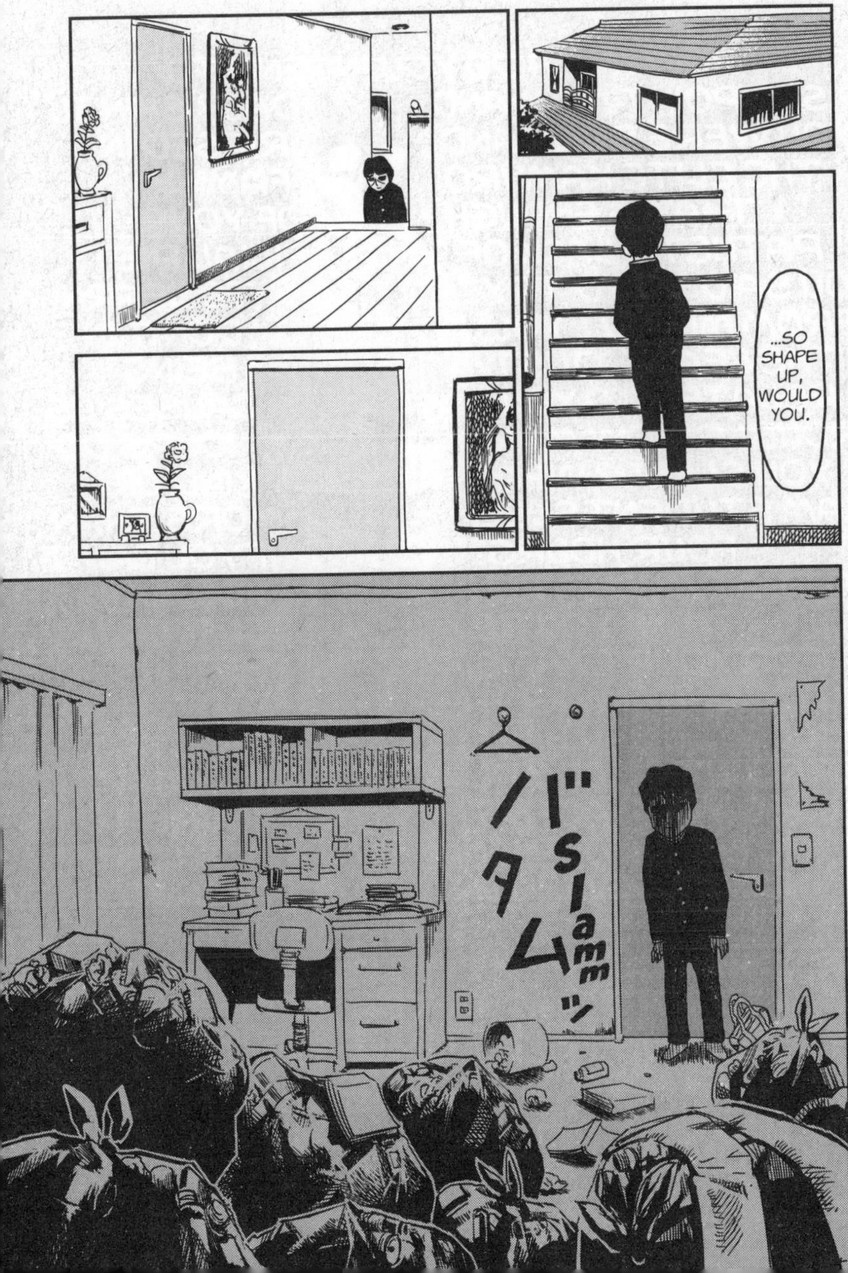
...SO SHAPE UP, WOULD YOU.
バタムッ
slamm

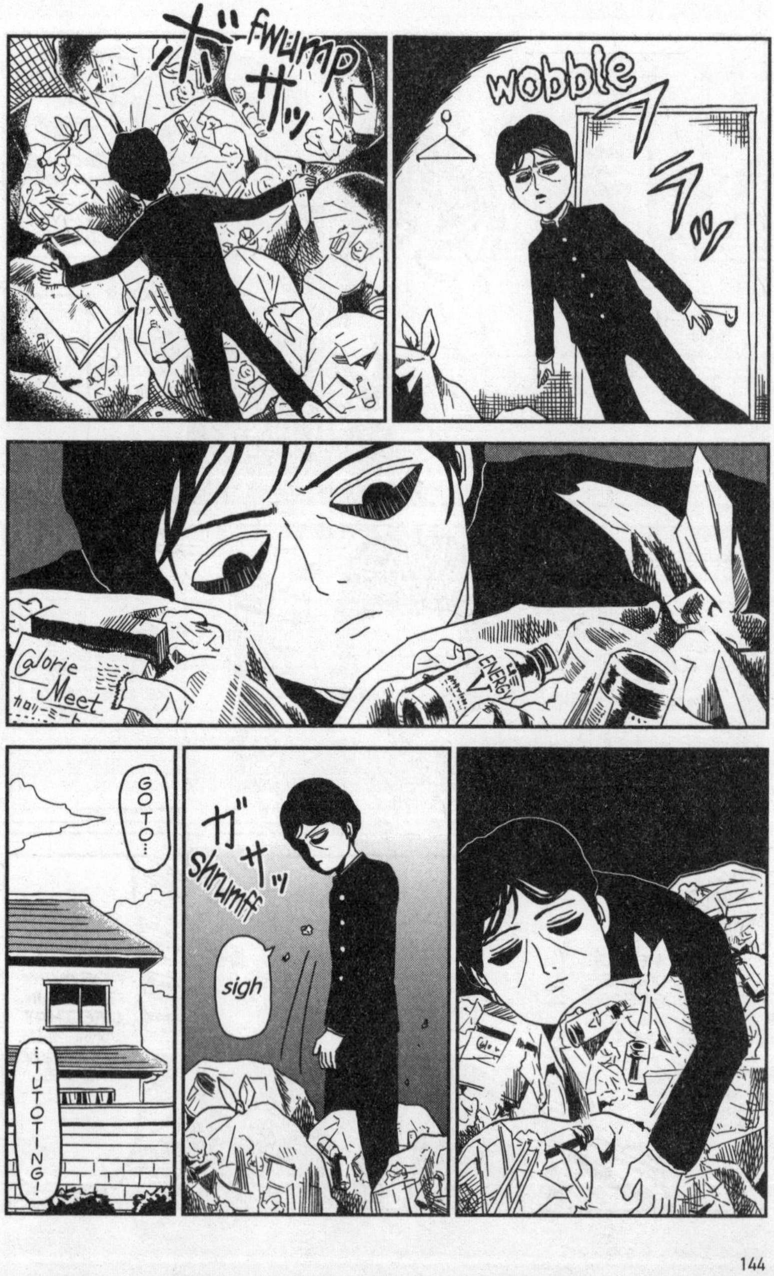
wobble
fwump
Calorie Meet
カロリーミート
ENERGY
ガサッ
shrumff
sigh
GOTO...
...TUTOTING!

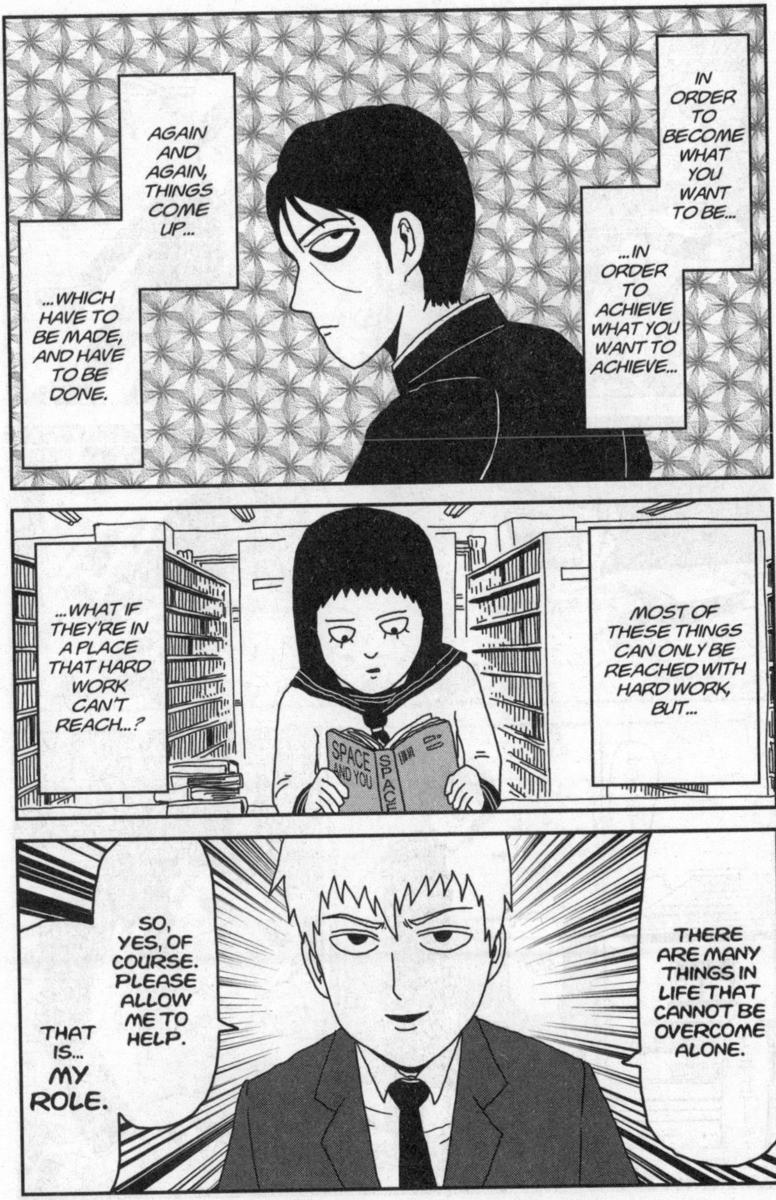
IN ORDER TO BECOME WHAT YOU WANT TO BE...
...IN ORDER TO ACHIEVE WHAT YOU WANT TO ACHIEVE...
AGAIN AND AGAIN, THINGS COME UP...
...WHICH HAVE TO BE MADE, AND HAVE TO BE DONE.
MOST OF THESE THINGS CAN ONLY BE REACHED WITH HARD WORK, BUT...
...WHAT IF THEY'RE IN A PLACE THAT HARD WORK CAN'T REACH...?
SPACE AND YOU
SPACE
THERE ARE MANY THINGS IN LIFE THAT CANNOT BE OVERCOME ALONE.
SO, YES, OF COURSE. PLEASE ALLOW ME TO HELP.
THAT IS... **MY ROLE.**

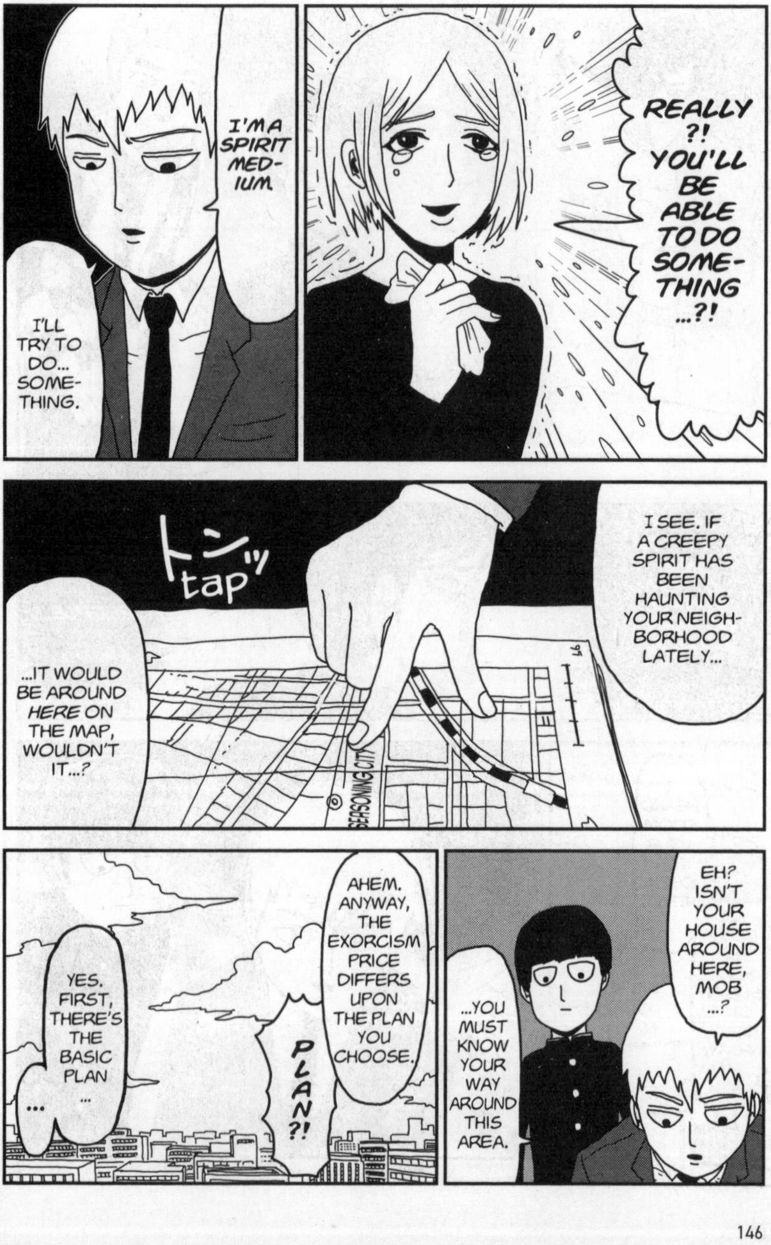
REALLY?! YOU'LL BE ABLE TO DO SOMETHING...?!
I'M A SPIRIT MEDIUM.
I'LL TRY TO DO... SOMETHING.
I SEE. IF A CREEPY SPIRIT HAS BEEN HAUNTING YOUR NEIGHBORHOOD LATELY...
トンッ tap
...IT WOULD BE AROUND *HERE* ON THE MAP, WOULDN'T IT...?
SEASONING CITY
EH? ISN'T YOUR HOUSE AROUND HERE, MOB...?
...YOU MUST KNOW YOUR WAY AROUND THIS AREA.
AHEM. ANYWAY, THE EXORCISM PRICE DIFFERS UPON THE PLAN YOU CHOOSE.
PLAN?!
YES. FIRST, THERE'S THE BASIC PLAN...
...

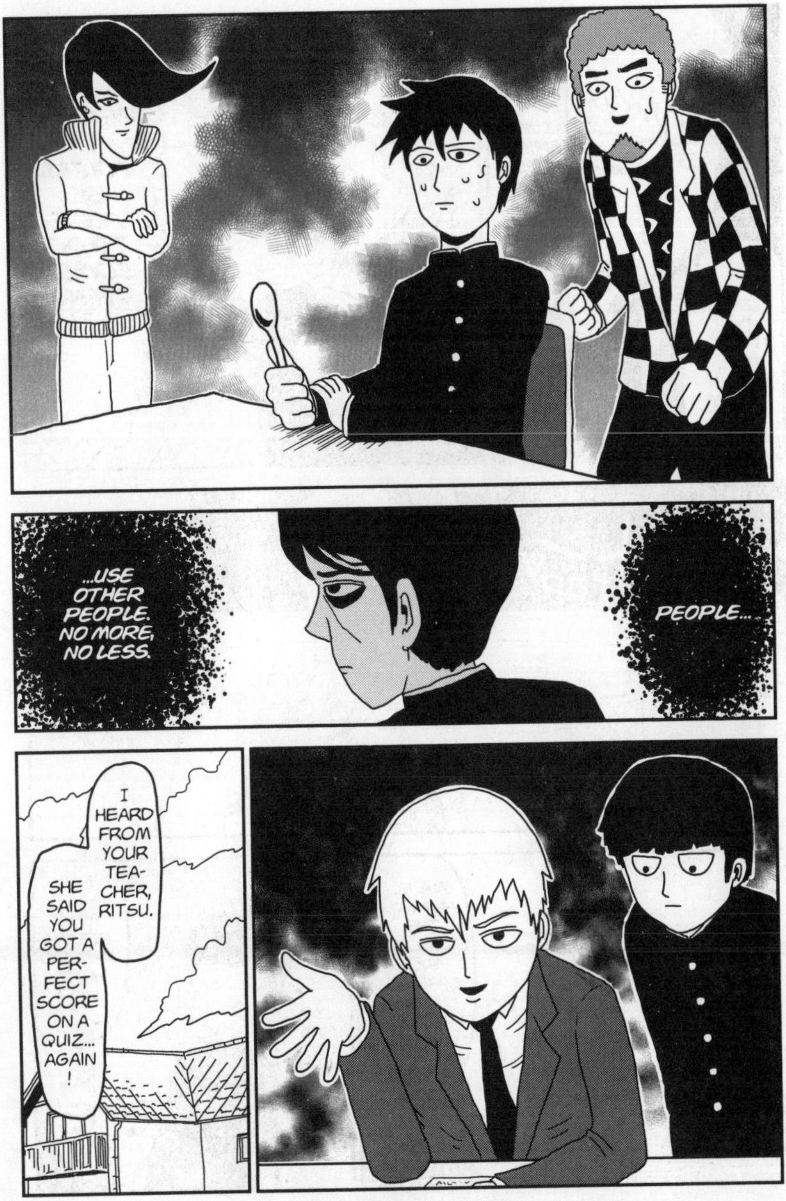
PEOPLE...
...USE OTHER PEOPLE. NO MORE, NO LESS.
I HEARD FROM YOUR TEACHER, RITSU.
SHE SAID YOU GOT A PERFECT SCORE ON A QUIZ... AGAIN!

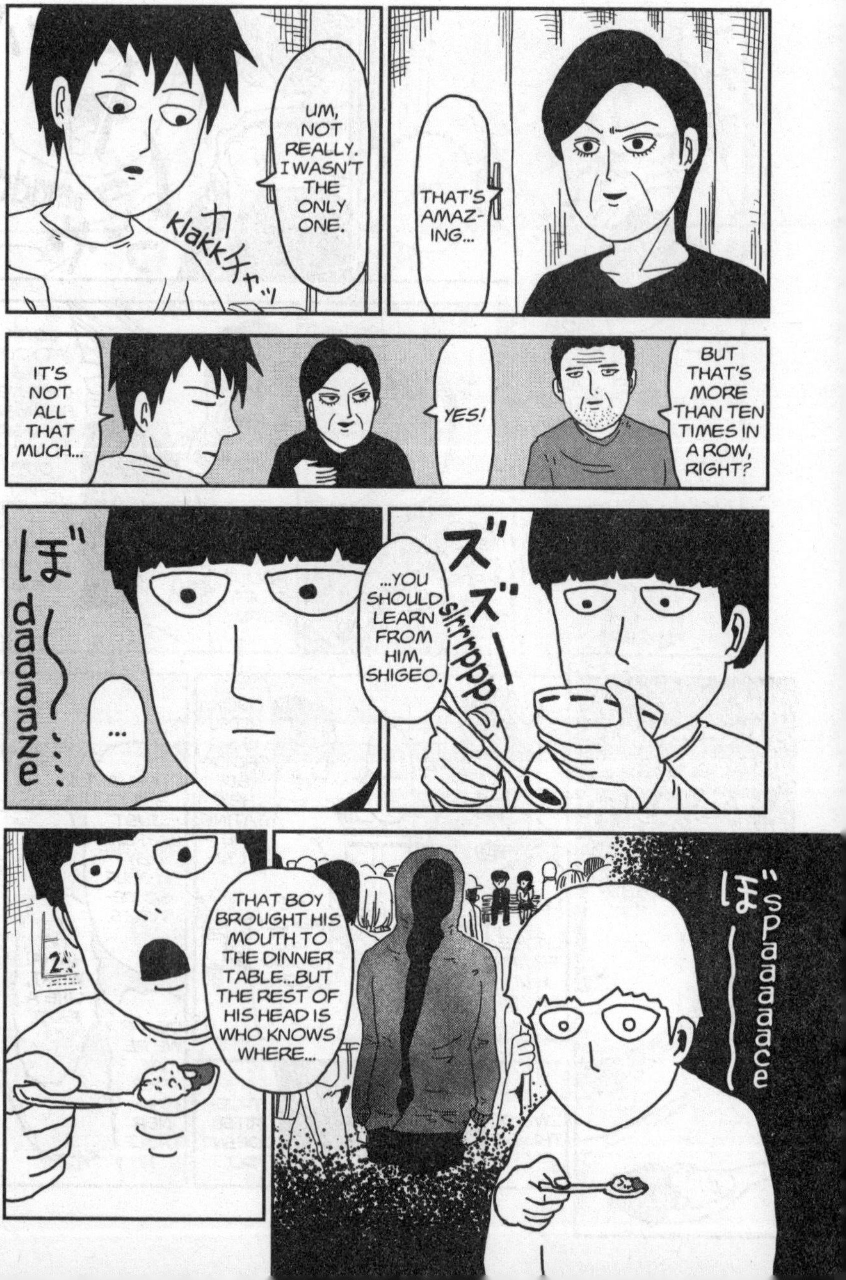
THAT'S AMAZ-ING...
UM, NOT REALLY. I WASN'T THE ONLY ONE.
klakk カチャッ
BUT THAT'S MORE THAN TEN TIMES IN A ROW, RIGHT?
YES!
IT'S NOT ALL THAT MUCH...
ズズー slrrrppp
...YOU SHOULD LEARN FROM HIM, SHIGEO.
ぼ～～ daaaaaze
...
ぼ～ spaaaaaace
THAT BOY BROUGHT HIS MOUTH TO THE DINNER TABLE...BUT THE REST OF HIS HEAD IS WHO KNOWS WHERE...

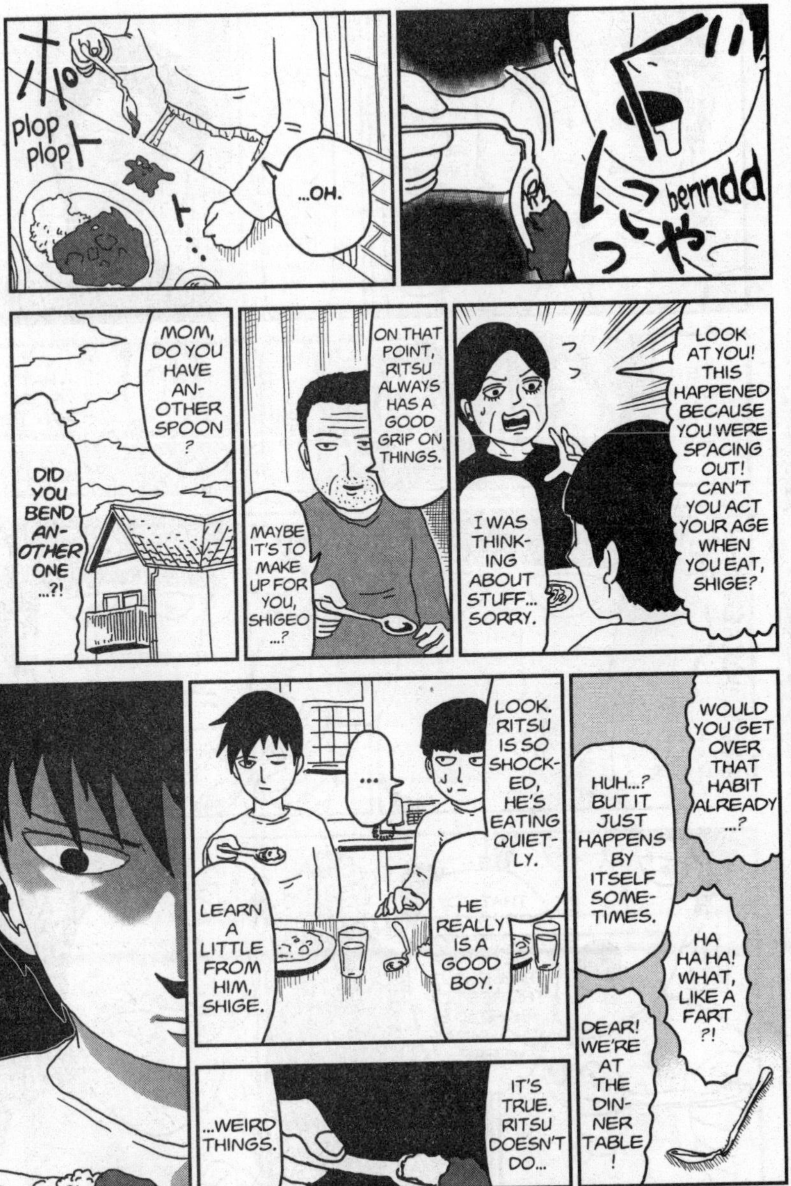
benndd
plop plop
...OH.
LOOK AT YOU! THIS HAPPENED BECAUSE YOU WERE SPACING OUT! CAN'T YOU ACT YOUR AGE WHEN YOU EAT, SHIGE?
I WAS THINKING ABOUT STUFF... SORRY.
ON THAT POINT, RITSU ALWAYS HAS A GOOD GRIP ON THINGS.
MAYBE IT'S TO MAKE UP FOR YOU, SHIGEO...?
MOM, DO YOU HAVE ANOTHER SPOON?
DID YOU BEND ANOTHER ONE...?!
WOULD YOU GET OVER THAT HABIT ALREADY...?
HUH...? BUT IT JUST HAPPENS BY ITSELF SOMETIMES.
HA HA HA! WHAT, LIKE A FART?!
DEAR! WE'RE AT THE DINNER TABLE!
LOOK. RITSU IS SO SHOCKED, HE'S EATING QUIETLY.
...
HE REALLY IS A GOOD BOY.
LEARN A LITTLE FROM HIM, SHIGE.
IT'S TRUE. RITSU DOESN'T DO...
...WEIRD THINGS.

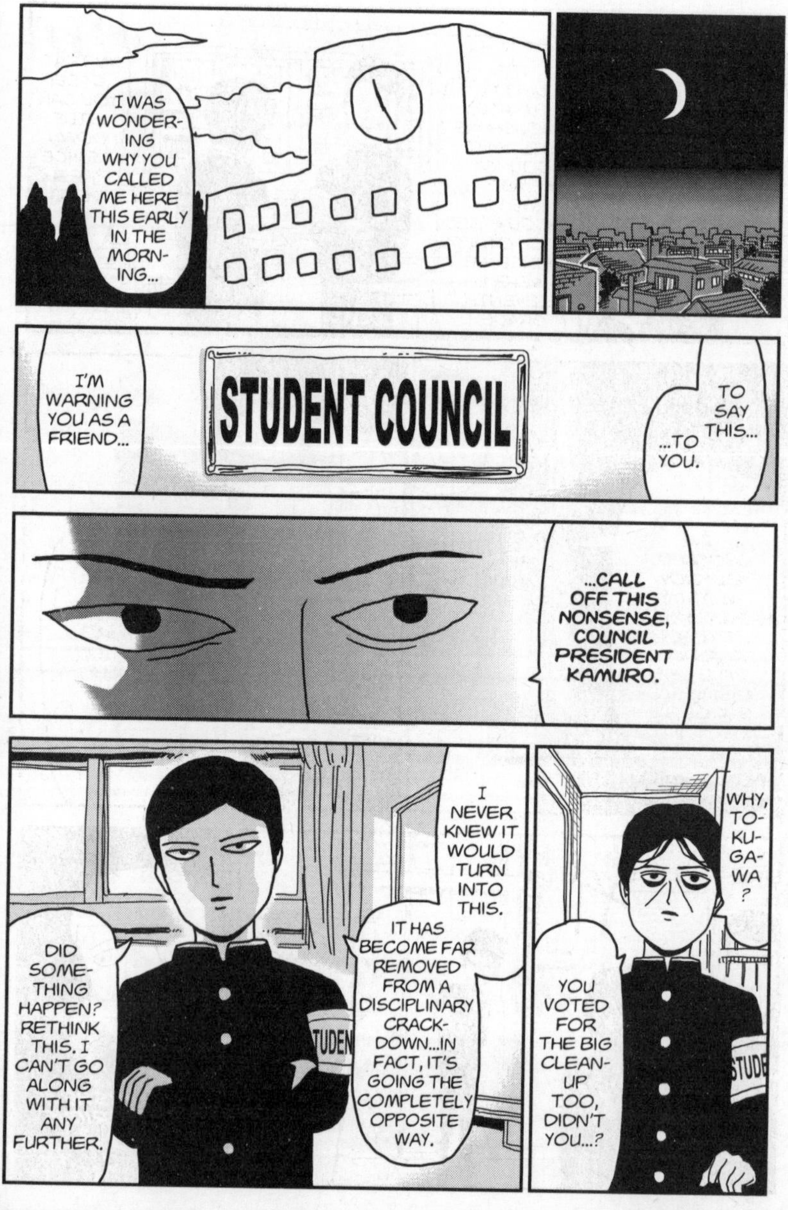
I WAS WONDERING WHY YOU CALLED ME HERE THIS EARLY IN THE MORNING...
TO SAY THIS... ...TO YOU.
STUDENT COUNCIL
I'M WARNING YOU AS A FRIEND...
...CALL OFF THIS NONSENSE, COUNCIL PRESIDENT KAMURO.
WHY, TOKUGAWA?
YOU VOTED FOR THE BIG CLEAN-UP TOO, DIDN'T YOU...?
I NEVER KNEW IT WOULD TURN INTO THIS.
IT HAS BECOME FAR REMOVED FROM A DISCIPLINARY CRACKDOWN...IN FACT, IT'S GOING THE COMPLETELY OPPOSITE WAY.
DID SOMETHING HAPPEN? RETHINK THIS. I CAN'T GO ALONG WITH IT ANY FURTHER.

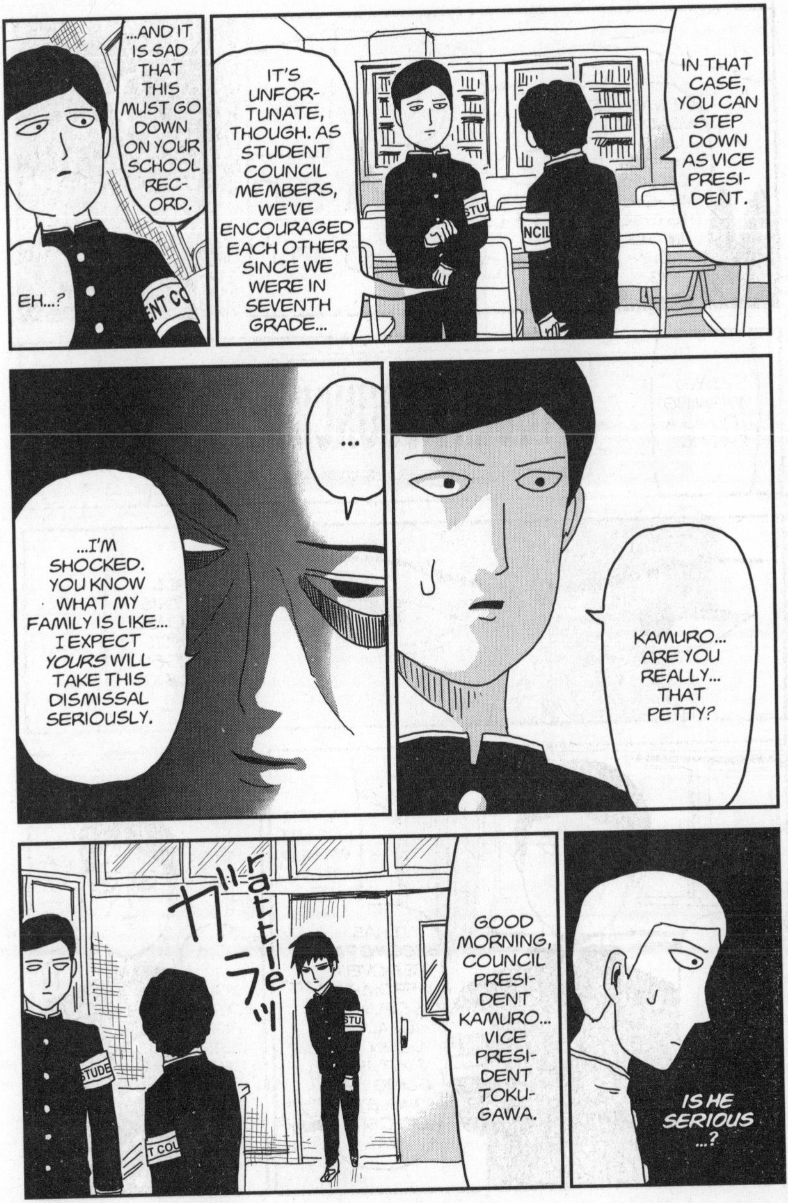
IN THAT CASE, YOU CAN STEP DOWN AS VICE PRESIDENT.
IT'S UNFORTUNATE, THOUGH. AS STUDENT COUNCIL MEMBERS, WE'VE ENCOURAGED EACH OTHER SINCE WE WERE IN SEVENTH GRADE...
...AND IT IS SAD THAT THIS MUST GO DOWN ON YOUR SCHOOL RECORD.
EH...?
KAMURO... ARE YOU REALLY... THAT PETTY?
...
...I'M SHOCKED. YOU KNOW WHAT MY FAMILY IS LIKE... I EXPECT *YOURS* WILL TAKE THIS DISMISSAL SERIOUSLY.
IS HE SERIOUS...?
GOOD MORNING, COUNCIL PRESIDENT KAMURO... VICE PRESIDENT TOKUGAWA.
ガラッ
rattle

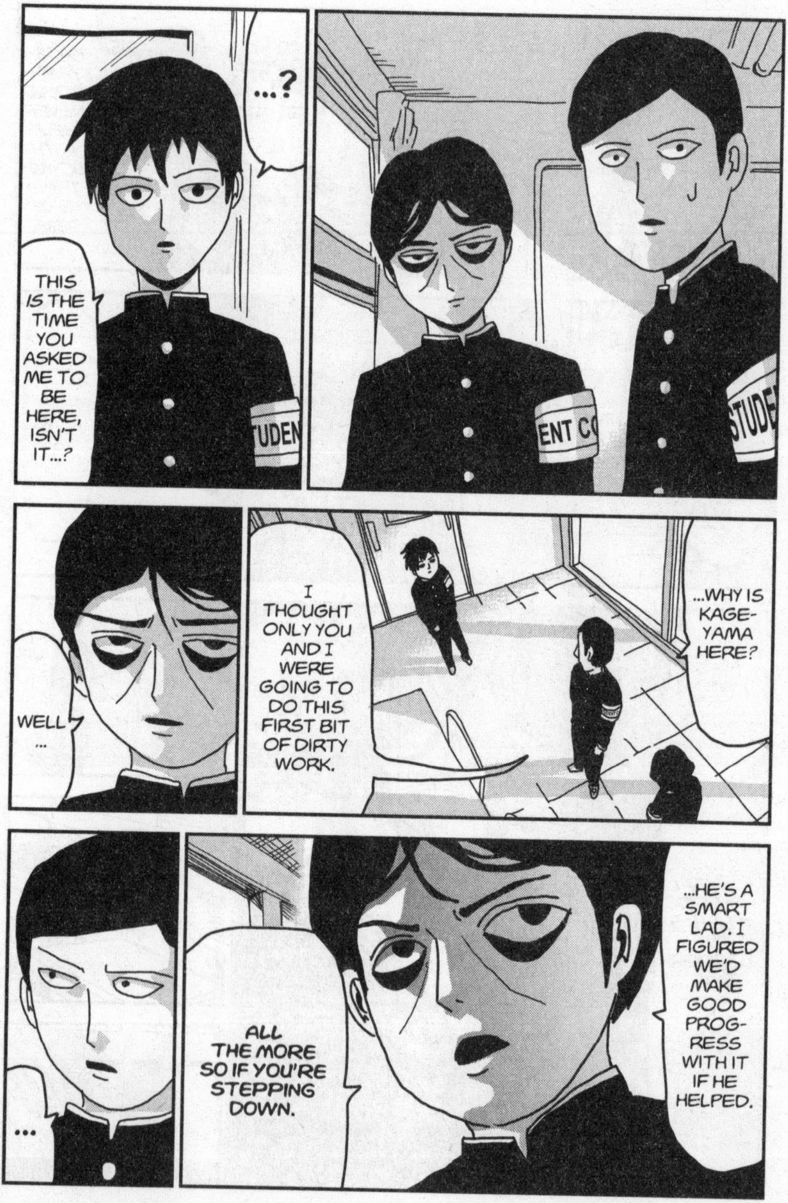
...?
THIS IS THE TIME YOU ASKED ME TO BE HERE, ISN'T IT...?
...WHY IS KAGE-YAMA HERE?
I THOUGHT ONLY YOU AND I WERE GOING TO DO THIS FIRST BIT OF DIRTY WORK.
WELL ...
...HE'S A SMART LAD. I FIGURED WE'D MAKE GOOD PROG-RESS WITH IT IF HE HELPED.
ALL THE MORE SO IF YOU'RE STEPPING DOWN.
...

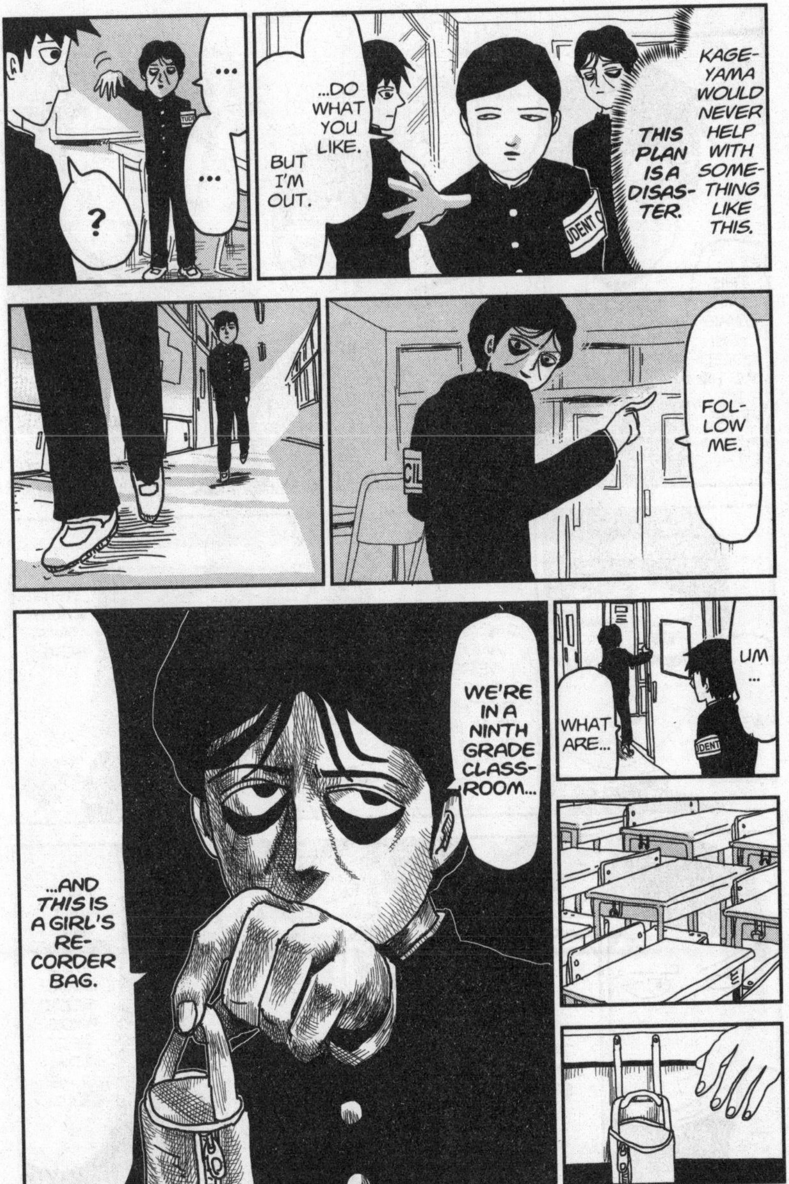
KAGEYAMA WOULD NEVER HELP WITH SOMETHING LIKE THIS.
THIS PLAN IS A DISASTER.
...DO WHAT YOU LIKE.
BUT I'M OUT.
...
...
?
FOLLOW ME.
UM ...
WHAT ARE...
WE'RE IN A NINTH GRADE CLASSROOM...
...AND *THIS* IS A GIRL'S RECORDER BAG.

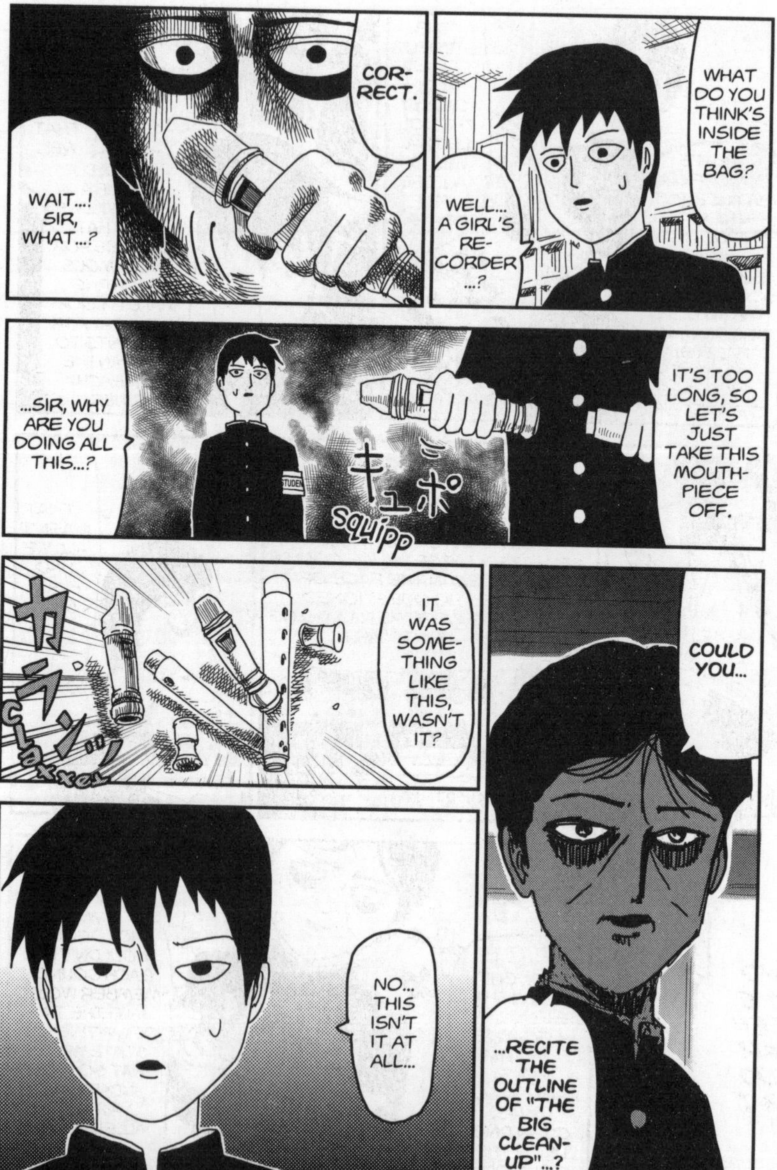
WHAT DO YOU THINK'S INSIDE THE BAG?
WELL... A GIRL'S RE-CORDER ...?
COR-RECT.
WAIT...! SIR, WHAT...?
IT'S TOO LONG, SO LET'S JUST TAKE THIS MOUTH-PIECE OFF.
キュポ
squipp
STUDEN
...SIR, WHY ARE YOU DOING ALL THIS...?
COULD YOU...
...RECITE THE OUTLINE OF "THE BIG CLEAN-UP"...?
IT WAS SOME-THING LIKE THIS, WASN'T IT?
カランッ
clatter
NO... THIS ISN'T IT AT ALL...

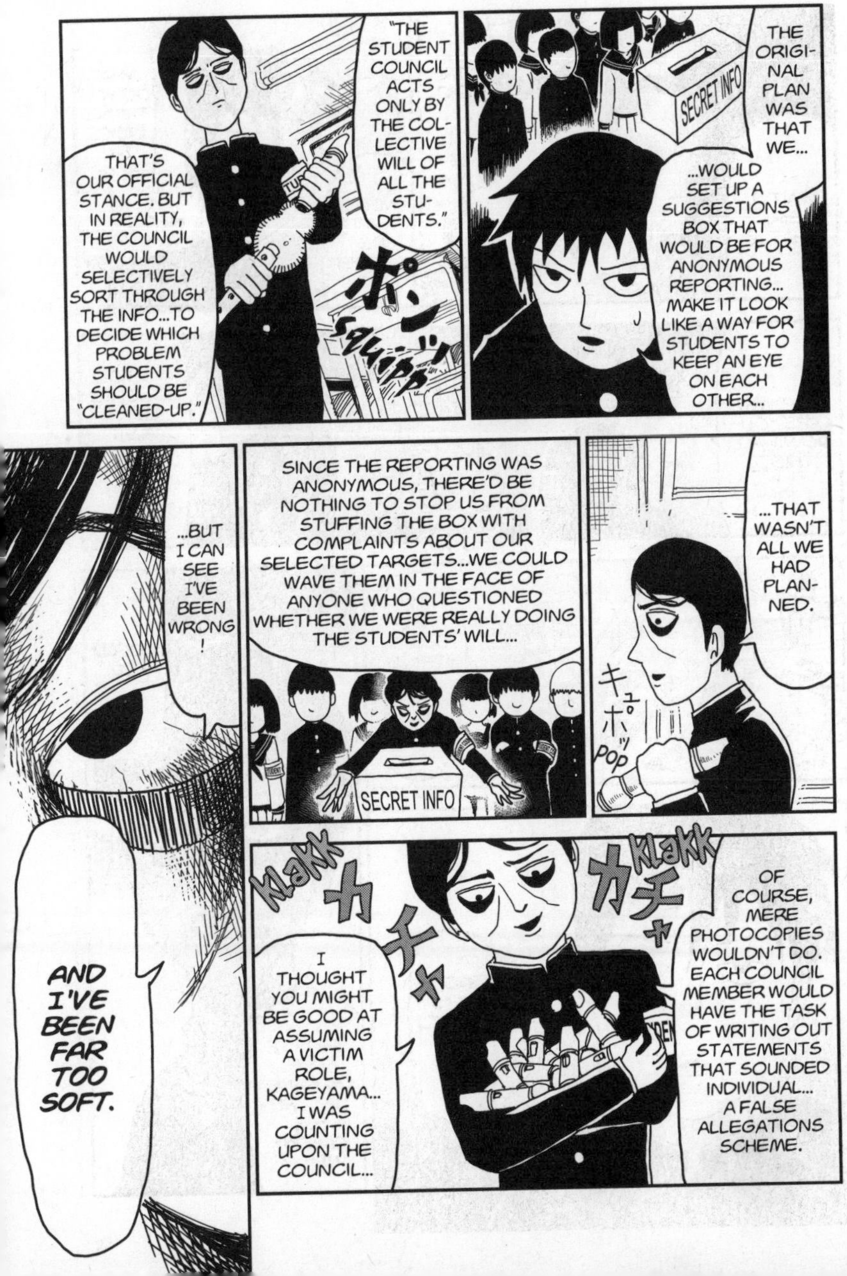
THE ORIGINAL PLAN WAS THAT WE...
...WOULD SET UP A SUGGESTIONS BOX THAT WOULD BE FOR ANONYMOUS REPORTING... MAKE IT LOOK LIKE A WAY FOR STUDENTS TO KEEP AN EYE ON EACH OTHER...
SECRET INFO
"THE STUDENT COUNCIL ACTS ONLY BY THE COLLECTIVE WILL OF ALL THE STUDENTS."
THAT'S OUR OFFICIAL STANCE. BUT IN REALITY, THE COUNCIL WOULD SELECTIVELY SORT THROUGH THE INFO...TO DECIDE WHICH PROBLEM STUDENTS SHOULD BE "CLEANED-UP."
ポンッ
...THAT WASN'T ALL WE HAD PLANNED.
キュポッ
POP
SINCE THE REPORTING WAS ANONYMOUS, THERE'D BE NOTHING TO STOP US FROM STUFFING THE BOX WITH COMPLAINTS ABOUT OUR SELECTED TARGETS...WE COULD WAVE THEM IN THE FACE OF ANYONE WHO QUESTIONED WHETHER WE WERE REALLY DOING THE STUDENTS' WILL...
SECRET INFO
KLAKK
カチャ
OF COURSE, MERE PHOTOCOPIES WOULDN'T DO. EACH COUNCIL MEMBER WOULD HAVE THE TASK OF WRITING OUT STATEMENTS THAT SOUNDED INDIVIDUAL... A FALSE ALLEGATIONS SCHEME.
KLAKK
カチャ
I THOUGHT YOU MIGHT BE GOOD AT ASSUMING A VICTIM ROLE, KAGEYAMA... I WAS COUNTING UPON THE COUNCIL...
...BUT I CAN SEE I'VE BEEN WRONG!
AND I'VE BEEN FAR TOO SOFT.

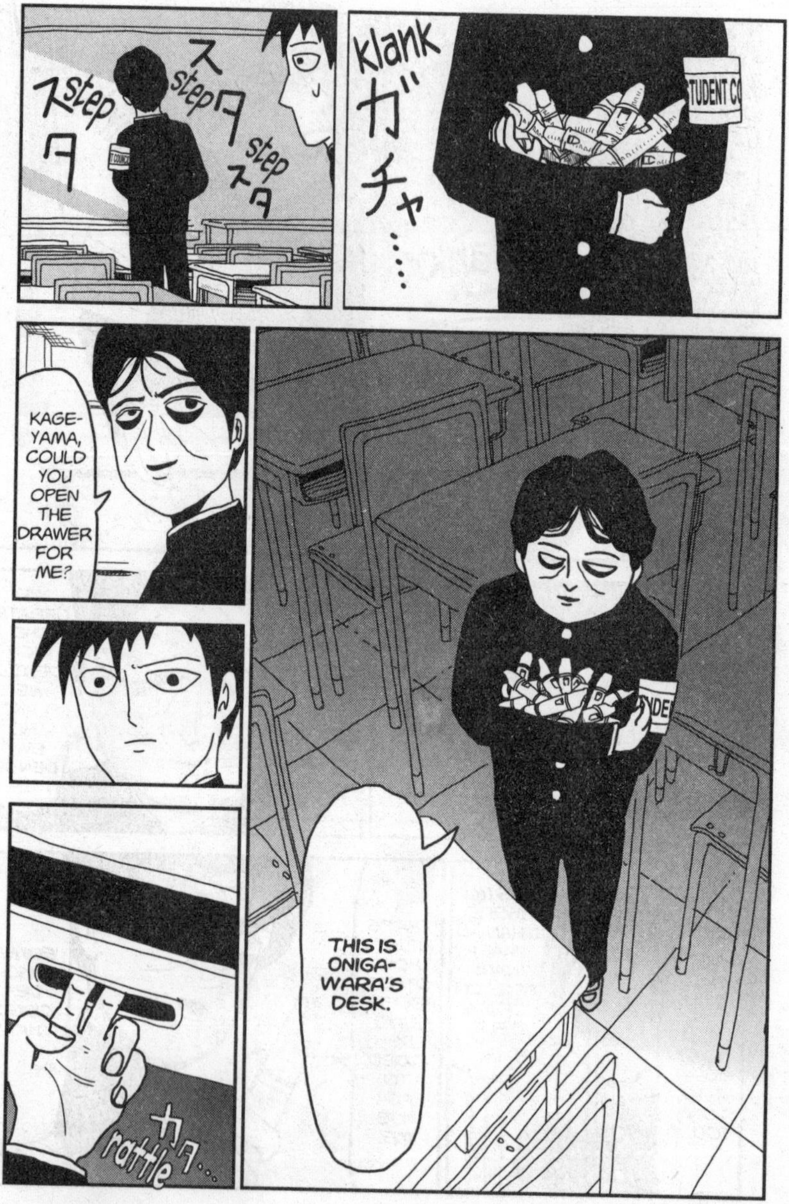
klank ガチャ…
スタ step スタ step スタ step スタ
THIS IS ONIGA-WARA'S DESK.
KAGE-YAMA, COULD YOU OPEN THE DRAWER FOR ME?
カタ rattle …

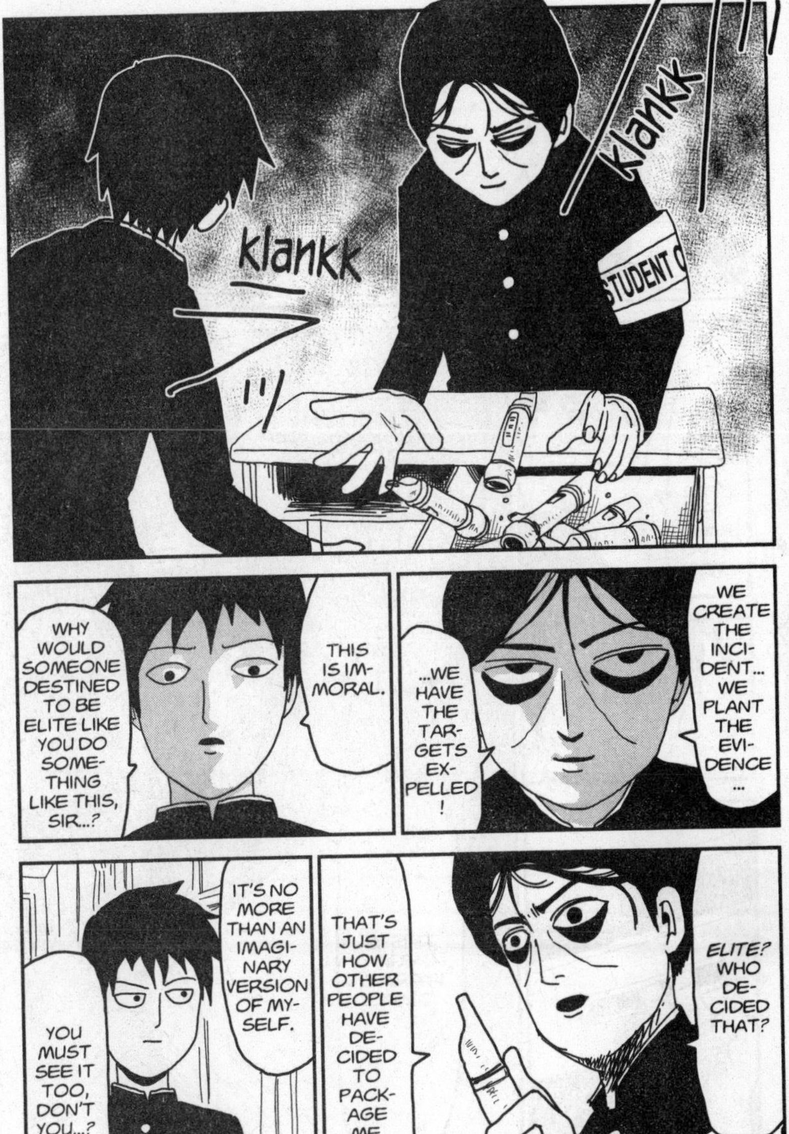
klankk
klankk
WE CREATE THE INCIDENT... WE PLANT THE EVIDENCE...
...WE HAVE THE TARGETS EXPELLED!
THIS IS IMMORAL.
WHY WOULD SOMEONE DESTINED TO BE ELITE LIKE YOU DO SOMETHING LIKE THIS, SIR...?
ELITE? WHO DECIDED THAT?
THAT'S JUST HOW OTHER PEOPLE HAVE DECIDED TO PACKAGE ME.
IT'S NO MORE THAN AN IMAGINARY VERSION OF MYSELF.
YOU MUST SEE IT TOO, DON'T YOU...?

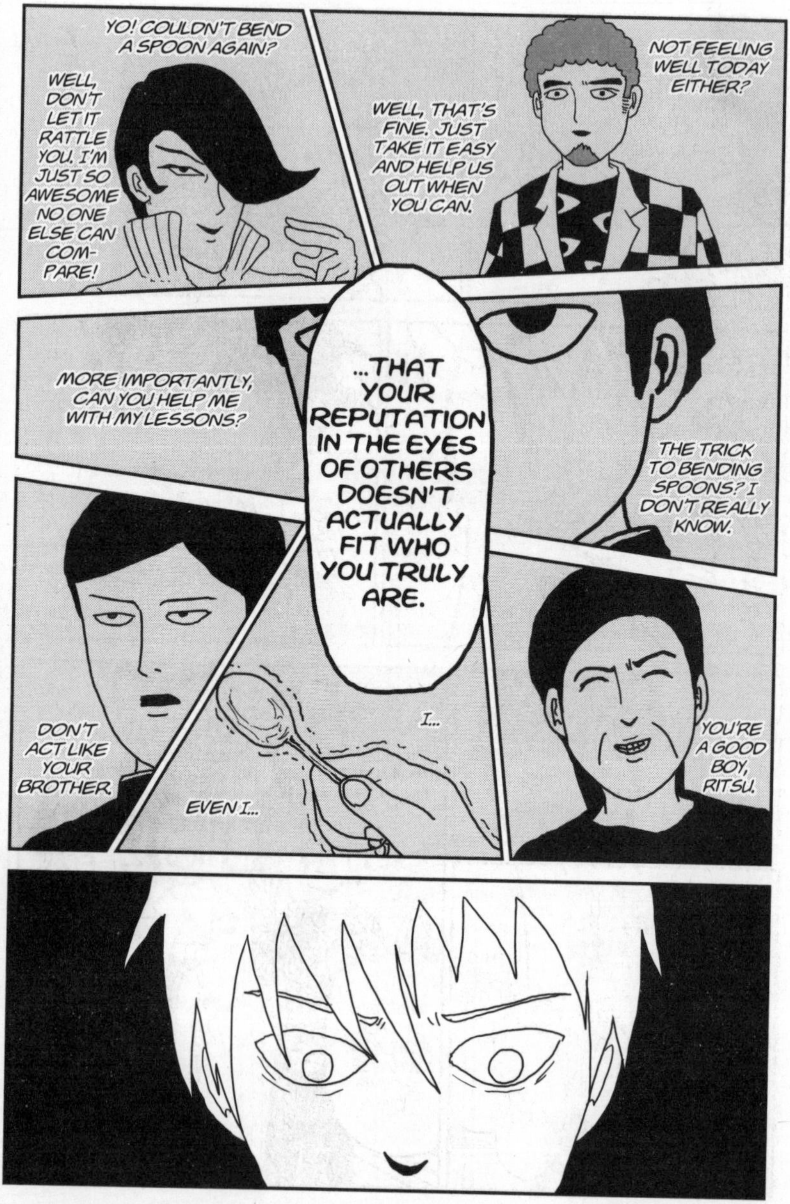
NOT FEELING WELL TODAY EITHER?
WELL, THAT'S FINE. JUST TAKE IT EASY AND HELP US OUT WHEN YOU CAN.
YO! COULDN'T BEND A SPOON AGAIN?
WELL, DON'T LET IT RATTLE YOU. I'M JUST SO AWESOME NO ONE ELSE CAN COM-PARE!
THE TRICK TO BENDING SPOONS? I DON'T REALLY KNOW.
MORE IMPORTANTLY, CAN YOU HELP ME WITH MY LESSONS?
...THAT YOUR REPUTATION IN THE EYES OF OTHERS DOESN'T ACTUALLY FIT WHO YOU TRULY ARE.
YOU'RE A GOOD BOY, RITSU.
I...
EVEN I...
DON'T ACT LIKE YOUR BROTHER.

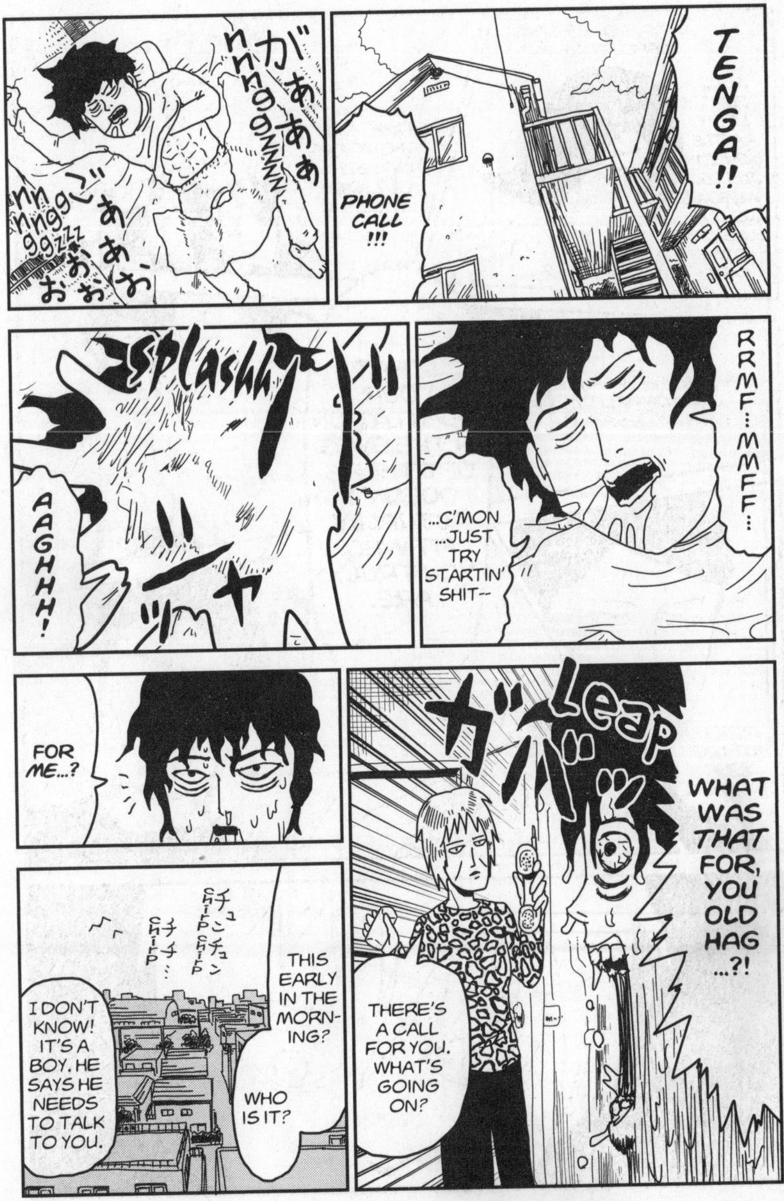
TENGA!!
PHONE CALL!!!
nnnggzzzz
nnngggzzz
RRMF... MMFF...
...C'MON ...JUST TRY STARTIN' SHIT--
splashh
AAGHHH!
Leap
WHAT WAS THAT FOR, YOU OLD HAG...?!
THERE'S A CALL FOR YOU. WHAT'S GOING ON?
FOR ME...?
chirp chirp
chirp
THIS EARLY IN THE MORNING?
WHO IS IT?
I DON'T KNOW! IT'S A BOY. HE SAYS HE NEEDS TO TALK TO YOU.

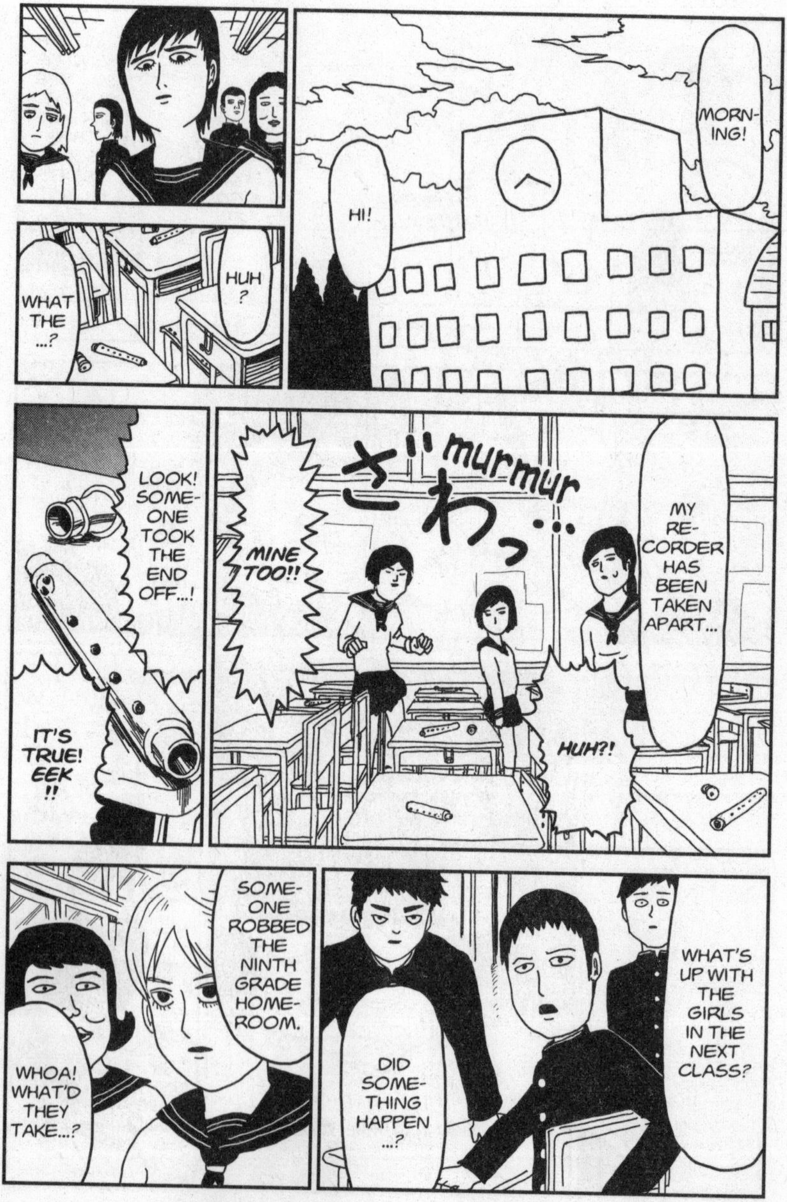

MORNING!
HI!
HUH?
WHAT THE ...?
MY RECORDER HAS BEEN TAKEN APART...
ざわっ murmur
MINE TOO!!
HUH?!
LOOK! SOMEONE TOOK THE END OFF...!
IT'S TRUE! EEK!!
WHAT'S UP WITH THE GIRLS IN THE NEXT CLASS?
DID SOMETHING HAPPEN...?
SOMEONE ROBBED THE NINTH GRADE HOMEROOM.
WHOA! WHAT'D THEY TAKE...?

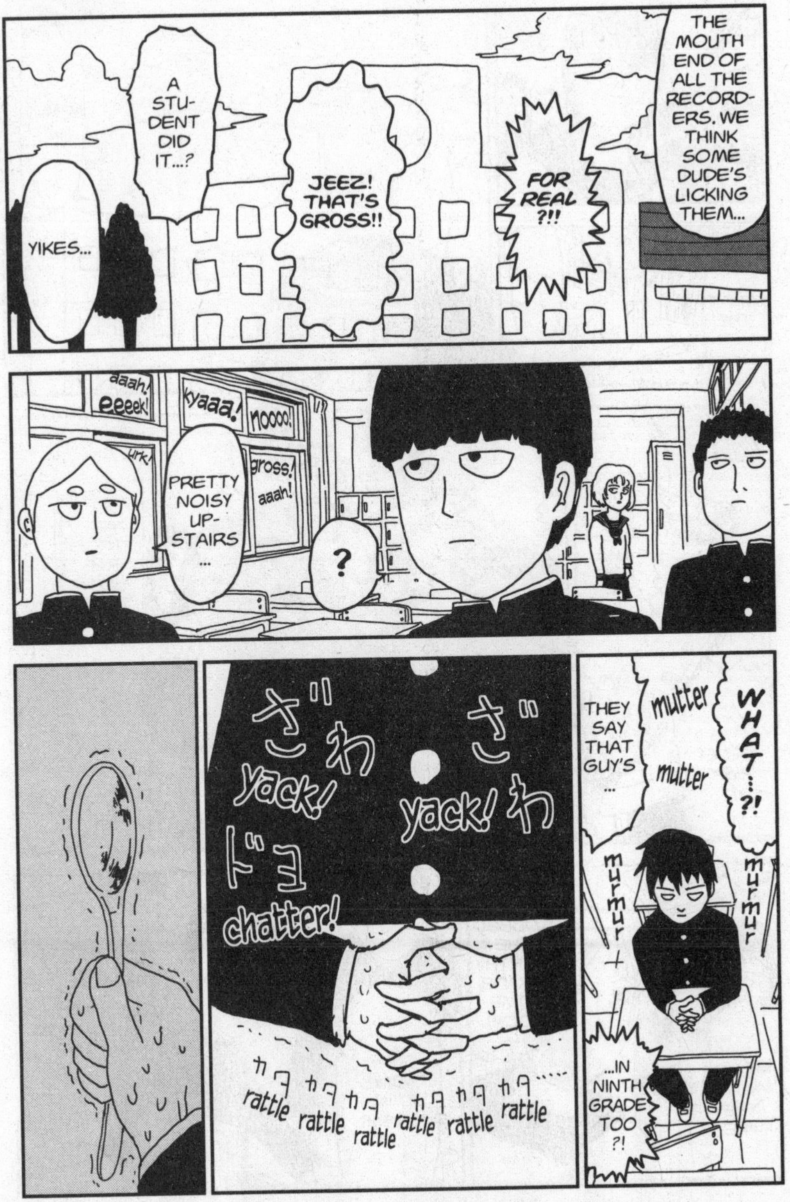
THE MOUTH END OF ALL THE RECORD-ERS. WE THINK SOME DUDE'S LICKING THEM...
FOR REAL?!!
JEEZ! THAT'S GROSS!!
A STU-DENT DID IT...?
YIKES...
?
nooo!
kyaaa!
aaah! eeeek!
gross! aaah!
urk!
PRETTY NOISY UP-STAIRS...
WHAT...?!
mutter
mutter
THEY SAY THAT GUY'S...
murmur
murmur
...IN NINTH GRADE TOO?!
ざわ
ざわ
yack!
yack!
ドヨ
chatter!
カタ カタ カタ カタ カタ カタ......
rattle rattle rattle rattle rattle rattle

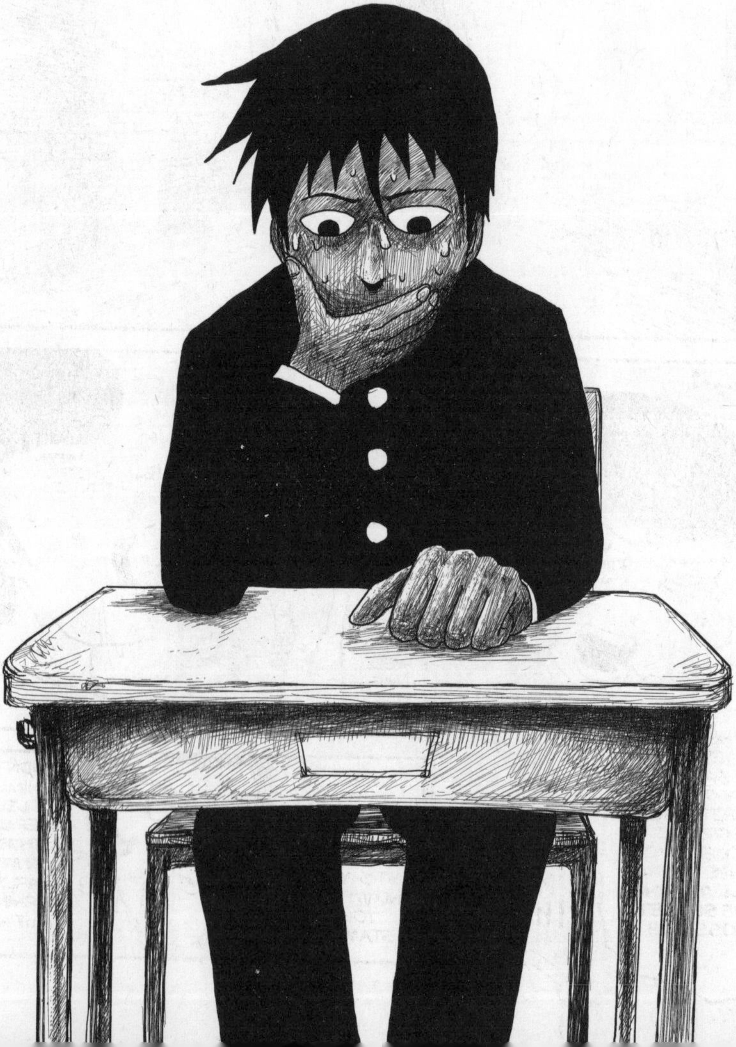

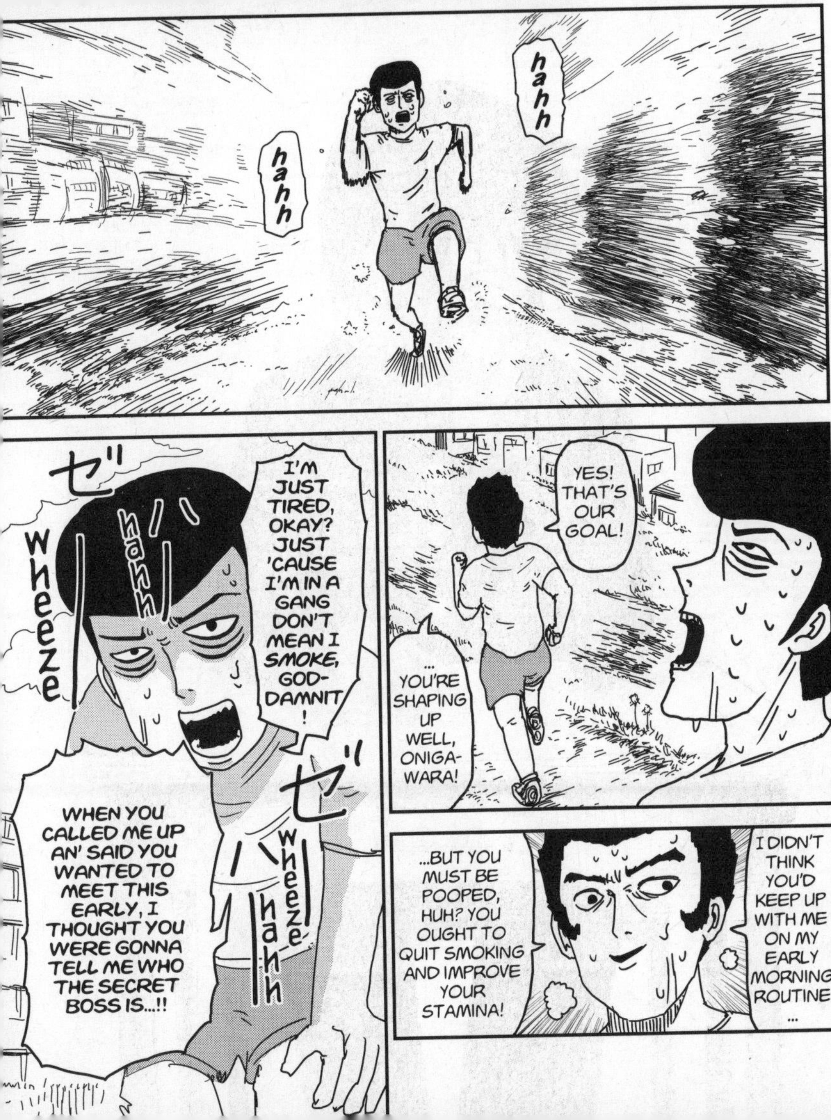
hahh
hahh
YES! THAT'S OUR GOAL!
... YOU'RE SHAPING UP WELL, ONIGA-WARA!
I DIDN'T THINK YOU'D KEEP UP WITH ME ON MY EARLY MORNING ROUTINE ...
...BUT YOU MUST BE POOPED, HUH? YOU OUGHT TO QUIT SMOKING AND IMPROVE YOUR STAMINA!
I'M JUST TIRED, OKAY? JUST 'CAUSE I'M IN A GANG DON'T MEAN I SMOKE, GOD-DAMNIT!
ゼハ
wheeze
hahh
ゼハ
wheeze
hahh
WHEN YOU CALLED ME UP AN' SAID YOU WANTED TO MEET THIS EARLY, I THOUGHT YOU WERE GONNA TELL ME WHO THE SECRET BOSS IS...!!

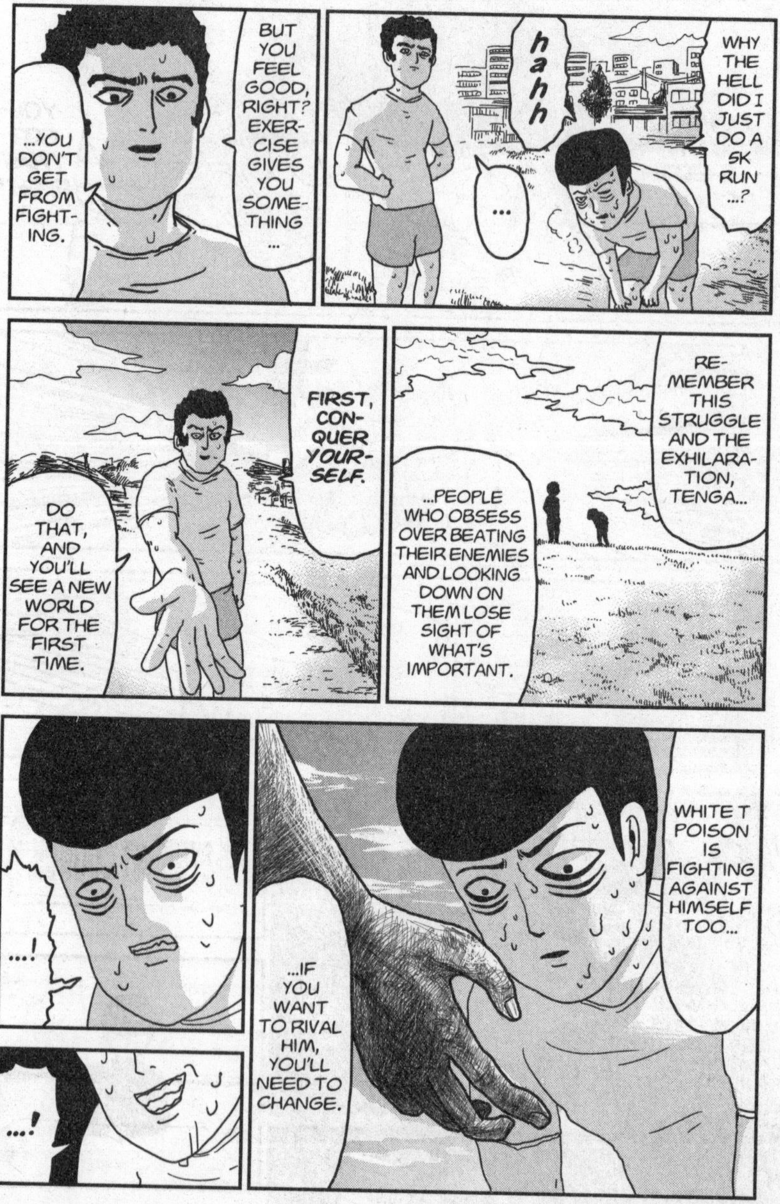
WHY THE HELL DID I JUST DO A 5K RUN ...?
hahh
...
BUT YOU FEEL GOOD, RIGHT? EXERCISE GIVES YOU SOMETHING ...
...YOU DON'T GET FROM FIGHTING.
REMEMBER THIS STRUGGLE AND THE EXHILARATION, TENGA...
...PEOPLE WHO OBSESS OVER BEATING THEIR ENEMIES AND LOOKING DOWN ON THEM LOSE SIGHT OF WHAT'S IMPORTANT.
FIRST, CONQUER *YOURSELF*.
DO THAT, AND YOU'LL SEE A NEW WORLD FOR THE FIRST TIME.
WHITE T POISON IS FIGHTING AGAINST HIMSELF TOO...
...IF YOU WANT TO RIVAL HIM, YOU'LL NEED TO CHANGE.
...!
...!

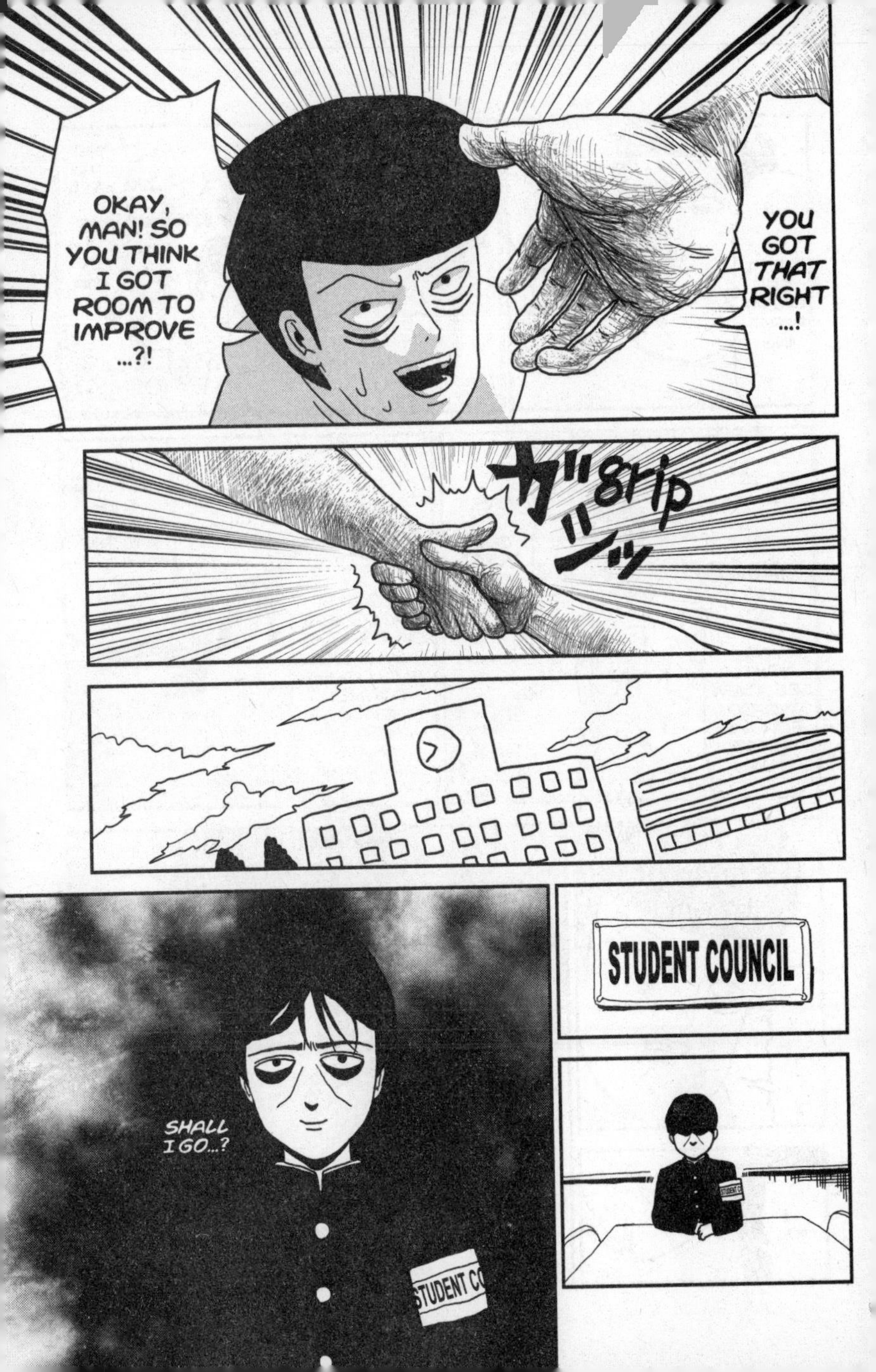
YOU GOT THAT RIGHT ...!
OKAY, MAN! SO YOU THINK I GOT ROOM TO IMPROVE ...?!
ガッ
grip
STUDENT COUNCIL
SHALL I GO...?

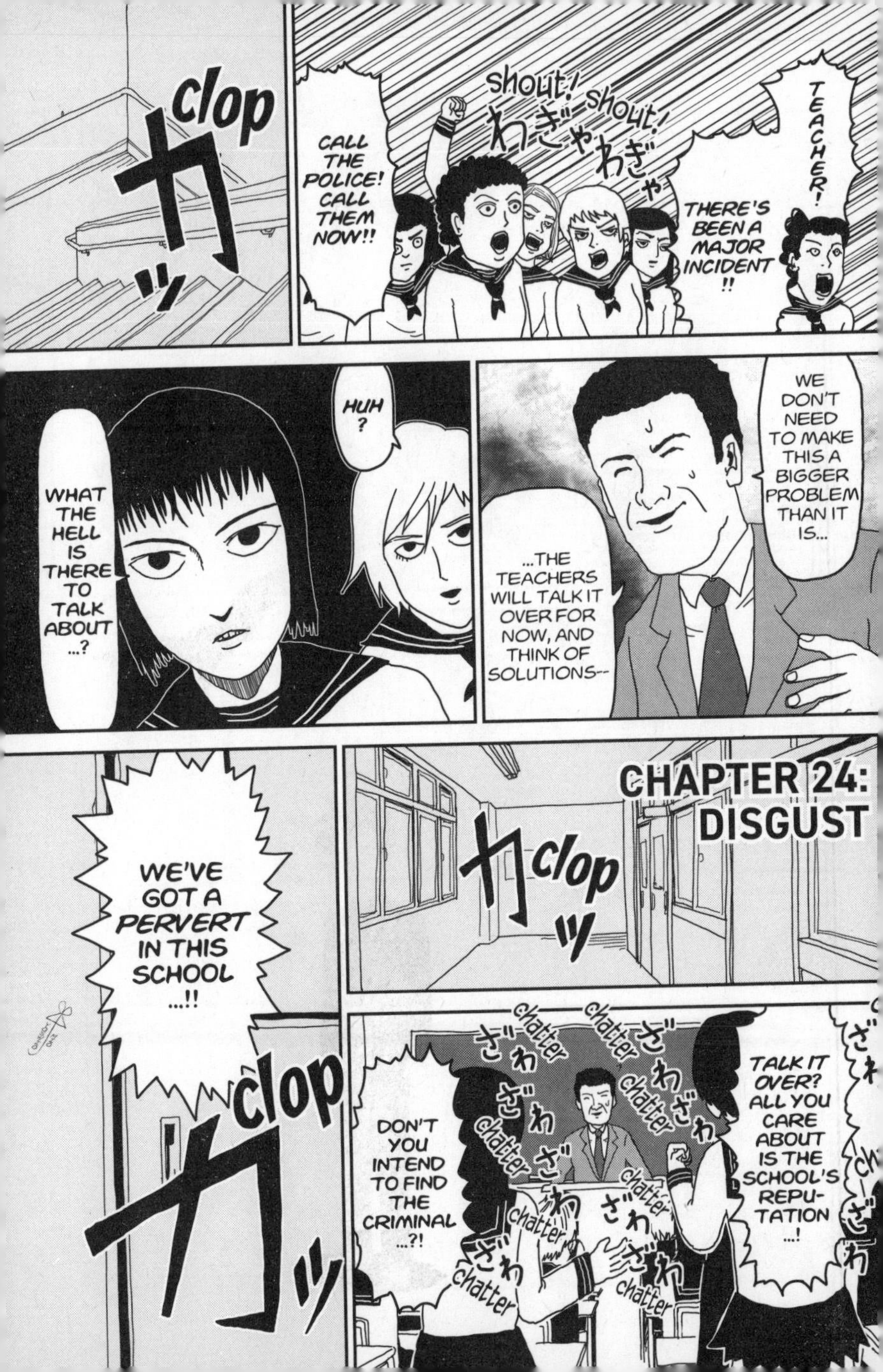
TEACHER!
THERE'S BEEN A MAJOR INCIDENT!!
shout! わぎゃ shout! わぎゃ
CALL THE POLICE! CALL THEM NOW!!
clop カッ
WE DON'T NEED TO MAKE THIS A BIGGER PROBLEM THAN IT IS...
...THE TEACHERS WILL TALK IT OVER FOR NOW, AND THINK OF SOLUTIONS--
HUH?
WHAT THE HELL IS THERE TO TALK ABOUT...?
CHAPTER 24: DISGUST
clop カッ
TALK IT OVER? ALL YOU CARE ABOUT IS THE SCHOOL'S REPUTATION...!
chatter ざわ chatter ざわ
DON'T YOU INTEND TO FIND THE CRIMINAL...?!
WE'VE GOT A PERVERT IN THIS SCHOOL...!!
clop カッ

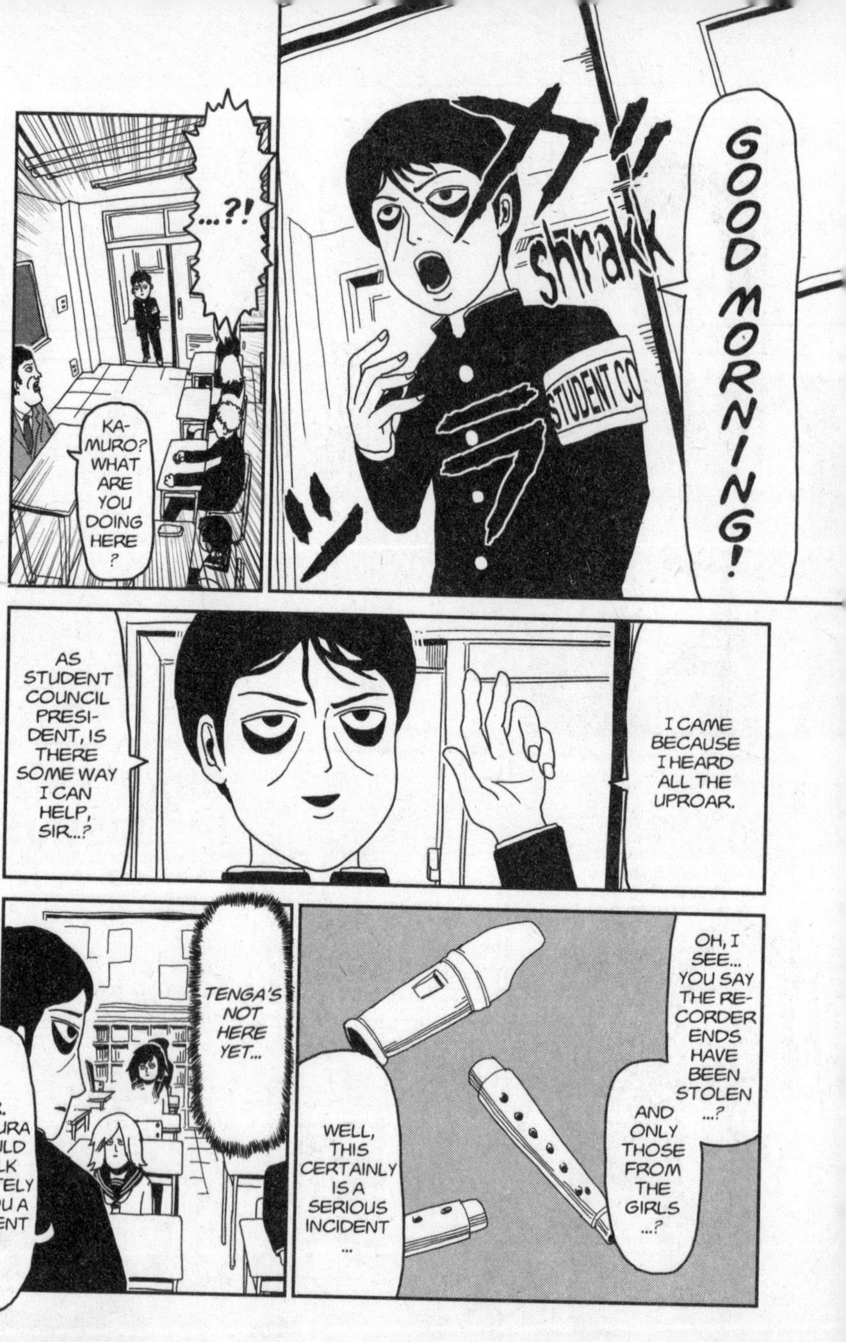
GOOD MORNING!
shrakk
STUDENT CO
...?!
KA-MURO? WHAT ARE YOU DOING HERE?
I CAME BECAUSE I HEARD ALL THE UPROAR.
AS STUDENT COUNCIL PRESIDENT, IS THERE SOME WAY I CAN HELP, SIR...?
OH, I SEE... YOU SAY THE RECORDER ENDS HAVE BEEN STOLEN...?
AND ONLY THOSE FROM THE GIRLS...?
WELL, THIS CERTAINLY IS A SERIOUS INCIDENT...
TENGA'S NOT HERE YET...
MR. KAKURA COULD TALK VATELY O YOU A OMENT ...?

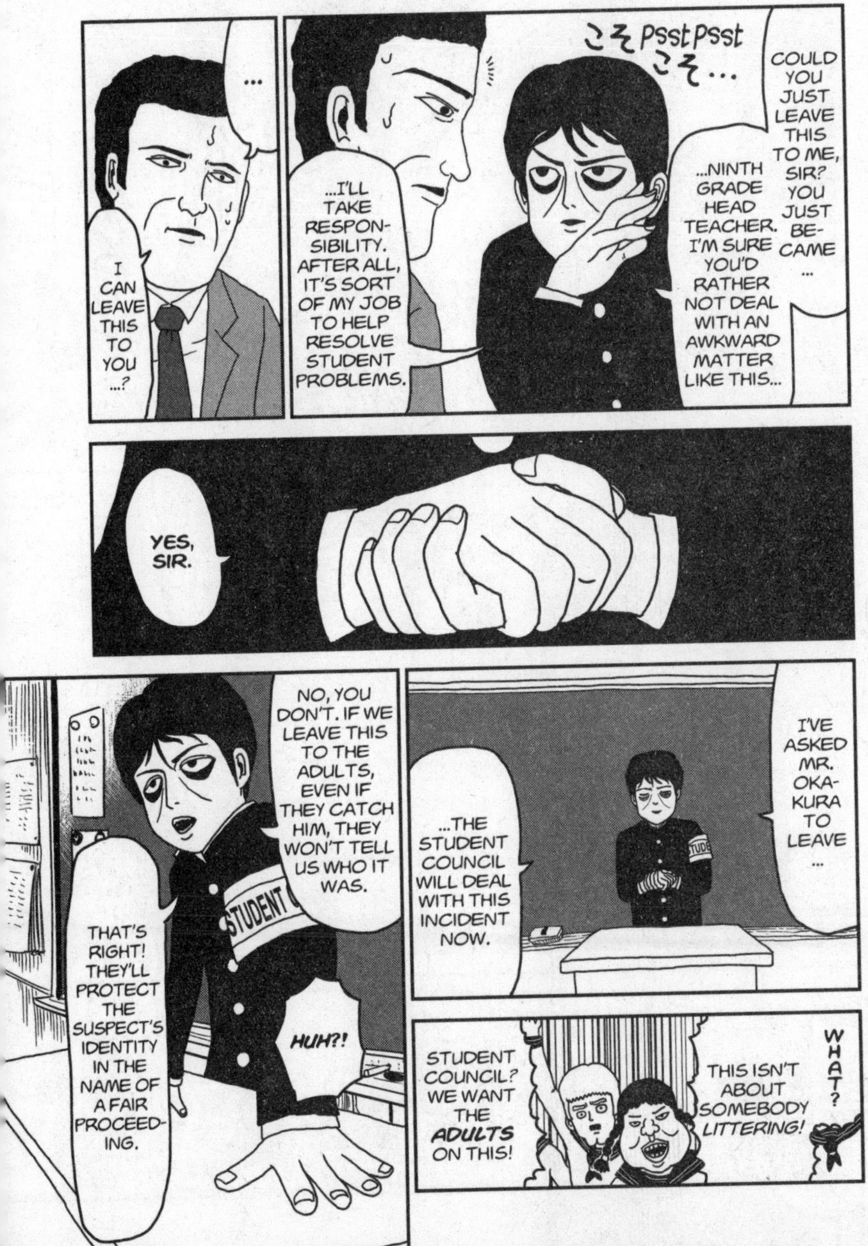
こそ PSST PSST こそ…
COULD YOU JUST LEAVE THIS TO ME, SIR? YOU JUST BECAME…
…NINTH GRADE HEAD TEACHER. I'M SURE YOU'D RATHER NOT DEAL WITH AN AWKWARD MATTER LIKE THIS…
…I'LL TAKE RESPONSIBILITY. AFTER ALL, IT'S SORT OF MY JOB TO HELP RESOLVE STUDENT PROBLEMS.
…
I CAN LEAVE THIS TO YOU …?
YES, SIR.
I'VE ASKED MR. OKAKURA TO LEAVE …
…THE STUDENT COUNCIL WILL DEAL WITH THIS INCIDENT NOW.
WHAT?
THIS ISN'T ABOUT SOMEBODY LITTERING!
STUDENT COUNCIL? WE WANT THE **ADULTS** ON THIS!
NO, YOU DON'T. IF WE LEAVE THIS TO THE ADULTS, EVEN IF THEY CATCH HIM, THEY WON'T TELL US WHO IT WAS.
THAT'S RIGHT! THEY'LL PROTECT THE SUSPECT'S IDENTITY IN THE NAME OF A FAIR PROCEEDING.
HUH?!

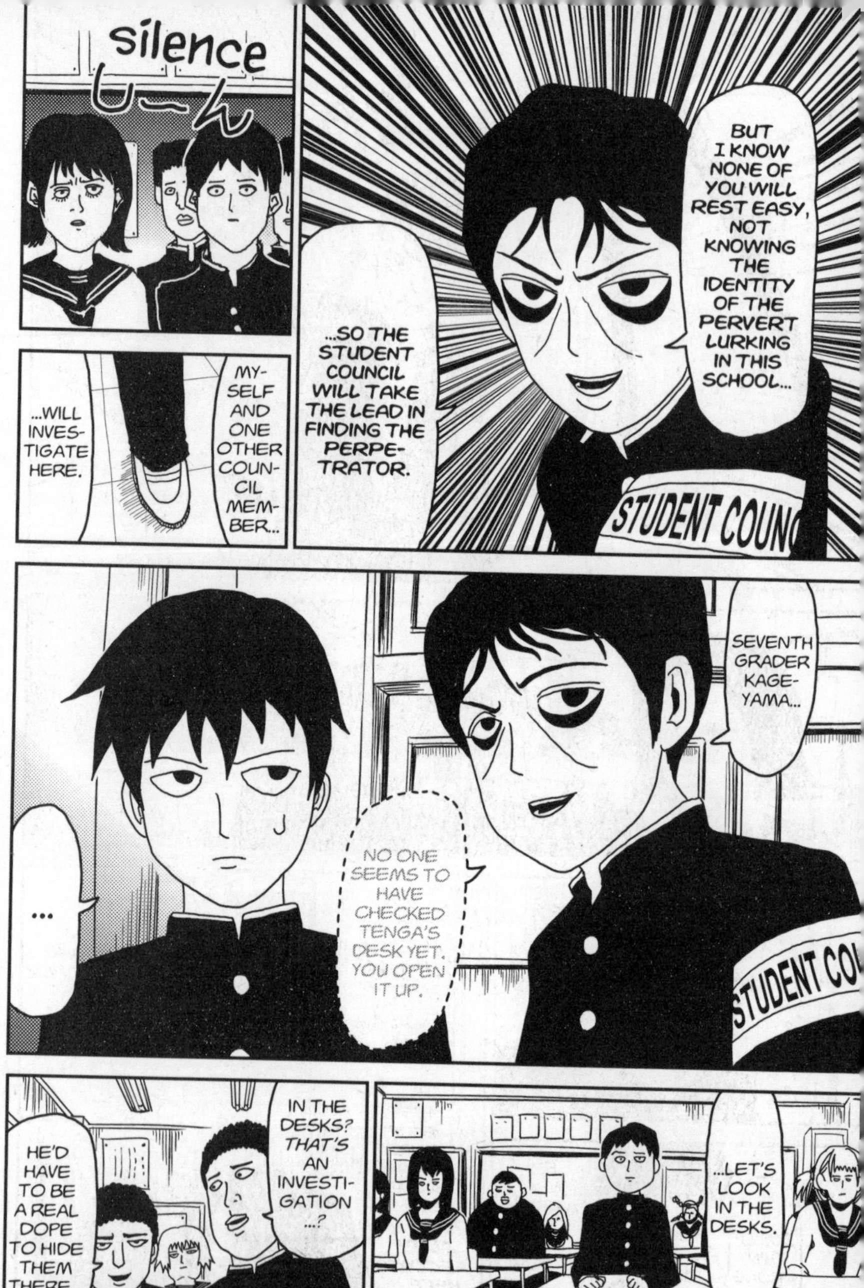
BUT I KNOW NONE OF YOU WILL REST EASY, NOT KNOWING THE IDENTITY OF THE PERVERT LURKING IN THIS SCHOOL...
...SO THE STUDENT COUNCIL WILL TAKE THE LEAD IN FINDING THE PERPETRATOR.
STUDENT COUNC
silence
しーん
MYSELF AND ONE OTHER COUNCIL MEMBER...
...WILL INVESTIGATE HERE.
SEVENTH GRADER KAGEYAMA...
NO ONE SEEMS TO HAVE CHECKED TENGA'S DESK YET. YOU OPEN IT UP.
STUDENT CO
...
...LET'S LOOK IN THE DESKS.
IN THE DESKS? THAT'S AN INVESTIGATION...?
HE'D HAVE TO BE A REAL DOPE TO HIDE THEM THERE...

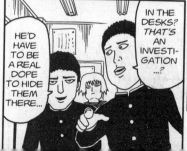

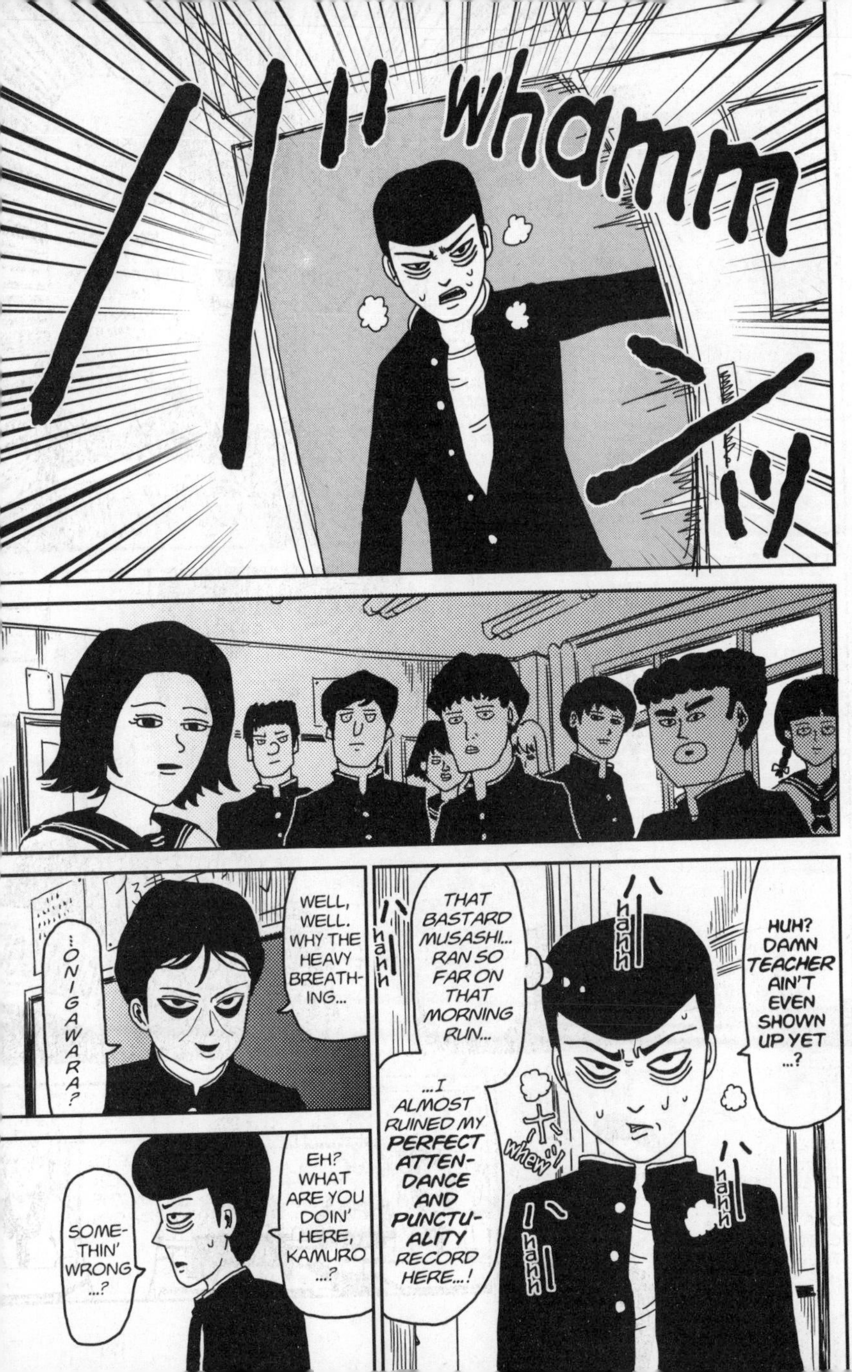
whamm
HUH? DAMN TEACHER AIN'T EVEN SHOWN UP YET ...?
hahh
hahh
THAT BASTARD MUSASHI... RAN SO FAR ON THAT MORNING RUN...
...I ALMOST RUINED MY PERFECT ATTENDANCE AND PUNCTUALITY RECORD HERE...!
whew
hahh
hahh
WELL, WELL. WHY THE HEAVY BREATHING...
...ONIGAWARA?
EH? WHAT ARE YOU DOIN' HERE, KAMURO ...?
SOMETHIN' WRONG ...?

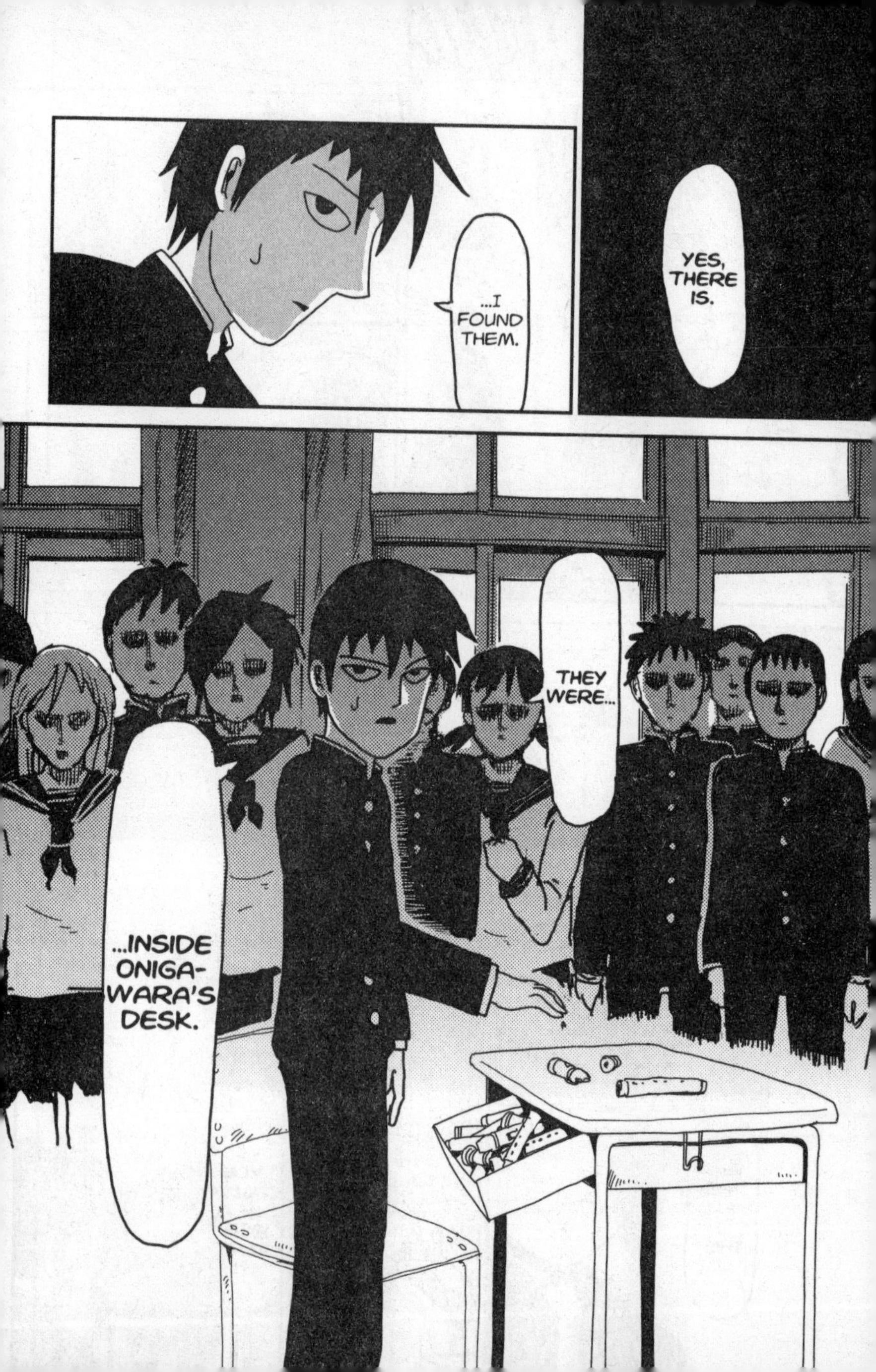
YES, THERE IS.
...I FOUND THEM.
THEY WERE...
...INSIDE ONIGA-WARA'S DESK.

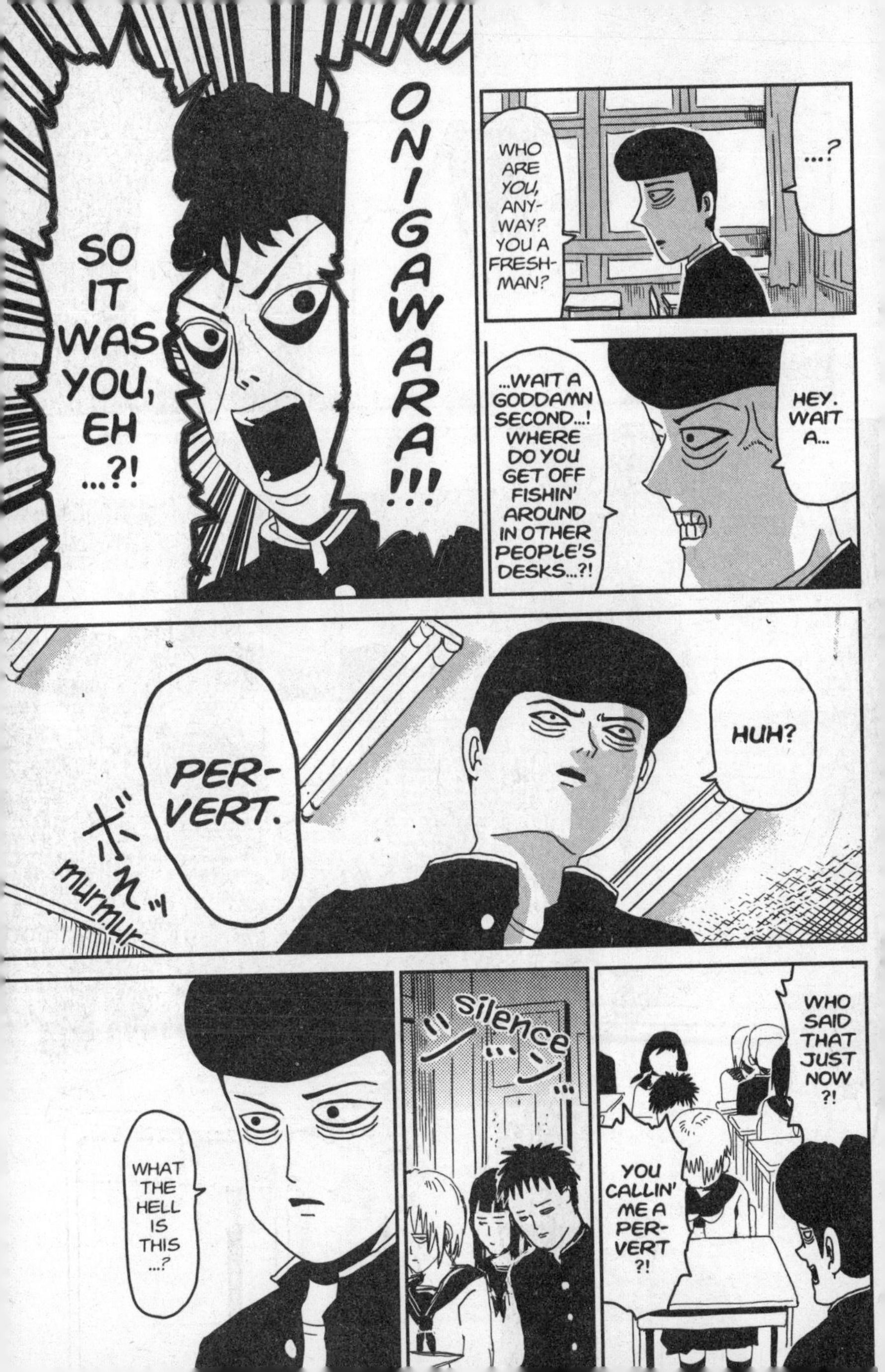
...?
WHO ARE YOU, ANY-WAY? YOU A FRESH-MAN?
HEY. WAIT A...
...WAIT A GODDAMN SECOND...! WHERE DO YOU GET OFF FISHIN' AROUND IN OTHER PEOPLE'S DESKS...?!
ONIGAWARA!!!
SO IT WAS YOU, EH ...?!
HUH?
PER-VERT.
murmur
WHO SAID THAT JUST NOW ?!
YOU CALLIN' ME A PER-VERT ?!
silence
WHAT THE HELL IS THIS ...?

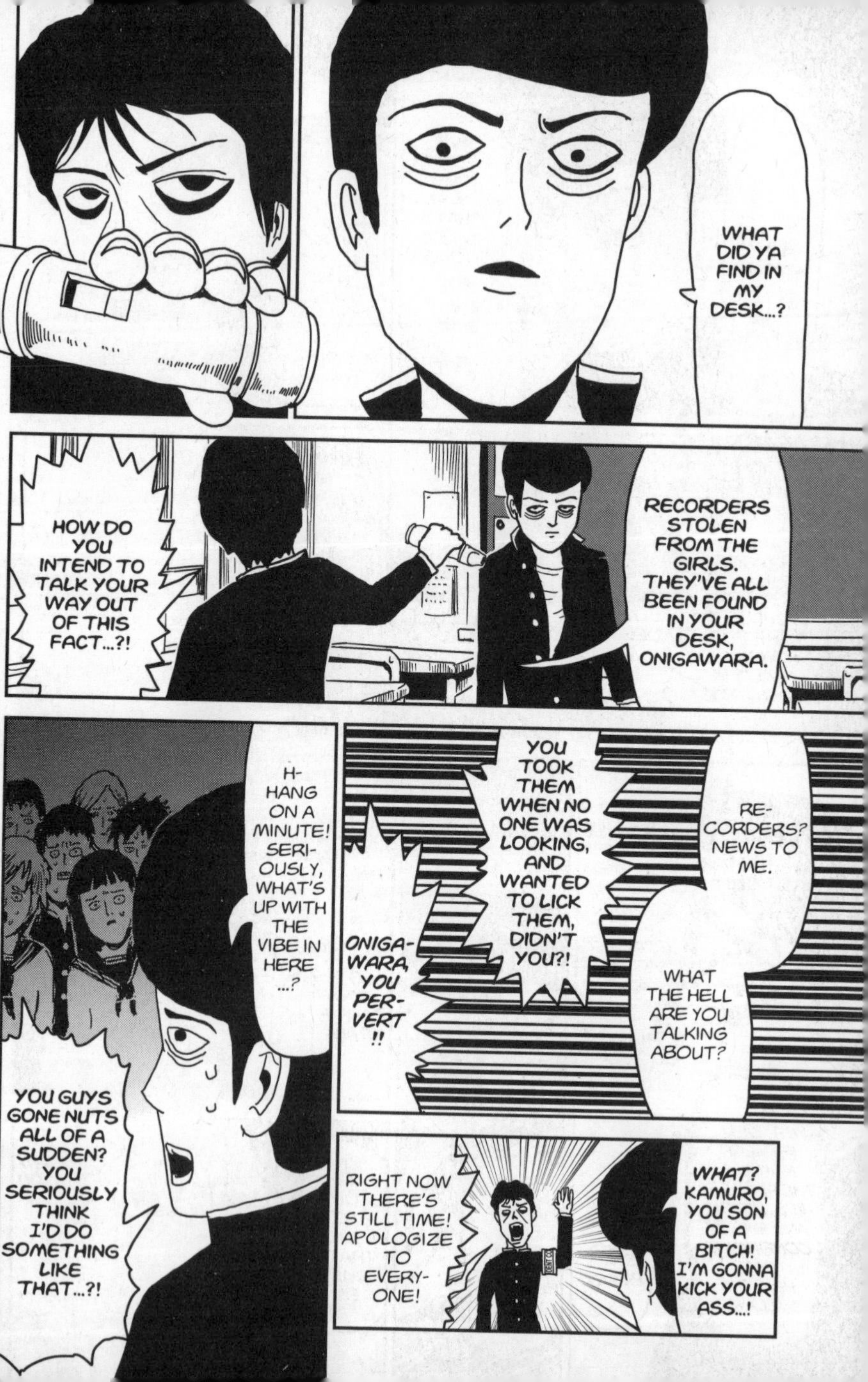
WHAT DID YA FIND IN MY DESK...?
RECORDERS STOLEN FROM THE GIRLS. THEY'VE ALL BEEN FOUND IN YOUR DESK, ONIGAWARA.
HOW DO YOU INTEND TO TALK YOUR WAY OUT OF THIS FACT...?!
RE-CORDERS? NEWS TO ME.
WHAT THE HELL ARE YOU TALKING ABOUT?
YOU TOOK THEM WHEN NO ONE WAS LOOKING, AND WANTED TO LICK THEM, DIDN'T YOU?!
ONIGA-WARA, YOU PER-VERT!!
WHAT? KAMURO, YOU SON OF A BITCH! I'M GONNA KICK YOUR ASS...!
RIGHT NOW THERE'S STILL TIME! APOLOGIZE TO EVERY-ONE!
H-HANG ON A MINUTE! SERI-OUSLY, WHAT'S UP WITH THE VIBE IN HERE ...?
YOU GUYS GONE NUTS ALL OF A SUDDEN? YOU SERIOUSLY THINK I'D DO SOMETHING LIKE THAT...?!

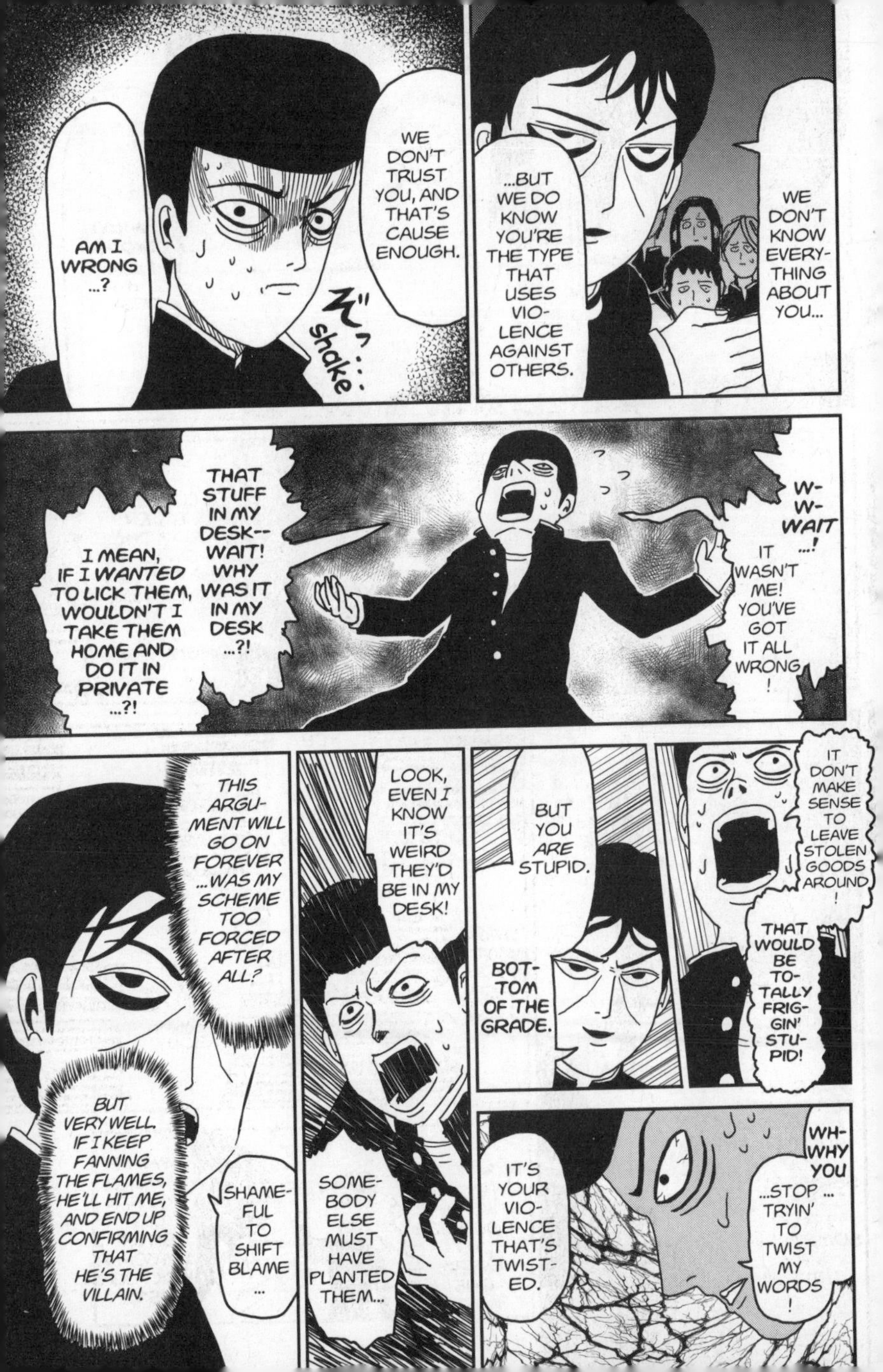
WE DON'T KNOW EVERYTHING ABOUT YOU...
...BUT WE DO KNOW YOU'RE THE TYPE THAT USES VIOLENCE AGAINST OTHERS.
WE DON'T TRUST YOU, AND THAT'S CAUSE ENOUGH.
shake
AM I WRONG ...?
W-W-WAIT ...!
IT WASN'T ME! YOU'VE GOT IT ALL WRONG!
THAT STUFF IN MY DESK-- WAIT! WHY WAS IT IN MY DESK ...?!
I MEAN, IF I WANTED TO LICK THEM, WOULDN'T I TAKE THEM HOME AND DO IT IN PRIVATE ...?!
IT DON'T MAKE SENSE TO LEAVE STOLEN GOODS AROUND!
THAT WOULD BE TOTALLY FRIGGIN' STUPID!
BUT YOU ARE STUPID.
BOTTOM OF THE GRADE.
WH-WHY YOU ...STOP ... TRYIN' TO TWIST MY WORDS!
IT'S YOUR VIOLENCE THAT'S TWISTED.
LOOK, EVEN I KNOW IT'S WEIRD THEY'D BE IN MY DESK!
SOMEBODY ELSE MUST HAVE PLANTED THEM...
THIS ARGUMENT WILL GO ON FOREVER ...WAS MY SCHEME TOO FORCED AFTER ALL?
SHAMEFUL TO SHIFT BLAME ...
BUT VERY WELL. IF I KEEP FANNING THE FLAMES, HE'LL HIT ME, AND END UP CONFIRMING THAT HE'S THE VILLAIN.

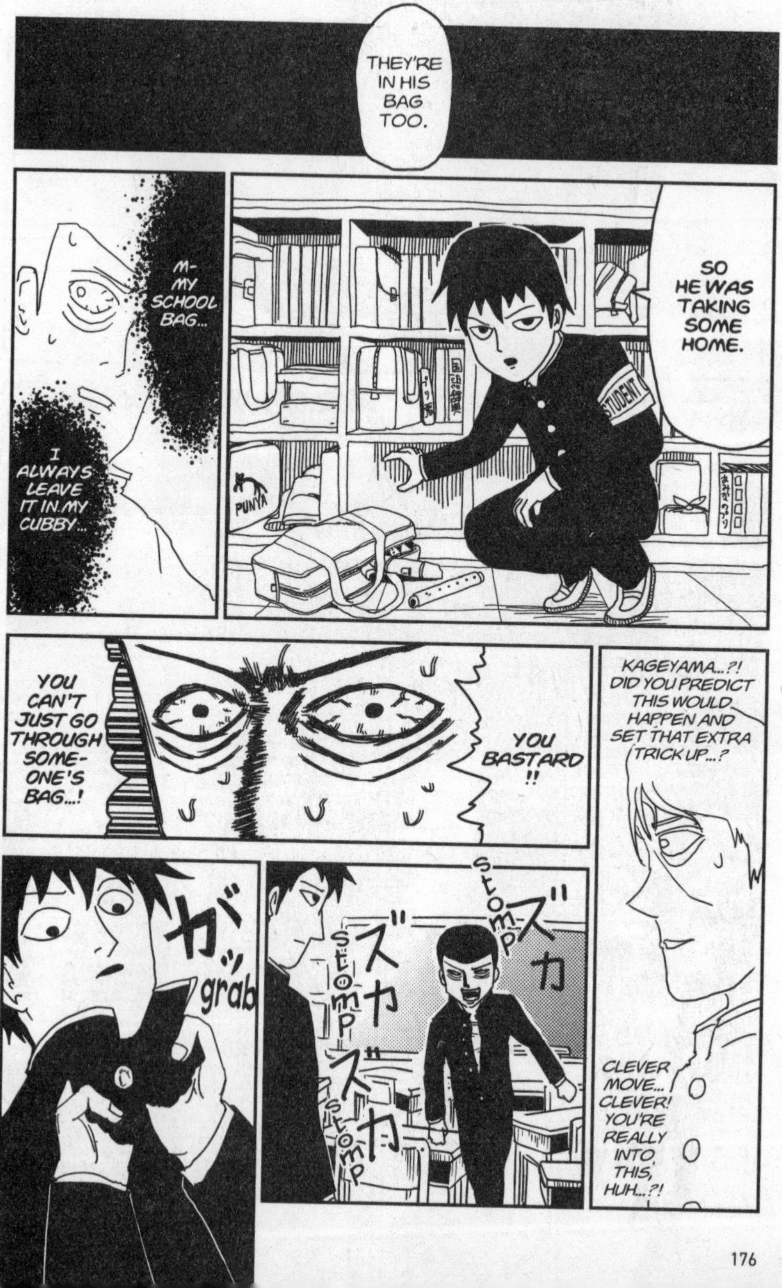
THEY'RE IN HIS BAG TOO.
SO HE WAS TAKING SOME HOME.
STUDENT
PUNYA
M-MY SCHOOL BAG...
I ALWAYS LEAVE IT IN MY CUBBY...
KAGEYAMA...?! DID YOU PREDICT THIS WOULD HAPPEN AND SET THAT EXTRA TRICK UP...?
CLEVER MOVE... CLEVER! YOU'RE REALLY INTO THIS, HUH...?!
YOU BASTARD !!
YOU CAN'T JUST GO THROUGH SOME-ONE'S BAG...!
ズカ stomp
ズカ stomp
ズカ stomp
ガッ grab

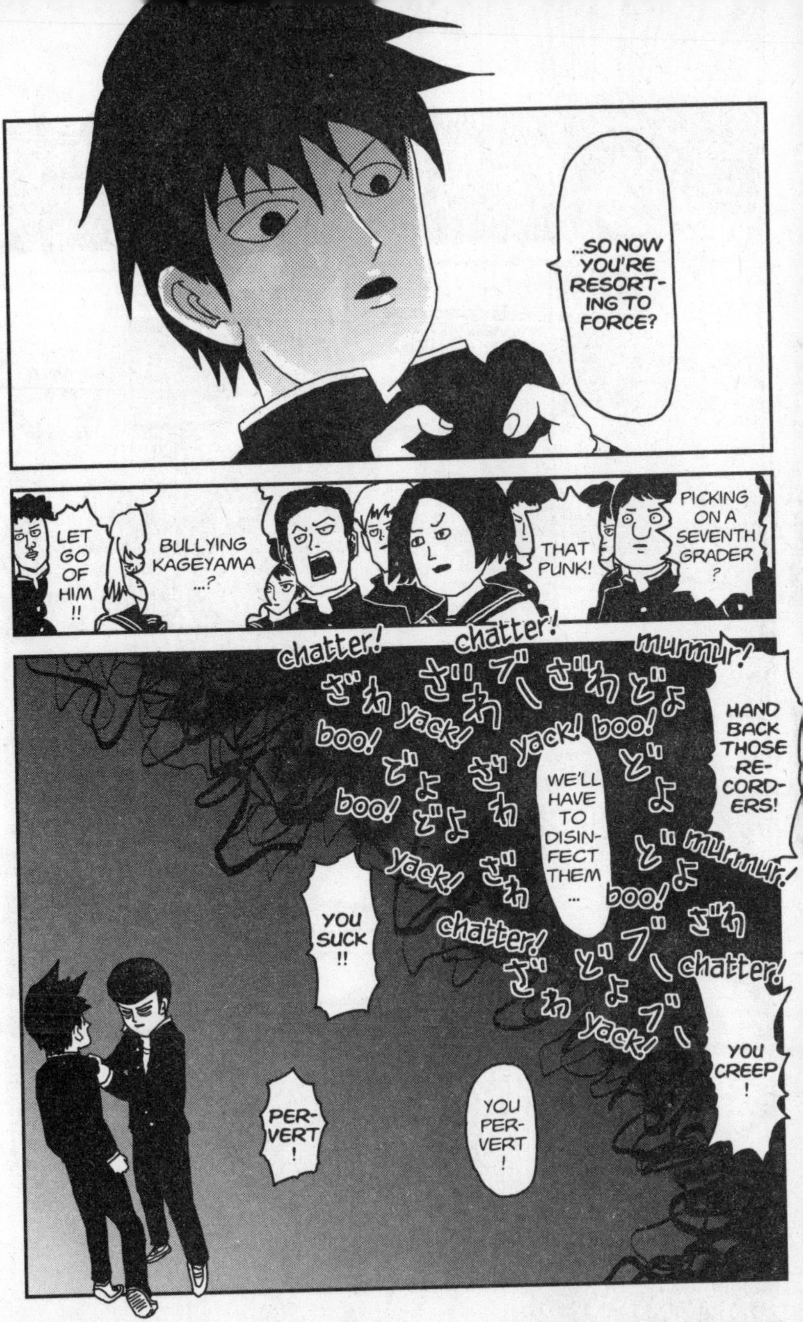
...SO NOW YOU'RE RESORTING TO FORCE?
PICKING ON A SEVENTH GRADER?
THAT PUNK!
BULLYING KAGEYAMA ...?
LET GO OF HIM!!
murmur!
chatter!
chatter!
HAND BACK THOSE RECORDERS!
WE'LL HAVE TO DISINFECT THEM ...
yack! boo!
yack!
boo!
boo!
murmur!
yack!
boo!
chatter!
chatter!
yack!
YOU CREEP!
YOU SUCK!!
YOU PERVERT!
PERVERT!

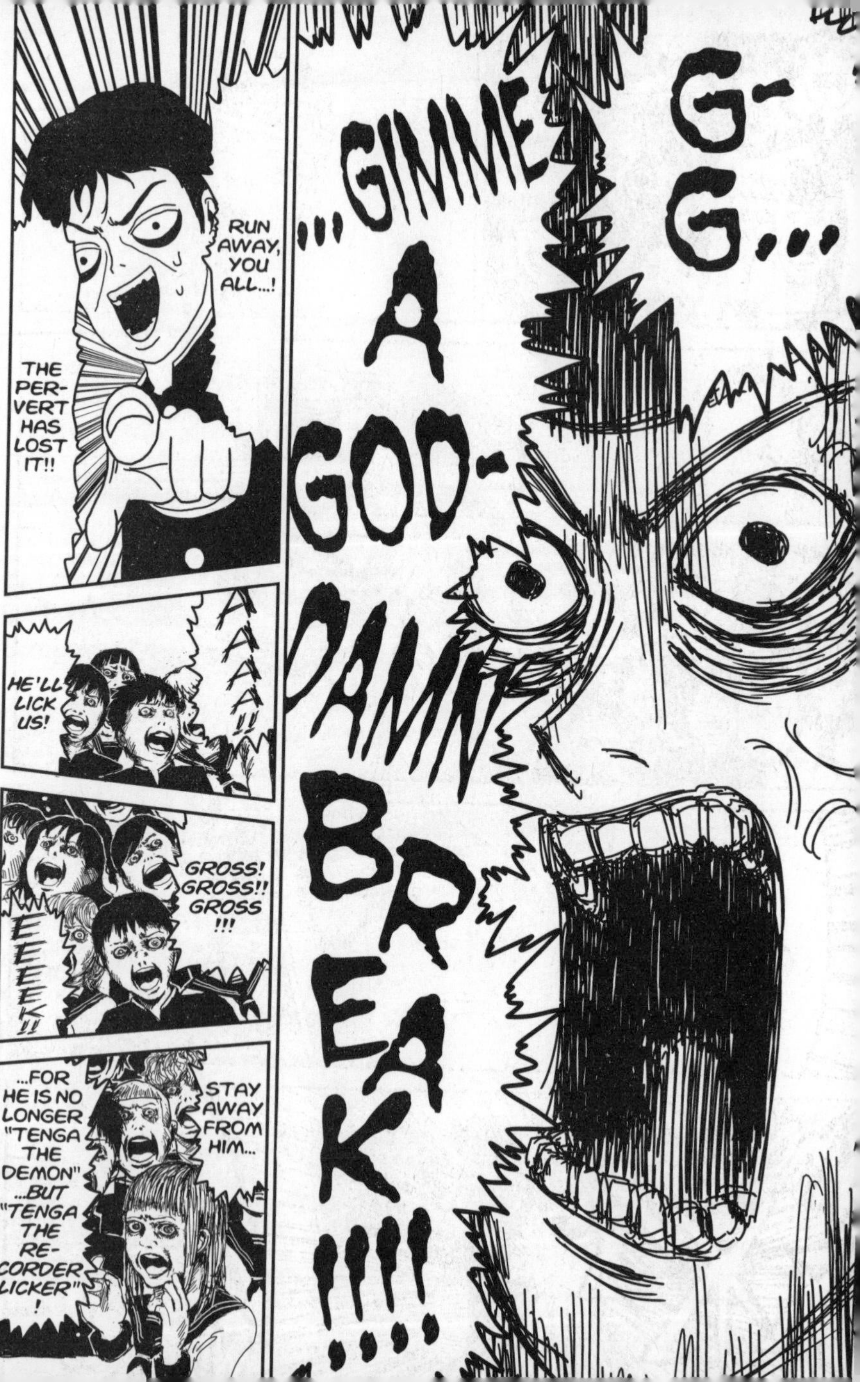
G-G...
...GIMME A GOD-DAMN BREAK!!!!
RUN AWAY, YOU ALL...!
THE PERVERT HAS LOST IT!!
AAAAA!!
HE'LL LICK US!
GROSS! GROSS!! GROSS!!!
EEEEEK!!
STAY AWAY FROM HIM...
...FOR HE IS NO LONGER "TENGA THE DEMON" ...BUT "TENGA THE RECORDER LICKER"!

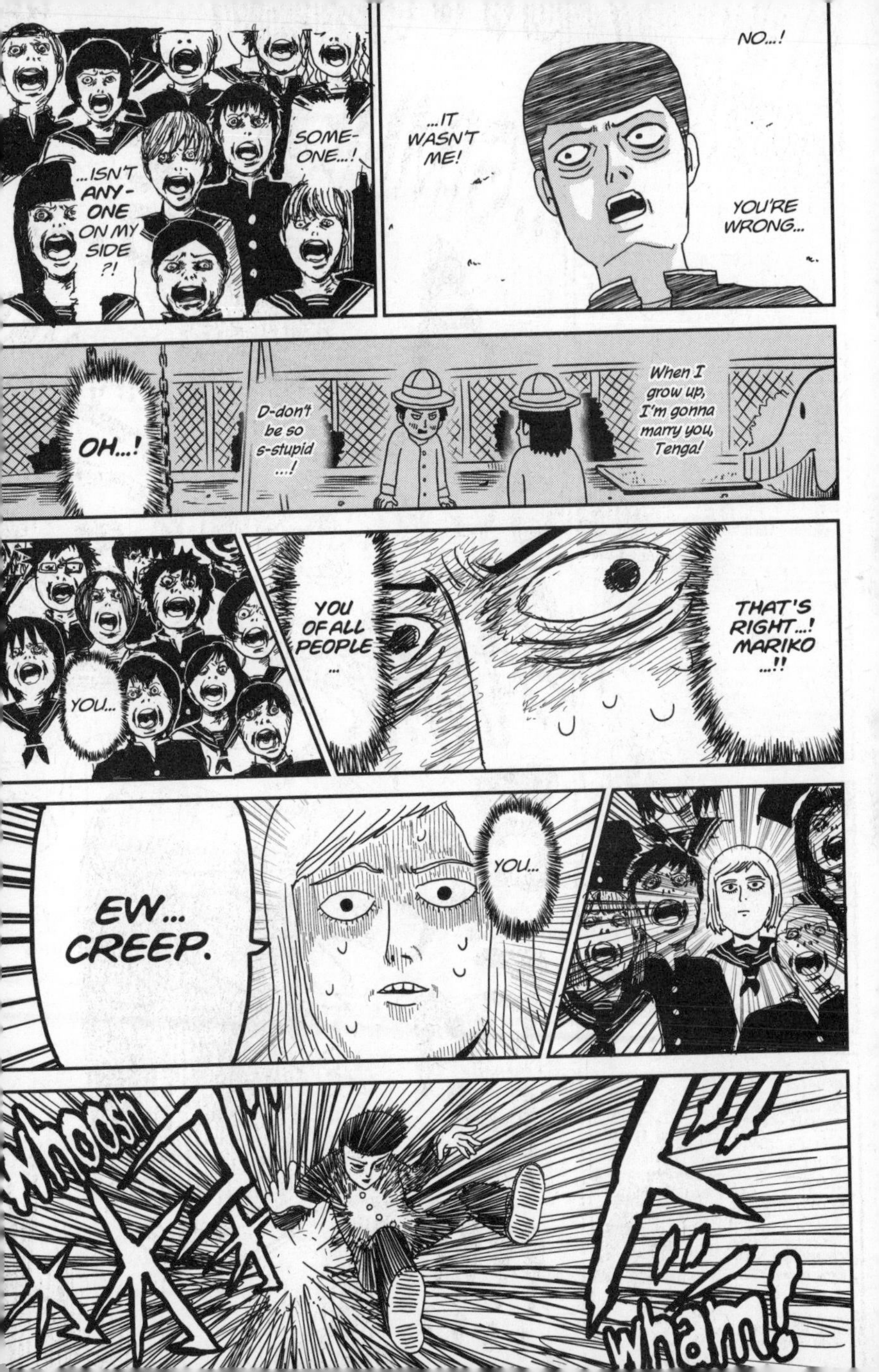
NO...!
...IT WASN'T ME!
YOU'RE WRONG...
SOME-ONE...!
...ISN'T ANY-ONE ON MY SIDE ?!
When I grow up, I'm gonna marry you, Tenga!
D-don't be so s-stupid ...!
OH...!
THAT'S RIGHT...! MARIKO ...!!
YOU OF ALL PEOPLE ...
YOU...
YOU...
EW... CREEP.
wham!
WHOOSH

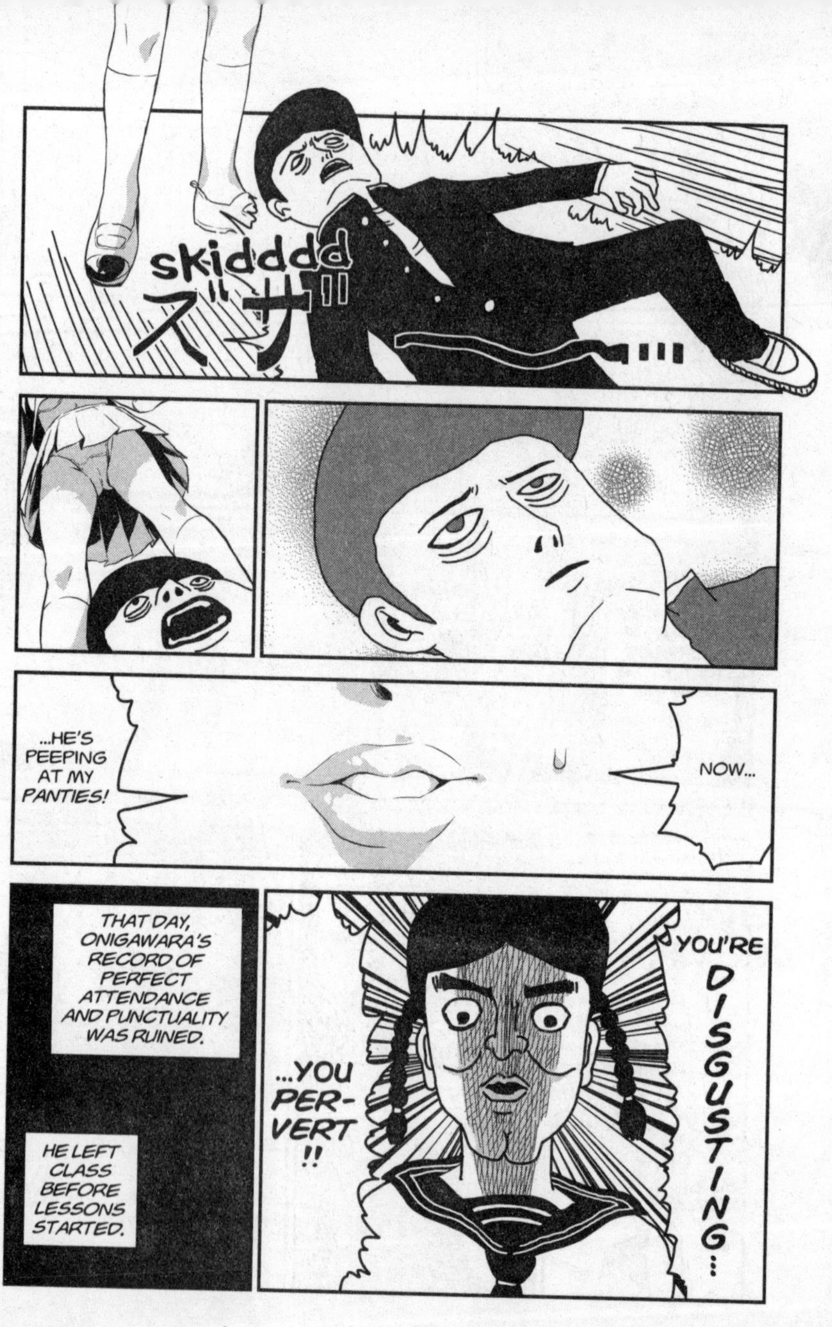
skidddd
NOW...
...HE'S PEEPING AT MY PANTIES!
YOU'RE DISGUSTING...
...YOU PER-VERT!!
THAT DAY, ONIGAWARA'S RECORD OF PERFECT ATTENDANCE AND PUNCTUALITY WAS RUINED.
HE LEFT CLASS BEFORE LESSONS STARTED.

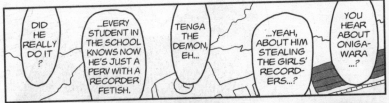

YOU HEAR ABOUT ONIGA-WARA ...?
...YEAH, ABOUT HIM STEALING THE GIRLS' RECORD-ERS...?
TENGA THE DEMON, EH...
...EVERY STUDENT IN THE SCHOOL KNOWS NOW HE'S JUST A PERV WITH A RECORDER FETISH.
DID HE REALLY DO IT ?
...WHAT'S WRONG, ONIGAWARA? YOU RAN IN SUCH GOOD SPIRITS THIS MORNING.
YOU DIDN'T DO IT, RIGHT ...?
...IN WHICH CASE, YOU OUGHT TO HOLD YOUR HEAD UP!
I'VE BEEN SET UP. SOME-THING ...
...IS GOING ON HERE.
LEAVE HIM BE. WE'RE GOING TO START OUR RUN, CHIEF.
KAGE-YAMA, LET'S GO.
...

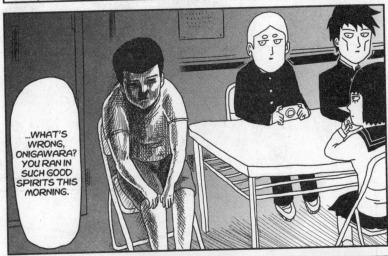

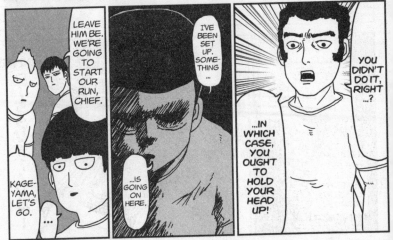

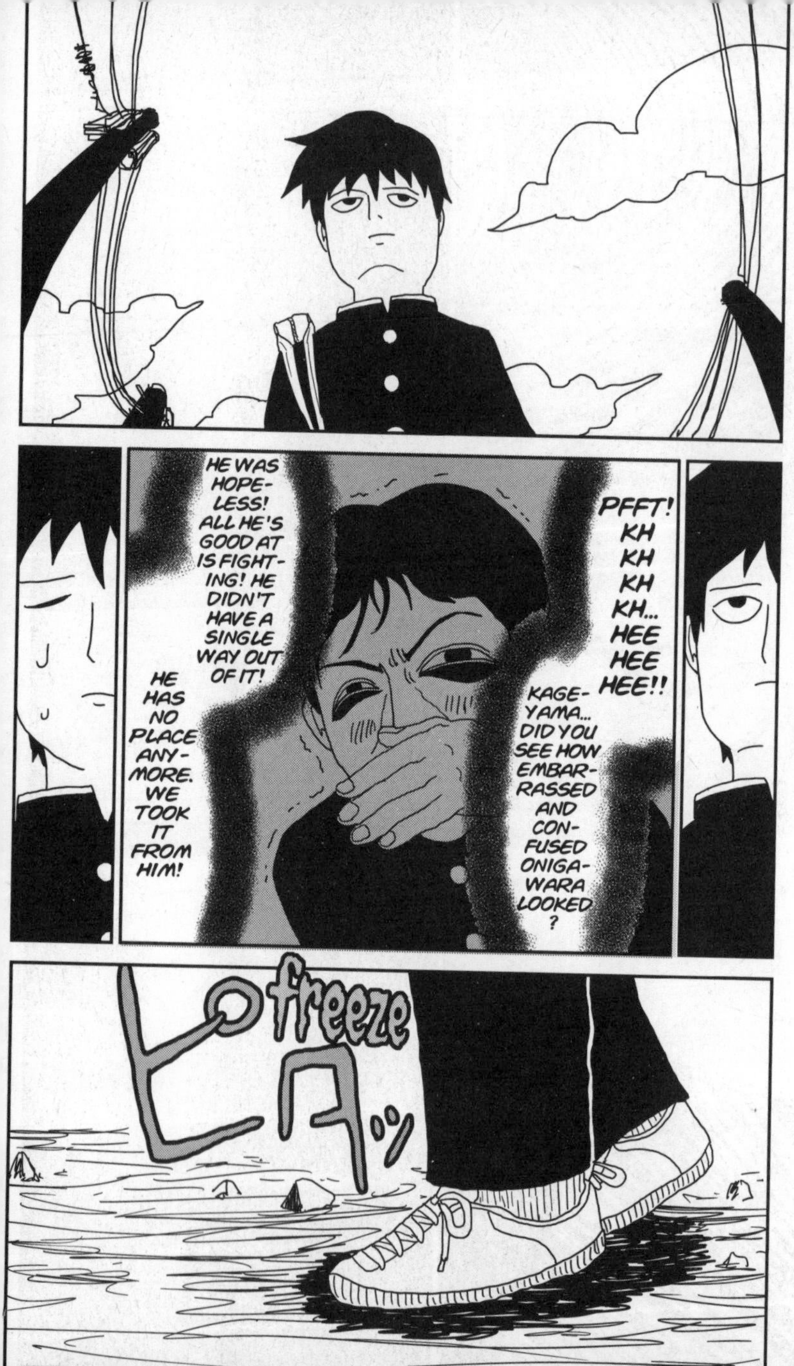
PFFT! KH KH KH KH... HEE HEE HEE!!
KAGE-YAMA... DID YOU SEE HOW EMBAR-RASSED AND CON-FUSED ONIGA-WARA LOOKED?
HE WAS HOPE-LESS! ALL HE'S GOOD AT IS FIGHT-ING! HE DIDN'T HAVE A SINGLE WAY OUT OF IT!
HE HAS NO PLACE ANY-MORE. WE TOOK IT FROM HIM!
freeze
ヒタッ

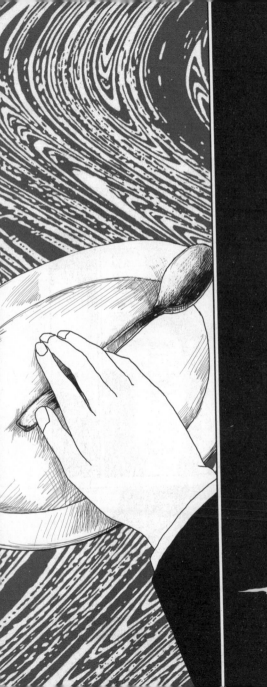

I'M THE
WORST...

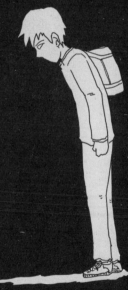

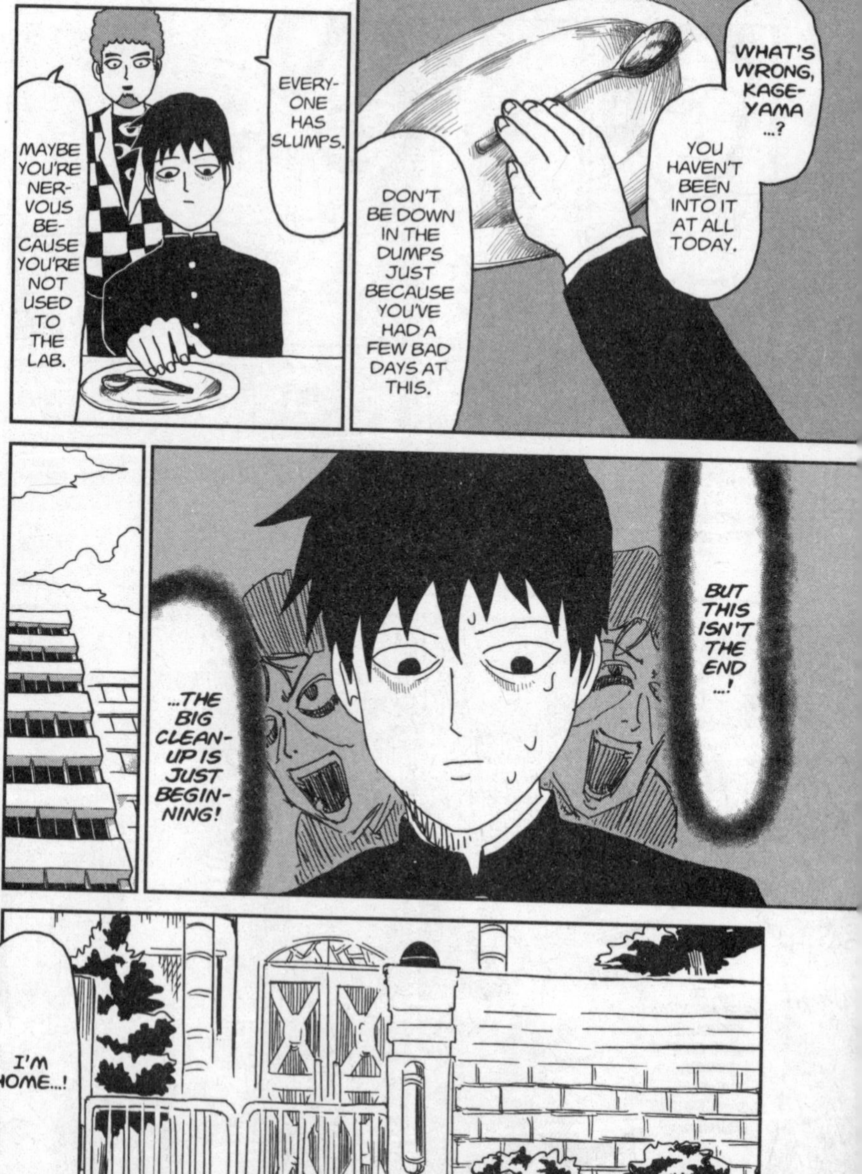
WHAT'S WRONG, KAGEYAMA ...?
YOU HAVEN'T BEEN INTO IT AT ALL TODAY.
DON'T BE DOWN IN THE DUMPS JUST BECAUSE YOU'VE HAD A FEW BAD DAYS AT THIS.
EVERYONE HAS SLUMPS.
MAYBE YOU'RE NERVOUS BECAUSE YOU'RE NOT USED TO THE LAB.
BUT THIS ISN'T THE END ...!
...THE BIG CLEANUP IS JUST BEGINNING!
I'M HOME...!

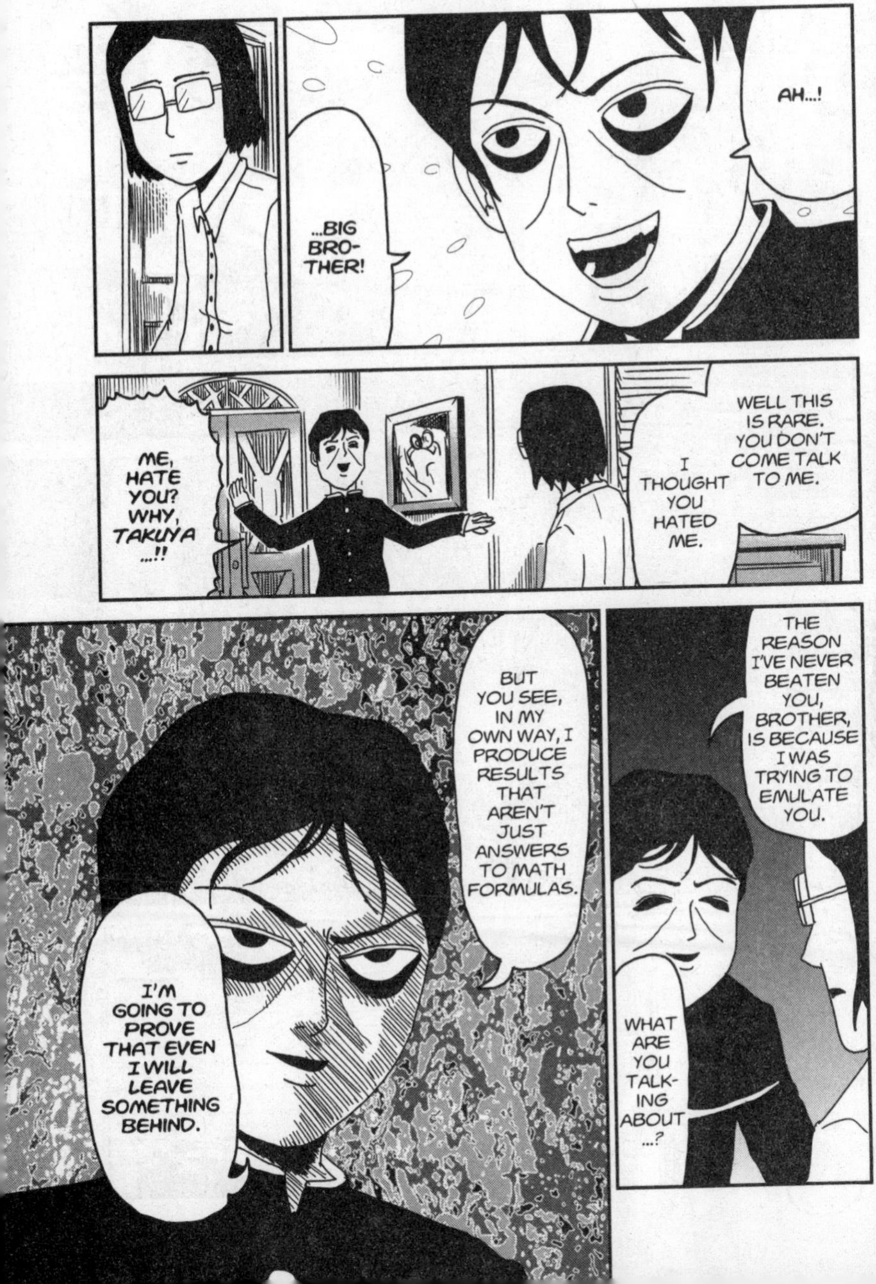
AH...!
...BIG BRO- THER!
WELL THIS IS RARE. YOU DON'T COME TALK TO ME.
I THOUGHT YOU HATED ME.
ME, HATE YOU? WHY, TAKUYA ...!!
THE REASON I'VE NEVER BEATEN YOU, BROTHER, IS BECAUSE I WAS TRYING TO EMULATE YOU.
WHAT ARE YOU TALK- ING ABOUT ...?
BUT YOU SEE, IN MY OWN WAY, I PRODUCE RESULTS THAT AREN'T JUST ANSWERS TO MATH FORMULAS.
I'M GOING TO PROVE THAT EVEN I WILL LEAVE SOMETHING BEHIND.

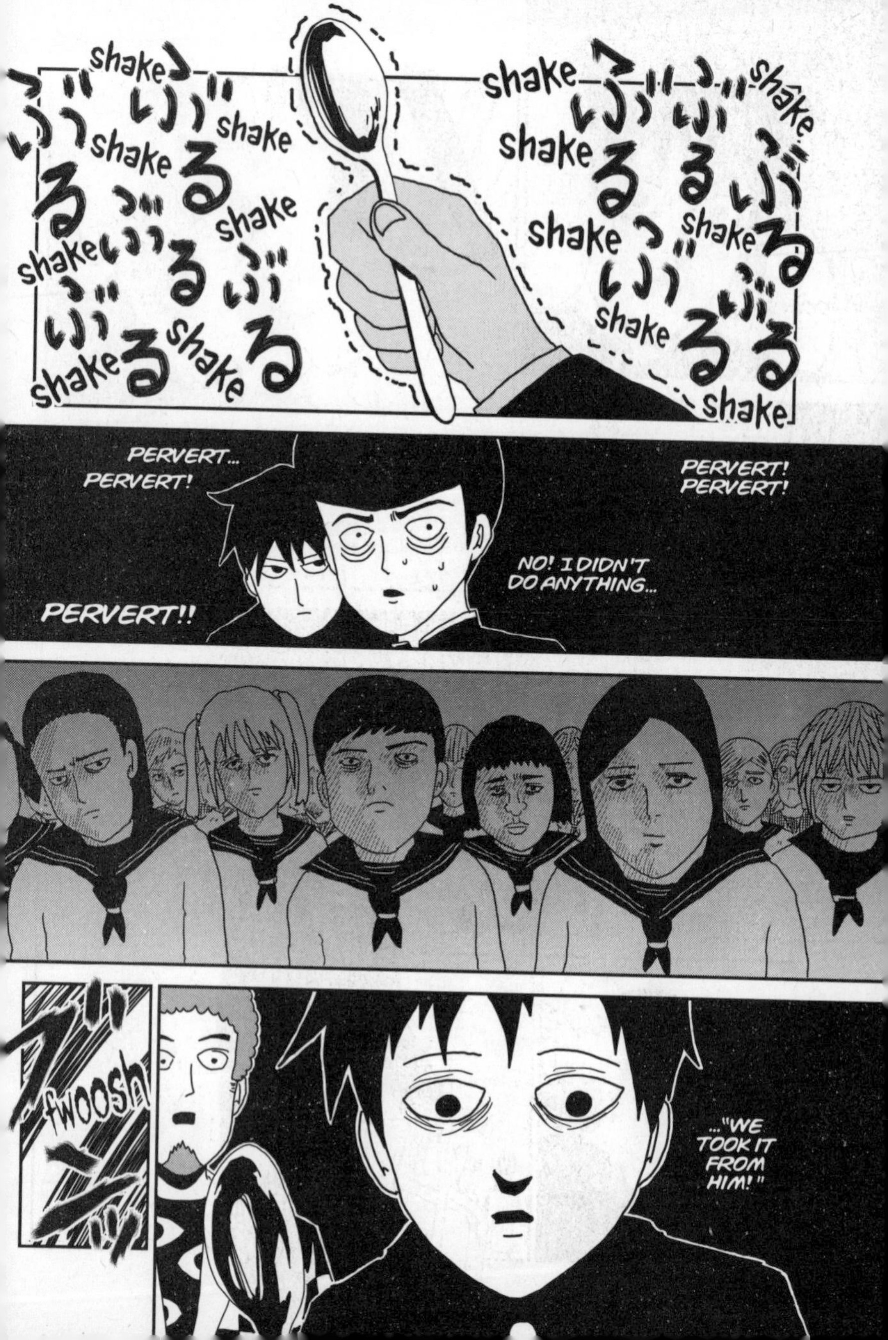
ぶるぶる
shake
ぶるぶる
shake
ぶるぶる
shake
PERVERT! PERVERT!
NO! I DIDN'T DO ANYTHING...
PERVERT... PERVERT!
PERVERT!!
..."WE TOOK IT FROM HIM!"
fwoosh

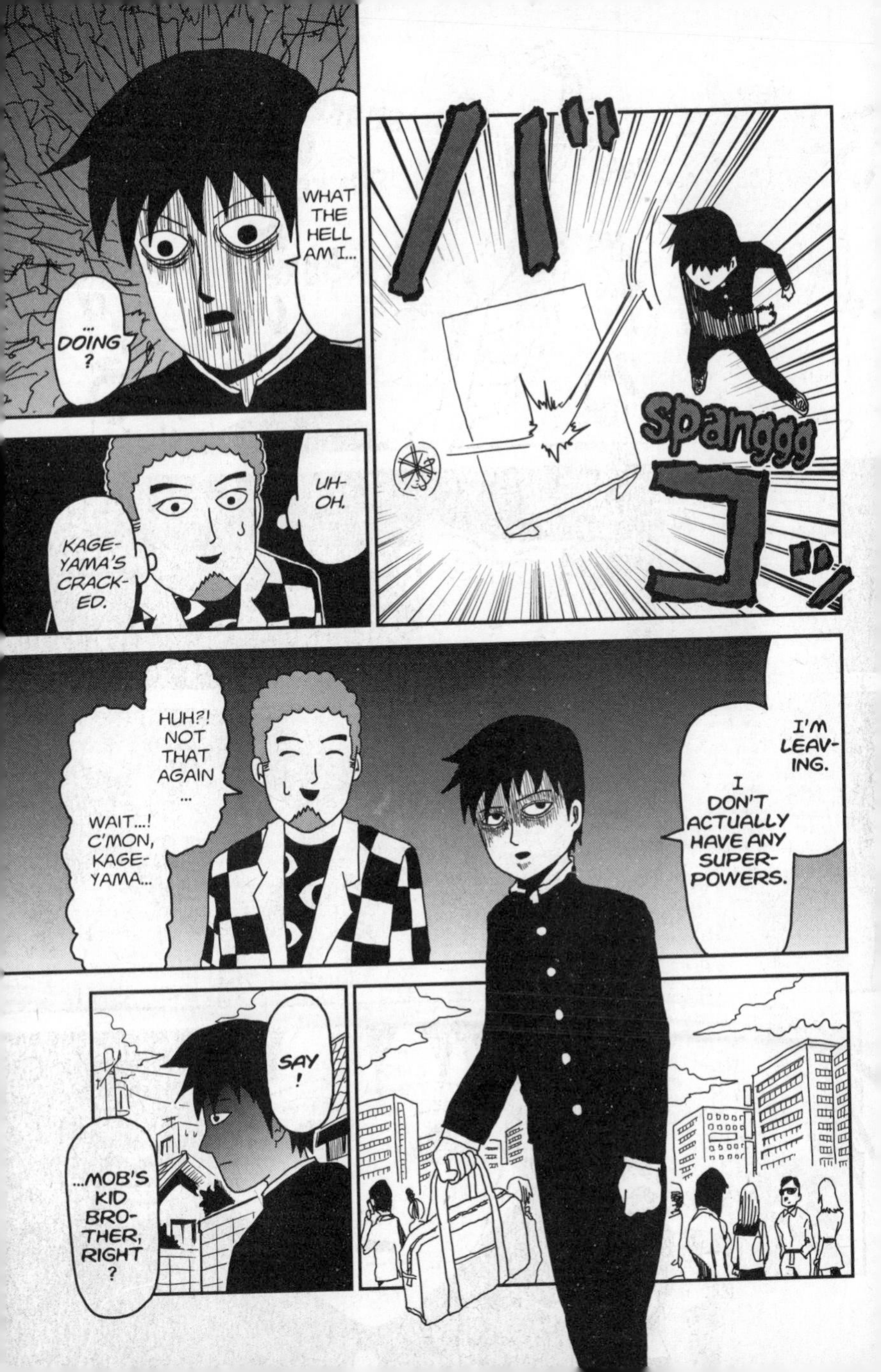
Spanggg
WHAT THE HELL AM I...
...DOING?
UH-OH.
KAGE-YAMA'S CRACK-ED.
I'M LEAV-ING.
I DON'T ACTUALLY HAVE ANY SUPER-POWERS.
HUH?! NOT THAT AGAIN ...
WAIT...! C'MON, KAGE-YAMA...
SAY!
...MOB'S KID BRO-THER, RIGHT?

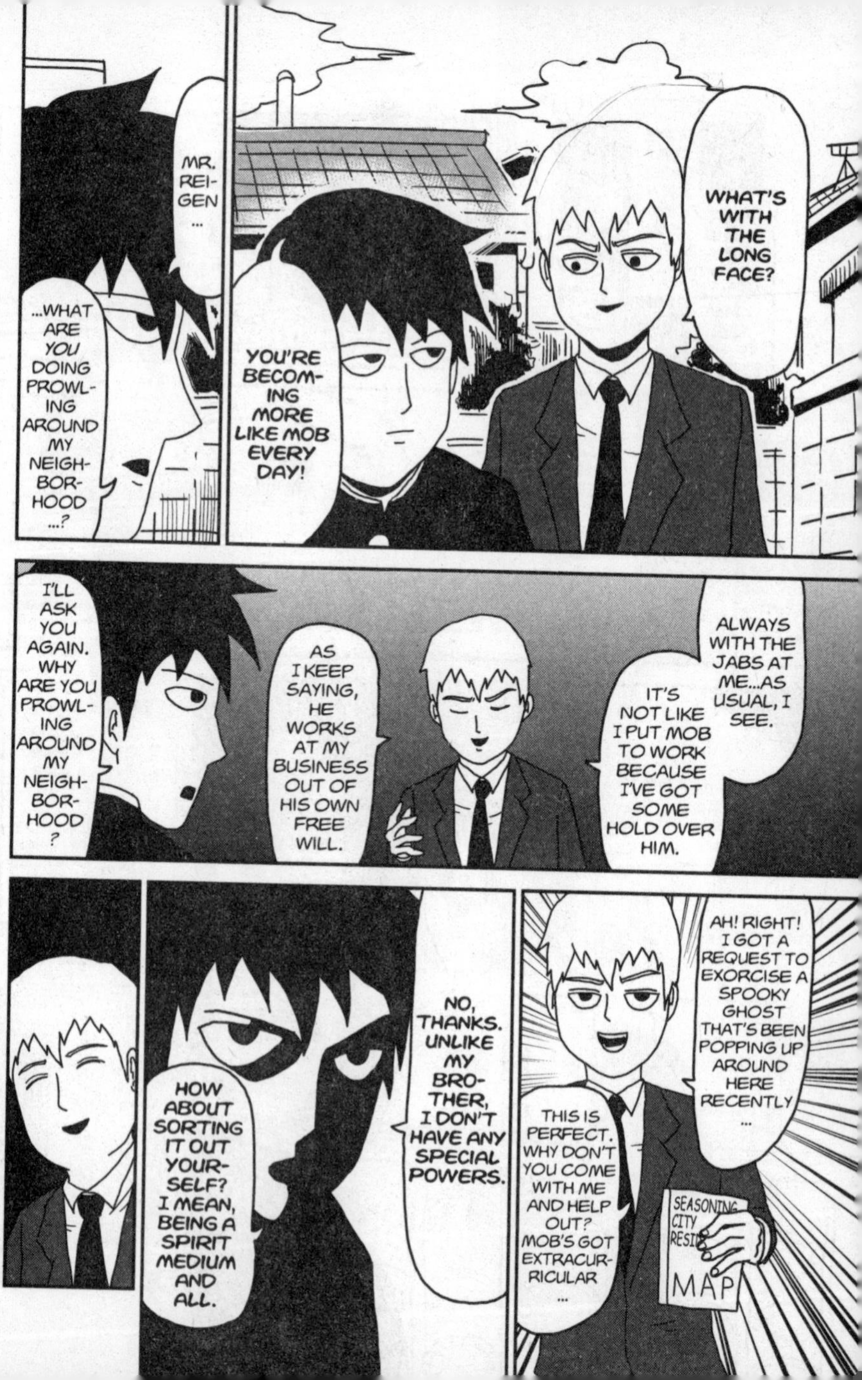
WHAT'S WITH THE LONG FACE?
YOU'RE BECOMING MORE LIKE MOB EVERY DAY!
MR. REIGEN ...
...WHAT ARE *YOU* DOING PROWLING AROUND MY NEIGHBORHOOD ...?
ALWAYS WITH THE JABS AT ME...AS USUAL, I SEE.
IT'S NOT LIKE I PUT MOB TO WORK BECAUSE I'VE GOT SOME HOLD OVER HIM.
AS I KEEP SAYING, HE WORKS AT MY BUSINESS OUT OF HIS OWN FREE WILL.
I'LL ASK YOU AGAIN. WHY ARE YOU PROWLING AROUND MY NEIGHBORHOOD?
AH! RIGHT! I GOT A REQUEST TO EXORCISE A SPOOKY GHOST THAT'S BEEN POPPING UP AROUND HERE RECENTLY ...
THIS IS PERFECT. WHY DON'T YOU COME WITH ME AND HELP OUT? MOB'S GOT EXTRACURRICULAR ...
SEASONING CITY
MAP
NO, THANKS. UNLIKE MY BROTHER, I DON'T HAVE ANY SPECIAL POWERS.
HOW ABOUT SORTING IT OUT YOURSELF? I MEAN, BEING A SPIRIT MEDIUM AND ALL.

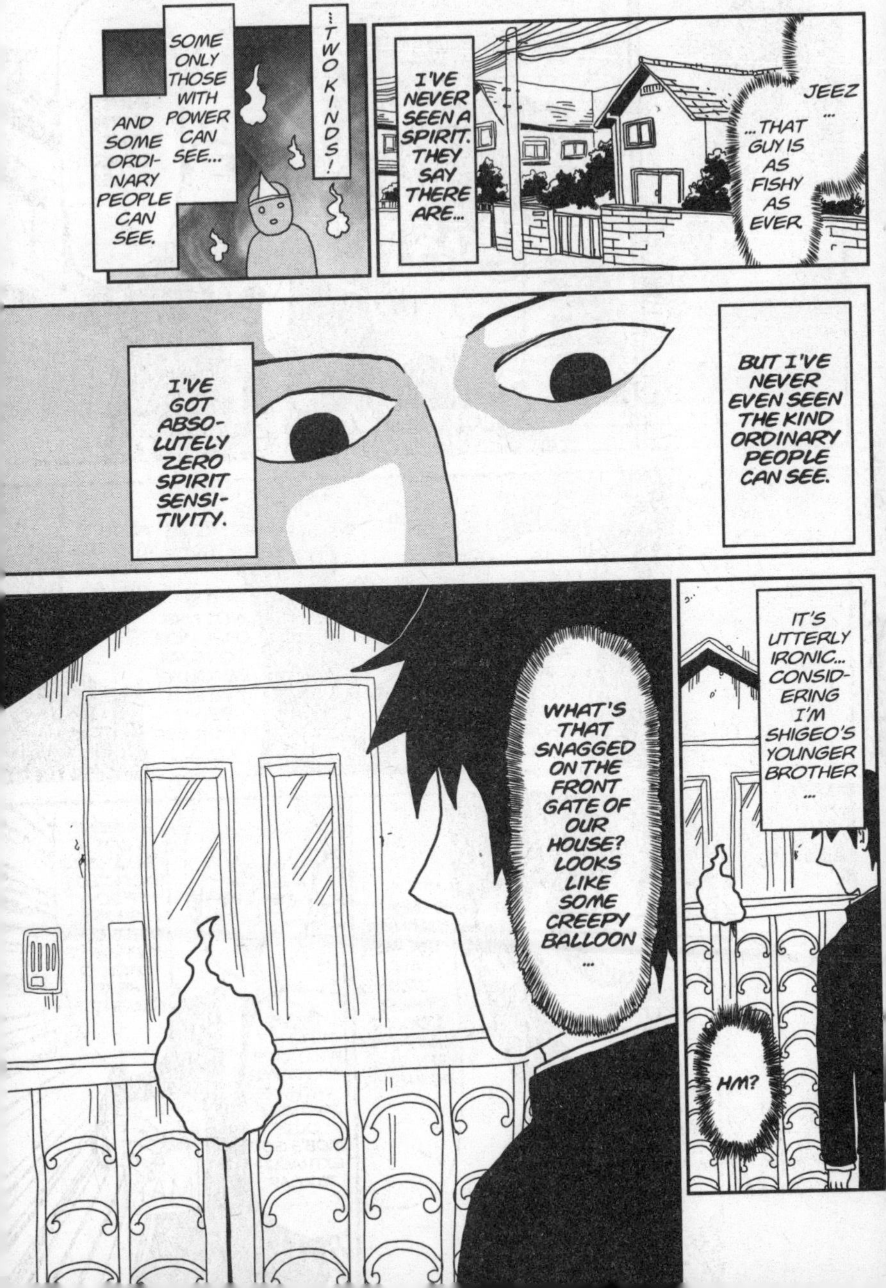
JEEZ...
...THAT GUY IS AS FISHY AS EVER.
I'VE NEVER SEEN A SPIRIT. THEY SAY THERE ARE...
...TWO KINDS!
SOME ONLY THOSE WITH POWER CAN SEE...
AND SOME ORDINARY PEOPLE CAN SEE.
BUT I'VE NEVER EVEN SEEN THE KIND ORDINARY PEOPLE CAN SEE.
I'VE GOT ABSOLUTELY ZERO SPIRIT SENSITIVITY.
IT'S UTTERLY IRONIC... CONSIDERING I'M SHIGEO'S YOUNGER BROTHER...
HM?
WHAT'S THAT SNAGGED ON THE FRONT GATE OF OUR HOUSE? LOOKS LIKE SOME CREEPY BALLOON...

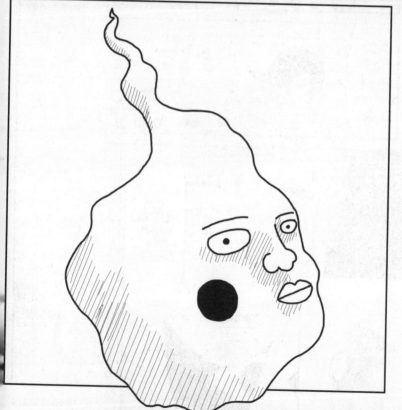

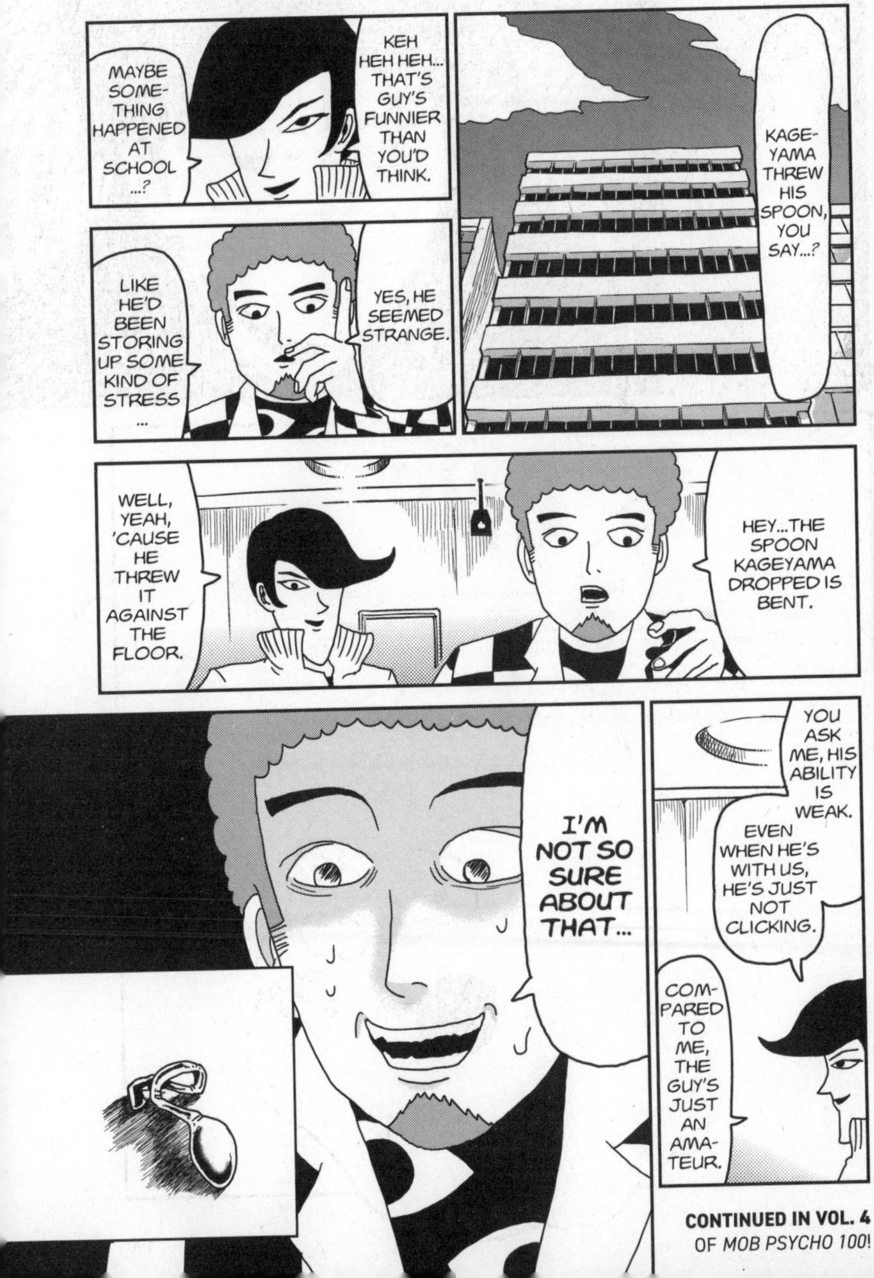
KAGEYAMA THREW HIS SPOON, YOU SAY...?
KEH HEH HEH... THAT'S GUY'S FUNNIER THAN YOU'D THINK.
MAYBE SOMETHING HAPPENED AT SCHOOL ...?
YES, HE SEEMED STRANGE.
LIKE HE'D BEEN STORING UP SOME KIND OF STRESS ...
HEY...THE SPOON KAGEYAMA DROPPED IS BENT.
WELL, YEAH, 'CAUSE HE THREW IT AGAINST THE FLOOR.
YOU ASK ME, HIS ABILITY IS WEAK.
EVEN WHEN HE'S WITH US, HE'S JUST NOT CLICKING.
COMPARED TO ME, THE GUY'S JUST AN AMATEUR.
I'M NOT SO SURE ABOUT THAT...

CONTINUED IN VOL. 4
OF *MOB PSYCHO 100*!

ONE

Thanks to the many thoughts sent by my readers, though I don't ordinarily meet a lot of people, I feel like I've been having many conversations. And it's thanks to you that I was able to produce Volume 3. Thank you!

president and publisher
MIKE RICHARDSON

editor
CARL GUSTAV HORN

designer
BRENNAN THOME

digital art technician
SAMANTHA HUMMER

English-language version produced by Dark Horse Comics

MOB PSYCHO 100

MOB PSYCHO 100 Volume 3 by ONE © 2013 ONE. All rights reserved. Original Japanese edition published by SHOGAKUKAN. English translation rights arranged with SHOGAKUKAN through Tuttle-Mori Agency, Inc., Tokyo. This English-language edition © 2019 by Dark Horse Comics LLC. All other material © 2019 by Dark Horse Comics LLC. Dark Horse Manga™ is a trademark of Dark Horse Comics LLC. All rights reserved. No portion of this publication may be reproduced or transmitted, in any form or by any means, without the express written permission of Dark Horse Comics LLC. Names, characters, places, and incidents featured in this publication either are the product of the author's imagination or are used fictitiously. Any resemblance to actual persons (living or dead), events, institutions, or locales, without satiric intent, is coincidental.

Published by Dark Horse Manga
A division of Dark Horse Comics LLC
10956 SE Main Street, Milwaukie, OR 97222

DarkHorse.com

To find a comics shop in your area, visit comicshoplocator.com.

First edition: July 2019 | ISBN 978-1-50670-989-5
Digital ISBN 978-1-50671-148-5

7 9 10 8

Printed in the United States of America

NEIL HANKERSON EXECUTIVE VICE PRESIDENT **TOM WEDDLE** CHIEF FINANCIAL OFFICER **DALE LAFOUNTAIN** CHIEF INFORMATION OFFICER **TIM WIESCH** VICE PRESIDENT OF LICENSING **VANESSA TODD-HOLMES** VICE PRESIDENT OF PRODUCTION AND SCHEDULING **MARK BERNARDI** VICE PRESIDENT OF BOOK TRADE AND DIGITAL SALES **RANDY LAHRMAN** VICE PRESIDENT OF PRODUCT DEVELOPMENT AND SALES **KEN LIZZI** GENERAL COUNSEL **DAVE MARSHALL** EDITOR IN CHIEF **DAVEY ESTRADA** EDITORIAL DIRECTOR **CHRIS WARNER** SENIOR BOOKS EDITOR **CARA O'NEIL** SENIOR DIRECTOR OF MARKETING **CARY GRAZZINI** DIRECTOR OF SPECIALTY PROJECTS **LIA RIBACCHI** ART DIRECTOR **MICHAEL GOMBOS** SENIOR DIRECTOR OF LICENSED PUBLICATIONS **KARI YADRO** DIRECTOR OF CUSTOM PROGRAMS **KARI TORSON** DIRECTOR OF INTERNATIONAL LICENSING · **CHRISTINA NIECE** DIRECTOR OF SCHEDULING

KEEP YOUR HANDS OFF EIZOUKEN!

By Sumito Oowara

Asakusa loves to design worlds. Mizusaki loves to animate. Kanamori loves to make money! And at Shibahama High, they're known as Eizouken—a club determined to produce their own science fiction anime! But with no budget and a leaky warehouse for a studio, Eizouken is going to have to work hard—together!—and use their imaginations if they want to create their vision of the ultimate world.

VOLUME 1
ISBN 978-1-50671-897-2
$12.99

VOLUME 2
ISBN 978-1-50671-898-9
$12.99

VOLUME 3
ISBN 978-1-50671-899-6
$12.99

AVAILABLE AT YOUR LOCAL COMICS SHOP OR BOOKSTORE

To find a comics shop near you, visit comicshoplocator.com. For more information or to order direct, visit darkhorse.com. *Prices and availability subject to change without notice.

EIZOKEN NIWA TE O DASUNA! by Sumito OOWARA © 2017 Sumito OOWARA. All rights reserved. Dark Horse Manga™ and the Dark Horse logo are registered trademarks of Dark Horse Comics LLC. All rights reserved. (BL7016)

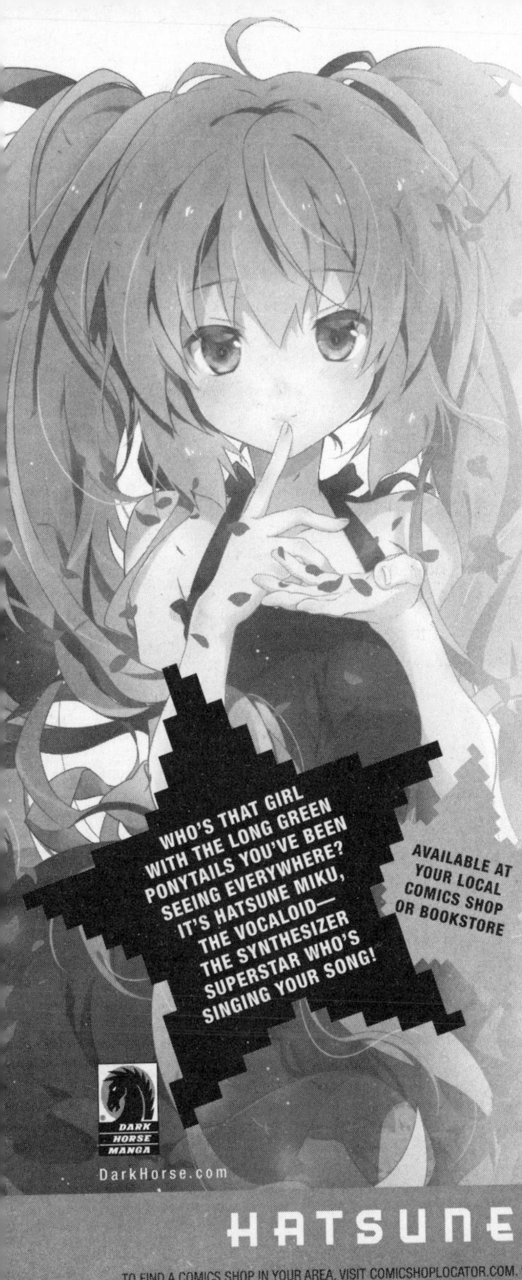
WHO'S THAT GIRL WITH THE LONG GREEN PONYTAILS YOU'VE BEEN SEEING EVERYWHERE? IT'S HATSUNE MIKU, THE VOCALOID—THE SYNTHESIZER SUPERSTAR WHO'S SINGING YOUR SONG!
AVAILABLE AT YOUR LOCAL COMICS SHOP OR BOOKSTORE
DARK HORSE MANGA
DarkHorse.com

HATSUNE MIKU: ACUTE
Art and story by Shiori Asahina
Miku, Kaito, and Luka! Once they were all friends making songs—but while Kaito might make a duet with Miku or a duet with Luka, a love song all three of them sing together can only end in sorrow!

ISBN 978-1-50670-341-1 | $10.99

HATSUNE MIKU: RIN-CHAN NOW!
Story by Sezu, Art by Hiro Tamura
Miku's sassy blond friend takes center stage in this series that took inspiration from the music video "Rin-chan Now!" The video is now a manga of the same name—written, drawn, and edited by the video creators!

VOLUME 1
978-1-50670-313-8 | $10.99

VOLUME 2
978-1-50670-314-5 | $10.99

VOLUME 3
978-1-50670-315-2 | $10.99

VOLUME 4
978-1-50670-316-9 | $10.99

HATSUNE MIKU: MIKUBON
Art and story by Ontama
Hatsune Miku and her friends Rin, Len, and Luka enroll at the St. Diva Academy for Vocaloids! At St. Diva, a wonderland of friendship, determination, and even love unfolds! But can they stay out of trouble, especially when the mad professor of the Hachune Miku Research Lab is nearby . . . ?

ISBN 978-1-50670-231-5 | $10.99

UNOFFICIAL HATSUNE MIX
Art and story by KEI
Miku's original illustrator, KEI, produced a best-selling omnibus manga of the musical adventures (and misadventures!) of Miku and her fellow Vocaloids Rin, Len, Luka, and more—in both beautiful black-and-white and charming color!

ISBN 978-1-61655-412-5 | $19.99

HATSUNE MIKU: FUTURE DELIVERY
Story by Satoshi Oshio, Art by Hugin Miyama
In the distant future, Asumi—a girl who has no clue to her memories but a drawing of a green-haired, ponytailed person—finds her only friend in Asimov, a battered old delivery robot. The strange companions travel the stars together in search of the mysterious "Miku," only to learn the legendary idol has taken different forms on many different worlds!

VOLUME 1
ISBN 978-1-50670-361-9 | $10.99

VOLUME 2
ISBN 978-1-50670-362-6 | $10.99

HATSUNE MIKU

REPENT, SINNERS! THEY'RE BACK!

Miss the anime?
Try the *Panty & Stocking with Garterbelt* manga! Nine ALL-NEW
stories of your favorite filthy fallen angels, written and drawn by TAGRO,
with a special afterword by *Kill La Kill* director Hiroyuki Imaishi!
978-1-61655-735-5 | $11.99

DARK HORSE MANGA

AVAILABLE AT YOUR LOCAL COMICS SHOP OR BOOKSTORE | To find a comics shop in your area, visit comicshoplocator.com
For more information or to order direct, visit darkhorse.com

Panty & Stocking with Garterbelt © 2010-2022 GAINAX/GEEKS, © 2011-2022 TAGRO. Dark Horse Manga™ is a trademark of Dark Horse Comics LLC.
All rights reserved. (BL 7065)

QUITE
POSSIBLY
THE MOST *fabulous*
EVANGELION MANGA EVER.

"IT'S A TRULY LAUGH-OUT-LOUD BOOK THAT *EVANGELION* FANS
SHOULD BE SURE TO PICK UP. **RECOMMENDED.**"–CHE GILSON, OTAKU USA

DON'T BE CONCERNED
THAT THERE'S NO REI OR
ASUKA ON THIS COVER.
THERE'S PLENTY OF THEM
INSIDE. OH, YEAH, AND
THAT SHINJI DUDE, TOO.

VOLUME 1
978-1-50670-151-6 • $11.99

VOLUME 2
978-1-50670-375-6 • $11.99

AVAILABLE AT YOUR LOCAL COMICS SHOP OR BOOKSTORE
To find a comics shop in your area, visit comicshoplocator.com • For more information or to ord
direct, visit DarkHorse.com

Neon Genesis Evangelion: Legend of the Piko Piko Middle School Students • Illustration by YUSHI KAWATA and YUKITO. © khar

TONY TAKEZAKI'S

NEON GENESIS EVANGELION

EMERGENCY

EMERGENCY

EMERGENCY

GENCY

Place a takeout order for this manga, containing twenty-three servings of satire in both color and black and white from prankster Tony Takezaki, voted a fan favorite in Japan! It's a meal instead of a snack!   978-1-61655-736-2 | $12.99

HUNGRY FOR MORE *EVANGELION*?

AVAILABLE AT YOUR LOCAL COMICS SHOP OR BOOKSTORE | TO FIND A COMICS SHOP IN YOUR AREA, VISIT COMICSHOPLOCATOR.COM
For more information or to order direct, visit DarkHorse.com
TONY TAKEZAKI NO EVANGELION. Illustration by TONY TAKEZAKI. Edited by KADOKAWA SHOTEN. Dark Horse Manga™ is a trademark of Dark Horse Comics LLC. All rights reserved. (BL 7046)

DRIFTERS

KOHTA HIRANO

Heroes from Earth's history are deposited in an enchanted land where humans subjugate the nonhuman races. This wild, action-packed series features historical characters such as Joan of Arc, Hannibal, and Rasputin being used as chess pieces in a bloody, endless battle!

From Kohta Hirano, creator of the smash-hit *Hellsing*, *Drifters* is an all-out fantasy slugfest of epic proportion!

VOLUME ONE	**VOLUME TWO**	**VOLUME THREE**
978-1-59582-769-2 | $13.99	978-1-59582-933-7 | $12.99	978-1-61655-339-5 | $12.99

VOLUME FOUR	**VOLUME FIVE**	**VOLUME SIX**
978-1-61655-574-0 | $13.99	978-1-50670-379-4 | $13.99	978-1-50671-546-9 | $14.99

AVAILABLE AT YOUR LOCAL COMICS SHOP OR BOOKSTORE TO FIND A COMICS SHOP IN YOUR AREA, visit comicshoplocator.com
For more information or to order direct, visit DarkHorse.com.

DARK HORSE MANGA

Drifters © Kouta Hirano. Originally published in Japan in 2010 by Shonen Gahosha Co., Ltd., Tokyo. English translation rights arranged with Shonen Gahosha Co., Ltd., Tokyo through Tohan Corporation, Tokyo. (BL 7092)

SOMETHING'S WRONG HERE . . .

You sense it, somehow. You suspect this story doesn't really go the way it should. You're suspicious! But a smooth talker like Reigen would know what to say at this point. *"Just flip the book around and start reading it the other way instead."* Aha! So this was really the last page of the book. You're saved! Thank you, Reigen-sensei! *"Now, about my fee . . . "*

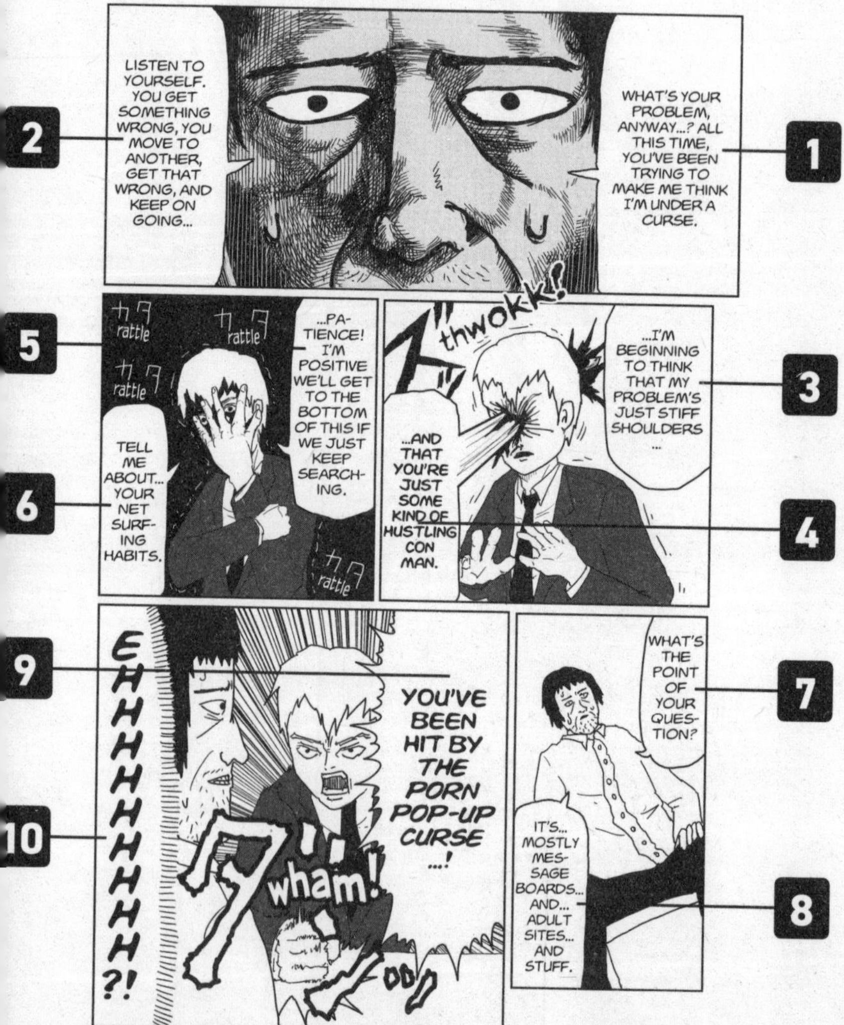
1
WHAT'S YOUR PROBLEM, ANYWAY...? ALL THIS TIME, YOU'VE BEEN TRYING TO MAKE ME THINK I'M UNDER A CURSE.
2
LISTEN TO YOURSELF. YOU GET SOMETHING WRONG, YOU MOVE TO ANOTHER, GET THAT WRONG, AND KEEP ON GOING...
thwokk!
3
...I'M BEGINNING TO THINK THAT MY PROBLEM'S JUST STIFF SHOULDERS ...
4
...AND THAT YOU'RE JUST SOME KIND OF HUSTLING CON MAN.
rattle
rattle
rattle
rattle
5
...PA-TIENCE! I'M POSITIVE WE'LL GET TO THE BOTTOM OF THIS IF WE JUST KEEP SEARCH-ING.
6
TELL ME ABOUT... YOUR NET SURF-ING HABITS.
7
WHAT'S THE POINT OF YOUR QUES-TION?
8
IT'S... MOSTLY MES-SAGE BOARDS... AND... ADULT SITES... AND STUFF.
9
YOU'VE BEEN HIT BY THE PORN POP-UP CURSE ...!
wham!
10
EHHHHHHHHHHHH?!